Author's Note

The Leadership Engine coined the term Teachable Point of View, which is at the core of how leaders develop other leaders. The book lays out a framework for developing leaders at all levels of an organization and argues that it is the major responsibility of the current leaders to develop the next generation, not something that should be outsourced to consultants and/or professors.

The examples of leaders teaching range from Jack Welch at GE to Roger Enrico at PepsiCo to General Wayne Downing, four-star head of the Special Operations Forces to Eleanor Josaitis, founder of Focus: HOPE, all of whom responded to Peter Drucker's leadership challenge, "Be a teacher."

Peter Drucker challenged a group of pharmaceutical executives in a workshop we both participated in several years ago. He said:

> ... force yourself to be a teacher, to get up in front of maybe your subordinates, maybe another group, and project to them, "This is what I am trying to do. This is what I have learned. This is what I am going to reach for."
>
> ... It isn't only that leaders are made, self-made mostly and not born, it is that continuing leadership is a matter of behavior and practices and not a gift or charisma. It is a responsibility.

Since the first publication of *The Leadership Engine*, the relevance of this idea has increased. First, the number of companies who have had to go outside for CEOs is increasing because of the failure to develop leaders. Note that AT&T went outside twice, 3M hired Jim McNerney from GE, Home Depot hired Bob Nardelli from GE, HP hired Carly Fiorina from Lucent, Albertson's hired Larry Johnston from GE, Polaris hired Tom Tiller from GE, Honeywell hired Dave Coddy from GE to name just a few. The biggest failure of a leader is not to develop a successor—GE had seven, not by accident as Jack Welch spent twenty years focused more on teaching and developing leaders than on any other task. *The Leadership Engine* shows others how to build this leadership pipeline.

The second change since the first publication of the book is that the success of institutions in the new millennium will increasingly be determined by how much smarter they can become every day through knowledge creation and through aligning members of the organization with new knowledge. The bursting of the new-economy bubble, the tightening of the capital markets, the death of many dot.com darlings, and the accounting debacles at Enron and elsewhere just reinforce my certainty that having leaders at all levels with aligned business ideas and values is the key to success.

The world has definitely changed. Markets are truly global. Intangibles carry premium value. New technologies create new capabilities every day. The revolving doors of the labor markets spin at the speed of turbines. In this lightning fast world old strategies and processes won't work. New ones that are much more versatile and that function much more smoothly are needed. But, the job of a leader has not changed. Enhancing the value of assets and sustaining growth are still the ultimate goals. This is accomplished by developing others to be leaders, creating leaders at every level, and getting them aligned and energized. The company that fields the better team with the smarter people and has them working most often on the things that create the most value will win out over its competitors.

—Noel M. Tichy
April 2002

Critical Praise for *The Leadership Engine*

"Periodically, all successful organizations have to change. Once a crisis has occurred, any organization will change, butwaiting for a crisis is not often the route to success. How do large organizations change without a crisis? Noel Tichy correctly finds the answer in leadership—a leadership that permeates an organization at all levels."

—LESTER THUROW, author of *The Future of Capitalism*

"Insightful, entertaining and practical.... *The Leadership Engine* provides a blueprint for more effective organizations."

—THOMAS J. TIERNEY, Worldwide Managing
Director/Bain & Company

"This book is the most valuable of the lot because it solidly confronts a vexing problem today—the lack of leaders who are willing to take their organization s through fundamental change. From Congress to the boardroom to the computer room, the qualities discussed are in short supply. If you think you've got what it takes, Tichy offers a comprehensive handbook for developing a leadership program at your workplace."

—*COMPUTERWORLD*

"It is no secret that the successful execution of any change strategy rests largely on the shoulders of those who lead. In *The Leadership Engine* Noel Tichy gives us an inside look at the process used to expand that leadership universe."

—PROFESSOR LEONARD A. SCHLESINGER, Harvard Business
School

NOEL M. TICHY is a professor at the University of Michigan Business School where he specializes in leadership and organizational transformation. A consultant to General Electric since 1982, he ran GE's renowned Crotonville executive development center for two years. As a senior partner in Action Learning Associates, Professor Tichy has consulted with clients around the world, including Royal Dutch/Shell, Coca-Cola, Mercedes-Benz, Ameritech, NEC, and Royal Bank of Canada. His previous books include *Control Your Destiny or Someone Else Will* (coauthored with Stratford Sherman) and *Every Business Is a Growth Business* (with Ram Charan).

ELI COHEN is an independent researcher and consultant, and partner in the firm Tichy Cohen Associates. He has consulted on strategy with a variety of clients while at Bain & Company. Prior to that he held operating positions at Procter & Gamble and Commerzbank AG.

Also by Noel M. Tichy

Control Your Destiny or Someone Else Will: How Jack Welch Is Making General Electric the World's Most Competitive Company (with Stratford Sherman). New York: Doubleday/Currency, 1993.

Managing Strategic Change: Technical, Political and Cultural Dynamics. New York: John Wiley & Sons, Inc., 1983.

Organization Design for Primary Health Care: The Case of the Dr. Martin Luther King, Jr., Health Center. New York: Praeger, 1977.

Global Citizenship (with Andrew R. McGill and Lynda St. Clair). San Francisco: Jossey-Bass, 1997.

Every Business Is a Growth Business (with Ram Charan). New York: Times Books, 2000.

THE Leadership Engine

How Winning Companies Build Leaders at Every Level

NOEL M. TICHY

with Eli Cohen

HarperBusiness Essentials
A HarperBusiness Book
An Imprint of HarperCollins*Publishers*

To my life partner and favorite leadership teacher,
Patricia Stacey,
and to our gang of emerging leaders,
Danielle, Donny, Joel, Leslee, Michelle and Nicole

HarperCollins books may be purchased for educational, business, or sales promotional use. For information please write: Special Markets Department, HarperCollins Publishers Inc., 10 East 53rd Street, New York, NY 10022.

First HarperBusiness paperback edition published 2002

Designed by Alma Hochhauser Orenstein

The Library of Congress has catalogued the hardcover edition as follows:

Tichy, Noel M.
The leadership engine : how winning companies build leaders at every level /
by Noel Tichy with Eli Cohen.—1st ed.
p.   cm.
Includes bibliographical references and index.
ISBN 0-88730-793-0
1. Leadership.   2. Executives—Training of.   I. Cohen, Eli D.   II. Title.
HD57.7.T5   1997
658.4'092—dc21   97–17607

ISBN 0-88730931-3 (pbk.)

04 05 06 ❖/RRD 10 9

At the end of the day, you bet on people, not on strategies.

—Larry Bossidy, CEO, Honeywell

Contents

Acknowledgments

There are many acknowledgments due when a book represents twenty-five years of experience and work. I would like to start, however, with a special thanks to the person who helped me find my voice and worked so hard to bring my ideas alive on the written page. Nancy Cardwell argued me into clarity on a number of issues and then wrote what I meant instead of what I said. Her partnership has been invaluable to me. Thank you Nancy Cardwell.

Because this book reflects a lifetime of work, it is impossible to name and adequately express my appreciation to all the individuals who have shaped me and my ideas and values and who have energized me over the years. So, I want simply to express my gratitude to the hundreds of young MBA students whose thoughtful questions and eagerness to learn have kept me excited about learning and teaching, and to the executives with whom I have had the joy of sharing journeys of mutual enlightenment in the Global Leadership Program at the University of Michigan and the other executive programs I have led at both Columbia University and the University of Michigan. I also want to thank the many people at General Electric who made my years there so valuable to my learning and development.

There are numerous leaders who have contributed to this book. I thank them for continuing to add value to the world. I am particularly indebted to Jack Welch who gave me the opportunity to put many of my ideas into practice at GE's Crotonville management development institute. Welch gets even better as a leader every day, reinforcing my prediction (in my previous book with Stratford Sherman) that he, along with Alfred Sloan, will be the two most remembered and respected business leaders in the twenty-first century.

Other leaders who have taught me much include, especially, Larry Bossidy of Honeywell, who continues to be a world-class benchmark, and John Trani of Stanley Works. Also at the top of that list are the late Father Bill Cunningham and Eleanor Josaitis, who taught me what visionary leadership is really all about as they built Focus: HOPE into the world's standard for development of human capital as a way to fight racism and poverty. Every one of the leaders we interviewed for this book has been a teacher for me.

My academic debts are large. James MacGregor Burns's book *Leadership* opened my eyes and heart to transformational leadership. This led to several years of work with my late colleague Mary Anne Devanna on our book *The Transformational Leader*. Burns's work continues to shape my thinking. Warren Bennis has also been a great influence on my thinking about leadership, along with Michael Brimm, John Gardner, Charles Kadushin, Andy McGill, Phil Mirvis, Tom Moloney, Edgar Schein, Len Schelsinger, Hiro Takeuchi, Karl Weick and my very special Indian guru Ram Charan. Professor Larry Selden has taught me to be a better thinker about business and the capital markets.

A book like this required tremendous cooperation from all the companies that participated in our research. The people who were excited by our ideas and supportive of our efforts helped us immeasurably. There are too many to name, but I owe special thanks to Larry Toole of GE Capital, Susan Peters of GE Appliances, Claudia Davis of Hewlett-Packard, Colonel David Abrahamson and Colonel Harold Jensen of the United States Special Operations Command, Rear Admiral Philip Dur (United States Navy, Retired) who is currently at Tenneco, Ben Porter and Mark Greenberg of AlliedSignal, Paul Russell of PepsiCo, Pat Asp of ServiceMaster, Joyce Hergenhan of General Electric and Jerome Adams of Shell Oil.

My colleagues who directly worked on this book were unbelievably committed, professional and tolerant of my pace, style and often absentee leadership. I thank them for hanging in there on this project. My administrator Launa Artz kept me and all the pieces together, while Lynda St Clair, Ellen Berger and Melissa Niglio helped to fill them in. Nancy Tanner provided essential project support. Chris DeRose played a key role in the early PepsiCo research and with the creation of the handbook.

It was wonderful to have a helpful and enthusiastic editor who is a great leader himself. Adrian Zackheim believed in me, in the team and in the project. He kept us on track while encouraging us to fully explore the complexities of the material.

Finally, my colleague and partner on the research, Eli Cohen, taught me that leading and teaching can be a partnership. A very special thanks to him.

Preface

One day over five years ago I watched Father Bill Cunningham stand before more than four hundred faculty members, students and executives at the University of Michigan Business School and lay out an incredible vision of Detroit as "the Broadway of civil rights" and then convince us that it could be brought to reality. Father Cunningham, who is a central figure in this book, died on May 26, 1997. But, he has left behind a powerful legacy. Focus: HOPE, the civil rights organization that he cofounded with Eleanor Josaitis, has changed—and is continuing to change—the lives of thousands of people in inner-city Detroit. He was one of my heroes and, as a master of stretch leadership, a role model for me. His boldness in setting enormously high goals and his ability then to energize people to reach them was so astounding that he will inspire and energize me—and hopefully you—for years into the future.

I have left my descriptions of Father Cunningham in this book in the present tense because he lives so vibrantly in my mind. I can still picture him, the charismatic orator, sharing his extraordinary vision for Detroit and telling us how Focus: HOPE would be a role model for twenty-first-century society. His words that day captured several of the essential themes of this book. He was an inspiring leader because he had a storyline that embodied an exciting vision of the future and he backed it up with concrete actions and evidence of success. His words opened up a whole new world of possibilities for us. That day, Father Cunningham got us to see declining, Rust Belt, "Murder City" Detroit in radical new terms. Here's an excerpt:

Here we have Detroit. A hundred and forty-one languages, burgeoning with revolution, radical, smoking all the time, on its knees, a tidal wave coming in, and I don't know of any other place I would rather be in this world, if I were to want to be where the world is going to survive. Thirty years ahead of Los Angeles. A hundred years ahead of Europe. Twenty years ahead of Chicago. Now, in this town, which is the Broadway of civil rights, is the final struggle to make something work that's never worked before.... We've got to knock down the last vestige of racist mentality: that black men and women are not suited, not fitted for, not capable of, the highest positions of contribution to our society.... We have at Focus: HOPE, this very day, hundreds of young men and women whom I will say can compete with the finest scientists and manufacturing people in the world. They are, today, world class and they haven't even begun.... We have the very finest American machine tools and labs, and we are watching our young people master these machines, master their maintenance, master design equipment that most automotive companies don't have in their fine labs, yet. The tool rooms make their own fixtures and tooling, program and process, and they're only in their first year. By the end of their third year, they are going to be masters of Japanese and German language. By the end of their sixth year, they are going to be cross-trained in six to eight major manufacturing disciplines. ... These young men and women know how to operate every one of those machine tools and how to correct any of the problems. When a machine crashes, they know how to repair it. ... Now, where do they come from? These gems? Are they imported from Japan? Do we bring them in from Germany? Or do we even bring them in from MIT? They come from the streets of Detroit.... So, we are making history. We are changing the way people think and the way people do things. And I promise you, in the next ten years, ... that we are going to turn this world around on the fulcrum of the city of Detroit, City of Destiny, the Broadway of civil rights. But it will require the highest expectations of us all. Highest expectations of our brothers and sisters. I will conclude my remarks by saying, "Yeah, you're right, I've never been accused of being reasonable. But I'd like anybody to compare miracles with us, right now. God bless you all."

In 1993, I introduced Father Cunningham to Bob Knowling (another role model leader in this book). I had thought that Knowling, then head of the Ameritech Institute, might be able to find ways for Ameritech to support the efforts of Focus: HOPE. Bob generously offered Father Cunningham more than one hundred used computers from Ameritech as a gift and said he would like to help with the great efforts under way at Focus: HOPE. But Father Cunningham's response was a confrontational rejection. He told Bob not only that he did not want hand-me-down equipment but that Bob obviously did not understand what Focus: HOPE was all about. Focus: HOPE was a civil rights organization designed to build the future by providing globally competitive, high-technology capabilities to minority men and women. They would work only on tomorrow's technology, not society's hand-me-downs. Father Cunningham went on to challenge Knowling by recounting the dismal track record of big companies that promised to help but didn't deliver. And, he particularly expressed his concerns about Ameritech and whether its local unit, Michigan Bell, would follow through on any offers of assistance. After that meeting, I had to work hard at damage control. I had convinced Knowling that Ameritech should spend millions of dollars and thousands of person days working with Focus: HOPE, and now Cunningham had told him off. The ultimate irony was that a white Irish-American priest was dressing down an African-American executive who had a proven track record of active community development involvement. Knowling was exactly the kind of role model that Cunningham wanted for his people. Knowling had grown up in poverty, developed competitive capabilities and was in the highest levels of contribution to society. He was a responsible and involved corporate and personal citizen. At the time I was furious at Cunningham's behavior and told him so afterward. But Knowling, once he got over his surprise, could see that Cunningham's tough position was based on high standards and uncompromising principles. As a result, Ameritech gave Focus: HOPE new computers and did donate thousands of person days of volunteer help. Eventually, Ameritech sold Focus: HOPE an old Ameritech Yellow Pages building for a pittance. The building is to become the home of Tech Villas, a new center that will help people from around the world create programs based on the Focus: HOPE model. Along the way Bob Knowling and Father Cunningham became mutually supportive colleagues and friends.

In 1996, I invited twenty-four senior Ford Motor executives to a benchmarking and teaching session with Focus: HOPE students and staff. The Ford executives spent the afternoon going one-on-one with the Focus: HOPE people, getting to know one another as individuals, discussing leadership and learning about Focus: HOPE. Then we held a workshop where the two groups analyzed why Focus: HOPE was such a high-performing organization and the implications for Ford. As always, when executives spend time at Focus: HOPE, they were awestruck by how much could be done with seemingly so few resources. They also could see the impact of having a focus on a single mission, strong commitment and leadership at all levels, where everyone takes responsibility for teaching and energizing everyone else. The session ended with Father Cunningham challenging the Ford executives. He shared his teachable points of view about taking risks and focusing on success with the Ford executives. Then he began to challenge the Ford executives to become stronger leaders and to stop searching for consensus because, "the exact synonym for consensus is mediocrity." Rather, he told them, leadership is about taking people to places where they have never dared to go. He then pressed them to develop a mission that would be as energizing for the people at Ford as the Focus: HOPE mission has been for over thirty years for the people of inner-city

Detroit. Finally, he offered them the bold goal of designing a new Taurus with twice the engineering at half the cost, a task, he told them, that would require them to stretch themselves with the highest expectations. At the end of his talk, they gave him a standing ovation. He had energized them to think of themselves as leaders who would control their own destiny.

Five months later Bill Cunningham was diagnosed with cancer of the bile duct. The prognosis was bad. Eleanor Josaitis took over as the primary leader of Focus: HOPE. But, as Cunningham fought valiantly with experimental cancer treatments, he stayed deeply involved, through Josaitis's daily visits and consultations with him. Together, they made plans for the Tech Villas program and other ways to insure that Focus: HOPE would continue and expand its mission well into the twenty-first century. His final act of leadership was telling Eleanor, when he knew that he had only a few days or hours to live: "Don't put my name on a building or a boulevard—make my work live on." There is no doubt in my mind that this will happen. I can think of no better example than Bill Cunningham of a leader with a teachable point of view who created a genetic code of leaders developing leaders. Through him and the other leaders in this book and my own experiences learning and teaching, I think I am beginning to understand the essence of winning leadership: building into the future by developing the abilities of others.

This book reflects a twenty-five-year journey for me. It tries to combine a number of deep themes running throughout my personal and academic life. These themes all have to do with how to successfully transform organizations to achieve the best they can for all their stakeholders: employees, shareholders, customers and communities. The journey was triggered by my fervor in the late 1960s for social change, civil rights and antiwar activities. This led me first to Columbia University, where I got a Ph.D. in social psychology and became even more committed to a better, more just, democratic world. After obtaining my degree, I became a professor of organizational behavior at the Graduate School of Business at Columbia University. While teaching at

Columbia, I spent most of the 1970s working to improve health care in poor and underserved areas. I spent five years working in the South Bronx of New York with the Dr. Martin Luther King, Jr., Health Center. The center delivered health care to fifty thousand indigent, mostly black and Puerto Rican, residents of the community, while at the same time aiming to stimulate community development, provide jobs and enhance the quality of life in the area. I wrote my first book, *Organization Design for Primary Health Care: The Case of the Dr. Martin Luther King, Jr., Health Center* (Praeger, 1977), on that experience. I then worked in Camden, New Jersey, to help a young doctor, Emmett Doerr, try to replicate the MLK experience. I also took a year off from Columbia to work in Hazard, Kentucky, to set up a rural version of MLK. Throughout this journey, I was both consciously and unconsciously learning that leadership was the key determinant of success, not processes, culture, techniques or scientific management but energized visionary leaders who could make things happen.

By the early 1980s, I had moved to the University of Michigan and become a real believer in the work of James MacGregor Burns, who had coined the term "transforming" or "transformational leadership" in his 1978 Pulitzer Prize–winning book *Leadership*. According to Burns, transformational leaders are people who fundamentally alter the institutions they lead, as opposed to transactional leaders who merely maintain or manage what they are given. Burns's work started my late colleague Mary Anne Devanna and me researching and writing about transformational leadership in business. Together, we co-authored a book, *The Transformational Leader* (Wiley, 1986). A key figure in that book was Jack Welch, who had started the transformation of General Electric in 1981. As a result of the book, I got to know him, and he invited me to take a two-year leave from the University of Michigan to head up GE's worldwide management development operation to try to put into practice the concepts of leadership and change that I was wrestling with at the time. The two years at GE taught me more about leadership than the previous decade and a half. I only partly understood it at the time.

Following GE, in the late 1980s, I returned to Michigan to write and apply my new lessons on leadership development to executives and MBA students. Writing a book on GE and Welch's transformation with coauthor Stratford Sherman taught me even more about leading through teachable points of view. The title of the book is one of Welch's major teaching points: *Control Your Destiny or Someone Else Will* (Doubleday/Currency, 1993). Despite all of these experiences and though I had helped the Michigan Business School and numerous client companies design and implement innovative leadership development and change programs, it wasn't until two years ago that the focus became crystal clear to me.

I had known for a long time that the goal was to have leadership at all levels in an organization. What had not been clear was how to develop those leaders. Now, I saw the answer. Organizations have leaders at every level, I realized, because other leaders teach them. Father Cunningham, Admiral Chuck LeMoyne, the courageous former second-in-command of the U.S. Special Operations Forces who also died of cancer while this book was in progress, along with the many other leaders in this book, show us how.

Leaders developing leaders is my new mantra, one that I repeat to my children, to MBA students, to executives and to those engaged in global citizenship and development programs. I wrote this book not just to reflect my teachable points of view but to challenge each reader to articulate his or her own teachable points of view and become a leader who develops other leaders.

ANN ARBOR, MICHIGAN
JUNE 1997

Introduction

In an eighteen-month period shortly before he became CEO of PepsiCo in early 1996, Roger Enrico spent nearly a third of his time at his house in the Cayman Islands or on his ranch in Montana. This may seem like a pretty unusual way for the vice chairman of a multibillion-dollar company based in Purchase, New York, to do his job. But his job is exactly what Roger Enrico was doing. And he was doing it extremely well. In this remote off-site setting, away from the daily demands of making potato chips, selling sodas and resolving assorted day-to-day problems, Enrico was preparing PepsiCo to survive and thrive into the twenty-first century. He was running his own personal "war college" to develop a new generation of leaders for PepsiCo.

In sessions running from early in the morning until late at night, Enrico would lead nine executives at a time through five days of action learning. He told them stories about his own varied experiences in the business and coached them on their personal operating styles. He shared his points of view about how to build, grow and change a business, and, more importantly, he worked to help them develop their own points of view and become leaders in their own right.

As a vehicle for learning, he had each student take on a "grow the business" project that would have a significant dollar impact on the company. He would coach them on developing a stretch dream objective and an implementation effort, and then send them out to work on their projects. Several months later, they would return for a three-day session to review their progress. In the meantime, Enrico would start another class. During that eighteen-month period, Enrico ran ten of these workshop series, dedicating over 120 days of his time to this activity. As a result, PepsiCo has nearly one hundred much better developed leaders who not only have implemented some great business ideas for PepsiCo but who are now following Enrico's example and developing other leaders.[1]

The Difference Between Winners and Losers

In the past decade, a number of corporate giants have fallen on their faces. GM, Apple, Kodak, Westinghouse, AT&T and American Express are some of the more prominent ones. Kmart, US Air, Philips Electronics, Digital Equipment, several Japanese banks, and lots more could be added to the list. These former titans of commerce have gotten out of step with their customers, watched unhappy investors flee and cut back operations as their businesses have crumbled. They have lost shares in the consumer markets, value in the capital markets and confidence in themselves. They have become, to put it bluntly, losers.

It would be easy to blame these companies' woes on the changing global marketplace and on the demands of operating in a new business environment where all the rules of competition have changed. But the truth is that during the same period, a group of clear winners has emerged as well. While Westinghouse was struggling, GE climbed from one success to another. While IBM rearranged the deck chairs on the *Titanic*, Compaq Computer recovered from its own earlier stumbles and surged to the forefront. Then Compaq stumbled, removed Eckhard Pfeiffer as CEO and IBM was revitalized under the leadership of Lou Gerstner. And entrepreneurial upstarts such as Starbucks and Staples have simply created entirely new highly successful organizations. There have been too many successes to blame companies' fates on outside forces. There are, within the companies, fundamental differences between the winners and the losers. There is something going on in the winning companies that sets them apart from the losers.

In my twenty-five years as an organizational psychologist and a management consultant, I have seen lots of troubled companies up close, from the inside. During that time, I have had first-hand experiences with an infinite variety of dysfunctional management practices. I have also developed a number of tools that have helped a lot of clients get back on track. And I have worked with a number of winning companies, including General Electric, where I worked full-time as head of leadership development at its Crotonville executive training center while on leave from the University of Michigan Business School in 1985–87. A major part of my job has always been figuring out what works and what doesn't. Several years ago, however, the great disparity between the track records of the corporate winners and losers prompted me to step back and specifically tackle the broader question: Why do some companies succeed while others fail?

Winning Organizations Are Teaching Organizations

The answer I have come up with is that winning companies win because they have good leaders who nurture the development of other leaders at all levels of the organization. The ultimate test of success for an organization is not whether it can win today but whether it can keep winning tomorrow and the day after. Therefore, the ultimate test for a leader is not whether he or she makes smart decisions and takes decisive action, but whether he or she teaches others to be leaders and builds an organization that can sustain its success even when he or she is not around. The key ability of winning organizations and winning leaders is creating leaders.

I like the concept of the teaching organization rather than the learning organization. To be an effective teacher, one needs to be a world-class learner. However, that is not sufficient. One also has to pass on the learning and energize others to also be teachers. An organization of teachers at all levels is what this book is all about. It is much tougher to take one's learning and translate it into a teachable point of view than to be just a competent learner.

The winning organizations and people who do this well come in all shapes, sizes and nationalities, and can be found in any industry. The goods and services they produce and the strategies and tactics they employ are widely divergent. But they all share a set of fundamentals.

• First, leaders with a proven track record of success take direct responsibility for the development of other leaders.

• Second, leaders who develop other leaders have teachable points of view in the specific areas of ideas, values and something that I call E-cubed—emotional energy and edge. Winning leaders/teachers have ideas that they can articulate and teach to others about both how to make the organization successful in the marketplace and how to develop other leaders. They have teachable values about the kinds of behavior that will lead to organizational and personal success. They deliberately generate positive emotional energy in others. And they demonstrate and encourage others to demonstrate edge, which is the ability to face reality and make tough decisions.

• Third, leaders embody their teachable points of view in living stories. They tell stories about their pasts that explain their learning experiences and their beliefs. And they create stories about the future of their organizations that engage others, both emotionally and intellectually, to attain the winning future that they describe.

• Finally, because winning leaders invest considerable time developing other leaders, they have well-defined methodologies and coaching and teaching techniques. Among these is the willingness to admit mistakes and show their vulnerabilities in order to serve as effective role models for others.

In this book, I am going to take you to visit a number of winning leaders so that you can observe them in their roles as leaders/teachers developing other leaders/teachers. Among them will be such well-known executives as Jack Welch, former CEO of General Electric; Roger Enrico former CEO of PepsiCo; Lew Platt, formerly of Hewlett-Packard; Larry Bossidy of AlliedSignal; Bill Pollard of ServiceMaster; and Eckhard Pfeiffer of Compaq Computer. Others include Gary Wendt, former CEO of GE Capital; Bob Knowling, former Vice President of U S WEST; and General Wayne Downing, former head of the U.S. military's Special Operations Forces and a member of President Bush's National Security Advisory; along with a host of other not-so-well-known leaders. They each have their own style, but the common denominator is very simple: They personally invest time and emotional energy in teaching and expect all other leaders to do the same thing. Teaching is a way of life for them.

In Santa Clara, California, Andy Grove, Chairman of Intel Corporation, goes into the classroom several times a year to teach Intel managers how to lead in an industry in which the product (microprocessors) doubles in capacity every eighteen months.[2] In Grove's teaching sessions, he discusses the role of leaders in detecting and navigating the turbulent industry shifts that many companies fail to survive.[3] Why does Grove take the time to do this? Because he believes that having leaders at all levels of Intel who can spot the trends and have the courage to act will enable Intel to prosper while competitors falter. So Grove is dedicated to teaching and developing others at all levels to be winning leaders.

During the Welch era, if you showed up on the right day every couple of weeks at GE's Crotonville leadership development institute, you would find Jack Welch, CEO of GE, teaching.[4] Welch spent an enormous amount of time giving speeches to employees and taking the hot seat in question-and-answer sessions, but he also interactively taught. He has a variety of modules, usually half a day at a time, that he used to teach leadership. In the most senior program, he asked among other things, "If you were named CEO of GE tomorrow, what would you do?" Welch used the question to orchestrate a no-holds-barred discussion in which he jousted with participants and honed their analytic abilities and leadership instincts by having them also joust with each other. He considered such sessions essential and is proud of his commitment. Says Welch, "I've gone to Crotonville every two weeks for fifteen years to interact with new employees, middle managers, and senior managers. I have not missed a session." Jeffrey Immelt, the current GE CEO, continues this commitment at Crotonville.

In the mid-1990s at Coronado, California, Rear Admiral Ray Smith, a Navy SEAL since the Vietnam War, visited a class of SEALs graduating from Basic Underwater Demolition SEAL training. Only 20% of the candidates who enter this elite six-month program survive its great physical and mental demands and graduate.[5] Throughout the day, Smith, in his fifties, participated in the same physical training as the SEAL candidates, all in their twenties. At the end of the day, he met alone with the graduates. Speaking as a successful leader who has been exactly where they are, he laid out for them personally his teachable point of view on the leadership duties of becoming a SEAL, the conduct, honor and teamwork required, and their need to develop other leaders.

In addition to holding formal teaching sessions, winning leaders also integrate their leadership development and coaching into the fabric of everyday activities. Dick Stonesifer ran GE Appliances for five years until he retired in 1996. During that time, his business produced many officers for GE's other businesses. Stonesifer's point of view on developing leadership is straightforward—you have to work at it, and you can always get better. So he had a policy of giving his executives real-time coaching. After every major meeting, he would go back to them to specifically discuss the things they had done well and the things they could do better. To improve himself, he also used to carry around a list of things he needed to work on. During the last five years of his career, he even had his subordinates formally review his performance and contribute to the list. In doing this, he not only learned, but he sent two other messages. One was that he expected each of his people to learn, and the other was that if they could teach Stonesifer about leadership they could and should teach others.

To highlight the lessons from the winners in this book, I will refer to some of the mistakes that losers make. But I'm not going to focus on them. That's because nobody but losers really want to spend much time writing or reading about other losers. It's depressing, and ultimately nowhere near as helpful as studying and learning from the winners. So this is a book about winners. Who are they? What separates them from the losers? And what can you do to make sure that you and your organization are winners as well?

I use the terms "winning companies" and "losing companies" to denote the disastrous results that some companies have turned in while other companies, subject to the same global and market trends, have prospered. I have no crystal ball and cannot predict, with 100% certainty, which companies will win in the future, nor can I guarantee that the "winning companies" I have studied will be winners in the future.

I do believe, however, that right now, each of them has found the key to sustained success. I would be willing to wager that the companies I will tell you about in this book will be successful for a long time. This is because, as you will see, they have developed into organizations with Leadership Engines, where leaders exist at all levels and leaders actively develop the next generation of leaders. Once this Engine gets running, it is hard for competitors to stop.

At any given point in time, I believe, this is the best predictor of whether or not a company will win in the near and long term. Technologies, products, even demographic shifts come and go. But a company that continually produces leaders at all levels is here to stay because it has people who anticipate and know how to deal with change.

Some of the losing companies may have been good at generating leaders in the past. Or maybe they grew for other reasons. But each of them fell apart because when they needed it, they did not have a Leadership Engine. Even winning companies stumble. Witness the recent difficulties at PepsiCo. But I believe PepsiCo will be a winner in the long term because of the leadership it has developed and continues to develop. There is no "free ride" or "coasting period." The companies that win will be those that build or maintain a steady focus on developing leaders at all levels of the company.

Are Leaders Made or Born?

I have a very simple thesis: All people have untapped leadership potential, just as all people have untapped athletic potential.[6] There are clear differences due to nature and nurture, that is, genes and development, as to how much untapped potential there may be. But no matter what level of athletic or leadership performance a person currently exhibits, he or she can make quantum improvements. Not everyone can be the CEO of a multibillion-dollar corporation, just as not everyone can be an Olympian or win at Wimbledon, but with coaching and practice we can all be a lot better than we are. The important teaching point is: Leadership is there in you.

I have a little exercise that helps people see this. First, I ask them to review their lives and think about a leadership success that they have enjoyed. I have tried this with literally thousands of executives and MBA students worldwide, and I am fully convinced that almost everyone has had such an experience. At some time, in high school or college, at work, on an athletic team or in a community or church group, they have made something happen through other people that would never have occurred without their leadership. In my own case, very early in my career, I took a leave of absence from Columbia University Business School to set up a model interdisciplinary health care clinic in Appalachia. But the week before I arrived, the mine workers' union cut back on health benefits, and the hospital where I was going to serve as a consultant setting up one model program was all of a sudden struggling just to survive. Over the next year, I had to step in and run the clinic. I found that I had the leadership skills to run the clinic and develop a team that could keep it going despite the loss of a major source of its funding.

Once the participants have a clear picture in their mind of the time in their lives when they were most proud of themselves as a leader, I ask them to tell the story to someone else. Inevitably, the room ignites with energy as the partners share their leadership stories. People love to tell their stories. After a few minutes, I ask the group to stand back from the stories and reflect on what made the leadership successful. Then, as a group, we generate a list of the characteristics of effective leadership built on what I call their personal benchmarking trip. As they articulate the important qualities of leadership, people realize that they know what winning leadership is about. Many, to their dismay, also realize that they haven't really exercised it in years.

The point in the workshop is to open people up to their own leadership potential, to challenge them to improve and to ultimately motivate them to want to develop other leaders. That is one of the goals of this book as well, to awaken the desire to improve yourself as a leader and to develop other leaders. The other is to help you do it.

It is never too early or too late to take on the challenge of improving your leadership abilities and of developing them in others. Tom Tiller, whom you'll meet in this book, was named the manager of a GE appliance plant at the tender age of 29, in large measure, I am certain, because he is so clear about his teachable points of view and his role as a leader/teacher. I've seen young professionals and MBA students pull together teachable points of view even as they are just embarking on their careers. And I have seen older executives nearing retirement age take miraculous strides. Bill Weiss, former CEO of Ameritech, had worked in the AT&T system for decades. While he had often resisted the telephone company's bureaucracy, he was perceived as a typical "Bellhead" telephone executive. Then, at the age of 62, he looked at the organization he would be leaving in three years, and realized that his legacy would be one of failure if he didn't prepare it to survive in the burgeoning telecommunications industry. In the last three years before his retirement, he started a revolution to completely revamp the company and develop new leaders. His amazing performance demonstrated to me that age and career tenure are not limiting factors.

The scarcest resource in the world today is leadership talent capable of continuously transforming organizations to win in tomorrow's world. The individuals and organizations that build Leadership Engines and invest in leaders developing other leaders have a sustainable competitive advantage.

The Leader-Driven Organization

Winning Is About Leadership

- Winning organizations have leaders at all levels
- Producing those leaders is what separates the winners from the losers

Leaders Have Ideas, Values, Energy and Edge

- Ideas and values guide their decisions
- Energy and edge get them implemented

Without Leaders, Organizations Stagnate

- They can't keep pace with changing markets
- They don't add shareholder value

In August 1991, Bill Weiss, the CEO of Ameritech, walked into my office with a problem. The company he headed was an old-style Baby Bell telephone company that suddenly found itself having to compete in a new, fast-moving telecommunications industry. In order to survive, it needed to expand its product mix, change its bureaucratic operating style and establish a new working culture based on intense competition rather than stifling regulation. After listening to Weiss describe the situation at Ameritech, my colleague Patricia Stacey and I came to a clear conclusion. "Bill," I told him, "you are 62 years old and retiring at 65. I don't think we should be talking about your leading any kind of transformation. Your agenda is to find a successor, make sure he or she is in place and get out of the way. You'll have to turn it over to that person to do the transformation."

Weiss was polite but firm. "I can't do that," he replied. "We'll lose two or three more years while that person is getting his or her act together. That would be catastrophic, because within five years, we've got to either transform this company or find our markets rapidly shrinking. Until now, our leaders have been unwilling to contemplate anything but gradual change. We've got to find a way to radically reform and reorient our company. We'll have to deal with succession in that context."[1]

Within six months of this meeting, two of the key potential CEO successors had left Ameritech, and four new potential successors from within the organization were leading a massive cultural change effort called Breakthrough Leadership. The company had also created a temporary organization to run parallel with the operating company. This temporary organization was designed to simultaneously screen and develop leaders for Ameritech's future, as well as to develop the vision, values and strategy for the new Ameritech. It involved hundreds of leaders and task forces, and intensive development activities throughout 1992. In 1993, this was expanded to thousands of Ameritech managers.

By May 1994, when Weiss retired, the company had been totally reorganized into new business units, and a new CEO was in place: 47-year-old Dick Notebaert. It had thousands of reenergized and motivated employees. And it was primed to take off in the new telecommunications world. From 1993 through 1996, Ameritech outperformed its peers, providing a 19.0% annual return to investors versus 13.9% for the Standard & Poor's Telephone Index.[2] For 1996, Ameritech posted net income of $2.13 billion, on revenue of $14.9 billion.[3] In 1998, Ameritech was acquired by SBC for $62.6 billion. In 2000, Dick Notebaert moved on to become CEO of Tellabs.

When Bill Weiss retired in 1994, he even left the board so

that Notebaert would have the freedom to run the business on his own. But Weiss gave Ameritech a lasting legacy: In a very short time, he had positioned the company to be a winner by developing a team of leaders who would continue to invest in developing other leaders. In his last three years, he gave a bravura performance of leadership, and he left the company not only in the hands of a strong successor, but also with a keen appreciation for and a culture of leadership.

Weiss himself readily acknowledges that he wasn't always a great leader. He became chairman in 1984, but for the first seven years of his tenure, he just tinkered, "because our performance was solid and life was comfortable." But finally he saw that big things had to change if Ameritech was going to survive, and someone had to make those changes happen. "I have to admit my first efforts were at gradual change, incremental change," he says. "I had to start thinking in terms of radical change; revolution, if you will. I should have done it sooner."[4]

Bill Weiss may have been a slow starter, but Ameritech was put on a winning trajectory because he came to understand a secret about winning organizations and winning people: Winning is about leadership. Winning individuals are leaders, people with ideas and values, and the energy and guts to do what needs to be done. And organizations are winners because they have good leaders, not just at the top, but at all levels. Winning companies value leaders, they have cultures that expect and reward leadership, and they actively put time and resources into developing them. Winning companies win because they have lots of leaders, and they have lots of leaders because they deliberately and systematically produce them. This is what separates the winners from the losers.

Most people in business will tell you that developing leaders is an important activity, and that organizations must carry it out in a thoughtful and systematic manner. The reality, however, is that while there is much talk and much surface activity, very few organizations do a good job of it. They talk a good game, but when the chips are down, they don't follow through very well.

Some companies don't do a good job developing leaders because they don't try very hard. Some have good intentions, but they just don't commit the time and resources necessary to do it. Others, such as General Motors, the former Digital Equipment and the former Westinghouse, like to talk about leadership but actively discourage it by punishing people who dare to think independently. And still others, such as AT&T, have committed huge amounts of time and resources to elaborate well-enforced human resources development processes, but they have been largely taught by consultants and academicians who aren't leaders themselves. So what they have tended to produce are very articulate managers who are masters of the latest "business-speak" and the fads and fashions of management gurus. But they end up acting like civil servants and bureaucrats, not leaders.

Winning companies, however, deliberately and systematically develop people to be real leaders, to be people with their own points of view who motivate others to action. They use every opportunity to promote and encourage leadership at all levels within the company, and their top leaders are personally committed to developing other leaders. At Ameritech, in one year, Bill Weiss personally spent over seventy days on Breakthrough Leadership activities. At PepsiCo, Roger Enrico devoted more than 120 days over eighteen months to running workshops and mentoring other leaders. And Jack Welch taught at General Electric's Crotonville management training center biweekly, in addition to availing himself of the many coaching opportunities that present themselves daily.

The big difference between winners and losers, whether they are organizations or individuals, is that winners understand that learning, teaching and leading are inextricably intertwined. Teaching is not some ancillary, nice-to-do activity that is left to the staffers in the human resources area or, worse yet, to outside consultants. Teaching is the central activity of winning organizations. It is hard-wired into everything they do. Larry Bossidy of Honeywell does not run a budget review or a strategy session without making it an important coaching and teaching opportunity. For both Bossidy and his subordinates, these interactions build energy and get the juices flowing faster. In most companies, meetings with the top boss evoke reactions that range from terror to narcolepsy, in which all the participants struggle to stay awake through mind-numbing bureaucratic rituals. In winning companies, any meeting that doesn't leave the participants better prepared and more eager to do a better job is considered a failure and a waste of time. As Andy Grove of Intel puts it: "It is not right for [the chairman] to allow people to be late and waste everyone's time. . . . Just as you would not permit a fellow employee to steal a $2,000 piece of office equipment, you shouldn't let anyone walk away with the time of his fellow managers."[5]

Further, in winning companies, leading and teaching are considered so essential to success that they aren't reserved for a favored few in the executive suite. Winning companies know that games are won and lost on the playing field, and victory goes to the team with the most good players. So they nurture, and expect, leadership everywhere. In winning companies, teaching, learning and leading are inherent parts of everyone's job description.

When one Chicago-area hospital threatened to cancel an important facilities management contract with ServiceMaster, it was chairman Bill Pollard who made the plea for a second chance to bring down costs and increase quality, but it was the ServiceMaster manager at the hospital who got together with his workers and figured out how to change their cleaning procedures to get the job done. The new procedures worked so well that crew members from the hospital were soon teaching other crews. ServiceMaster is a low-tech service company making world-class returns of 25%[6] a year for the past twenty-five years because it expects all of its workers to lead, and it follows them when they do.

Winning companies are, to be sure, smart operators and savvy competitors. They have the same goals as everyone else in business, to create value for their shareholders, employees and customers. And they grow—and keep growing—by efficiently delivering a constant stream of desirable goods and services to those customers. But rather than concentrating on coming up with winning strategies for the marketplace, winning organizations start by getting smart, energized people in the right places so they will make the right decisions. The philosophy of winning companies, as Larry Bossidy puts it, is, "At the end of the day, you bet on people, not on strategies."[7]

In the 1980s, if you asked investors and managers if companies would need lots of people who could creatively destroy and rebuild businesses, many would say, "Sure," and promptly turn back to managing their balance sheets. Leadership wasn't a topic that grabbed a whole lot of attention, and when leaders did attract interest, it was mainly about who was going to make the next $600 million in a leveraged buyout.

In the early 1990s, leadership nearly slipped off the screen as a relevant management topic as popular new theories focused on corporate cultures or on work processes as the keys to success. But, as many executives have learned, leadership does matter. The results of leadership matter. And failure to deliver those results can be professionally fatal.

It's true that leadership is harder to quantify than "net income" and "operating costs." Its components are "soft" qualities, such as ideas, values, energy and edge. There's no line on the profit-and-loss statement that says "Leadership—$240 million." But the existence of leaders and the need for leadership are hard facts. Just look at the continuing successes of General Electric, ServiceMaster, Intel, PepisCo and Royal/Dutch Shell versus the dismal failures—which led to the ousters of the CEOs—at Eastman Kodak, Lucent, Westinghouse, Philips, General Motors and IBM. And look at IBM today. In 1992, IBM lost close to $5 billion. Since Lou Gerstner arrived, under a new team of leaders that he has both hired from the outside and developed within, IBM has provided investors with a better return than competitors every year but one. In 2001, the company made close to $5.5 billion.[8]

Companies with strong leaders win in their industries and in the capital markets. And the companies that are good at producing leaders win most often. In fact, one of the markers, or corollary traits, that I have noticed about winning organizations is that they are usually net exporters of talent. They are so good at producing leaders that other companies routinely hire them away. When AlliedSignal's board decided it was time to find a successor to chief executive Edward Hennessy, it raided GE to get Larry Bossidy.[9] 3M hired former GE executive Jim McNerney as CEO and Home Depot hired former GE executive Bob Nardelli as CEO.[10]

What Is Winning?

Before I go further in talking about the qualities of winning organizations and winning leaders, let me start by defining what I mean by "winning." I have just two criteria:

- **Success in adding value**

    There are many ways you could choose to measure this, but for corporations, I don't think there's a better one than the capital markets. For not-for-profit organizations, the test is whether they are growing and improving their use of assets (productivity).

- **Sustained excellence**

    For established companies to qualify as winners, they must have a continuing track record of success in the capital markets. A quarter or two in the limelight as a "darling of Wall Street" doesn't do it. For start-ups, especially in high-tech businesses where products have the shelf life of an ice cube on a hot sidewalk, the question is: Have they been able to redefine themselves as their businesses have grown and their initial products faded? The test for nonprofits is: Do they have a continuing impact, and are they growing to impact more people?[11]

Lots of people will argue that success in the capital markets isn't the same thing as, or doesn't even necessarily require, success in adding real value. This was true during the dot.com mania years when many high-priced initial public offerings were examples of the capital markets rewarding companies without solid track records. But their incredible valuations were almost always based on a gold rush mentality that doesn't last, and the bubble did burst, causing the prices to tumble when the initial euphoria wore off, and created huge numbers of bankruptcies all culminating in the biggest one in history—Enron.[12] There is also the big debate over the influence of Wall Street on corporate decisionmaking. Many people are worried that the health of our society and the long-term prospects for the economy are being sacrificed to meet the demands of "greedy" stock traders and institutional investors. It is true that some short-sighted and small-minded executives may have found quick rewards in the stock market by downsizing and laying off hundreds of thousands of workers. But despite these seemingly "irrational" examples, the markets in my opinion are in fact the fairest and most objective measure of leadership. Long-term market performance measures whether or not a leader is truly enriching shareholders (which is after all their primary, or one of their primary, missions).

The truth is that the capital markets have given bigger and more lasting rewards to well-managed companies that have good leadership. Studies have shown that downsizing to prosperity does not work. A study by New York–based Mitchell & Co. looked at firms that had cut more than 10% of their workforce in the mid-1980s. While Wall Street initially applauded the moves with higher stock prices, two years later the majority of the firms were trading below the market and their comparable industry groups.[13] Another study of 1,000 American companies found that investors place a higher value on companies that improved earnings through growth in revenue than on those that did so by cutting costs.[14]

The roots of some of the confusion about how to enrich shareholders (grow vs. cut) can probably be traced to General Electric, where CEO Jack Welch slashed approximately 100,000 jobs and sold off $8.5 billion in assets in the early 1980s.[15] After these actions (which won Welch the title "Neutron Jack"), the company's stock price soared. GE is now No. 1 in total market value in the world, topping $230 billion in July 1997.[16] There is, of course, a connection between GE's stock price and the asset sales and layoffs, but it isn't as direct as many Welch wannabes may think. The layoffs were never his goal, nor did he ever set any layoff target. Rather, Welch used the asset sales, layoffs and concurrent acquisitions to reposition GE and prepare it to be a better competitor in the future. He was exercising good leadership. After fifteen years, the capital markets aren't rewarding GE for downsizing; they are rewarding it for the results of good leadership.

According to research by Columbia University finance professor Larry Selden, the companies that are the most successful in the capital markets, the ones that are consistently in the top quartile of the S&P, maintain annual growth rates of 12% in revenue and a 16% operating return on assets. These numbers are not just financial abstractions. They are the real measures of whether a company is pleasing customers and making a profit, the two things that will ultimately determine whether it stays in business and employs anybody.

Since the late 1980s, the capital markets have been signaling that they understand the importance of good leadership. In the slower-paced "good old days" before global competition and international capital markets pushed everything into fast forward, executives could keep their jobs by plodding along and making small adjustments to the status quo. But those days are gone. The world is moving too quickly for bureaucratic caretakers to stay on top. Success in the new global marketplace requires constant innovation, redeployment of resources and risk. Investors are demanding success, and they are holding executives responsible. The ones who don't deliver are soon unemployed. Just talk to John Akers, Kay Whitmore or Jim Robinson. On Akers's watch, IBM's market value plunged nearly $50 billion, and he was ousted by the board.[17] While Whitmore headed Eastman Kodak, the company failed to grab the lead in digital imaging technology while diverting its resources to such misguided acquisitions as Sterling Drug. In 1993, Whitmore was let go by Kodak's directors because he didn't "move faster and further on ... enhanced earnings."[18] And at American Express, Robinson missed the fact that the marketplace was changing, and sat by while customers traded the prestige of holding an American Express card for the more tangible benefits offered by issuers of the new affinity cards. As a result, American Express has seen its share of the market drop from 26% in 1985 to 15% in 1996. But that's not Robinson's problem anymore. The board fired him in 1993.[19]

While the capital markets have caught on that leadership is what makes the difference between winners and losers, they are still missing a critical piece of the puzzle. They treat leadership as something of a "black box" that contains just the chief executive; if you change him or her, that's all you need to do. The reality is that while the CEO is a crucial player, it isn't just the top leadership that's important. The companies that consistently win, the Intels, the PepsiCos, the GEs of the world, don't just have one strong leader, or just a few at the top. They have lots of strong leaders, and they have them at all levels of the organization.

In slower, more predictable times, command-and-control hierarchies may not have been a bad idea. They provided a fairly simple system for consistent decisionmaking; all questions were passed up the ladder to the same one or few people, and their decisions were handed back down. But in today's wired-together, global marketplace, pleasing customers and making a profit is a function of quick thinking and agile action. Companies can win only if they can quickly deliver the goods and services that customers want. This means that they must always be alert for new ideas and new ways to win customer loyalty. They must be willing to tailor their products and delivery schedules to respond to individual customer needs, and they must be prepared to make instant decisions and adjustments to their work processes to meet those needs.

This requires an organization that isn't built to last but one that is built to change. In the future, the real core competence of companies will be the ability to continuously and creatively destroy and remake themselves to meet customer demands. Everyone in the organization must take responsibility for taking responsive actions. This means that a company needs leadership everywhere in the organization, from the corner office, in the customer service rep's cubicle, and on the shop floor. Leadership is the ability to see reality as it really is *and* to mobilize the appropriate response.

In the time it takes for a question to be passed up the ladder and a decision handed back down, the customer will have gone somewhere else or the opportunity will be missed. "Everybody else in the world is doing the same things we are," remarks Larry Bossidy. Therefore, if AlliedSignal wants to succeed, it must "get there faster with better-prepared people," he says.[20] In Allied-Signal's case, this means, for example, making sure that its engineers and production staff have sufficient knowledge and self-confidence so they can be assigned to work with customers, even in customers' plants, to solve problems and develop needed new products.

The importance of speed and customer responsiveness is not a new idea: "How Managers Can Succeed Through Speed" was the cover story of a 1989 issue of *FORTUNE* magazine. But the degree of responsiveness and speed required today is astounding by older standards. "The only differentiator you have in the marketplace is speed of action," says Dick Notebaert, the current chairman of Tellabs. "Cycle time is the key."[21] And the only way to get speed is to have leaders—people who are prepared to make smart decisions and implement them efficiently.

This need for quick thinking and instant responsiveness isn't confined to profit-making enterprises. The Special Operations Forces units in the military are replacing their old hierarchical leadership style with something more appropriate for the new roles they find themselves fulfilling. Today soldiers in these units are far more likely to be deployed on a crowded street than in an invasion force. The young soldier confronted by an angry crowd of Bosnian or Haitian citizens doesn't have time to contact his superior for instructions. So that soldier, probably under the age of thirty, has got to be thinking not only about the physical safety of his or her unit and their specific orders; he or she must also consider the geopolitical ramifications of his or her actions. An act to maintain the safety of a unit or the security of a checkpoint may cause a fissure in a peacekeeping alliance, or it may result in condemnation from important parts of the international community. Suddenly this soldier has to adopt the mindset of the President of the United States and make a decision in a nanosecond—without advisers, pollsters, politicos or perhaps even a radio that works. Over the last four or five years, the military has more than doubled the number of assignments its Special Operations Forces conduct. In most cases, this has meant a significant shift of focus from their old mission of unconventional warfare to a new one that more often than not falls under the heading of Foreign Internal Defense.[22] Leaders from the United States Special Operations Command have had to redirect the military's strength in leadership development toward these new types of missions.

Many of the leaders cited in this book are CEOs or other senior-level executives. They are redefining corporate missions, reshaping cultures and facing challenges of an enormous magnitude that most employees will never face. But the same traits that are necessary to bring off huge corporate transformations are equally important at other levels of the organization. You may not need a grand strategy for building a global telecommunications business if you are a service technician you can leave that assignment to the CEO. But you do need to have a clear vision of your job, some good ideas about how to fix customers' phones promptly and well and the ability to get it done. At heart, that's what leadership is about. It's about having smart ideas and getting them implemented well. As Mike Walsh, the late CEO of Tenneco, once put it, "Every person in a key position has to see himself or herself as a mini-CEO. They have to conceptualize what has to be done in the same way the CEO has. Then it cascades."[23]

Throughout my study, I found leaders who are developing the people in their companies to be these mini-CEOs. Larry Bossidy develops Mary Petrovich, the plant manager who is trying to turn around AlliedSignal's underperforming five-hundred-person St. Clair Shores, Michigan, safety restraint plant. ServiceMaster chairman Bill Pollard and former CEO Carlos Cantu make sure they develop people like Bob Hutchins, the account manager at the Chicago hospital. Leaders at these companies know that the game is for everyone to see opportunities and seize them.

"Everything that we do happens through our people," notes Patricia Asp, Vice President for People at ServiceMaster. "Any productivity improvement, any delighting of customers, service of customers or responding to customers is all done through people." Further, she adds, the front-line workers go into customers' homes and offices every day. They are the company's eyes and ears. The company, therefore, invests a lot in making sure that they understand what they see. "We want them to see not just how to do their jobs today, but to look at what's out there, what we could be doing. . . . We try to cause them to think about what are the best opportunities . . . What will have to change within our company and within our business units?" based on what they see.[24]

Losing organizations sometimes understand the need for leadership but make the mistake of betting on the wrong horses. They handicap their field of employees, select the ones they think will go farthest, and pour resources into training and developing them. Unfortunately, their too-early designation of an elite class of "high potentials" (HI-POs) often weeds out the people who could ultimately turn out to be the best leaders and irritates many other solid players. At Exxon, they used to jokingly refer to the "HI-POs" and the "PO-POs," standing for "pissed on and passed over." In such a system, it's highly likely that creative leaders like GE's Jack Welch, PepsiCo's Roger Enrico and AlliedSignal's Larry Bossidy would have been lost in the "passed over" class.

Winning companies do quite a bit of handicapping as well, but they wait longer before making their decisions, and they base them on broader leadership skills rather than simply the ability to complete individual assignments. Further, they continue to pour resources into developing everyone else, including the people that they don't think are going to make it all the way to the top. This means not only that they don't prematurely eliminate the late bloomers and nontraditional leaders, but also that they get the best out of everyone.

Winning companies understand that not everyone can be an Olympian, but through training and encouragement, and by offering opportunities to exercise leadership, they make the most of every player. Some people have a natural talent for coming up with good ideas and getting other people to help carry them out. Others have to work at expanding their own horizons, thinking bigger ideas and persuading others to go along. But winning companies know that, like athletes, no matter how good or bad a person's inherent leadership skills are, they can be improved with coaching and practice. And they systematically work at it.

In researching this book and looking for the core traits and competencies that separate winning organizations from losing ones, it became increasingly clear to me not only that leadership is the key trait that distinguishes the winners, but that the ability to *teach* leadership is their core competence. Lots of companies talk about leadership and try to teach it, but winning companies do it remarkably well. Winning organizations consistently improve and regenerate themselves by effectively developing the leadership skills of all their people. So I looked further to see *how* the winners teach leadership and *what it is* that they teach that makes them so successful. What I discovered were the same principles embodied in the program Bill Weiss began designing for Ameritech that day in August 1991. Winning organizations are successful at teaching leadership because:

- Proven leaders do the teaching. They have a teachable point of view about running and changing the business, as well as about leadership. They personally act as coaches and role models, and they share their mistakes as well as their victories.

- The leaders are avid learners. They draw from their pasts and reflect on their experiences to develop lessons for the future.

These leaders have:

IDEAS

They have clear ideas of what it takes to win in their marketplaces and how the organization should operate. They update their ideas to keep them appropriate to changing circumstances, and they help others to develop their own ideas. Jack Welch, for example, changed the central idea about how GE would make money from a product company to a global service company. Similarly, Andy Grove reshaped the central ideas for Intel as he witnessed the decline of the company's traditional business in computer memories and moved it into making microprocessors.

VALUES

The leaders and the organizations have strong values that everyone understands and lives up to. The values support the business ideas and are deeply embedded, and everyone is held accountable to them, even in seemingly minor everyday decisions and actions. Ameritech, for example, had to change its old bureaucratic values in order to compete in the fast-paced telecommunications industry. Establishing or revitalizing values is one of the most crucial and toughest jobs of leaders.

ENERGY

Leaders are not only highly energetic people themselves, but they also actively work to create positive emotional energy in others. They do this by structuring the organization to get rid of bureaucratic nonsense, and by stretching and encouraging everyone they meet. At Focus: HOPE, which you will hear a lot about later in this book, the late Father William Cunningham helped thousands of people in inner-city Detroit escape from lives of dependency by following one simple formula: Energize people through ever-greater challenges.

EDGE

Winning leaders are willing to make tough decisions, and they encourage and reward others who do the same. Some people call this quality "showing the courage of one's convictions." I use a term I stole from Jack Welch, the former CEO of General Electric: "edge."

A Leader's Teachable Point of View

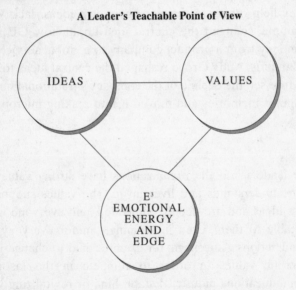

IDEAS

VALUES

E³
EMOTIONAL
ENERGY
AND
EDGE

Finally, the leaders communicate and teach through:

STORIES

Winning leaders personalize their visions and ideas by telling stories that touch people's emotions as well as their intellects. They drive their messages home with words and actions that engage and excite followers. Roberto Goizueta, former CEO of The Coca-Cola Company, spins a story that helps people in the company understand the strengths of this unique company and the opportunities that still lie ahead of the world's most power-ful brand. Coca-Cola, he tells them, accounts for just two of the sixty-four fluid ounces that each of the 5.7 billion people in the world consumes on average each day. Thus, Coca-Cola has sixty-two more ounces to capture. His story is symbolized by the infin-ity sign on the first page of his 1995 annual report. Coca-Cola, says Goizueta, has a world of infinite opportunity.

In the rest of this book, I will talk specifically about what win-ning leaders do that makes them winners and how they develop other winning leaders at all levels of their organizations.

Why Are Leaders Important?

Leaders Manage Through Times of Change
- They determine direction
- They move organizations from where they are to where they need to be

Leaders Make Things Happen
- They shape the culture
- They use the management tools

Leaders Are Revolutionaries
- They face reality and mobilize appropriate responses
- They encourage others to do the same

Show me a great company, and I'll show you one that has radically changed itself and is looking forward to the opportunity to do so again.[1]

—*LARRY BOSSIDY, FORMER CEO OF HONEYWELL*

This book is about leadership, and how winning leaders build winning organizations by developing other leaders. It isn't a tome on general management theory, and it isn't about how to set up efficient work processes, build quality products or use new technologies. It is about winning leaders, and how they think and behave differently from losers. To put this information into context, however, I do need to talk just a bit about my theory of business and the crucial roles that leaders play in making their organizations successful. If the last chapter made the case that leaders are what separate winning organizations from losing ones, this one will continue the discussion by exploring why. The rest of the book will talk about how.

In previous books, I have laid out in detail my general theory of business. Fundamentally, it is that success requires the ability to master revolutionary change. It requires taking on the dramatic challenge of creatively destroying and remaking organizations in order to improve them, and doing so repeatedly. In order for organizations to win, revolution, driven by leaders with ideas and the heart and guts to bring them alive, must become a way of life.

There is no doubt that revolutionary change can be painful. But in all facets of life, including business, one must master change. Faced with increasingly difficult, large and frequent shifts in economies, societies and marketplaces, organizations need leaders who can redirect life's emotional energies. Leaders of any institution, private or public, must be willing to repeatedly let go of old ideas and old ways of doing things and adopt new and better ones. And they must be able to help each and every employee generate the high levels of positive energy needed to do the same.

If winning is about constantly changing, you might ask: "Why should I bother with this book? By the time I've read it, it will be outmoded." But that's not true. The only thing that *never* changes is the fact that *everything* changes, and this book is about creating organizations and developing leaders who survive and thrive through change. The specific topic of transformational management can be left for another day. In fact, you don't really even have to subscribe to my theory of transformational leadership[2] to learn lots of valuable things about leading and developing other leaders from this book. No matter what their situation, leaders can improve their performance if they do a better job of generating ideas, instilling values, creating positive energy and making tough decisions. And they can build stronger organizations by teaching others to do the same. But you should remember that the people who succeed and maintain that success over time do so through successive periods of change; hold that thought as a backdrop in your mind as you read about winning leaders and what they do to build winning organizations.

The Crucial Role of Leaders

As I mentioned in the last chapter, a number of management theorists don't buy the argument that leadership is the key factor in determining an organization's success. They assert that a winning culture, or efficient work processes, or any number of other ancillary attributes are the *sine qua nons* for success. I agree with them that those things are important. But leadership takes precedence over everything else.

One reason leadership takes precedence is that leaders are the people who decide what needs to be done and the ones who make things happen. Just about everyone knew long before the 1960s that many Americans were being denied basic rights and freedoms, but it took a Martin Luther King Jr. and a handful of other determined leaders to bring about the civil rights movement. In the 1960s in Detroit, poor children were starving because their parents couldn't afford to buy them food. But it took a Father Bill Cunningham and Eleanor Josaitis to start Focus: HOPE, a feeding program that they expanded into a full-scale community organization that has trained over a thousand local residents to become highly paid and highly sophisticated machinists.

It's true that one person alone can't change the world, or even a moderate-sized organization. It takes the concentrated energy, ideas and enthusiasm of many people. But without a leader, the movement doesn't get started in the first place, or it quickly dies for lack of direction or momentum. Without leaders, good results are a matter of random chance, and therefore unsustainable.

Another reason that leadership takes precedence over the contributions of culture and management tools is that it's the leaders who create the cultures and use the tools. The management theorists who assert that corporate culture—not leadership—is the key that determines the success of an organization originally based their arguments on studies of the Japanese automakers and technology companies that took U.S. markets by storm in the 1970s and early 1980s. They bolstered their case by pointing to the strong cultures that made such U.S. companies as Hewlett-Packard, General Electric, IBM and Xerox leaders in their fields. It's an attractive theory, in part because it holds out to non-leaders the hope that they can attain excellence if they can only get themselves into the right culture. But the lesson that they draw from the examples is not the right one. These successful cultures didn't just spring up by themselves and start shaping their members.[3]

As Professor Edgar Schein of MIT's Sloan School of Management has clearly shown, corporate culture is developed at the birth of an organization by its leaders.[4] Folksy Sam Walton, with his down-home, we're-all-in-this-together attitude, created a family of "associates"[5] (as Wal-Mart store personnel are called), all dedicated to low prices and good service. Tom Watson, with his strict dress codes and company songs, fashioned IBM into a triumphal army. Watson figured that you couldn't be the world's No. 1 company unless you thought you were, so from day one, he established an image of success.

As long as a culture fits the marketplace, it succeeds, but when the external realities change, the culture has to change as well. That's where the proponents of cultural determination go astray. They argue that good cultures will mend themselves. But that's simply not true. At certain critical stages, radical cultural shifts are needed, and without leadership, they just don't happen. IBM's buttoned-down army was a perfect vehicle to quickly establish dominance in the fledgling computer industry. But by the 1980s, it was a drag. Under John Akers and other home-grown managers, the army lumbered along, missing opportunity after opportunity and losing market share to faster, more agile competitors such as Compaq, Dell and (until the early 1990s) Apple. Now, not only has IBM had to bring in a new CEO from outside the company, but the new CEO, Lou Gerstner, had to hire key managers from outside the company to run finance, accounting, human resources, strategy, the consumer division, and for other key posts.[6]

General Electric's culture is often cited as a paragon of successful durability, and its production of Jack Welch is held up as the proof. But the truth is that Reginald Jones selected Welch to succeed him as CEO because Welch was a radical deviant from the prevailing culture. Welch was an entrepreneurial player who spent his early formative years in GE's Plastics Division scoring successes by avoiding, thwarting or manipulating GE's rigid corporate bureaucracy. He knew the stifling effects of the old, incremental, overly analytic, internally focused, arrogant, don't-rock-the-boat culture. So when he became CEO, he immediately set about replacing it with a new externally focused culture that prizes speed, radical change and constructive conflict. His history as CEO was a story of selecting and developing leaders who, with him, have ripped apart the old culture and continually regenerated the company.

Another school of management theorists who disdain leaders—and who are rapidly disappearing over the horizon—are the reengineers. Reengineering came on the scene as its close cousin the total quality movement peaked. Both of these have very solid conceptual ideas and useful techniques. Unfortunately, their reputations have become tarnished because they were applied too often by the wrong people, by non-leaders.

There is a multibillion-dollar consulting industry in the world today that thrives largely on the fact that most managers don't want to lead. When non-leaders try to apply Total Quality Management or reengineering, they call in the consultants because, first of all, they don't know what to do, and, secondly, they are afraid of the tough part, the execution. But this, of course, dooms the effort. If the people inside the company don't know what to do or are afraid to do it, the consultants aren't likely to come up with an appropriate and effective plan. And there's absolutely no way that even if the outsiders did, against the odds, come up with a good plan, it could be implemented without solid leadership on the inside, from the people who live there every day. I recently uncovered a $60 million expenditure in a *FORTUNE* 50 company to reengineer the organization, where the results were a disaster. The turf battles were worse than before, teamwork did not exist and neither layers of management nor unproductive work had been removed. And management couldn't figure out why operations hadn't improved.

In the small number of cases, such as Motorola and GE, where the tools of Six Sigma total quality and reengineering have been wielded by real leaders, the results have been phenomenal. During Larry Bossidy's first year at AlliedSignal, all 105,000 employees were trained in total quality. Productivity, which had been growing at about 2%, grew on average 5.6% annually over the next five years.[7] But, more often than not, TQM and reengineering never get anywhere near the desired finish line.

When I started to work with Ameritech in 1991, there were 100 full-time quality facilitators and 5,000 quality groups. As current CEO Dick Notebaert recalls, "We used to spend days of time going through the process, but we weren't really interested in results. We had celebrations about the process; 'You just made it to Step Four in a seven-step process. Let's celebrate.'"[8]

Then Bill Weiss named Notebaert and three others to form a new top leadership team. They got rid of all the full-time facilitators, sending most of them back to real jobs adding value. Then they gave the 5,000 quality groups 90 days to deliver financially measurable results or be killed. Guess what? When Ameritech looked closely, only about 10% of them could point to any financial results or any hope of financial results. The rest had gotten lost in the morass of quality tools.

In some cases, enormously painful reengineerings have set ailing companies on the road to good health by realigning work processes and eliminating unnecessary tasks. In other, all-too-frequent instances, the effort was called reengineering, but involved nothing more than wholesale firings that resulted in "corporate anorexia." They destroyed people's lives and communities, and only left the companies less able to compete in the marketplace and weaker than ever. A survey by the American Management Association found that only 45% of downsized companies reported any increase in operating profits.[9] In almost all the cases, whether successful or not, the radical surgery was necessary because managers in the past had failed to exercise the leadership needed to refocus the company and make smaller cuts sooner.

What Do Leaders Do?

In a broad sense, what leaders do is stage revolutions. They are constantly challenging the status quo and looking around to see if they are doing the right things, or if those things can be done better or smarter. And, most importantly, when they do spot something that needs to be changed, they do something about it. In more concrete terms, they do two specific things:

- See reality—size up the current situation as it really is, not as it *used to be* or as they *would like* it to be, and
- Mobilize the appropriate responses

This is a lot harder than it sounds. Seeing reality requires that leaders remove the filters that screen out the things they might not want to see, acknowledge their own and their companies' shortcomings and accept the need for change. When you miss a delivery, it's easy to blame a supplier for not getting the parts to you on time, or to blame the customer for having demanding specifications. It's a lot tougher to admit that your procurement system is messed up or to accept that the failure to give the customer what he wants is *your* failure to deliver and not *his* failure to be satisfied.

Facing reality is about personally accepting the case for change. This is often referred to as "acknowledging the burning platform." At Ameritech, former CEO Bill Weiss faced reality by grasping the fact that the Chicago-based Baby Bell could not survive without entering new businesses. Merely offering phone service, even reliable, economical phone service, would no longer be enough. In a global telecommunications market, it needed to be playing in more arenas. It meant making the tough calls to stop doing some of the things it had always done, and the even gutsier calls to build new businesses.

Founders of new businesses often see realities that older competitors in the field miss. Fred Smith started Federal Express because he saw the reality that there would be an enormous demand for rapid delivery of packages in the new global market-place and that this would make the economics of setting up such a service highly favorable. While people already in the business fretted and complained about the difficulty of modernizing older delivery systems, Smith set out to build a completely new one. In retailing, while others were battling for the pocketbooks of America's increasingly urban populace, Sam Walton saw the reality that there was a huge customer base in small towns across the country that was being ignored. His response was to create a company that revolutionized the concept of the general merchandiser. The founders of Southwest Airlines had a different sense of reality about air travel when they began offering short-haul, low-fare, no-frills flights. That Southwest Airlines has become the most consistently profitable American airline is a testament to the reality that Herb Kelleher and his colleagues defined. While their competitors were looking inward, trying to maintain "business as usual" and doing a bit of fine-tuning around the edges, Smith, Walton and Kelleher were looking outward to see what was actually going on with real customers, in the real marketplace, and taking the radical actions needed to please them.

In established businesses, seeing reality is often more difficult because it means letting go of ingrained ways of thinking and working. Andy Grove of Intel, in his book *Only the Paranoid Survive*, describes the shakeouts in the computer industry in the 1980s as some companies—including Intel and Microsoft—adapted to new realities, while others such as IBM, DEC, Sperry, Univac and Wang failed to do so. As Grove explains it, around 1980, there were several successful computer companies that had proprietary designs for the chips and hardware in their computers, as well as proprietary designs for the operating systems and application software that ran them. These companies sold their large and expensive machines through their own sales and distribution networks, and they all made lots of money. Grove calls this the vertical period of the computer industry, because each company was a self-contained, vertically integrated player.

Then the invention of the microprocessor changed everything. The microprocessor carried the same power as its bigger brethren, and the same microprocessor could be put into any desktop computer. Suddenly, a dozen different companies, including Compaq, Packard Bell, Hewlett-Packard, IBM and others, were able to start making and selling virtually the same high-powered computers.

As advances in microprocessors accelerated, Compaq was quick to adopt the latest technologies. In 1983, it introduced its first portable computer—eighteen months before IBM's hit the market.[10] The company, founded only in 1982, reached $1 billion in sales in 1987, the shortest time ever for an American public firm to reach this milestone.[11] Michael Dell also spotted the opportunity. As a college student at the University of Texas in Austin, Dell had lots of energy and a love for computers and risk. He did not, however, have much love or patience for attending classes. So rather than go to lectures about business, he set about creating one. He would toil away in his dorm room lashing together standard parts into uniquely configured PCs that delivered just what his customers wanted. Dell saw that the new reality of interchangeable components meant a massive opportunity for his business to reach millions of buyers.[12] The company now does over $5 billion[13] a year in sales and continues to build all of its computers to order.

Among those who ignored the tide and clung to their old-line industry maps was IBM. At first it appeared that IBM was embracing the PC revolution. Its PC machines were among the hottest-selling in the market. But deep down, IBM fundamentally misunderstood the new shape of the industry. Grove, who personally witnessed the revolution as a supplier to IBM, says the company was "composed of a group of people who had won time and time again, decade after decade, in the battle among vertical computer players. The managers who ran IBM grew up in this world. When the industry changed, they attempted to use the same type of thinking regarding product development and competitiveness that had worked so well in the past."[14] As an example, Grove cites the development of OS/2. This operating system was technically outstanding. However, IBM didn't see the importance that open architecture and interchangeability had come to play in making PCs attractive to customers, so it was painfully slow in making OS/2 available for computers from other manufacturers. It took IBM almost three years to sell 600,000 copies of OS/2 (of which very few were used), while Microsoft only needed ten months to sell approximately 13 million copies of Windows 3.0.[15] When IBM finally decided to make some aggressive changes to OS/2, it was too late. Microsoft had captured people's imagination with Windows. OS/2 was a dismal failure, and a waste of money for IBM.

The same misunderstandings that plagued IBM's development of OS/2 virtually killed its efforts in PCs. Initially strong in PCs, IBM squandered its lead in the 1990s by being a "laggard with products," according to Bob Stephenson, who took over the PC business in 1995. The company was a "wholly unreliable supplier" as it clung to its vertical model for the industry and behaved antagonistically toward retailers and resellers, who actually sell a majority of the PCs in the U.S. It started to turn this around in 1993 and was losing billions as late as 1994. It took the company until 1996 to fully revamp its attitude and operations.[16]

Similarly, DEC failed to see the realities of the PC revolution. The company had burst on the scene and broken into the mainframe-dominated market in the 1960s with its mini-computers. But, faced with the next wave of technological development, the company was nearly killed in the early 1980s because it stuck with proprietary designs. In 1984, its leaders were still describing PCs as "cheap, short-lived and not very accurate machines."[17]

DEC and IBM both almost died as the result of their leaders' failures to confront reality. As I think about their blunders, I imagine knights headed for the battlefield. Decorated with medals from past wars, and flush with praises of others, they enter the battle confidently. But they enter it blindfolded, and are slaughtered mercilessly. From its peak value of $106 billion in 1987, IBM had destroyed approximately $80 billion in stock market value by 1993.[18] It also went from being ranked No. 1 in *FORTUNE*'s 1986 list of America's most admired companies to No. 206 in 1993.[19] In 1987, DEC's sales were growing at more than 20% a year. It was the darling of Wall Street when its stock hit a peak price of $199 before the 1987 crash.[20] After demand for their once-popular mini-computers began to lag, its "matrix" management system of interlocking and overlapping committees was too slow to stop the company's downfall.[21] At the close of the 1990 fiscal year, DEC reported its first-ever loss as a public company.[22] What followed were three years of poorly executed and ineffectual turnaround plans that robbed even more value from shareholders. The company's market value, which peaked at $26 billion in 1987, had shrunk to $4.6 billion in July 1992. That's when founder Ken Olsen was ousted[23] and Robert Palmer was asked to try to save the sinking ship—a job he failed at when DEC was finally bought by Compaq.[24]

Facing reality is the first crucial step that leaders must take if their organizations are going to respond appropriately. But that is just the starting point. Once the leader has figured out the problem/challenge/opportunity, he or she has to:

- Decide on a response,

- Determine what actions need to be taken to deliver that response and
- Make sure those actions get implemented promptly and well

Selecting the Response

Finding the appropriate response to a new set of circumstances (or deciding where to place the new platform) requires both ideas and the willingness to take risks. In Ameritech's case, the response that Weiss, Notebaert and their team came up with was to enter growth businesses that were new to the company. All of the new businesses capitalized on Ameritech's history as a communications provider, but they were definitely gambles. Signing up long-distance customers, constructing an electronic commerce network, offering enhanced cable TV services, and buying and running phone companies from Hungary to Australia all could have failed miserably. But Notebaert stuck with simple growth logic and encouraged people to get over their fear of trying something different. A real "home run," says Notebaert, has been security monitoring. "They all use telephone lines, they use the same wire and basically do the same work that we do. . . . Why should there be two trucks going out doing the same thing?" But, he adds, he had to "step outside the box," and adopt a new mindset, in order to see this opportunity. Looking back to 1991, he says, "We would have growth rates of two and a half percent in telephone lines, for example, and I can remember people saying, 'Well, we're in the Rust Belt,' and then in the southeastern part of the United States, they'd have growth rates of four percent. And we'd say, 'Well, there's nothing we can do. . . . They got dealt a better hand.' In the fourth quarter of 1995, our growth rate was higher than the southern and southeastern United States. I look out my window and I see the same economy. It's called . . . getting on the ball and not being a victim."[25]

At Intel, Andy Grove has had to respond to new realities several times with equally radical changes in the company's direction.[26] In the 1970s, Intel had built a great business providing semiconductors, primarily memory chips to the computer industry. As Grove puts it, the company's total identity was tied up in memories. "The company had a couple of beliefs that were as strong as religious dogmas. Both of them had to do with the importance of memories as the backbone of our manufacturing and sales activities."[27] It and a few other companies, including Unisem, Advanced Memory Systems, Advanced Micro Devices and Mostek, filled nearly all the industry's memory chip needs. In Santa Clara, California, where Intel was and is headquartered, life was great. Revenues and profit were both at record levels.

Then, when Intel sat atop the PC revolution making memory chips, unsettling rumblings began to come out of the Far East. While the U.S. memory chip makers enjoyed their expanding market, competitors were approaching from Japan. Steadily they built market share on a simple formula that is by now familiar: deliver quality products at costs beneath those of their American competitors.

At Intel, finding the appropriate response involved a long process of trial and error. At first it tried to focus on value-added products. Then it tried to focus on narrow segments of the memory market where it thought it had technical advantage. Its engineers worked harder trying to accelerate development of a next generation of products. Production people innovated and wrung cost out of Intel's system. But the company was overwhelmed. The Japanese could seemingly copy any invention before Intel had even gotten it right. And their pricing was brutal. At one point Intel "got hold of a memo sent to the sales force of a large Japanese company. The key portion of the memo said 'Win with the 10% rule. . . . Find AMD [another American company] and the Intel sockets. . . . Quote 10% below their price. . . . If they requote, go 10% AGAIN. . . . Don't quit until you WIN!'"[28]

By 1984, Intel was in a crisis. The Japanese were continually strengthening when the market coincidentally slumped. Suddenly Intel, no longer the strongest kid on the block, was having to fight for its space in a shrinking, not expanding, sandbox. The memory business was slowly bleeding the company. Finally, Grove describes one day staring out the window of an office at the company's campus in Santa Clara. The only two people in the room were Grove and Gordon Moore, one of Intel's founders.[29] Grove knew that everything that they had built was on the line. He asked Moore a very tough question: "If we got kicked out and the board brought in a new CEO, what do you think he would do?" Moore responded, "He'd probably get us out of memories." Grove reflected for a moment. And then he said, "Why shouldn't you and I walk out the door, come back and do it ourselves?"[30] The solution they ultimately reached was to abandon Intel's biggest business. Memory chips had become a commodity to which they could add little value, so they decided to start out almost entirely anew, designing and building the best microprocessors in the world. It was a painful and gutsy decision that probably saved the company.[31]

Strategic Actions

Once a strategy has been selected, leaders must figure out what actions have to be taken to successfully implement it, and they must take *all* of them. Often that means walking away from old systems and setting up entirely new ones.

At Ameritech, the decision to enter new fields meant actually lobbying to give away the company's monopoly on local phone service in order to get permission to enter new fields. As a result, Weiss and Notebaert found that they had to address every aspect of the business from redefining winning (they expressly mentioned the importance of rewarding shareholders for the first time) to reorganizing the company into business units, to redefining leadership through personnel changes and leadership development. Fundamentally, they saw that they had to rebuild the company from the ground up.

At Intel, Grove and his colleagues faced a similarly daunting challenge. Once Grove had made up his mind to leave the memory chip business, he had to figure out how. What impact would this have on customers, for example? Did the company need a full product line to offer computer manufacturers? Was the technology in memories so central to Intel's other products that it had to stay a part of the company?

To answer these questions, Grove conducted discussions with Intel employees and others over lunches and at technical conferences, staff meetings and product planning sessions. Even despite his firm conviction that the decision he and Moore had made was correct, when Intel managers asked, "Are we getting out of the memory business?" Grove still struggled with actually saying, "Yes." He, as much as anyone, had built Intel and identified the company with its success in the memory business. It was hard for him to abandon it. He subsequently found himself taking half-steps to get out of the memory business. He would at one moment decide to do it, but then approve the R&D budget for new memory chip designs. Finally Grove started to turn the corner. He was ready to make the strategic moves necessary to implement the new plan. In what was for Grove the crossing of the Rubicon, he told the sales force to notify customers that Intel would be getting out of the memory business.

Implementation

Implementation of a massive organizational change is the hardest part, because it requires selling the new response—including the case for change—and weeding out the resisters and the superfluous work. Implementation of an idea requires values, emotional energy and the edge, or guts, to see it through to the end.

Implementation is where you tackle the tough day-to-day issues. It's one thing to decide to consolidate operations and eliminate 25% of the workforce. It's another to tear down the corporate bureaucracy and streamline the processes so that 25% of the work disappears as well. This requires that leaders change their behaviors and teach others to do the same. If this doesn't happen, any boosts in the bottom line will be short-lived.

For Andy Grove at Intel, implementation meant shuttering plants and research centers and reassigning the company's best people to produce the company's products of the future—microprocessors. Moore stated at one meeting, "If we're really serious about this, half of our executive staff had better become software types in five years' time." After that meeting, Grove recalls looking around the room and wondering "who might remain, who might not." In the end, half of the members of Intel's senior leadership team were put in other jobs or left the company because they could not make the transition.[32]

Grove also made a personal commitment to change. If he was going to successfully lead a new microprocessor company, he would need to rebuild himself as well as the company. So he wrenched his calendar, his lifestyle and his approach to leading the business. He went back to school. Rather than cling to the details of his declining business, he learned about microprocessors and software, and how microprocessors should be built to run software. He was open about his own weaknesses, going to internal people and saying, "I don't know about this, help me." He also visited software developers and asked them to teach him about their business. His calendar showed someone who was building a company rather than running an existing one.

Today, Intel is one of the most successful companies in the world. The realization that its memory chip business was unsustainable led Grove to take all the actions to cast its future with microprocessors. All of these actions, from redirecting R&D to learning about new technologies to closing some production lines and opening others, built a new company that grew to $20.8 billion in revenue and $5.2 billion in net income in 1996 from a company that had about $2 billion in revenue and about $248 million in net income in 1987.[33] Today, Intel owns 88% of the market for microprocessors.[34] Compare that with companies such as Unisem, Mostek and Advanced Memory Systems,[35] which saw the same things that Intel did and felt the same pain but did not take the tough actions.

Industries like microprocessors, and computing, are traditionally thought of as turbulent. It is in these industries that leadership, or the lack of it, is often most visible. But these days just about every industry qualifies as turbulent. Look at telecommunications, health care, retail banking, even your local travel agent. No one is safe. Times are changing, and the organizations that thrive in the future will be the ones that change with them. And in order to do this, they must have leaders who will relentlessly search for reality and demonstrate the courage to act.

How Do Leaders Bring About Change?

Just as the word implies, leaders accomplish things by leading, that is, by guiding and motivating other people. Dictators issue orders, using fear and punishment to command compliance. Leaders shape people's opinions and win their enthusiasm, using every available opportunity to send out their message and win supporters. For many of the best leaders, the full-court press is instinctive. Others take a more systematic approach, but whether consciously or instinctively, leaders always operate on three distinct levels— on the organization's technical, political and cultural systems.

At first this may sound academic, but if you think about it for a minute, you'll see that it is true. Every group that exists for a purpose has a technical system that organizes its resources to accomplish the purpose; a political system that determines how power, influence and rewards are used to motivate people; and a cultural system consisting of norms and values that bind people together. All of them affect how people think and behave. China, for example, is struggling with a technical (economic) system that is rapidly moving toward market-driven capitalism, while its political system is clinging to old-fashioned totalitarian communism, and its cultural system is torn between the two. In the U.S., on the other hand, the three systems are more aligned. The technical system is firmly rooted in capitalism, the political system is democratic, and the cultural environment values the supremacy of personal freedom, as embodied in the Bill of Rights. Sometimes it's hard to differentiate among the systems because they are so intertwined, but all three are always at work, and the leader who wants to make a lasting difference has to work on all three.

At General Electric, Jack Welch tackled the technical system by designing a "GE business engine." This engine would consist of stable, highly profitable units that generate cash, and fast-growing businesses that would use the cash to produce even greater returns. Welch's shorthand slogan for this was that the company must be "No. 1 or No. 2 in every business that GE is in, or we fix, close or sell it." In fact, being No. 1 or No. 2 was not enough. To remain in the GE portfolio, he declared, a business also must have well above average real returns and a distinct competitive advantage. In 1981, when Welch became CEO, one-half of GE's $27.2 billion in revenue came from aging slow-growth businesses. Welch decided that the company was wasting capital by staying in businesses that weren't going to be champions. So, over his tenure, he has divested $16.2 billion of marginal businesses, including such old standbys as small appliances and aerospace, and spent $53 billion on acquisitions such as RCA and Borg Warner Chemicals.[36] These massive changes shook up the old order about how GE was going to use its resources to earn profits and clearly sent the message that GE was now playing a new game.

In the political arena, Welch took on GE's massive bureaucracy. For decades, GE's "scientific management" system had been considered one of the company's greatest strengths. It allowed the company to discipline and control its far-flung and diverse businesses. But by the early 1980s, the bureaucracy had taken control, and the company was choking on its nitpicking system of formal reviews and approvals. People were judged and paid according to how well they responded to the bureaucratic rules, even though the procedures delayed decisions and often thwarted common sense. Mastering the system had become a stylized art form and a requisite for advancement. The result was that many of GE's best managers devoted far more energy to internal matters than to their customers. As GEers sometimes expressed it, the company was operating "with its face to the CEO and its ass to the customers."

Jack Welch knew this well because, as head of GE Plastics, he had spent many years hassling, and being hassled by, the enforcers at GE headquarters in Fairfield, Connecticut. He believed in risks and fast action, and grew the Plastics business rapidly by doing what he thought needed to be done and apologizing later if he got called down by the corporate staff. Welch made it to the CEO's job by outwitting the bureaucrats. He understood that they liked documentation and reports, so he became a master of the game. He became famous throughout GE for his beautifully packaged multivolume presentations that were filled with charts, graphs, timelines and whatever other eye-catching gimmicks he could think of. The fact that he didn't get kicked off the ladder and now sits in the chairman's office is evidence that the strategy worked. But as soon as he took over, he called off the game. "One of the first things Jack eliminated when he became CEO," recalls Larry Buckley, a member of Welch's Executive Management Staff, "was fancy reports, because he knew how much money he had spent making them."[37]

Welch has replaced the bureaucracy at GE with a new political system based on "integrated diversity." The headquarters staff has been slashed to several hundred from thousands, and control over planning and much of the capital spending has been pushed out into the operating units. The headquarters in Fairfield still does allocate key resources, especially people, and teaches best practices on leadership, but the units now have the freedom, and responsibility, to play the smartest game possible in their industries.[38]

As Welch described it in a letter to shareholders: "We cleared out stifling bureaucracy, along with the strategic planning apparatus, corporate staff empires, rituals, endless studies and briefings, and all the classic machinery that makes big-company operations smooth and predictable—but often glacially slow. As the underbrush of bureaucracy was cleared away, we began to see and talk to each other more clearly and more directly. . . . Freed from bureaucratic tentacles, and charged to act independently [the businesses have done] so, with great success. Corporate management got off their backs, and instead lined up behind them with resources and support."[39]

Welch's letter paints a glowing picture of success, but his upbeat tone belies the months of anguish he experienced as he watched tradition-bound managers and workers thwart his dreams of a speedy, responsive and cooperative GE. The problem, he finally decided, was that its corporate culture continued to value hierarchy and me-firstism. If GE was going to enjoy the benefits of the new growth engine it had so painfully built, and if its workers were going to use their new freedom from bureaucratic meddling to work faster and smarter, the corporate culture had to change as well. In the United States, you could mandate communism and start allocating power and rewards through a totalitarian government, but unless you got rid of the populace's cultural notions of personal freedom and inalienable rights, compliance wouldn't last long.

At GE, there were hundreds of thousands of workers and managers who had grown up in a business that was full of little fiefs, where control of knowledge was control of power, where nobody felt any stake in the success of other fiefs, and where very few people ever got fired. For several years, Welch worried and preached, but nothing changed. He wondered whether he wasn't being clear enough, or if people were just tuning him out. Finally, he came up with the term "boundarylessness" to describe the cultural environment that he wanted.

In a hallmark speech to several hundred GE managers in 1994, Welch explained the concept of boundarylessness using a simple analogy. "In this company, if you can picture the house, the house got taller and taller and taller. As we grew in size, we added floors. The house got wider and wider and wider. As we got more complex, we built walls functionally. The objective of all of us in this place is to blow up the internal walls—the floors vertically and the horizontal ones. That's the game we're at, that's what we are fundamentally after." He went on, changing metaphors, to explain that the "layers are insulators. They're like sweaters. When you go outside and you wear four sweaters, you don't know that it's cold out. You haven't faced reality. You're not getting the straight scoop on the temperature. You're all covered up. As you peel each sweater off, you learn more about the temperature. That's the same thing about layers."[40] The boundaryless culture Welch wanted instead was one in which information would flow freely, in which people could honestly assess reality without fear and in which the company would capture "the speed of a small company in the body of a big one." At the core of a boundaryless company, he told them, are people who act without regard for status or functional loyalty and who look for ideas from anywhere—including from inside the company, from customers, or from suppliers.

Welch used every technique he could think of to teach this message and help people live it. He preached it over and over. He provided mechanisms for people to begin to live the new way. GE's vaunted Work-Out effort involved hundreds of thousands of GE employees, suppliers and customers in "town hall" problem-solving meetings. Work-Out was not an elective—Welch mandated that every business conduct the sessions. And he prescribed their format—people from across functions and at different levels would come together to work on specific issues. Hierarchy and functional boundaries had to be left at the door, and everyone was asked for their ideas. The meetings were designed to produce results, and leaders were expected to implement the recommendations from workers. He followed Work-Out with other, more sophisticated tools to help people come together in teams to solve problems, such as the Change Acceleration Program and an aggressive Quality program.[41] He rewarded people for benchmarking and capturing ideas from other parts of GE or other companies.

In addition to all of these programs, tools, and exhortations, he confronted those who did not believe in the cultural values.

In the old days, GE may have fired a few unpleasant people who didn't meet their performance goals, but nice guys who didn't deliver and complete jerks who did deliver were welcome to stay. In the new GE, Welch declared, performance and behavior would both count. People who embraced boundarylessness but couldn't quite deliver would be helped along and given second, maybe even third chances, but stellar performers who insisted on keeping up the old walls and floors would be dismissed. And he backed up his statement by personally getting rid of some boundaryful people at the top of the company. Finally, he held others responsible for doing the same thing in their parts of the company. He once sternly told a conference of GE's several hundred managers, "People throughout this company hear us talk about boundarylessness and taking out layers, and they look at what we've done. Where we have multiple layers still left, they rightly question our integrity. . . . The only way I am going to get at this thing is to ask you to do it, to simply treat it as an integrity issue. We have no room for boundaryful people at GE, and we must become boundaryless if we are going to get the speed we need to survive."[42]

The magnitude of this GE transformation may or may not make it an extreme example of change. However, the point isn't the change, but the importance of having technical, political and cultural systems that support and reinforce one another. Winning companies do a lot better job than losers of keeping the three working together, because their leaders are ever-mindful of the need for alignment and to keep them in step with the changing demands of the marketplace.

When you look at winning organizations and compare them with the losers, the first things you notice may be good market strategies, efficient operations and agile response times. Winning companies are exceptionally good at listening to their customers and giving them what they want. But these important qualities are really just intermediate products. From the outset, and in the end, winning is really about leadership.

Winning individuals are leaders, people with ideas and values, and the energy and edge to do what needs to be done. And organizations are winners because they have good leaders, people who understand the importance of selecting the right things to do and who are able to manage the complex forces required to get them done. Because of this, winning organizations are leader-driven. They value leaders, they have cultures that expect and reward leadership, and everyone in the organization actively puts time and resources into developing leaders. Finally, winners win because of their ability to continually and consistently create more leaders at all levels of their organizations.

Leadership and the Teachable Point of View

Great Leaders Are Great Teachers

- They accomplish their goals through the people they teach
- They teach others to be leaders, not followers

Winning Leaders Make Teaching a Personal Priority

- They consider teaching one of their primary roles
- They use every opportunity to learn and to teach

Winners Have a "Teachable Point of View"

- They have clear ideas and values, based on knowledge and experience
- They articulate those lessons to others

How am I doing as a leader? The answer is how are the people you lead doing. Do they learn? Do they visit customers? Do they manage conflict? Do they initiate change? Are they growing and getting promoted? You won't remember when you retire what you did in the first quarter of 1994, or the third. What you'll remember is how many people you developed. How many people you helped have a better career because of your interest and your dedication to their development. . . . When confused as to how you're doing as a leader, find out how the people you lead are doing. You'll know the answer.[1]

—LARRY BOSSIDY, FORMER CEO OF HONEYWELL

If winning organizations are distinguished from losers by their ability to produce leaders at all levels, winning leaders are distinguished from wannabes—from bureaucrats, dictators and managers—by their extraordinary success at teaching others to be leaders as well.

Teaching other leaders certainly isn't the only requirement of leadership. As I mentioned in the previous chapters and will discuss further in later chapters, leaders must have ideas about the purpose of their organization and how to organize its resources. They must have values that prescribe how it will operate and behave as a member of society. They must have energy and the ability to energize others. And they must have "edge," the courage to make hard choices and take tough actions. These are all essential characteristics of leaders that I will explore in detail later. However, after observing Roger Enrico at PepsiCo, Jack Welch at GE, Andy Grove at Intel, and a number of other winning companies and leaders, I have noted an additional trait that helps implement the others and, I believe, is ultimately responsible for the success of their organizations. It is that these leaders engender leadership traits in others. They teach others to be leaders.

The notion that teaching and leadership go hand in hand is not new. The standard definitions of "leadership" generally state that leaders are people who motivate one or more other people to do a specific thing. This involves teaching those other people to see the desirability of reaching that specific goal and, usually, showing them how to get there. More sophisticated definitions of leadership shift away from the idea that leaders set concrete targets or that they specify the actions to be taken. Warren Bennis, who teaches and runs a center that studies leadership at the University of Southern California, has written about leadership for decades. He states that "the basis of leadership is the capacity of the leader to change the mindset, the framework of another person."[2] In other words, according to Bennis, leaders get people to reach for common goals by helping them see aspects of the world differently.

I'd like to build on Bennis's definition. It certainly describes the activities of people with broader and more lasting impacts than manufacturing vice presidents who simply decree that more cars will be built. What needs to be added is an essential characteristic of winning organizations: sustainability. Winning organizations not only fulfill their desired goals today, but they also continually redesign those goals as circumstances change, and go on to meet those new goals. In order to do that, they must have a constant supply of new people with ideas, values, energy and edge. They need leaders. Therefore, if a leader is to be successful, he or she must develop others to be leaders. A person may have all the other traits of leadership, but if he or she doesn't personally see to the development of new leaders, the organization won't be sustainable, and the person is not a true leader—or at least not a winning one.

If you look across history and across all fields of endeavor, you will see that this is true. Institutions and movements succeed over the long term not because of their cultures, or their core manufacturing competencies, or their use of modern management tools, but because they continually regenerate leadership at all levels. These dynamic leaders then go on to shape strong cultures, develop needed core competencies, and employ appropriate management tools such as total quality or reengineering—but the key to their success is the development of these leaders in the first place. Jesus, Gandhi and Martin Luther King Jr. all understood this. They all had strong ideas, values, energy and edge, but without disciples to spread their mission, both during their lifetimes and after their deaths, their legacies would have been short-lived.

Other examples of successful leaders who fulfilled their goals by training others to be leaders include General George Marshall. Marshall didn't win World War II single-handedly for the Allies, but he built a crushing army by teaching others. He was known for his ability to develop other military commanders and served in prestigious military training posts for almost sixty years.[3] In the corporate world, Jack Welch has made General Electric the most valuable company on the planet, not by making every decision himself, but by teaching and encouraging all 200,000-plus of GE's employees to think, take initiative and become leaders.

And one of my favorite examples is Phil Jackson, former coach of the Chicago Bulls, now at the L.A. Lakers. In his book *Sacred Hoops*, Jackson talks about his work with Michael Jordan. Jordan is such a prodigiously talented athlete that there isn't much that any coach could do to improve his basketball playing. So Jackson focused his efforts with Jordan on making the superstar athlete a true leader of the team. And it worked. In 1989, five[4] years after joining the league and the very same year[5] Jackson became head coach of the Bulls, Jordan began to see his role not as just scoring points and blocking shots, but as a leader whose job also was to help raise the level of play of every other player on the team. Phil Jackson says that it is this contribution, Jordan's ability to help his teammates be better players, more than his superb athletic talent that has made the Chicago Bulls the world's winningest basketball team.

I don't mean to suggest that it isn't possible to build an organization that is successful—for a while—without generating new leadership. Autocrats such as Harold Geneen at ITT, Ed Hennessy at AlliedSignal, and Edzard Reuter at Daimler Benz built highly acclaimed corporations through their own forceful initiatives. But leaders like this usually don't see the need to develop any other leaders, and thus can discourage the leadership efforts of others, so their companies don't have the depth of resources needed to steer them through complicated times. IBM had a highly talented leader in its founder, Tom Watson Sr. The strength of his vision and charisma carried the company for several decades after his departure. However, because of overreliance on Watson's outdated formula for success, IBM failed to raise new leaders who would come up with the fresh ideas and strategies needed in the future. By the early 1990s, it found itself without world-class leadership at a critical time when the industry was structurally changing. Under nice-guy bureaucrat John Akers, it didn't have the capacity to transform ahead of the tidal wave, and it was inundated. To solve the problem, the board not only had to fire Akers,[6] but also had to go outside the company to find a successor. IBM had 256,000 employees[7] at the time, and not one of them was deemed strong or creative enough to take the helm. Similar stories could be told about Kodak, Westinghouse and the many other companies that have had to go outside to replace their faltering CEOs. Like Akers, Kay Whitmore at Kodak and Paul Lego at Westinghouse were well-intentioned, but given my criteria, they hadn't been developed into leaders themselves and they couldn't teach anyone else.

Teaching and learning are inextricably interwoven aspects of leadership. Leadership is the capacity to get things done through others by changing people's mindsets and energizing them to action. Successful leadership must accomplish this through ideas and values, not through coercion or Machiavellian manipulation.[8] This is true at all levels, whether it is the new engineer having to play a leadership role by influencing peers and managers, or the middle-level project leader who must lead up, down and horizontally, or senior executives atop multibillion-dollar corporations. Organizations need leaders if they want to win, and the only way to get them is for other leaders to consciously mentor and prepare them.

Leaders Teaching

When I say that successful leaders teach others to be leaders, I mean that literally. The winning leaders I have met all view teaching as one of their major jobs, and they spend a lot of time doing it.

Like many other companies, winning organizations do, of course, have well-organized and well-funded human resources departments, and they usually do offer lots of career development and management training programs. But the programs taught by development specialists and consultants provide only an array of tools that leaders can use. They don't teach the more critical leadership skills of figuring out where the organization needs to go or when to use the tools. The essence of real leadership is assessing changing situations and motivating others to act in an appropriate manner. Leadership is more about thinking, judging, acting and motivating than it is about strategies, methodologies and tools. Leadership reflects a person's mindset and his or her approach to the world. Even though these intangible qualities are extremely difficult to teach, winning organizations are remarkably successful at it. And that is because their most senior executives, their most proficient and talented leaders, as well as all of their front-line subordinates, are personally involved in the teaching.

Jack Welch of General Electric is one of the most dedicated teachers I know. For twenty years he has made biweekly visits to GE's Crotonville executive training center to enter into dialogue with thousands of his employees each year. His schedule was also filled with hundreds of video conferences, meetings, factory visits and workshop sessions. For Welch, every organizational process from strategic reviews to budget meetings to the annual general managers meeting were teaching and learning events. Jeffrey Immelt, current GE CEO, now does the same.

The world of business pays great homage to Welch, and other organizations emulate many of his programs and practices, such as the Crotonville executive training programs, GE's Change Acceleration Program, the "No. 1, No. 2, fix, close or sell" strategy and his concept of the "boundaryless" organization. But what most people fail to see is that the best Welch practice to emulate is his work as a teacher. The person who has really made a difference at GE is not Jack Welch, the guy who completely rethought the business, or the guy who acquired over $53 billion of assets and divested more than $16 billion.[9] The person who made the biggest difference is Jack Welch the world-class teacher. For example, look at the note on page 57 that he sent to thirty participants in his Executive Development Course. The note is important because it shows the level of engagement at the session. Welch sparked and led a mutual dialogue that stimulated participants to think about the most basic issues in leadership. This is the essence of teaching.

September 26, 1996

EDC—

I'm looking forward to an exciting time with you tomorrow. I've included here a few thoughts for you to think about prior to our session.

As a Group (perhaps 3 groups)
Situation -
Tomorrow you are appointed CEO of GE.
- What would you do in first 30 days?
- Do you have a current "vision" of what to do?
  - How would you go about developing one?
  - Present your best shot at a vision.
- How would you go about "selling" the vision?
- What foundations would you build on?
- What current practices would you jettison?

Individually--
  I. Please be prepared to describe a leadership dilemma that you have faced in the past 12 months, i.e., plant closing, work transfer, HR, buy or sell a business, etc.
  II. Think about what you would recommend to accelerate the Quality drive across the company.
  IIIa. I'll be talking about "A, B & C" players. What are your thoughts on just what makes up such a player?
  IIIb. I'll also be talking about energy / energizing / edge as key characteristics of today's leaders. Do you agree? Would you broaden this? How?

I'm looking forward to a fun time, and I know I'll leave a lot smarter than when I arrived.

Jack

Andy Grove is another great leader who teaches others to be leaders. Grove says his teaching is the result of deep reflection about what has allowed him to be successful. "I'm an engineer and a manager, but I have always had an urge to teach, to share with others what I've figured out for myself. It is that same urge that makes me want to share the lessons I've learned," he says in his book *Only the Paranoid Survive.*[10] So in addition to his hands-on teaching at Intel, he has taught courses at the Stanford Graduate School of Business and written several books.

Intel operates in an extremely fast-paced environment, with some of the shortest product life cycles and greatest leaps in technology of any industry. This has given Grove a clear point of view on his industry. "There is at least one point in the history of any company when you have to change dramatically to rise to the next performance level. Miss the moment and you start to decline."[11]

Grove eschews any sophisticated strategic models and instead focuses on the core abilities and character of its leaders. "How a company handles the process of getting through [these times] depends on a very 'soft' almost touchy-feely issue: how management reacts emotionally to the crisis." So Grove spends his time teaching leadership. The ability to groom leaders who share his sense of paranoia and can respond when they see change "has been instrumental to Intel's success," he says.[12]

Anatomy of a Teaching Program

Roger Enrico, the former CEO of PepsiCo, has perhaps set the performance high bar as an executive leader/teacher. In 1994 and 1995, the two years before he became CEO, Enrico devoted more than 120 days exclusively to coaching and mentoring the next generation of PepsiCo leaders. He personally designed a program called Building the Business, and over eighteen months he ran the program ten times, with classes of nine participants each time. His example of direct hands-on teaching has inspired leaders at other companies to start teaching their own courses.

The Building the Business program, says Enrico, was designed not to teach people how to come up with the answers he would have come up with, but to teach them how to come up with their own good answers to whatever challenges and opportunities might arise. "Somewhere along the way, we either told people, or they surmised, . . . that it was a paint-by-the-numbers system. It's like, if you use these tools in this sequence in this way, success is inevitable, as opposed to: these are tools to help you gain an insight into what you're doing, or help you to create a strategy from the insight that you get." If everything were so easy, he says, "I wouldn't need a manager, I'd have a machine."[13]

Enrico attributes the creation of his unique program to an insight that came to him during a conversation he had one day with Paul Russell, PepsiCo's vice president of executive development. Several months earlier, PepsiCo chairman Wayne Calloway had pointed out to his senior executives that if the company continued to grow at its historic 15% rate,[14] the ranks of its core of "key executives" would swell to 1,500 people by the year 2000. With only about 20% of those executives currently in place, Calloway had pressed his senior leaders to make a front-and-center commitment to raising up a new generation of Pepsi-Co leaders.

Enrico had volunteered and energetically started working with Russell to design the program. But after months of reading management literature and listening to a parade of well-known consultants (including me), Enrico's enthusiasm had waned. Finally, he was ready to throw in the towel. Why, he asked Russell, should he spend his time leading a program based on professors' models and other companies' experiences? Why not just bring in the consultants and let them teach it?

It wasn't a question that Russell had been expecting, but he had an immediate answer that lit a spark in Enrico. "You should do it," he told Enrico, "because the people at PepsiCo don't need leadership models with fuzzy applications. They need to hear about leadership at PepsiCo and about your experience and insights, and they need to hear it from you." Later, Enrico would say that this had been a breakthrough moment for him. At that instant, he decided to "shit can the academics" and create a program built on what he, Roger Enrico, knew about leadership. He picked up the foot-high stack of consultants' reports and threw them in the trash. Now he was excited. He would run the leadership program, but he would do it his way.

The inspiration that hit Roger Enrico that day is one that needs to hit many more executives. It was that the only way PepsiCo was going to remain successful was if its current leaders took personal responsibility for developing other leaders. And in order to do that, they must develop their own "teachable points of view" about running, growing and changing a business as well as about leadership. Enrico knew that he had lots of material in his head that would be valuable to the next generation of PepsiCo's leaders, but he had to figure out a way to articulate it so that it would be clear to them. He had to develop a teachable point of view, and then teach it.

During the next few days, Enrico spent every spare minute with Russell, pouring out his thoughts and memories, figuring out what he had learned, how he had learned it, and how he might teach it to others. They also videotaped interviews with other key PepsiCo executives for Enrico to use as benchmarking examples. Then, only eight weeks later, Enrico opened his own personal leadership "war college."

Enrico says that he first began seriously thinking about teaching in 1991 while recovering from a heart attack. After twenty-four[15] years as a rising star in PepsiCo's executive ranks, he was financially independent at the relatively young age of 48. "I was young enough to have a whole other career,"[16] he says, and he realized that he didn't want to be remembered only for how many soft drinks or potato chips he had sold. He wanted to be "someone who opened the minds of people to see what they might have missed."[17] He considered quitting PepsiCo to do community service and teach a course or two in a business school.

When Calloway and Russell and another colleague, Joseph McCann, encouraged Enrico to do his teaching at PepsiCo, he said yes partly out of loyalty. In the process of responding, however, he not only opened the minds of other PepsiCo executives, he also developed a strong team to support him when he was named chairman and CEO in early 1996, and a leadership model to keep PepsiCo a winner well into the next century. He had cracked the code to teaching leadership.

Enrico's methodology was one of intense interaction. He would begin the program with five days at a remote site, where he would spend from 8:00 A.M. until late at night every day talking to the participants individually and as a group about his own personal experiences rising through the ranks in PepsiCo. He talked about his successes and his failures and the lessons he had learned from them. He talked about how he solved problems, met challenges and viewed the world. "I try to talk . . . the way former PepsiCo CEO Don Kendall talked to me—frankly, openly, matter-of-factly. He didn't pontificate; he told stories,"[18] says Enrico.

He also pressed them for their own ideas and reactions, and to take seriously their responsibilities as leaders of PepsiCo. His opening line at many of these sessions was: "No longer can you look upward and blame the idiots at the top of the company for what is wrong. You're now one of them."[19] Bill Nictakis, a vice president of marketing at Frito-Lay, says Enrico's remark changed his view of his role, but it "scared the hell out of me. All of a sudden, my job wasn't just to manage volume variance: I had to think about planning strategies for five years from now."[20]

As the vehicle for learning, Enrico required each participant to bring with him or her a real project that had the potential to dramatically affect PepsiCo's revenue, quality, costs or customer satisfaction. They each laid out their challenge to the group, including Enrico, and then they all discussed how it might be refined and accomplished. The participants then would go back to their jobs for ninety days and try to implement their projects, using the ideas and lessons they had learned at the workshop. While the participants from one group were back at their jobs working on their projects, Enrico would start up a new group with a new set of projects. Meanwhile, he remained available for consultation and assistance. At the end of the ninety days, each group would reconvene with Enrico for three days to get feedback, report their progress and review what they had learned.

Peter Waller, then senior vice president for Kentucky Fried Chicken (KFC), a PepsiCo division, brought his idea for a family meals campaign to the program. When he was marketing director of KFC Australia, Waller had noticed that families were ordering four value meals at a time. So he had the idea to package the meals into a combination with enough variety for one family. He arrived with binders of data and market projections, but never dug them out of his briefcase. Instead, he and the other participants were prodded by Enrico to expand his idea into a broader international marketing program. He ended up with the slogan "Take Back the Family," and a Mega-meals campaign that boosted KFC's revenue growth into double digits in all its major markets.[21]

Teachable Point of View

Enrico's Building the Business program produced a number of new campaigns and projects that had the immediate effect of significantly improving the company's operations. More importantly, it got a whole new generation of PepsiCo leaders familiar with Roger Enrico and how his mind works. But perhaps most importantly, it made Enrico himself a better leader. Before starting the program, Enrico had been like the Bulls' Michael Jordan, an excellent solo player. In order to design and teach the program, however, he had to organize his vast knowledge and articulate explicitly what he had learned implicitly over the years. It pushed him to develop, or sharpen, a crucial component of leadership, which I call a "teachable point of view."

Having a teachable point of view is both a sign that a person has clear ideas and values and a tool that enables him or her to communicate those ideas and values to others. It is not enough to have experience; leaders must draw appropriate lessons from their experience, and then take their tacit knowledge and make it explicit to others. This requires not only that they have a point of view in their own minds, but that they can explain, or teach, it to others.

In Enrico's case, this was a particular challenge. Enrico had steered Pepsi through the so-called "cola wars," when the famous Pepsi Challenge caused Coke to change its formula.[22] He had also run its Frito-Lay division and turned it into one of the world's most powerful food brands. For Enrico, building businesses was instinctive; it was what made him tick. But he had never thought about how he did it. To teach others, he had to understand how first, and then teach it. He began to boil his experiences down to a set of leadership principles focused on quickly making decisions and implementing them. In addition to conveying his own points of view, an important part of Enrico's teaching was also aimed at helping his students learn to develop their own ideas and teachable points of view.

To influence and lead, one needs teachable points of view not only in the form of teachable ideas and values themselves, but also about how to nurture and develop good ideas and strong values in others. In Chapter 9, I will talk about how the very best leaders personalize these points of view and spin them out as stories that engage followers emotionally as well as intellectually. But the point I want to make here is that great leaders are great teachers not only because they know what they think, but also because they take the time to organize their thoughts in ways so that they can communicate them clearly.

I have started the practice of beginning workshops by asking people to think about their own teachable points of view. What are the central ideas driving their business? What are their own and their business's core values? And how do they link them together to direct their own actions and to energize other people? Then I have them stand up and actually give a three-minute presentation. A few are great, but most stumble a lot. These are usually experienced managers who have been professionals for years. So why can't they get their thoughts out and explain them? Because the ability to do something, even do it well, and the ability to articulate how they do it are two different skills. We all recognize that good athletes aren't necessarily good coaches.

And we know that many good artists and musicians aren't good teachers, either. We recognize the difference in sports and the arts, but when it comes to managing and leading, very few people understand the difference. Winning leaders do, and they act on that understanding. Most of us take our experiences and stick them in our hip pocket for use at a later time. But leaders keep taking them out and examining them, looking to see exactly what are the lessons they learned, and searching for effective ways to express them.

Most of us have teachable points of view about little things. For example, we not only put the milk in the refrigerator, but we can explain the why and how of spoilage and the beneficial effects of refrigeration. Leaders, however, have teachable points of view on a broad range of less tangible and much more complicated topics. And they are always coming up with new ones because they are always looking around to see what is to be learned from any situation.

Roger Enrico has a wonderful teachable point of view about developing new ideas and getting them implemented that he says he learned while he was teaching one of his early Building the Business workshops. He calls it "bundling." Here's how he explains it:

> When we did the follow-up session, some of the questions I asked were: "What did you really learn in the program? Were you able to apply it? What worked? What didn't work? What seemed to make sense?" And one guy said: "What I figured out was that if what you're working on is of really great significance, there is no way to make it happen unless you get it into the top five positions [on the priority list]." . . . And then some others said, "But my project isn't important enough to get to the top five. It's an important thing to do, but I can't get to the president."
>
> So, I asked one of them: "How do you do that? . . . Why didn't it get up there?" He said, "Well, because there were other people working on this and this and this." So, I thought about it, and I said to him, "Aren't these things connected? Isn't there a

knee bone connected to the thigh bone kind of thing here?" He said, "Well, yeah, there could be." And I said, "Well, why don't you guys band together? I mean, literally, why don't you get together [with the other people in your unit who are working on other problems]. . . . They all have the same problem you have [and you are all probably] working on a component of a larger thing." . . . So, together we came up with this concept of bundling. . . . What you've got to do is bundle these things into a business proposition, which in fact will make money, and don't worry about [the components]. . . . The organization will optimize these components as you go down. But you can't . . . get the components by themselves over the hurdle.

So, now part of what we do is we talk about bundling. I've now decided that bundling is one of the biggest ideas in leadership. Maybe it's another way of saying, getting up on a higher plane to see the horizon better. Sometimes people don't realize that seemingly unrelated things are related. It's the people who have the ability to see seemingly unrelated things going on in the organization and bundle them together into a proposition who are the great leaders.

Enrico cites an example from Pizza Hut.

When you're going out there to talk to customers in the field or to the franchisees, you shouldn't expect to find the answers. You might. Somebody might actually be doing something you can just roll out nationally. But you may not find the answer. You may find elements of it, and you have to bundle it together. . . . The one that got bundled together at Pizza Hut is [something that] will have an enormous effect. What this guy came up with is a simple thing, that the drivers are going out with 1.2 orders per trip, and if we can get it to 1.4 orders per trip, it's worth tens of millions of dollars. Not only that, it helps the drivers, and their tips go up. The whole thing will work in a synergistic way. And he said the way he wanted to do that was to have a device to aggregate orders by grid [location]. Well, and there was another guy working on the problem that our pizzas are cold by the time the drivers take them. Then, there was another guy working on the fact that we need a new computer system because we're not answering the telephones right. Well, this one guy saw that we could bundle them together. What he needed in order to do that is a computer that would, first of all, answer the damn telephone, and get the order taken. We think we can hold an order for seven minutes and still make our deliveries. So, the computer will hold the order for seven minutes searching for a match in the grid. If it doesn't get one, it will print the ticket anyhow. What we do now is we produce first-in and first-out. So, we may have a pizza sit there waiting for a match, and it gets cold. If we have a computer that will hold the order until we get a match, the two pizzas that are going with the same driver are produced at the same time. The point is that this whole thing got bundled together in this way, and now we can justify the cost of the computer. So that was the bundling idea that came out of some feedback from some of the participants.[23]

Teachable Moments

Another organization that does an outstanding job of teaching people to be leaders is the United States military's Special Operations Forces (SOF). The Special Operations Forces make up a critical component of the United States' defense and international relations plans. It has only 32,000 active duty personnel and another 14,000 reservists, accounting for only 1.3%[24] of the nation's defense personnel and budget, but they have garnered an inordinate share of the work being done. Somalia, Haiti, Bosnia, and Liberia all employed the Special Operations Forces heavily. Increasingly, as weapons of mass destruction proliferate, the sophistication of terrorists increases and regional conflicts heat up, the SOF are called on to broaden the scope of their activities. Their assignments may range from multilateral peacekeeping operations to rescue missions to anti-drug activities to training local police and military units.[25] The SOF, made up of Army

Rangers, Green Berets, Navy SEALs and the Air Force wings that support their rapid deployment, require people who are not only supremely skilled at extraordinarily difficult tasks, but who can react instantly with appropriate responses in crisis situations.

The late Rear Admiral Chuck LeMoyne, who was a Navy SEAL in Vietnam and taught special warfare for many years, described some of the training. "We provide the ultimate simulations, as real as possible, with [simulated] civilians in the way. The goal is to give these young men a sense of the confusion they'll face in a real operation."[26] This is because the truth is that when the metal starts to fly in battle, "training" goes out the window. The real goal of the preparation, therefore, is not to give people proficiency in the latest warfare technology. It is to create leaders, men and women who will react with the right instincts in hostile, confusing and unpredictable environments.

Basic Underwater Demolitions SEAL training (BUDS) is where candidates for Navy SEAL duty are weeded out. Its physical training is grueling, with only about 20% surviving the six-month course (27 out of a recent entering class of 137).

The real test and teaching of BUDS, however, is not what the students do, but what they become. BUDS is taught by SEAL veterans who are chosen for their strong leadership and all-around performance rather than their specialized abilities. Their primary function is to serve as role models and coaches. It is an honor to be chosen as an instructor for these units, and it is a job that is taken very seriously.

One of the most prized qualities taught is teamwork and a willingness to focus on the good of the entire mission. To drive this home, BUDS's physical regimen includes exercises lifting, carrying and handling a twelve-foot, 175-pound[27] log in teams. The point is that no one can do the job of a SEAL alone. As Admiral LeMoyne said, "We aren't looking for the Rambo or Lone Ranger types here."[28]

Hell Week at the finale of this first phase tests whether the aspiring SEALs have achieved the necessary personal transformation. By the time this week arrives, many will have already dropped out, and after the five days of Hell Week, another 35% to 40% percent will leave. During Hell Week, a SEAL will get four hours of sleep the entire week. Training is done in frigid waters in the early mornings and late nights off the coast of Coronado near San Diego. At the same time, most recruits endure sunburn and exhaustion because of the daytime exercises. During Hell Week, it is likely that a SEAL will have to depend on others to physically save him or her from danger and that he or she will, in turn, do the same for his classmates.[29]

In a crisis situation, SEALs can derive confidence from knowing they survived this week, and that their teammates did as well. In a short time, they have learned important lessons about leadership: that the human spirit can and must endure many things, that leaders must lead with high expectations and that teamwork is the key to accomplishing a mission.

An extraordinary feature of BUDS under Rear Admiral Ray Smith's command was the last day of physical training. After six months at BUDS, the remaining SEAL candidates are given probationary six-month assignments with active duty SEAL teams. At this crucial moment, before they departed for their probationary assignments, Admiral Smith, who ran the Naval Special Warfare Command between 1992 and 1996,[30] would visit them. But Smith did more than visit. He actively participated in all the day's activities. To prove that he would ask nothing of them that he wouldn't do himself, the admiral *in his fifties* would undergo the same physical regimen as men in their twenties.

Later that day, Smith would pose in the photograph taken of every graduating SEAL class. The men, about thirty of them, are wearing swim trunks. (I have shown one of these photos to dozens of people. Not one of them has been able to identify the 50-year-old in the picture.) In the middle of the photograph is a sign with a simple sentence: "I will do nothing to dishonor my unit, my navy, or my country."

After the photo was taken, Smith would sit alone and talk with the new graduates—giving them his teachable point of view about what it means to be a SEAL at a teachable moment in their careers. Like Jack Welch, who meets with every executive training class that goes through General Electric's Crotonville training facility, Smith knew that there are special turning points and situations in people's lives when they are most open to learning and accepting the guidance of others. This was one of them, so he went out of his way to touch each of these young people at that moment.

Smith used his time to help the graduates understand the experience they had just been through and prepare them for the future at the precise moment when they were likely to be most receptive. He would explain his point of view on the role of SEALs in furthering the interests of the United States. He framed the experience as the beginning of a commitment to leadership by "any man, anywhere, anytime." Then he would talk about how they should live their lives to uphold the honor of the SEALs.

In describing these sessions, Smith told me: "I talk about behavior and I talk about citizenship, the roles of being a SEAL, how they are viewed by the public as special and how they have to live up to that expectation. . . . I tell them, 'You have to comport yourself at all times above and beyond the normal American citizen. That's your burden now. You can't be called Navy Special Warfare and expect to be treated special. You've got to behave special.'"[31]

For twentysomething aspiring hotshots who have just proven that they can perform nearly superhuman feats and survive unimaginable difficulties, advice about personal peccadilloes and meeting public expectations of decorum may not have been something they were eager to hear. But if there was ever a moment when they needed to hear it, it was then, and if there was anyone who can tell them, it was the Admiral himself. And the fact that he did it at that precise moment made it all the more powerful.

The Teaching Organization

While it's essential that top leaders teach, one of the most intriguing aspects of winning organizations is the degree to which all leaders at all levels actively work to develop other leaders. Teaching is truly part of these organizations' genetic code of leadership, and one of the primary tools that their leaders use to lead.

I once had a discussion with a middle manager at Intel's Folsom, California, facility. I didn't mention that I was writing a book about leaders and teaching, but when we began to talk about Intel's success, he brought up the subject and expounded on it for thirty minutes. Spontaneously, he laid out the entire case for why teaching is important and who ought to teach.

Basically, he said, Intel went through some tough times in the mid-1980s "that led us to be very conservative in our hiring. For a long time, we grew and grew, but didn't hire anyone. But, in the past three years, we've practically doubled in size. As a result, half of our managers have never been through a downswing, and we are losing some of the hungry, paranoid culture."[32] To counteract this, Intel has made teaching an explicit part of everyone's job. Andy Grove teaches new-hire orientations and senior manager courses, and Grove and other top leaders hold regular question and answer sessions with employees.

Further, every leader at Intel "from Grove down to experienced managers [who have been there on average twelve to fifteen years] is required to teach, and part of their bonus is based on whether or not they do it," my acquaintance continued. Some of them teach formal corporate courses. Others teach courses at the company's sites across the world. "It's not a big part of the bonus. But it's Andy's way of saying, 'This is important and we want you to do it.' If you don't have managers who have been there teaching, you end up like IBM in the early 1990s. All of their teaching was done by people who weren't leaders or weren't even in the company. When things changed, their people didn't know how to make tough decisions, because you can only learn that from people who have been there."

The person with whom I was speaking said he teaches a class to new hires on how to initiate and manage constructive conflict. He says his most valuable teaching, however, takes place in the office. "When one of my people is dealing with an issue and they are not confronting it, I will confront them. I support them if that's what they need. But I make sure they confront it. When I am getting copied on e-mails, and there is a chain of reply messages attached to a certain issue, I know people aren't confronting. That's when I get involved. I tell people, 'I'll go with you if you want. I'll stay in the meeting you need to have the whole time.' But it's important that they learn to confront it, and it's my job to help them do that." It is this attitude about leading and teaching that helps make Intel a winning company.

Leading Is Teaching

Although many of the people I have highlighted in this chapter are senior executives at the top of huge organizations, as the Intel middle manager indicates, teaching cannot be confined to the rarefied upper reaches of senior management. It's true that seasoned leaders such as Roger Enrico, Admiral Smith, and Jack Welch have an invaluable legacy to pass on by virtue of their many years of experience and their proven records of success. It's also true that the most important lessons often come from the tough, even failure, situations, so losing these hard-won lessons would be especially wasteful and costly to their organizations. But the fact is that the importance of teaching goes far beyond the specific content of what is taught.

Teaching is at the heart of leading. In fact, it is through teaching that leaders lead others. Leading is not dictating specific behavior. It is not issuing orders and commanding compliance. Leading is getting others to see a situation as it really is and to understand what responses need to be taken so that they will act in ways that will move the organization toward where it needs to be. Whether it is teaching something as simple as what concrete tasks need to take precedence over others this week, or something as complex as how to make good decisions, teaching is how ideas and values get transmitted. Therefore, in order to be a leader at any level of an organization, a person must be a teacher. Simply put, if you aren't teaching, you aren't leading.

Past as Prologue

Learning from Experience

Winning Leaders Draw from Their Pasts

- Events early in life shape lessons that they use in the future
- They consciously capture these lessons and use them as guides

Leaders' Stories Reveal Their Teachable Points of View

- Tom Tiller's grandfather taught him, "You gotta try"
- Fidel Castro taught Roberto Goizueta to take risks

Everyone Has a Usable Past: Leaders Just Use Theirs Better

- Leaders recognize the defining moments in their lives
- They communicate the lessons through words and actions

Each of us tells our own personal life story to ourselves, every day. The "mind chatter" that rushes through our brains at two hundred words per minute when we're not concentrating on something else becomes the story we are living. I should have done this, or I'll never get over that.

The mind is formed to an astonishing degree by the act of inventing and censoring ourselves. We create our own plot line. And that plot line soon turns into a self-fulfilling prophecy. Psychologists have found that the way people tell their stories becomes so habitual that they finally become recipes for structuring experience itself, for laying down routes into memory and finally for guiding their lives.[1]

—GAIL SHEEHY

One of the things that makes leaders such great teachers is that they are extraordinary learners as well. Life is full of lessons that we all learn every day. To a large extent, that's what living is about. But leaders are much better than most people at recognizing those lessons and using them.

We all have worldviews, complex webs of ideas, values and assumptions about how the world operates. We all have fundamental beliefs, for example, about whether people are naturally generous or greedy, or whether we are victims of fate or controllers of our own destinies. And we develop these views, which shape our responses to the world, out of our past experiences. But most people don't consciously recognize these views and can't trace their origin. In my experience, winning leaders not only can, but do.

Winning leaders consciously think about their experiences. They roll them over in their minds, analyze them and draw lessons from them. They constantly update and refine their views as they acquire new knowledge and experience. And they store them in the form of stories that they use not only to guide their own decisions and actions, but also to teach and lead others. When you hear leaders talk about their lives, you learn their teachable points of view.

Many leaders point to their childhoods as the source of important ideas and values, and the time when they began to develop emotional energy and edge. Bob Knowling, a former vice president at Ameritech, who is CEO of a privately held software company, InternetAccess, Inc., for example, traces his self-determination and edge to a nasty encounter in a welfare office one day when he was seven years old. Knowling, an African-American, was one of thirteen children. He had gone to the office with his mother to get food stamps. When she asked if she could use the stamps to buy more peanut butter and less of something else, the woman behind the counter told her: "You wouldn't be here asking for more peanut butter if you had thought twice about having all those kids." At that moment, Knowling says, "I witnessed the transformation of my mother, and my own began as well. She took my hand, and as we walked out of the office, she declared, 'I am off welfare for good.'"

As Knowling's mother worked to make good on her vow, he says, she also began focusing on teaching her children that they must take responsibility for their own lives. As a result, instead of hanging out on the street, he joined the Boys Club and played basketball and football. This won him a scholarship to Wabash College, where he was named a division All-American. Poverty defeats many people. Knowling has several older siblings who are still struggling to get by. But thanks to his mother's transformation, Knowling says he and the younger ones learned valuable lessons from their poverty and are all successful professionals. "We learned," he says, that "hardship is there to overcome. If you adapt and adjust, you can get along. And no matter how bad the situation, everyone has the potential to succeed."[2]

In this chapter, I want you to listen to the life stories of some of the leaders I have met while researching this book. I have deliberately left them in the form of extended quotes because one of the most interesting and important things about how leaders use their pasts is their ability to pick out the lessons and articulate them clearly. To paraphrase them would give me the opportunity to edit and shape them. I want you to hear how well they do it themselves. I want you to observe firsthand how their minds work.

Tom Tiller, CEO of Polaris

Tom Tiller was one of the most successful young men in America. At 33, he became head of manufacturing for General Electric's $6 billion Appliance division and the youngest officer at GE. At age 34, he was named by GE's CEO Jack Welch to head the company's $1 billion silicone business. From there he went on to become CEO of Polaris. When I asked Tiller how he got to where he is, he immediately started telling me about his childhood. After just a few minutes, it was clear that Tiller has a clear image of who he is, and he knows how he got that way. More importantly, he applies the lessons from his past to his current circumstances. What follows is his largely unedited reply when I asked him to tell me about his own development.[3]

My story is a pretty simple one, really. I grew up in a very small town in northern Vermont, a place called Essex Junction, which is just about as big as it sounds. It's about thirty miles from the Canadian border. And as a kid up through high school, that's the only place I lived. It was a very small community. I had very deeply rooted values from a very young age and sort of the Yankee work ethic. The whole state is only 500,000 people. There are more cows than there are people. . . . So, I have a lot of small-town values, a sense of community, doing what's right, treating people like you're going to be with them for twenty or thirty years, not twenty or thirty minutes. And I think that had a lot to do with who I am and the way I try to live my life.

A person who had a very, very large impact on me as a person and as a leader was my grandfather. Everyone has someone, and for me it was my grandfather. . . . He dropped out of school in ninth grade and was part of a family where his dad died and he had to support the family. He became a self-made person. He was an entrepreneur, a very, very successful entrepreneur. He ran several different businesses and did very well, largely through the idea that anything can be done if you put your mind to it, anything. He was willing to try and experiment with about any idea or concept with people as young as you can imagine. For example, when I was seven or eight years old, he would give me his Jeep and let me go drive it by myself. Not out on the main road, but he happened to have a sawmill and he would let me drive it around the sawmill, and I had to bump it into a few things, but he let you do that. He let me drive a 50,000-pound bulldozer, an enormous bulldozer, when I was eleven years old. I could barely reach the pedals. I built an airplane runway strip when I was seventeen years old. He said to me, "I want a runway built between now and the end of the summer." I told him, "I've never built one." He said, "I know you haven't, but go figure out how to do it." It was just the idea of "go do it." "Try it." It's great to talk to people, but there is no substitute for getting in the game and "Just go do it."

At GE, we talk about it as "stretch" or "empowerment." He didn't have fancy words like that for it, but, you know, he'd give you a chainsaw, show you a half a million trees and say, "Between now and the end of the week those got to be cut down." It was just the idea of giving you impossible problems with just very rough kinds of ideas on how to do it, and then just demanding that you got to figure out a way to do it.

He and I have a very special relationship. It's the way he lived his life. He struggled, made a lot of mistakes up until he was thirty-five or forty years old, and then did very, very well financially and professionally. And to him, the idea that you can't do something wasn't in the universe—or the idea that you got to go to a whole bunch of people before you try doing something. His idea was don't be afraid to make some mistakes. I mean, you don't want to cut your leg off. You've got to understand the basics about doing something, but he was very much on the side of let's go try it, figure it out and adapt, as opposed to taking six years and hiring fifty-three consultants and getting a bunch of outside people involved. A really big, big piece of what he gave me is that there's no limit to what you can do. You know, I came from a very modest background, my dad ran a gas station, my mom worked, was a homemaker first and then worked, eventually, in the family business, but I know that there's no limit to what you can do. Your only limit is what's inside of you. . . .

The worst thing you can do in life is tell somebody that they can't do something, or to assume that they can't do something. People continuously amaze me with the unlimited capability of the human spirit, whether it's a physical thing like running the Hawaii [Ironman] Triathlon or a project at work, or whatever. But people can do whatever they want to do. And, you know, a lot of people talk about limits and you can't do this, but the human spirit is unlimited. It's one of the few truly unlimited things.

Tiller went on to tell me a story about how he learned that "a problem is a golden thing because it's a huge opportunity."

Our wrestling team in high school was absolutely terrible. We were the Bad News Bears. Even the coach was going to quit. We were 2–14, we were getting killed. . . . So we decided that we were going to get better and made a commitment to each other that even though we were the Bad News Bears we could be the best team. And we did everything together as a team to try to really capture that. . . . We went from 2–14 to 16–0; a championship season the next year. And we did that by getting the whole team committed. We wanted to go to wrestling camp in the summer, and some of the kids couldn't afford to go. So we figured out a way to financially help them to go, so the whole team would go. The whole team would run stairs together. The whole team would practice like dogs together. It was getting that whole group of people to participate and commit, rather than just one or two of the people. And that was a big, big deal.

Tiller later extrapolated from his wrestling experience to tell me another big lesson.

You wouldn't think of wrestling as a team sport at first, you know? It feels more like cross-country, or whatever, but wrestling is very much a team sport because how you perform on Saturday or Sunday depends on how well you practice. How well you practice depends on how good the people are that you practice with. You will notice, if you look at successful wrestling teams, state champions tend to come in pairs. A team with a state champion 145-pounder will have a very good 138-pounder and 155-pounder, guaranteed. . . . So there's a very high level of interdependence. And if you can bring the level of the whole team up, every individual benefits. It's just like in manufacturing: You can have a terrific job in a fabrication area, but that fabrication area is much better off if the finishing area and assembly area are working together. So you got to improve the individual performance, but there's huge synergy in getting the whole team there. And that's a big deal: Being able to build those teams, create that common sense of purpose, is a big part of what I do every day. And I learned a lot of that in the wrestling room back at Essex Junction High School.

As Tiller recalled other important lessons and influences on his life, he also told me about Mrs. Magnet.

You've got to have, in my mind, an inspiration, somebody that can really help you see what's possible. My third grade teacher was—everybody has a special teacher—one of the people who really helped me understand how much fun it is to learn. One of the things that drives me, inside, that excites me every day, is the opportunity to learn. That's a core value of mine. The thing that I really get out of a job or a project is the ability to learn something. This teacher was phenomenal. Mrs. Magnet was her name. And just to give you an idea of what a crazy loon she was: The last day of school she stood on her head and took out her false teeth as a result of a bet she had made with the class. Talk about leaders being vulnerable, I mean, she was absolutely about as vulnerable as she could be. And she ran her classroom very differently than most public school classrooms. She had this concept of, you know, "You got to do your work." And we used to do the work between eight o'clock and eleven o'clock in the morning. But then the rest of the day you could grow. We had a very unstructured classroom. I remember we worked on a giant project that involved how cities are formed and so forth, and we built a project probably the size of this room. This is third grade, now. We built this huge, creative project that she really challenged us to do, and the bet was a result of that project.

You've just got to do, I mean, don't make life into a drudgery. Make life into fun. There's a certain amount of work that is just kind of drudgery. You've got to learn your addition and subtraction. But you've got to create that emotional bond with people that there's more there. Okay? It's not just about making 6,200 washing machines a day, but it's part of the launch of a lifetime.

It's part of a higher purpose. And that's what really gets people excited and gets that kind of creativity.

When I think of the core values that really shaped me, I think treating everyone the same, regardless of their background, is a big deal to me. You know, my grandfather, who I consider one of the smartest people I've ever met, had no formal education. And I can learn as much from my three-year-old kid as I can from a Ph.D.—in a different way. Treating everyone the same, with the same kind of level of dignity and respect and worth [is important to me]. Different people play different roles on the team, but you got to have that same, basic level of respect. The work ethic is huge as a core value. Taking risks, taking chances is another. Making the small mistake so that you can hit the home run later on is a big thing. Don't try to make everything absolutely perfect before you try to do something, is a big value. Getting a whole team of people involved rather than just one or two is a big, big deal; trying to create that win. Not just for the 126-pound wrestler, but for the whole wrestling team, so that each person can have their individual part of the contribution, part of a much larger part of the contribution is a big deal.

It's fun to listen to Tom Tiller and energizing to watch his body language as he tells his stories. As they roll out one after another, he gets more and more into them. It's clear that they define who he is in his own eyes, and that they are part of the fiber of his everyday life. Moreover, because he has been able to apply repeatedly the lessons contained in them, he won a reputation as one of GE's most successful turnaround artists. One of the most significant of these turnarounds, which I will discuss in a later chapter, was at GE's Appliance division, where as a twenty-nine-year-old straight out of business school, he saved a kitchen range plant from almost certain death by engaging everyone in the plant in fixing its problems.

In each one of these situations, Tiller has taken the lessons from his growing up and taught them to others. His life story has led to his teachable point of view—winning is about taking the bull by the horns. And through his stories and self-examination, he has been able to translate his point of view to other people and to energize them. He even says it isn't all that difficult, because—citing yet another homespun lesson that he's learned—"People fundamentally don't want to be third." He has taken these learnings with him to Polaris, where as CEO he has driven the new levels of performance.

We All Have Stories

One of the great myths of leadership is that extraordinary leaders are created by extraordinary events or circumstances. Alexander the Great was able to conquer most of the known world by the age of 32 because the geopolitics of the time positioned him uniquely to do it. Winston Churchill's aristocratic upbringing and unique experience as a young member of Parliament and Lord of the Admiralty prepared him to step in at a crucial moment and become one of Great Britain's greatest prime ministers. But the argument that you need extraordinary experiences to become a winning leader is nonsense. Everyone's life is filled with experiences—traumatic, frustrating or exhilarating—that can be the source of valuable learning.

Larry Bossidy's formative years were spent working in the family shoe store in Pittsfield, Massachusetts. Dick Stonesifer, former head of GE Appliances, spent his youth in a working-class family in Baltimore. Mary Petrovich, the young manager of AlliedSignal's St. Clair Shores safety restraint plant, spent her teenage years playing softball (for which she won a scholarship to the University of Michigan) and helping her widowed mother raise seven younger siblings. None of their stories are particularly Olympian. Lots of people have similar ones—some even more striking. The key thing, however, is that great leaders craft their histories into usable stories and continually revisit them for inspiration and guidance. Tom Tiller does this, and the result is a crystal-clear teachable point of view about stretching people by setting high goals and the value of teamwork. When people challenge him on these subjects, Tiller does not need to resort to the GE standard line because he can tell his own personal story: as a grandson, as a wrestler and now as an executive. This ability to use the past to provide lessons for the future is like any other leadership skill: Some people are better at it than others, but anyone who makes a conscious effort to examine his or her experiences and to learn from them can become a better leader.

Roberto Goizueta of Coca-Cola

The late Roberto Goizueta, the former chairman of The Coca-Cola Company, increased the value of his company more than any other CEO in the history of business. When he took the helm of Coke in 1981, it was already one of the nation's most successful and respected businesses. Nonetheless, in fifteen years, he increased its profits over seven-fold and increased market value thirty-fold.[4] His success reflected a business philosophy that he said he learned on his family's sugar plantation in Cuba, and an almost unlimited willingness to take risks, which he got from Fidel Castro. Because I didn't talk to Goizueta directly about his learning experiences, I can't give you his story entirely in his own words. But the facts are well known because he often talks about them publicly, and by his actions he demonstrates the lessons that he has learned. So I have included him here because he was a world-class leader whose winning formula for success so clearly reflects his past.

Goizueta was a mild-mannered man whose gentility could be deceiving when you first meet him. When selected to be Coke's chairman, his quiet, understated demeanor made him seem an odd choice to lead a company where the image of excitement plays such an important role. Goizueta himself once told *FORTUNE* magazine, "We don't know how to sell products based on performance. . . . Everything we sell, we sell on image."[5] But behind the unassuming facade is a determined and thoughtful man who has woven a winning philosophy out of his many varied life experiences.

When you first look at Goizueta's actions, a clear underlying business philosophy isn't always immediately apparent. Over the years, he has made a number of missteps and repeatedly backtracked. When he first took over as head of Coke, he pushed its diversification into the fruit juice market, only to reverse himself and later sell off most of the business. In 1982, he acquired Columbia Pictures, which proved to be a profitable but diverting investment that he also off-loaded after just seven years. And in 1985, he committed what many considered one of the biggest follies in business history by abandoning the hundred-year-old formula for Coca-Cola's flagship product and introducing New Coke, which proved to be a colossal failure.[6] He appeared to be a man who didn't know which way to turn. But despite these seeming diversions, he has steadily led Coca-Cola to new heights of profitability and shareholder value. And if you read any of his published interviews or his annual letters to shareholders, you will see that he has done this by following a philosophy developed through years of examining and learning from his experiences. Like other successful leaders, he is a man who knows what he knows, and knows where he learned it.

Goizueta traced two fundamental premises of his business philosophy to his grandfather Marcelo, who immigrated to Cuba from Spain in the 1800s and founded a sugar and real estate empire. By the time Roberto was a young boy, his grandfather was retired, so he would spend days talking and reading with Roberto in his study. Out of these long conversations grew many of the truths that still guide Goizueta at Coca-Cola decades later. One of the things Goizueta says he learned from his grandfather was that you should focus on the things that matter. As a self-made businessman, Marcelo knew how easy it was to lose focus and get lost in complexity, so he taught Roberto to be vigilant about concentrating on the few things that really mattered. To this day, says Goizueta, "I am a great believer in cash flow. Earnings is a man-made convention, but cash is cash. The larger the company is, the less it understands cash flow."[7]

The other lesson that Goizueta attributed to his grandfather is about the responsibilities of being an owner and adding value to the business. Technically, Goizueta's stockholdings represented only a tiny piece of Coca-Cola's capital, but he nurtured that capital as if it were all his. He evaluated performance on two measures. The first is Market Value Added. This measure determines whether or not a company has fattened investors' pocketbooks. Introduced by the consulting firm Stern Stewart, it measures the difference between a company's market value—what investors could get out of a business by selling it—and the capital that investors have put in over the company's lifetime. Internally, Goizueta also introduced in 1987 a formula called Economic Value Added that calculates returns on invested capital.[8] Goizueta evaluates every expenditure from the point of view that if a project earns 10% but the cost of the capital is 15%, the project has destroyed economic value. The idea, says Goizueta, came straight from his grandfather. "You borrow money at a certain rate and invest it at a higher rate and pocket the difference. It is simple," he says.

As a teenager, Goizueta's wealthy family sent him to high school in the United States to learn English. After that, he studied chemical engineering at Yale, because he thought it would be helpful when he took over the family business. But when he returned to Cuba he was restless. Inspired by his grandfather's example, he wanted to test himself, to see if he could make his own mark on the world. So he answered a blind ad in the newspaper and joined Coca-Cola as an entry-level chemist in Havana. But, sooner than he thought, Fidel Castro gave him the opportunity to really test himself and build a life out of nothing. In 1959, when Castro took over Cuba, the Goizueta family fled. Roberto arrived in Miami with his wife and their three children, $40 in cash and 100 shares of Coca-Cola stock held in trust in New York.

The experience, Goizueta said, taught him a third important lesson: that it is possible to survive and prosper even after you have lost everything. In a very real sense, Castro taught him to be fearless about taking risks. You can create opportunities if you are willing to go out on a limb. As a result, from his first day as CEO, he has routinely asked questions and suggested experiments just to see what might happen if things worked differently. In a document laying out his strategy for the 1980s that he presented to the board when he became CEO, he said, "Our behavior will produce leaders, good managers, and—most importantly—entrepreneurs. It is my desire that we take initiatives as opposed to being only reactive and that we encourage intelligent individual risk-taking."

Goizueta's risk-taking manifested itself with such successful product introductions as diet Coke and caffeine-free Coke products. It also led to New Coke. New Coke is a good example of how the pieces of Goizueta's philosophy came together and shaped Coca-Cola as it is today. Goizueta's fearlessness about risks allowed him to dare to change the old formula. And then, when it proved to be such a disaster, he recognized that the public had provided him with an invaluable piece of information. His grandfather had told him to focus on "things that mattered," and now it was abundantly clear to him that the thing that mattered most for Coca-Cola was its unique original product. It was only when he saw the market reaction to New Coke, he told *FORTUNE* in 1995, "that I came to learn how special this product was." Said one observer who was close to the situation, "It was like a light bulb went on. Aha! This is the essence of what we own."[9] As a result, Goizueta accelerated his assault on noncore business units—generally selling them at a profit—and reduced the company basically to its trademark. From then on, Goizueta turned all his energies to selling Coke products. This involved undoing many of his previous actions, including selling Columbia Pictures and most of the company's ancillary businesses. Now, The Coca-Cola Company[10] exists almost solely to sell Coca-Cola.

To say that Goizueta returned Coca-Cola to a singular focus on its primary asset isn't to say that he stopped pushing for growth or change. On the contrary, his willingness to take risks and his belief that people can make their own opportunities have led him to adopt a new sales strategy based not on the size of the conventional soft drink market but on the total fluid intake of everyone in the world. The theme he preaches to his troops is that there are 5.7 billion people in the world who each consume sixty-four ounces of liquid a day, and currently Coca-Cola's products account for only two of those ounces. The real growth opportunities, therefore, he says, are not limited to emerging markets where Coca-Cola's products aren't available, but are also in the densely populated markets such as Southern California, where the remaining sixty-two ounces remain to be captured. To symbolize his aspirations, he placed on page one of the Coca-Cola 1995 Annual Report a big infinity symbol. Coke people around the world are translating this aspiration into innovations such as marketing partnerships with retailers in the U.S. and equipping special taxis in South Africa to sell Coca-Cola products.[11]

In looking back at the New Coke debacle, Goizueta expressed no regrets. "Whether or not we were smart or dumb, right or wrong was and is irrelevant. . . . The job of management is to provide results and those have been produced in spades."[12] As for his teaching to others, Goizueta would offer, "An old boss once told me I was too much a man of action. But I like to quote the poet Antonio Machado, who said, 'Paths are made by walking.'"[13] And Roberto Goizueta pressed Coke managers to take risks. "Don't wrap the flag of Coca-Cola around you to prevent change from taking place. It is extremely important that you show some insensitivity to your past in order to show the proper respect for the future."[14]

In Goizueta's own words in the Coca-Cola 1995 Annual Report, he wants his legacy to be a culture that "will institutionalize the process of rapidly learning from every aspect of our environment: our consumers, our customers, our partners, our competitors, seemingly unrelated organizations, and, yes, our own mistakes." The culture, according to Goizueta, "includes me. And I am proud to say that I learned more in 1995 than any year before, but not as much as I will this year [1996]."

Roberto Goizueta's life story is one of high expectations and sudden loss, followed by even higher rewards. His grandfather taught him to work hard, stay close to the business, avoid complexity and reach for your dreams. Fidel Castro taught him that nothing is insurmountable. His success at Coca-Cola was a direct result of the fact that he learned those lessons and lives them every day.

Debra Dunn of Hewlett-Packard

When I asked Hewlett-Packard to introduce me to some of their best young leaders, Debra Dunn was at the top of the list. At forty years old, Dunn was a general manager in the company's Test and Measurement business. She was in charge of products, including video servers, cable modems and wireless data communications technologies—all uncharacteristically high-tech products for HP's oldest division. Dunn is one of Silicon Valley's highest-ranking women, and one of the company's most senior line executives without an engineering degree. She is also one of its toughest, most effective and best-liked leaders. She now reports to Carly Fiorina, CEO of Hewlett-Packard, with responsibility for strategy, and has been a key architect of the transformation.

When I met Dunn, I was surprised by both her appearance and demeanor. Her stylish clothes and two-toned punk haircut gave her a look that I would have expected of a rock star or a show business promoter, but not of the leader of a multimillion-dollar segment of Hewlett-Packard. At the same time, her manner was unusually open and friendly.

That Debra Dunn is a bit of a maverick is not surprising. She has a background that is highly unusual for a heavy-hitting corporate executive. But she has drawn on her difficult youth and her early career running food and housing co-ops to develop effective points of view and a no-nonsense leadership style that rank her among the best.

When I asked her to tell me about herself, she said, "I grew

up in West Palm Beach, Florida, in a very working-class environment. . . . Probably the most significant catalyzing event for me,
from a leadership perspective, was that when I was fourteen, my
dad died. And my mom, who had worked all her life and was
very competent, was at a loss about doing a lot of the things my
dad had done. . . . So when I was 14 I started managing the family finances and doing that kind of stuff. On one level, it was kind
of terrifying, but on another level it gave me a self-confidence
that has carried me through the rest of my life. I think that's
really the most fundamental element of being a leader, because
when you're thrown into a situation that seems impossible and
you do it, then nothing ever seems quite so impossible again."

The determination and self-confidence that Dunn developed
as a teenager led to many early accomplishments. She played
sports and graduated as valedictorian of her class. Then she won
a scholarship to Brown University, where she says she met a new
set of challenges and learned some more important lessons that
have shaped her thinking. "Most people who go to Brown are
from a different part of society," she says. "It was an influential
time in terms of my sense of myself, about how I could fit into
various situations or how I could not fit in and still succeed on
my own terms." So, while availing herself of an Ivy League education, she pursued interests that were shaped by her clearly
unaffluent upbringing. "I did an independent concentration—
what does it say on my diploma?" she asks rhetorically, searching back in her memory. "I remember—it says: Classical and
Marxist Theories of Economics and Social Organization—in
Latin."

After "succeeding on my own terms" at Brown, Dunn chose
what she describes as "a pretty alternative career path." While
many of her classmates took traditional jobs on Wall Street or
headed for graduate work, she joined a tiny nonprofit organization. "I had done a thesis on consumer cooperatives . . . and was
interested in them as a democratic economic form. I decided
that I really wanted to work in that environment. So I found this
little organization in Ann Arbor, Michigan, called NASCO:

North American Students of Cooperation. It was an organization of maybe ten people, including the student temps . . . and we all made $8,000 a year. We were young kids with lots of energy, and we were going to change the world. But we didn't really have any resources. . . .

"What I did at NASCO seems tangential from what I am doing now," she says, "but it was actually an interesting experience from a number of perspectives. All these co-ops had a large element of volunteerism. So there was a very big challenge to figure out how to motivate people who were volunteers. You didn't pay them, you couldn't fire them. It required me to think about a lot of fundamental issues of how people are motivated, how you can get people to effectively work together. At the time, I didn't understand the relevance of that to things I would do later, but subsequently reflecting on that experience, it was very useful to realize that fundamentally you have to get people hooked into a higher vision of what they're trying to do and help them understand how they are part of a bigger whole."[15]

As Dunn spent the next four years working in the nonprofit community, she continued to learn about leading and motivating people. But she also began asking herself why she wanted to lead. What drove her to be out in front? Acknowledging that there may be some "rationalization and self-delusion" involved in her answer, she says that she finally decided that what really interested her was "affecting how people deal with each other. . . . When I go and visit my relatives in Oil City, Pennsylvania, and talk to them about their life at work, it's shocking and horrifying to me the way their organizations work and people aren't respected. . . . I [decided that I] could have a far more positive impact being in the power structure, acting in a way that I thought was based on solid values. And that's what really drove me out of the alternative community and into this. I decided that if I really wanted to have impact, I would become part of the mainstream and impact the way people really worked and how their lives functioned."[16]

Living in Boston at the time, and having learned like many

other leaders that you should always aim high, she applied and was admitted to Harvard Business School. From Harvard, Dunn was hired by HP, where she has turned her social values and the lessons she learned in the "alternative" economy to becoming an extremely effective leader in corporate America. For example, when given an assignment early in her career, before the era of reengineering, to design the "factory of the future" for HP, she flew in the face of conventional wisdom to eliminate layers of supervisors and give more decisionmaking to the people on the shop floor. And throughout her career, she has repeatedly been willing to step outside the box to solve problems that have defied conventional approaches.

From her struggles in a fatherless family and her success at Brown, she learned how much you can accomplish if you just face challenges and tackle them directly. Working as a community activist, she learned to deal with resistance to change. And growing up with her working-class relatives, she came to value the importance of respecting everyone. These lessons have given her a solid foundation for success at HP.

Finally, she says, "The legacy I want to leave is helping people understand that sometimes it's really good if people aren't like you. There are different packages that work, and different styles that work. And not it's just OK to be different, sometimes it's better." [17]

Emotional Journey Lines

To help people draw lessons from their own experiences, I have developed a little exercise I often ask them to perform. Take out a sheet of paper and draw a simple graph. At the middle of the vertical axis write "neutral emotional energy," at its bottom write "negative emotional energy," and at the top write "positive emotional energy." Make the horizontal axis a timeline from your childhood to today. Then plot on the chart the times in your life when you have felt particularly good about yourself, the times when you were particularly stressed or bummed out, and the times you were just plain bored. The result will be what I call an "emotional journey line." Then recall what was going on at those times, and think about how those experience shaped you as a person and as a leader. This usually turns out to be a powerful exercise that reveals many of the tacit lessons that people have learned in their lives and helps them draw a teachable point of view from them.

As an example, I want to share the emotional journey of Gary Wendt, former CEO of GE Capital, which he recounted for me one afternoon in his office. GE Capital is the financial services arm of General Electric and operates in dozens of businesses, from rail car leasing to insurance to credit card processing. The company's net income has been growing at nearly 20% a year for over a decade. It is one of the largest financial institutions in the world.[18] Wendt's story is an illustrative one because it has clear turning points and moments of crisis from which he says he drew specific lessons. Wendt is by nature an optimistic person, with a droll, self-deprecating sense of humor. He isn't one to dwell on pain, so even when he describes periods that were enormously difficult, his eyes twinkle, and he chuckles as he looks back at his distress. But despite the lighthearted tone—it's another characteristic of winning leaders that they don't nurse their wounds—Wendt's story makes it clear that he has learned some of his most important lessons in times of difficulty.

Gary Wendt grew up in the tiny farming community of Rio (rhymes with Ohio), Wisconsin, population 700, where, he says, "If you were going to be part of the social structure, you worked." So, even though he was a kid from a family that didn't need the money, some of his earliest recollections were doing chores around town for sixty-five cents an hour. He then attended a high school that was so small that "We would play basketball, at halftime put on a suit and play in the pep band and then after the game dress for the B team game in case they needed anyone." When I first sat down with Wendt to talk about leadership, he joked to me, "I'll impress you. I was president of my class in eighth grade, ninth grade, tenth grade and twelfth grade. The only reason I wasn't in eleventh grade is because I wanted a year off. What won't impress you is there were only twenty-eight people in my class."

After leaving Rio, Wendt went to the University of Wisconsin and then Harvard Business School. "During graduate school," he says, "somehow I got the impression that when I came out of there . . . I could do anything I wanted and I had all the answers. And it was at that point that I got two of the best educational lessons that I ever had, no question." They are lessons, he adds, that an organization as large and complex as "GE could never give anybody."

While Harvard was spitting out its normal cadre of investment bankers, consultants and budding professional managers, Wendt says he was attracted to real estate. So, when he saw an ad at the Harvard Business School that announced boldly, "I am going to build a dome city in Houston, and I would like some people from the Harvard Business School to help me with the financial aspects," Wendt applied. It turned out, however, that this urban development magnate was a used car salesman named Harlan Lane. Lane had gotten wealthy in the used car business by making celebrities out of his customers. If you bought a car from Lane's dealership, he would put you on television. He did this by buying large blocks of TV time in the middle of the night from local affiliates and broadcasting images of his new customers when they bought their cars.

In a Texas drawl, Lane told Wendt "what a great man he [Lane] was" and that if Wendt came down to work with him, "Boy, I'll make you a millionaire. I made a lot of people before, and I'll make you." Wendt was intrigued but decided to do something a bit more standard. Lane, however, wouldn't give up. "I was sitting there with the company I was going to go to work for, negotiating the deal . . . and somehow Harlan finds me, and he gets me on the phone." Lane proclaimed, "Boy, I need one of you Harvard Business School boys. You come down and work for me, I'll buy you a brand new Cadillac car." Wendt's resistance melted. Not at the Cadillac, but at the fun this would be. "I thought, 'This guy's a hustler, so what the hell?'"

Wendt arrived in Houston with his Harvard degree, ready to "rebuild Harlan's company," he says, but Lane immediately took the wind out of his sails. He was ready to give Wendt one of the most important lessons in his life. "Boy," he told Wendt, "before you can do anything for me, you need to prove to me you can sell. You go out there and you start selling lots." According to Wendt, "The Harvard pedigree I was wearing around proudly was just ripped from me." Devastated, not knowing what to do, he pondered for three days. "I had no money, I had just moved my wife down to Texas. So I went back to Harlan. 'OK, Harlan, I'll sell some lots for you. Give me the price list.' 'Boy,' he says, 'we don't have a price list.' Now, this is a used car dealer: 'You go and make the best deal you can and I'll tell you whether it's good enough. Okay?'" Not many people in a company like General Electric, says Wendt, ever get the experience to learn that business "is negotiating price between two parties. Now, sometimes you have a very sophisticated way like television, and sometimes you do it by sitting across the table and telling them this car is really the best car they can possibly get. But Harlan taught me about values and pricing. That was lesson number one."

As it turned out, Wendt "sold more lots than anybody at a higher price for a month, and Harlan came in and said, 'Okay, you're in charge now.'" Then he left, went to Arkansas, and bought a bank. He left Wendt "in charge of this little subdivision, which was like shooting fish in a barrel, I mean Houston, Texas, in 1967, a freeway going through this property, and it really wasn't very hard to sell the property, and we built houses. But Harlan went up and got in a very complicated deal in a number of ways, which did make me a millionaire. On paper I was made a millionaire within two years of the time I went to work for him. But it was a very thinly traded stock, and he had driven that sucker up. Eventually, he got in financial trouble and our company was liquidated. In the meantime, I was running my own small business. What I learned then was how to meet a payroll.

And it was tough because after things turned bad, we didn't have any money. Literally, every Friday, my bookkeeper would make out all the checks and I'd put them on the desk and ask her how much money we had and make decisions on who was going to get paid and who wasn't going to get paid. The line was pretty easy to figure out. The first thing you paid was your taxes to the government because they'd put you in jail if you didn't do that. The second people you paid was yourselves. And then after that, it was however much you had money for. And I can remember having a whole drawer full of checks and people would come up and the people who hollered the loudest got paid. . . .

"I'm telling you this story because you don't get experiences like that very often in a large business, of being able to go out and worry about having enough money coming in the door to pay the bills that are also coming in the door. And I always considered that lesson, plus the value lesson, two extremely important things in business. Both lessons would be hard to teach unless you had the personal experience." The challenges were scary, Wendt says, but because they were "emotional experiences," they are engraved in his heart. If they had been easy, he probably wouldn't have learned so well.

After leaving Texas with two small children and nothing to show for his time with Harlan but the Cadillac that he got to keep, Wendt went to work for a small real estate investment trust in Coral Gables, Florida. And when that industry went bust in 1973, he was hired by General Electric to clean up the many problems in its real estate portfolio. It wasn't more than a blip in General Electric's huge financial portfolio, but it was an embarrassment, says Wendt, and Reg Jones, GE's chairman, wanted it cleaned up.

From the beginning, Wendt says, "I behaved differently than I think most GE people did . . . because I had come out of this culture that you had to do things. You had to keep moving. And I didn't understand the culture of signatures on a page to get approval to do things." Further, he says, "the really good news was that the people in GE were so embarrassed about the real estate stuff that they didn't want to talk about it. And so I just did things. I wasn't a rocket scientist, but I figured out that GE had a lot of money. We had a thousand units that were unfinished, and a half-finished condo unit was worth zero. So I decided that we might as well get the damn things done and they might be worth something someday. So I went ahead and finished all the units, and lo and behold, by the middle of 1976, the market came back and we were the only ones to have anything for sale. Everything else was like bombed-out buildings and we had all these very nice units, flags were flying out in front and everything. So we sold all thousand units in 1976 and took orders for another thousand units. I don't think that could have happened as easily had I been trained in the system. . . . I didn't ask [anybody], I just went out and did it."

Unlike the rough times with Harlan, Wendt says that this was an emotional high period. "I felt like an entrepreneur who had money at his disposal for the first time in his career." And it was during this period that Wendt says he first noticed "that the people who succeed at GE or anyplace are the people that go after things and get them done. I came in here and went after things and got things done because I didn't know that there was another way to do it . . . I really take my defining moment in GE as that first year when I didn't know you weren't supposed to do it any other way."[19]

As GE Capital grew and Wendt gained more prominence in the organization, he continued to act as an entrepreneur and "behave differently." GE Capital had started as a way for people to finance appliances during the Depression, but it had grown into a diversified financial institution that, like others, managed portfolios of loans and leases but stayed away from managing assets. That is, until Gary Wendt came along. Today it is the fifth-largest financial institution in the U.S.,[20] and it has attained that ranking, in part, because Gary Wendt's financiers understand business, not just portfolio management, and they are willing to get their hands dirty.

Finishing the condos in Florida was the first of a long string of successes that Wendt and GE Capital have achieved by stepping up to the plate and managing the assets it finances. But it was the Houston Astros that Wendt says crystallized the learning into a solid business philosophy.

"One of the assets we had was a participation in a loan with six other banks and Ford Motor Credit on all the assets owned by Judge Roy Hofheinz, including the Houston Astrodome, and the Houston Astros baseball team," he told me. "The judge was a hell of a businessman in addition to being a visionary, but he had a stroke and it basically made him incapacitated. The people who took over weren't able to run the business. So our loan was in default. For about a year and a half, we, as part of this big group of participants, did one thing: sent money down every time they told us to send money down, or, if not, they were going to shut the Astrodome. After a while, though, I decided that we had to get tough. We couldn't sit still. And so I made an offer to all the other institutions to buy them out at thirty cents on the dollar. Not surprisingly, all six banks said yes. Ford Motor said, No, we won't do that, but we'll go in with you as partner. So we and Ford ended up actually buying out the Hofheinz family and taking over a lease on the Astrodome and ownership of the Houston Astros baseball team. I'll never have more fun in my life, ever. . . . We didn't know anything at all about how to run a baseball team, but we ran it. And at the end of two years, we got back all our money, every penny, and every penny of interest that we had in it. And our only mistake was we sold it too soon. We should have kept it. You know what I sold the Houston Astros for in 1978? Eleven million dollars. Then it sold for $165 million six years later. The banks, of course, took it right in the chops. They were out seventy cents on the dollar.

"The leadership part," says Wendt, "was getting in there, actually taking control and applying business logic to a recreational thing. It was amazing to us: We had a good general manager, and he was honest with us. We said, 'What kind of a baseball team have you got?' He said, 'Not a good one.' And the first year there was free agency, and believe me, Reg Jones [the chairman of GE] was not going to let us pay more for a center fielder than he got paid. Could you see the proxy statement for GE back then? 'Left-handed, power-hitting first baseman for one million two hundred thousand'? Yeah. So we couldn't do that. We knew we were going to have a bad ball team. They actually went from fourth to fifth place in the standings during the four years that we owned them, but we had the largest increase in attendance in major league baseball. And we did it by marketing entertainment and not baseball. We switched our strategy from advertising the players and talking about the great team we were going to have, to advertising on Saturday morning television that if you came to the game you got a bat. We were the first ones to do that promotional stuff. You came to all the Astros games during the year, you had a full set of clothes and equipment. The idea of managing problems and managing assets and not being a financial institution, but being an operator of financial assets, came from the Houston Astrodome situation."

Wendt's leadership journey line makes amusing fare. But, because he has thought about and understood both the good times and the bad, it has provided him some powerful lessons. Growing up in the farming community of Rio, Wisconsin, he learned the work ethic and the need for a take-charge attitude. And struggling with Lane's seat-of-the-pants real estate business made him ready to act independently and entrepreneurially at GE Capital. In fact, the lessons that he pulled out of these experiences became hallmarks at GE Capital. Wendt's emphasis on thinking differently from others led to a business model for GE Capital different from other financial institutions. "When a bank has a loan that goes bad they write it off or sell it at a discount. We'll try to run that hardware for a while," says Wendt. Moreover, his belief in entrepreneurship led to GE Capital's decentralized structure, which Wendt says is "one of the top three reasons why we've been so successful."[21]

How Leaders Use Their Stories

The most effective leaders are those who are in touch with their leadership stories. This is in part because, as the Gail Sheehy quote at the opening of the chapter states, the story we tell to ourselves "becomes the story we are living." The story itself shapes our attitudes, actions and reactions. When we know our stories, we know ourselves. Stories, however, are equally important because they allow other people to know us. Stories create real, human connections by allowing others to get inside our minds and our lives. With their human protagonists, dramas and climaxes, they engage listeners on an emotional and intuitive level that is rarely touched by the purely rational argument.

It is much easier for Tom Tiller, for example, to explain stretch goals with his grandfather's "cut down a million trees" story than with Jack Welch's annual report letters. Everyone had a grandfather, and most people have at some point succeeded at doing something that seemed impossible at the time. Mary Petrovich of AlliedSignal has a story about being a "young, blond girl engineer" and how she and a group of UAW workers turned around their operation once they began working together. That makes a much clearer point about teamwork between management and hourly workers than any management consultant's studies of productivity. And Gary Wendt demanded that GE Capital leaders negotiate better deals when they knew that he knew what it's like to be a salesman and live by negotiating prices.

In these first four chapters, I have made the case (1) that organizations win if they have the ability to continually produce leaders at all levels and (2) that leaders are people who learn, develop teachable points of view and then teach others to be leaders. In the rest of the book, I am going to talk about specific qualities I have found in leaders and about how winning organizations and leaders succeed in fostering them in others.

Because leadership isn't a discrete set of traits, there aren't any simple, or even complicated, formulas for being or becoming a leader. Leadership is a holistic pattern of thought processes, attitudes and behaviors. Each leader has different weights placed on different attributes, and each has his or her own teachable points of view. One thing they have in common, though, is that they have developed their winning attitudes, behaviors and points of view by reflecting on their lives and by examining their experiences. And at the end, they have developed a complete and workable leadership style.

The Heart of Leadership

It Starts with Ideas

Winning Organizations Are Built on Clear Ideas

- "Quantum" ideas set a direction for everyone
- "Incremental" ideas are about strategy, structure and implementation

Leaders Make Sure the Ideas Are Current and Appropriate

- They assess changing realities and amend the ideas as necessary
- The ideas lead to significant added value

Ideas Are the Framework for Actions at All Levels

- They provide a context for everyone's decision making
- They motivate people toward a common goal

When Phil Knight started a little athletic shoe company in 1964, he named it Nike for the Greek goddess of victory. Knight chose the name not so much as a statement of his aspirations for the company as of its purpose. Nike, he declared, would be dedicated to helping athletes win. If this meant pouring resources into the best design department in the industry, Nike would do it. If it meant paying Michael Jordan and other talented athletes millions of dollars to serve as product testers, confidence-builders and role models, Nike would do it. Nike would become a winner by helping its customers do the same. Every decision and every action by every Nike employee would be aimed at furthering that goal. Nike's game would be making its customers winners, or at least feel like them.

This singular idea that Phil Knight articulated over thirty years ago, and continues to propound today, has propelled Nike to become the premier athletic shoe and sportswear company in the world, with a market value of $21 billion.[1] It has served as the organizing principle that guides all of its activities. Like its customers, Nike's markets are fast-paced. Every day brings new demands and challenges that require instant responses from Nike's 14,000-person[2] workforce. But because everyone at Nike clearly knows what they are aiming for, they continue to create the right innovative responses needed to get there. It's what makes Nike a winner.[3]

Ideas provide the intellectual underpinning of every human activity. In sports, it's obvious that an athlete needs to know what game he or she is playing in order to win. What is being tested? What does the playing field look like? Where is the goal? What is the aim? But in business, a great many companies—and some of them very large ones—spend decades on the field without any idea of what it is that they are aiming to accomplish. Like Woody Allen, they seem to believe that "eighty percent of success is showing up."

Most companies start out with a good central idea. Otherwise they would never get up and running. Over time, however, a great many of them lose their way. As they grow, they get caught up in diversification for its own sake. Or they achieve their initial goal and, like NASA after it put a man on the moon, fail to come up with a new one. Or they get distracted by something else. In any event, they eventually lose sight of their guiding principle, and often they forget that they even need one. Winning companies and winning leaders never forget.

Winners are always firmly grounded in clearly stated ideas.

They have an explicit central idea that explains why they are in business and how they intend to add value. They have organizational ideas about how the various parts of the organization will interact with each other. They have well-defined values about what constitutes desirable and unacceptable behavior. And, most importantly, these ideas are shared and understood by everyone working in the organization. They provide every member with an intellectual framework and an internal yardstick for measuring the rightness of his or her actions. By defining the game and setting the rules, these ideas allow each individual to act independently and to take actions that will move everyone together toward success.

In the early 1960s, when John F. Kennedy said he wanted the U.S. to put a man on the moon, NASA mobilized tens of thousands of scientists and engineers around this central idea. Each one of them, in hundreds of separate laboratories, directed all their research toward achieving this goal, and within just a few short years, Neil Armstrong was there. A century ago, Theodore Vail organized American Telephone & Telegraph Company around the idea of "universal service." The goal of the company would be to provide every home in the U.S. with basic, standardized telephone service. For nearly a hundred years, this idea drove all of AT&T's behavior and decisions, about running a regulated monopoly, about technology development and about organizational structure. Henry Ford started Ford Motor Company on a central idea he stole from the textile industry, namely, mass production. Ray Kroc founded McDonald's on an idea stolen from Henry Ford, namely, mass production of fast food. And Tom Monahan built Domino's Pizza on the central idea of "30-minute delivery of a standard pizza" to your house or apartment. In each case, these fundamental ideas served as the organizing principles for getting thousands of people to achieve a common goal.

Winning leaders understand that ideas are an essential tool for shaping and motivating an organization. They consider the generation of ideas one of their most important functions. And they generate these ideas by constantly seeking new information, reflecting on their own experience and searching for insights— not only about markets, technology and human behavior, but also about the larger world around them. Bill Pollard, a world-class leader who is the chairman of ServiceMaster, told me that he learns and gathers business ideas everywhere he goes. "You know, I get ideas from what I read. I got ideas from helping to start a project in an Indian village in Ecuador. . . . I think one of the risks that I continue to see is what I call the 'arrogance of ignorance.' Successful people get to a level and then, subliminally or other-wise, say, 'I know what I know . . . and don't bother me with more.'" Pollard adds that "how a person gets fed by other ideas, by philosophies, by thinking through the basic issues of life, I think is the fundamental question in leadership and is a fundamental question in business leadership."[4] I couldn't agree more.

As Pollard points out, the generation of ideas is a cross-fertilization process. Good ideas arise out of exposure to and rumination on other ideas. As a result, while most successful lead-ers are usually very good at generating winning ideas—especially the "quantum" ones about the course and purpose of the organi-zation—this doesn't have to be the case. One of the best leaders I know is Lew Platt, the CEO of Hewlett-Packard, who describes himself as "not the most likely person to come up with a good idea. . . . Give me a blank sheet of paper and tell me to write down fifteen approaches to something, and I might be lucky to get five, whereas other people would produce twenty-five in that period of time." But, he says, he does "have some skill at sorting out the good from the bad." So he surrounds himself "with a lot of people who are good at generating ideas" and picks out the best.[5]

In winning organizations, the source of the ideas isn't what matters; it's the fact that the top leader embraces the ideas, spreads them throughout the organization and encourages oth-ers to have good ideas. In all the winning organizations I have studied, ideas cascade through the ranks. Workers at each level draw off the central ideas of the company to develop ideas for improving their own operations and to generate ideas for the units under them. Good ideas at all levels drive these organizations to success.

The Power of Ideas

AlliedSignal, which merged with Honeywell, was a company where a couple of simple straightforward ideas have made a world of difference. Before the arrival of Larry Bossidy as CEO in 1991, AlliedSignal was a company without a clear operating principle. The previous CEO, Ed Hennessy, had built AlliedSignal into a conglomerate spanning three sectors—automotive, engineered materials (primarily plastics and chemicals) and aerospace. But he had no central idea of what he wanted the businesses to accomplish. His primary focus had been growth through acquisitions. And he rewarded managers for finding new acquisitions, so nobody paid a lot of attention to actually running the businesses. This strategy carried the company for some time. However, as the company entered the 1990s, it was suffering badly. It had poor margins relative to market positions, too much debt and a negative cash flow.[6]

When he arrived at AlliedSignal from General Electric in 1991, Bossidy sized up his situation. "When I came in here ... the company was a strange marriage of disparate companies that no one had really tried to weld together. There were 52 separate fiefdoms ... and at least three different companies."[7] So he quickly formulated a set of unifying ideas that would serve as the basis for running all of the businesses. First of all, he declared, AlliedSignal would act as one company; each unit would operate in a manner designed to maximize the success of the combined company rather than as an independent fief. And, he added, its success would be measured not by top-line growth acquired for its own sake, but by returns to shareholders. AlliedSignal's purpose would be to provide shareholders with a consistently better return than they could get on other comparable investments, and its employees would be rewarded for their ability to operate within the company, rather than their ability to find another company to acquire.

The results of Bossidy's efforts have been astounding. Since he began the transformation, AlliedSignal's total return to investors has been over 500% versus the Dow Jones Industrial Average at just under 200%.[8] In his first year as CEO, market value went from $3.6 billion to $6.1 billion[9] and was $22.2 billion[10] as of June 6, 1997. After a net loss of $273 million in 1991,[11] it posted a profit of $1.02 billion for 1996.[12] Revenue growth, which averaged 1.14% for the five years prior to his arrival, has averaged almost 5%[13] annually since he took over. AlliedSignal has continued to make acquisitions, but they are a disciplined part of solid growth strategies at each of the company's three businesses.

The amazing thing about Bossidy's transformation, which shows the astounding power of a central idea, is that AlliedSignal turned around its performance while keeping many of the same people at the top of the organization. During the turnaround, he kept his three sector heads, Dan Burnham, Fred Poses and John Barter, in place. They were all at AlliedSignal before Bossidy arrived.

Barter credits Bossidy's clear statement of direction with kick-starting the turnaround. "Before we had been run as a deal company. The focus was on the next acquisition. Why did we perform the way we did? Because operations was not the focus. What Larry did was to provide that focus and expectation."[14]

The Paradox of Ideas: Incremental and Quantum

Larry Bossidy's two precepts about unifying the company and performing for shareholders are what academics call "quantum" ideas. They are big, overriding principles that set direction and are essential to keeping everyone working toward a common goal. But by themselves they wouldn't have been enough to make AlliedSignal a winner, because they don't suggest a strategy or any specific actions that people might take to reach that goal. For that purpose, every business unit in the company must come up with its own "incremental" ideas.

For leaders, the need for quantum and incremental ideas presents something of a paradox. A paradox is "holding two seemingly inconsistent truths simultaneously to discover a deeper truth." For the leader, one truth argues that a lot of incremental ideas drive continuous improvement, the evolutionary model of change. Another truth argues that you need big, frame-breaking ideas to create revolutionary changes, a transformational model. The overriding truth, which successful leaders have learned to embrace, is that you need both. You need incremental ideas and quantum ideas, and the two must work in concert. Quantum ideas provide the framework on which incremental ideas hang, and incremental ideas shape the actions that get the quantum ideas implemented.

The problem at many companies is that they spend too much time on incremental ideas, and nobody ever steps back to look at the big picture. A few years back Toyota generated a constant flow of the incremental ideas necessary to master continuous improvement, *kaizen*. Every company in the world wanted its just-in-time manufacturing system to be as lean and flexible as Toyota's. Toyota's bottom line was in great shape, but the company wasn't generating the kind of quantum ideas that produce bold new products and top-line growth.[15] Only after Honda took the lead with the innovative Accord and Acura did Toyota wake up. Soon, however, a wiser Toyota introduced its successful Lexus and Camry lines, proving itself to be a master of the quantum and incremental paradox.[16]

The need for quantum and incremental ideas isn't confined to the executive suite. In winning organizations, everyone at all levels is expected to, and does, generate both kinds of ideas. At ServiceMaster, Bob Hutchins, account manager at the Chicago hospital, was faced with a major challenge: reduce costs and improve quality. For his operation, he realized, this required a quantum change, a total rethinking of the cleaning of the hospital. Once he got clear on the quantum idea, he then mobilized people to work on incremental ideas to achieve the needed improvement. Hutchins's idea for transforming his unit's work would not qualify as a quantum idea for Bill Pollard or Carlos Cantu, who are responsible for the entire $4.9 billion[17] company. But because it required a total change in Hutchins's own sphere, his unit's operations, it was quantum for him.

Similarly, Ameritech's remaking has required that people at all levels of the company come up with quantum and incremental ideas. When Ameritech decided to intensify its focus on shareholders, it determined that growth and return on assets were going to be its key yardsticks based on the work of Professor Larry Selden. The company's Breakthrough program—which I referred to in Chapter 1 and will describe again later—educated people as to the importance of both these metrics, but then they had to come up with the ideas that would produce results. In Cleveland, the manager of an Ameritech garage that dispatches service trucks, for example, had the quantum idea that Ameritech could become more cost-efficient by increasing the utilization of its assets (the trucks in his garage). He then asked his drivers for incremental ideas to get that done. The combined ideas completely changed the way the garage dispatched trucks. Drivers took them home at night and were dispatched to their calls via phone each morning. This eliminated unnecessary trips into the garage. Drivers who had been making their first calls between 9:00 and 9:30 A.M. began doing them at 8:15 A.M., and staying out later in the afternoons as well. This effectively added almost two hours to the productive workday of each installer.[18]

Good Ideas Are Teachable

At AlliedSignal, Larry Bossidy's special talent was his ability to clearly formulate ideas so that they are teachable and could be translated by others into action. As a leader, it was important that Bossidy come up with a core set of quantum ideas about AlliedSignal's purpose. But this would have been of little value if he hadn't also been able to teach them to others in such a way that they could act on them. Winning organizations succeed because leaders at each level draw off the ideas of those above them to frame both large quantum and more specific incremental ideas that help their units reach the desired goal. In order to do this, they must clearly understand and embrace the underlying ideas themselves.

Each year Bossidy produced a list of three specific objectives that were to be the goals of everyone at AlliedSignal. The articulation shifted each year, as Bossidy refined his ideas and adapted them to changing conditions. But the core vision remained the same: We will become a premier company, distinctive and successful in everything we do. We will do this by focusing on shareholders, operating as one company, satisfying customers and improving productivity to gain market share or grow profit margins. In 1996, the three priorities were:

- Make customer satisfaction our first priority
- Drive growth and productivity through integrated world-class processes
- Make all of our commitments, including net income and cash flow[19]

Bossidy designed the yearly priorities to help leaders at all levels of AlliedSignal develop and implement the quantum and incremental ideas needed to achieve the overall corporate goals. As my research team and I conducted dozens of interviews at AlliedSignal, we were amazed to see how well Bossidy had succeeded in getting his message across. In every business unit we visited, we could see his ideas cascading down and spreading throughout the organization.

Mary Petrovich was the general manager of AlliedSignal's St. Clair Shores, Michigan, safety restraint plant. She is blond, blue-eyed, in her thirties and grew up not far from the plant. She was the oldest of eight children, and the first in her family to go to college. After graduating with a degree in engineering, she worked for three years at General Motors before returning to Harvard

Business School.[20] She has been at AlliedSignal since 1993.[21] In February 1996, when we asked her what the three priorities for her plant were, her reply mirrored Bossidy's statement:

- Make customer satisfaction our first priority
- Integrate activities and processes; make sure people work together
- Make the numbers, meet the commitments

Her statement was very similar to Bossidy's, but it wasn't a mere parroting of the boss, because she then went on to frame the goals in the context of her specific plant and to explain what they meant for her and her five hundred employees at St. Clair Shores:

This month we are holding a town hall meeting. And I'm going to spell out for people exactly what our priorities for the year are. The first one is to make customer satisfaction our first priority. Our future here, whether it's a year, two years, or ten years, is going to be dependent on our ability to make a quantum leap in our customer satisfaction. When I came here, our quality and delivery levels were abysmal. They're improving, but we've got to get better. . . . And the way we're going to know whether or not our customers are satisfied is by looking at three things. It's going to be (1) our quality and (2) the number of complaints we get . . . and (3) it's going to be our on-time delivery. . . .

The way I'm going to explain the second priority is . . . we can't make the numbers unless we have a process to get there. We've got a lot of initiatives. We've got a lot of people spending energy, but we've got to work smarter, not harder. We've got to align those people. We've got to integrate these select initiatives. . . . If we focus on zero defects we're going to have a happier customer, and we're going to have a lower cost. But we've got to do that in collaboration with the quality engineers. We can't just have these black belt [quality specialists] task forces that are working on special projects and have the quality organizations working on their own problems. They've got to work together. So it's integrating the processes and the initiatives. . . . The idea there is we are doing these initiatives not just to check off the column so that everybody [at headquarters] in Morristown and Southfield feels happy, but we're doing them because they're critical to getting us to where we need to be in terms of our operating performance and in terms of our customer satisfaction. . . .

The third thing is making the numbers, meet the commitments. . . . In the AlliedSignal environment, you make the numbers or you're gone. [A while back] we weren't making the numbers, we deserved to be gone. . . . I think if you do the first two things, then make the numbers is going to happen. If you make the customer satisfied, and you're working on the right high-leverage opportunities [with the right people] . . . you're there.

After explaining what Bossidy's 1996 list would mean specifically for St. Clair Shores, Petrovich went on to describe how it was subtly different from the year before. The big change in 1996, she said, was that Bossidy rearranged the items on his list. Bossidy's list, she says, has always had the same general elements, which she described as: "make the numbers," "a total quality, work together kind of thing," and "some level of growth or customers kind of thing." But in 1996, she said, "Now he's taking the numbers and saying, Well, it's not really our first thing, we'll make it the last thing. . . . People out there were saying, 'Gosh, we've got to make the numbers at any cost.' I think Larry's philosophy is, yeah, we got to make the numbers, but the focus should be, How do I get this number? The focus shouldn't just be on slash to get the number, it should be, okay, what are the processes that I've got to fix so I can make the numbers?" That's why Bossidy moved customer satisfaction and teamwork above it on the list, she said. "It's pretty simple."

Mary Petrovich's ability, and willingness, to discuss Larry Bossidy's ideas is a clear signal that both of them are doing their jobs well. Bossidy has framed his ideas in a way that Petrovich finds easy to understand, and he has spent time making them understood through one-on-one coaching with Petrovich and her bosses, and through large-scale communications programs. Petrovich has taken the lead from Bossidy and reframed them for her employees at the St. Clair Shores plant. A crucial fact here is that Petrovich's ideas don't mirror Bossidy's just because Bossidy said they needed to, but rather because Bossidy has convinced her and others like her that they are the right ones. What Petrovich has done, as a leader, is to translate those priorities, which she believes in, into quantum ideas for her organization. She also has incremental ideas for getting her people on board. One of them is that she constantly displays her own personal commitment to reaching the goals and constantly holds her workers accountable for reaching them as well. For example, she says, if General Motors complains that a belt had the buckle sewn on backwards, she takes the defective belt down to the assemblers and tells them, "You guys, you ten people, you did this. What are we doing about this kind of action. . . . See, you localize the message to the relevant people you're talking to."[22] Petrovich is doing the same thing Bossidy does—setting a course and making it real for everyone involved.

Together, Petrovich and her team have turned around the St. Clair Shores plant, raising quality and service levels to standards in line with other AlliedSignal plants and turning an annual loss into a profit.

We had a similar experience when we interviewed Curt Clawson. Clawson is the general manager of AlliedSignal's Filters and Spark Plugs business.[23] A tall, lanky man in his mid-thirties, Clawson is in charge of $200 million in sales to external customers and hundreds of millions of dollars in goods provided to other divisions at AlliedSignal. His slow southern Indiana drawl belies his competitive intensity (he was a captain of the Purdue basketball team while in college). His first words to us were an apology for being dressed in a suit for our interview. "Usually I'm not like this," he said. "But I was up in Detroit with a customer today."

Clawson is one of a number of rising leaders at AlliedSignal. Unlike Jack Welch, who combined a number of autonomous units at GE because he thought they were creating too much redundancy, Larry Bossidy has purposefully kept as many business units with their own profit-and-loss accountability as he can. The reason: It gives Curt Clawson and others like him a chance to develop as business leaders by coming up with their own ideas and running their own shows.

As one of these leaders, Clawson takes Bossidy's priorities and creates his own central ideas for Filters and Spark Plugs. Like Bossidy, he eschews complicated strategies and focuses on a few clear ideas. "You get into a lot of trouble when you start treating a business like a Harvard Business School [from which Clawson graduated] case study," he says. He adds that "At AlliedSignal, my job is very complex. I have an incredible amount of information coming at me from above and below. At the same time, I've got latitude and have to make my own decisions." And this is exactly how Bossidy wants it. Having provided the direction, he lets Clawson and his team, who are closer to the market, make their own decisions.

Clawson's priorities for the Filters and Spark Plugs business for 1996 were to:

- Aggressively reduce costs
- Grow selectively
- Empower people

Clawson's list isn't as close to Bossidy's as Mary Petrovich's, but it serves the same purpose, which is to point his employees down the road that he believes will take them to success. Clawson says he doesn't explicitly repeat Bossidy's priorities because Bossidy himself makes his agenda so abundantly clear. "Thanks to Larry," he says, "you walk into any building and you see what you've got to do: Boom. Make the numbers."

Clawson crafts his message based on the specific realities of his business, and he freely talks about the factors that brought those realities about. For example, he says that "grow selectively" is important because AlliedSignal makes its investments very carefully. "We have to be selective because we don't have a lot of money [to throw around] . . . and we have to have selected customers because we have such a high operating income margin hurdle to get over," he explains.

Basically, says Clawson, if his people keep Bossidy's list in mind and add on his list, the choices they make will lead them where they need to be. He explains that it is his role to interpret an otherwise complex environment for his people. "It got all convoluted before. . . . What they constantly hear is, low-cost provider, world-class goods, global market, blah, blah, blah. . . . I mean, half the things that we used to say just seemed to be oxymorons. . . . What does that mean to them? What we have to do is translate from this complex world to two or three things that they have to do to make us successful. So I paint the picture to them. I had a hundred of them here the day before yesterday and we reiterated it again. Our environment says that we have all these things going on. At the end of the day, if we want to be successful, we need to do two things: We need to have growth . . . and [we need to have] aggressive cost reduction. End of story."

Clawson, like Petrovich, spends a lot of time with his workers, translating and making sure that his ideas are as clear and as important to his employees as Bossidy's are to him. He says he seeks to make the priorities as tangible as possible to people, and he encourages them to come up with ideas of their own. He does this, like Petrovich, in part by showing his own interest in details. "I have to be able to walk on the shop floor and pick up a filter like this [he holds up the part] and say, How can we go from this design to something less complicated? So we can take two people off the line and pay less in material? I have to be able to do that. If I can do that two or three times when I go to a plant, everybody in the company will find out. And so, not only will it help me understand the business, but it will help them understand. They'll know that I'm interested in the details of what they're doing. . . . [Then, the result] is infectious. The next time I go back to the plant you've got a string of people who show you what they've done since the last time you were there."[24]

Bossidy's "quantum" ideas for AlliedSignal certainly weren't exotic. In fact, once he stated them, they seemed pretty self-evident: AlliedSignal is in business to reward shareholders, and this is done by satisfying customers. Nonetheless, his forceful propounding of these ideas has led to an enormous improvement in the company's operations simply because they have aligned the efforts of all of AlliedSignal's workers toward a common goal and a common understanding of how to get there.

Ideas: The Building Blocks of a Business Theory

The AlliedSignal example illustrates the power that a leader can exert simply by having a central idea or organizing principle that is understood throughout the organization. This central idea unites people around a common goal and allows them to act independently in ways that will move them all toward the same desired end. However, having a teachable central idea by itself isn't enough to assure success. The leader must have an idea that is appropriate to the marketplace and to the economic and technological environment. In other words, he or she must have a good idea, because if it is a bad idea, it will still organize and swiftly move people—straight toward disaster.

This happens to organizations all the time. They start out and grow because they have a good central idea, but ideas have a life cycle and eventually become stale. They become inappropriate for the marketplace and for the economic and technological conditions. That's when losers lose their way and when winning companies and winning leaders come up with new central ideas to radically transform their organizations.

Many recent highly visible corporate debacles have been blamed on sluggish action or poor implementation by company executives. IBM's managers are often blamed for failure to capitalize on the company's leadership in computing and to maintain that lead in the PC era. Xerox is cited for its failure to capitalize on its lead in important technologies as it gave away the graphic user interface found in many computers today and lost market share to Japanese copier producers. But while I agree that implementation in these cases could have been much stronger, the real problem lies elsewhere.

People do fail because of a lack of execution. But more fail because they are pursuing bad, or at least untimely, ideas. In his book *Managing in a Time of Great Change,* Peter Drucker asserts that companies fail because "In most cases, the right things are being done—but fruitlessly. . . . The assumptions on which the organization has been built and is being run no longer fit reality. These are the assumptions that shape any organization's behavior, dictate its decisions about what to do and what not to do, and define what the organization considers meaningful results. These assumptions are about markets. They are about identifying customers and competitors, their values and behavior. They are about technology and its dynamics, about a company's strengths and weaknesses. These assumptions are about what a company gets paid for."[25]

When Drucker remarks that "the right things are being done," he means that individuals in the organization are doing the right things based on the company's wrong-headed ideas or assumptions. He cites General Motors to make his case. For fifty years, GM was one of the most successful companies in the world. It achieved this success by assuming that people would constantly trade in their current vehicles for more expensive (and more profitable) models. GM established autonomous divisions, each aimed at a different income segment, and geared its manufacturing operations to produce long runs of mass-produced vehicles.

During the 1970s, however, the reality of the automobile market shifted into high gear, while GM's central business ideas idled in neutral. Buyers became more sophisticated, blowing up the once-predictable income projection path. New production techniques wrenched the economics of car-making to make short runs and variation less costly than before. Yet GM stuck to its old ideas about its divisions and manufacturing. Rather than rethink its product development strategy, each of its divisions began to offer a "car for every purse," which confused customers.

By the end of the 1980s, GM had seen its market share erode and its profits disappear, and it had virtually ignored the real growth market in light trucks and minivans. The company laid off thousands of workers and provided abysmal return to shareholders. The so-called leaders of GM had failed in the crucial job of developing and maintaining a business idea that was appropriate to the realities of the marketplace.

The importance of an appropriate understanding of the business is highlighted by the fact, Drucker points out, that Hughes and EDS, two businesses acquired by GM, flourished at the same time the core car business floundered. The EDS and Hughes units were run by GM managers who had been raised in the same system as the managers still running the car business. The key difference was that in the EDS and Hughes units, managers learned a new business, where they developed good ideas. By contrast, in the car business, GM managers refused to alter their ideas about running an auto company despite market shifts.[26]

In an ideal world, this updating of business ideas would be continual, and the incremental changes would add up to quantum ones. As circumstances changed, the old ideas would evolve into new ones appropriate for the new times. To some degree, this does happen in the real world. Good leaders like the ones I discuss in this book do constantly scan the horizon, assess the current environment and refine their central ideas to reflect the reality of the day. However, incremental changes that optimize the results of an old theory can only go so far. At some point, a whole new idea, a transformation and a transformational leader are needed. As Roger Enrico of PepsiCo puts it, it is possible "to optimize to the point where [you] begin to actually deteriorate the fundamental things. . . . That's when the wheels fall off." That's when you need a whole new wagon. Enrico says his own personal rule of thumb is: "If you have a business that more than one year in a row is burning the furniture to make a profit, then you're in deep trouble. The wheels are falling off." At that point, he says, it is the job of the leader to "break out of the tyranny of incrementalism" and to come up with "a new platform of growth."[27]

At Compaq Computer, Eckhard Pfeiffer did just that within weeks of becoming CEO in the midst of a crisis in 1991, and now he is moving to build yet another new platform that will position the company to reach bold new goals and ultimately avoid another crisis. When it comes to defining and redefining central ideas, I know of few leaders who do a better job.

Pfeiffer came to Compaq's headquarters in Houston after building the company's European operation from nothing, with only $20,000[28] to start. Silver-haired, immaculately dressed and manicured, he is the model executive: smart, straightforward and articulate. He is also intensely competitive and tenacious, attributes he honed as an athlete on tennis courts and alpine ski slopes and continues to use today in sports and business. When Pfeiffer took over, the company was not quite ten years old and had been a roaring success. The core business idea—to be a maker of premium quality PCs—had been refined to make Compaq the leading company in the field with growing market share, and a soaring stock price. However, by 1991, the company's core ideas were out of step with the market. The development of high-performance, low-priced Central Processing Units (CPUs) had shifted the balance of the market. So, within just a few weeks of being named CEO, Pfeiffer expanded the company's target from relatively price insensitive high-end users to more segments of the market. Further, he wanted to increase overall demand.

In order to do this effectively, Pfeiffer completely revamped Compaq's marketing and manufacturing operations to focus on delivering the right machines at the right prices rather than delivering machines at prices out of reach for most buyers. This meant coming up with ideas for changing just about everything in the company, and making sure that those new ideas were aligned to produce the desired results.

Drucker uses the term "business theory" to describe the family of ideas that leaders must tie together into a clear mandate for how an organization will run internally and externally. And, he offers a very helpful framework both for stimulating the generation of new ideas and for putting them together. I often use it in working with executives, and I will use it here to show how Compaq has shaped and reshaped its central ideas. Drucker's framework is based on these questions:

- What are your assumptions about your organization's environment, mission and core competencies? Do they fit reality?
- Do the assumptions in all three areas fit one another?
- Is the theory of the business known and understood throughout the organization?
- How often and how well do I test the theory of the business?

Taking a look at each of these, you can see how Compaq has evolved and continues to evolve.

Compaq was founded in 1982[29] by a group of investors including chairman Ben Rosen and Rod Canion, its first CEO. Originally, they saw an opportunity in providing high-end portable PCs. As the company grew it built a variety of PCs that had "the best and latest designs with everything but the kitchen sink and which could be dropped off the table repeatedly, plugged in and started again without a problem."[30] Their pricing strategy of "premium products, premium prices"[31] set it apart from its competitors who simply tried to underprice IBM. Their justification was plain and simple—the market would clearly pay for the best. So, they built most of their core competencies around their products' superior functionality and quality, perhaps best put in their then-advertising theme, "It simply works better."[32]

Well, this did simply work better. For eight strong years, at least. A short time after developing this business theory, Compaq had the momentum over IBM and everyone else in PCs. Compaq had correctly identified opportunities in the marketplace and organized itself to exploit them. Employees understood the business model very well, and their "no compromises" philosophy brought them repeated success in the marketplace.[33] Compaq was the fastest company ever to achieve $1 billion in sales,[34] and it reached $2 billion in sales only six years after its birth.[35] It was a darling of Wall Street and saw its stock price rise from an initial $1.02 to $24.75 at its peak in 1991.[36]

Then, the computer market suddenly shifted, and Compaq was caught flatfooted. As Rosen, put it "in the second quarter of 1991, a funny thing happened on the way to prosperity. . . . What had happened was that competition was intensifying and product price was becoming much more important to customers. Yet we were locked in to a product line characterized by high costs and high prices."[37] Consumers shifted as PCs moved into more homes and onto more desktops. Companies interested in putting a PC on every desk were more concerned about price than when they had been putting them only in engineering labs. Universities and schools that wanted to increase access also favored price over the latest technological advancements. Families who wanted PCs for their children had to make them fit within tight budgets. At the same time, exponential leaps were made in the power of the computer chip, which pushed down the price/performance ratio of each previous generation of chip. Performance, good enough for most, was now available cheaply. Finally, Microsoft and Intel were teaming up to provide open standards which lowered the barriers to entry into manufacturing PCs and helped level the playing field in the PC business in general. Almost instantaneously, Compaq's assumptions about its markets and its business theory no longer fit reality.

The new market realities required Pfeiffer and his new management team to also reconsider their assumptions about Compaq's mission and the core competencies needed to fulfill it. In very broad terms, Pfeiffer didn't change Compaq's mission to be a worldwide leader in making and selling PCs. But he changed its market orientation from being technology-centric to customer-centric. Pfeiffer believed that there were specific segments in the market that had their own preferences in technology and function and their own price points. Pfeiffer wanted Compaq to design computers backward—working from the preferences of these segments so that products could be profitably delivered at the customer's price points. Prior to this, computer companies had basically built the computers they wanted to and priced them to make a profit, and then sold them to whoever would pay that price. In many of the segments, Pfeiffer's new strategy meant a 180-degree turn for Compaq to offer lower-priced products.

At the same time Pfeiffer was looking for growth opportunities, he decided to expand Compaq's presence in networked PC-servers. To capture the leading position in this market, Pfeiffer also used a competitive price–based strategy. Finally, Pfeiffer believed that to reach and expand all segments of the market for which Compaq would offer PCs, he needed to radically expand the number of distribution partners across the globe.

Pfeiffer's predecessor Rod Canion had perceived some of the same changes in the marketplace as Pfeiffer, but he resisted making the necessary changes in the company. After Compaq's performance started to slump, Canion had presented a recovery plan in September of 1991, but he believed that the company could hold out on implementation until the first quarter of 1993. He trusted that his customers would continue to be drawn by the company's old promise of superiority,[38] so he continued to pursue the high-price strategy. When Pfeiffer arrived in Houston in February of 1991, his job was to be Chief Operating Officer. However, when the company reported its first-ever loss in the third quarter of 1991, the board fired Canion[39] and named Pfeiffer to replace him.

In identifying the first steps of implementing the turnaround, Pfeiffer says, "We had to recognize our key strengths and define the new market requirements in order to build our new strategy."[40] This meant changing ideas about how the company and its employees would work. Mainly, this meant replacing Compaq's long held assumption that success would be built on painstaking perfectionism and putting new emphasis on speed and agility. Compaq wouldn't sacrifice its reputation for quality, but it would pull back from the expectation—especially among its workers—that all of its products would reflect absolute state-of-the-art technology.

The new theory became well known and understood, because Pfeiffer concentrated on making it so. He committed himself to communicating what he calls "one clear crisp message" to his troops.[41] Thinking back, he recalls, "Communication was our greatest need and our toughest challenge throughout the first two hundred days."[42] One of the ways Pfeiffer spread the word and signaled his firm commitment to change was by kicking off an initiative focusing on six new priorities for the organization. At the top of the list were products and costs. For a company that prided itself on performance leadership, Pfeiffer introduced ridiculous goals—he wanted to take costs and prices down 35%.[43] This brash goal signaled to everyone that the company's business theory had changed. Pfeiffer then went about reworking each element of the business theory. The company that had approached every product with the same over-engineering zeal began to change every aspect of its manufacturing to shave costs that weren't necessary. Pfeiffer and his team also took the R&D budget from 6.0% of revenue in 1991 to 2.3% in 1993.[44] And, he boosted manufacturing capacity from 30,000 units in a good month to 30,000 units over the Thanksgiving weekend alone in 1993.[45] In addition, Pfeiffer's team added forty-five new products to the line and, within just a few years, added tens of thousands of distribution partners in the U.S. alone.

The results of Compaq's turnaround were amazing. In June 1992, when the company announced price cuts of up to 32%, revenues rose 75% in less than a year.[46] Over the six years from 1990 to 1996, gross margins at Compaq declined from 43% to 23%, but its profits have almost tripled to $1.3 billion.[47] Meanwhile, the stock, after the troubles of 1991, is up 745% vs. 78% for the S&P 500 and 64% for the S&P Computer Index from the end of 1991 to the end of 1996.[48] In 1992, Pfeiffer had said he wanted Compaq to be the No. 1 PC company in the world by 1996. It achieved this in 1994, two years ahead of schedule.[49]

Eckhard Pfeiffer's leadership was incredibly powerful for one reason: he focused his entire organization not on optimizing the last business theory but on changing the business theory frequently. As a result, he set up Compaq internally to constantly test and redesign its business theory. "We learned from the crisis in 1991, that we had to be willing to act very quickly," he says.[50] Pfeiffer had a flat organization structure that can easily sense changes to the environment, communicate them upward, and then implement decisions. He also started high-energy weekly meetings of his senior executives to keep the entire company abreast of new developments.

When use of the Internet took off, Pfeiffer and his team wasted no time changing their assumptions about their markets. In an effort called Crossroads Pfeiffer formed fifteen task forces of leaders within the company to redefine the company's business theory and take action. Bob Stearns, Compaq's Senior Vice President for Technology and Corporate Development, summed up the changing assumptions for me one day in the spring of 1996. "I think we're at a major inflection point in the industry. . . . This thing we've been working with, the PC, is really a communications device, not a personal productivity device, and therefore it's going to replace the black telephone, not just be a bigger computer." The task forces saw Compaq at the center of the network revolution, not marginalized by it.[51]

In typical Compaq fashion, the company moved quickly and aggressively. The teams had only nine weeks during the spring and summer of 1996 to make their plans, and then the company began immediately taking actions. Pfeiffer wanted to increase Compaq's leadership in the worldwide information technology industry. So he set a new goal to move from the No. 5 computer company in the world to one of the top three by the year 2000, which means it will have to more than double in size to $40 billion in sales in three years. To achieve this goal, the company implemented the plans of the Crossroads teams to improve Compaq's world-renowned efficiency.[52] This helped fund new products in existing markets as well as entirely new businesses such as professional workstations, Internet products and services, networking equipment and system integration and solutions for large, medium and small businesses. To support this, Compaq reorganized into four global product groups.[53] By the end of 1996, Compaq was poised to successfully complete its second transformation in five years. In 1997, it completed its boldest move to date—the multibillion-dollar acquistion of Tandem Corporation.

In the computer business, the devastating effects of holding on to old ideas may become more apparent more quickly than in some other businesses. Pfeiffer had to rethink Compaq's entire theory of the business twice in less than five years. And he began his last transformation while the stock was at an all time high and the company was doing well.[54] For most leaders in other industries, challenges of this magnitude don't come along so often. But inevitably, they do come along. For every business, no matter how successful it has been nor for how many decades, the day will come when the old ideas don't work anymore and a radical rethinking is required. Winning leaders know this, and they remain winners by making sure, not only that the organization is always focused, but that it is focused on ideas that are right for today. Pfeiffer's big misstep that eventually got him fired was the acquisition of Digital Equipment Company. He became so isolated and inflexible that he lost his own team and his job. He stopped being a good leader/teacher.

Ideas as Energizers

In the previous sections, I have talked about how good ideas unify a workforce by giving people an intellectual understanding that allows them to come up with their own good ideas for reaching a common goal. Before I move on to talk about how winning leaders develop good ideas, however, I want to point out one more important role that ideas play. And that is that they excite and motivate people to action.

Ideas engage people's minds and open them to new possibilities. And when those possibilities are attractive, they rally people to action. When John Kennedy dared to articulate the idea that America could put a man on the moon, millions of people, not just Americans, were instantly eager to make it happen. Ideas about rights and freedoms inspired the English in 1215 to rise up and force King John to sign the Magna Carta. Five and a half centuries later, some of those same ideas impelled the American colonists to declare independence and stage a revolution against the British. And in this century, communist ideas about the fair allocation of wealth moved the Russian peasants to overthrow their ruler. The sheer power of these ideas led these people to risk their lives and stage bloody wars to establish and preserve them.

In business, ideas excite people not only by expanding their perceptions of what's possible, but also by offering them a goal that is interesting and seems worth achieving. Before Phil Knight came along, industry pros thought the $2 billion Adidas empire would be the leader forever. No one foresaw Nike ousting Adidas from its long-time position of international dominance.[55] But the uniqueness of Knight's idea about helping Nike's customers to become winners got his employees interested and excited. Nike offered its workers a chance to focus on the playing field and measure their performance in games won and speed records set. It offered them an opportunity to be winners as well, and they jumped in enthusiastically to "Just Do It."

Knight has found a formula that works so well not just because it is a smart concept for the market, but also because it is a great rallying cry for the people who work at Nike. Today, Knight is challenging them to redefine the game, to make Nike a total sports company by providing everything from equipment to apparel to management of sports stars' contracts.

Leaders Generating Ideas—Think Revolution

With all the consulting and academic fanfare these days about "learning organizations," there is surprisingly little discussion about ideas, which are the substance of learning. Consultants and academics talk about processes for implementing ideas, but they don't talk about the ideas themselves. And there is almost no practical help offered to organizational leaders in generating those ideas. This is in part because there are no simple rules, and I am not going to try to give you any, either. But I have observed a couple of things about winning leaders and how they develop ideas that provide a good starting point. My two big pieces of advice are:

- Think the unthinkable
- Use everything you've got

One of the biggest mistakes that most people make in looking for new ideas is that they don't look far enough. We think about moving the furniture or repainting the walls, but we don't consider rebuilding the room. And that is often what needs to be done. One of the major contributions of *Reengineering the Corporation* is that in it Michael Hammer and James Champy urged companies to stop trying to fix their current work processes and instead come up with new processes more appropriate for what needs to be done. They urged executives to throw out their old assumptions and start all over again.

Much of this chapter has been devoted to discussing the fact that successful companies have central ideas about their businesses. Because they are well understood and accepted, these ideas unify everyone in the organization and help them work toward a common goal. The power of these ideas comes from their constancy and their widespread acceptance. Nonetheless, successful leaders never view their ideas as carved in stone. Rather, while winning leaders are clear about the ideas they hold, they hold them very loosely. They are constantly challenging them and looking around for even better, more appropriate ideas.

Peter Drucker calls this willingness to scrap everything and start over "abandonment." An organization must periodically "challenge every product, every service, every policy, every distribution channel," he says, in order to avoid being "overtaken by events." If it doesn't do this, he adds, "it will squander its best resources on things it should never have been doing or should no longer do. As a result, it will lack the resources . . . needed to exploit the opportunities that arise."[56] Drucker is absolutely right. Certainty and complacency are the two biggest enemies of creativity and positive change. But it isn't the organizations that must do the challenging and the rethinking. It is their leaders.

Bill Gates proved himself the master of abandonment in 1995 when Microsoft did a 180-degree turnaround on its Internet strategy. After months of disdaining the Internet and touting its plans to build a proprietary on-line service, Microsoft virtually dropped dozens of projects and embraced the Internet. It cost Microsoft millions to make the about-face. But "people aren't asking anymore if Microsoft will be killed by the Internet. [They ask] whether Microsoft will dominate the Internet," says Scott Winkler, vice president at the market research company Gartner Group Incorporated.[57] True leaders have a desire to win that overrides their attachment to the past, and they have the courage to face reality, even when it means eating their pride.[58]

Eckhard Pfeiffer is another great "abandoner." Within weeks of becoming CEO, he completely revamped Compaq, and now he is redesigning it again. Pfeiffer says he is not only comfortable with change, he thrives on it. He traces his urge for constant improvement to his childhood. Born in what is now Poland, he and his family were forced to move after World War II. His father was a POW of the Allies, and the family moved without him when Eckhard was only four. "That feeling of absolute poverty, of absolute helplessness," he says, "shaped my life and the will and the energy . . . to get somewhere where these things would not matter . . . to move on in my life and in my career." It also taught Pfeiffer to be constantly vigilant and to expect permanence from nothing. After that experience, he says, "I've never been afraid to change everything."[59]

The longer an idea remains in place, the harder it is to change, and the harder it is for its leaders even to think about changing it. That's one of the reasons that Jack Welch's transformation of General Electric is so remarkable. Welch joined General Electric right out of college and has worked his entire career there. Still, when he became chairman in 1981, he had the vision and the edge to throw out the central idea that had been motivating the company for nearly one hundred years. When GE was founded in 1892,[60] Charles Coffin, the company's first CEO, had the idea that the company would be "general electric," that is, a company that did everything related to electricity. The company's actual success or competitiveness in a given market was not really an issue. Coverage, or comprehensiveness, was what mattered. At first, when electricity was new, this might have been a good idea. It gave the company a stake in all the related emerging technologies. Over time, however, electricity became ubiquitous, and General Electric became a sort of "Mega Monster, Huge We-Do-Everything Company." It rarely left a business once it had entered it, regardless of how poorly it fared in it. As a result, when Welch took over, the company had no organizational focus and was in 241 businesses, many of them quite mediocre.

One of the first things Welch did as CEO was to look around and say: "Forget it." GE was one of America's corporate behemoths, and still surprisingly profitable. But Welch saw that it was squandering its resources and could do a lot better if it didn't have so many losers. So he declared that in the future General Electric would be No. 1 or No. 2 in each of its businesses, and if it couldn't achieve that position it would fix, close or sell the business. Today GE has twelve businesses, and it is No. 1 or No. 2 in each one.[61] This was a gutsy move on Welch's part. He thought the unthinkable. And it's paid off handsomely. GE's profits have more than quadrupled off of an already huge base in fifteen years.

In the last chapter, I talked about leaders learning from their life experiences, and earlier in this chapter I quoted Bill Pollard, the chairman of ServiceMaster, as saying that he learns and gets business ideas from everything he does. That's a quality that I've found in all the successful leaders. They are magnets for information. They collect it everywhere, they remember it and they use it.

Gary Wendt at GE Capital used his experience working for small companies to formulate the business idea that achieving large goals rests not on thinking big, but on thinking small. His small business approach, Wendt says, is possibly "the secret, and if not the secret then one of the top three or four secrets for why GE Capital has grown."[62] At GE Capital, Wendt says, he designed an organization to break away from the insulation that large organizations provide. He wants to give people experiences that deliver basic lessons such as meeting a payroll and negotiating directly with customers, suppliers and acquisition targets. For that reason, Wendt ran GE Capital as a collection of twenty-seven distinctly focused businesses serving specific markets, with a business leader and team in charge of each. This has been a key ingredient in GE Capital's growth. "A lot of businesses have one strategic planner trying to jam growth into their organizations. When I want growth, I've got twenty-seven leaders looking for opportunities."[63]

"Looking for opportunities" . . . that's the other big thing that winners are always doing. Nothing ever happens to them, no piece of information crosses their desk or their dinner table, no idle comment is heard in the hardware store that they do not examine and evaluate for new ideas. Dick Notebaert, formerly CEO at Ameritech, says he came up with the idea to enter the home security market by observing that the home security companies were sending trucks to customers' homes to install and repair wiring just like his telephone people were. ServiceMaster, which started out in the mothproofing business, got into carpet cleaning after workers reported to the founder, Marion Wade, that lots more homeowners were installing wall-to-wall carpet. He figured that since he was already sending his employees into people's homes, he could offer two services instead of one.

Today, ServiceMaster provides other in-home services such as pest control, lawn care and appliance servicing.

While winning leaders do get ideas serendipitously, they don't leave a lot to chance. They are surprisingly systematic and diligent in seeking out information. Most executives spend time schmoozing with important customers, but winners also go out and talk to non-customers, to figure out what their needs are and why they aren't buying from him or her. And they look at their competitors and at other industries, not just to see how well they are doing but to see what they are doing.

Winning leaders also seek out people in their organizations to feed them information. Curt Clawson at AlliedSignal has his chocolate budget. "You've got to know the details of the business," he says, and one of the most effective ways he has found is "just walking around with a box of chocolates and stopping to chat. Then everyone, even your computer science people, wants to tell you what they are doing that's cool."[64]

On a very practical level, leaders create ways for both themselves and others to learn and create new ideas. They do this personally, and in so doing, they help future leaders learn to generate ideas as well.

Gary Wendt, formerly of GE Capital, says, "In a big company, none of us would have to ever think about new ideas and we could still keep totally busy. There is enough garbage that takes place in these companies, there are enough papers to move, responsibilities for old things, reviewing this, reviewing that, that we wouldn't have to spend one minute on growth and we'd be totally busy."[65] Wendt, therefore, held "dreaming sessions" with each of his business units. At these unstructured sessions, he challenged core assumptions and asked people to look at their customers and markets in new ways. These sessions were much more exciting and helpful than the old-fashioned strategic planning process for both Wendt and his people. In the old sessions, the plans were virtually finalized before he got to see them, and his ability to make contributions was marginal. By then, "Everyone's mind is made up [and questions lead to] confrontation."

Wendt's personal role in the sessions was critical. He was sitting down and talking as one businessperson to another. When someone bought a completed business plan to his dreaming sessions, "My role is to take the plan and throw it on the floor. . . . " He pantomimes with great glee. "Then you get out the flip charts and you start saying, 'Now wait a minute. What are the issues for this customer?' Whatever themes you do decide to go on, you build it from scratch. And you get them to think about it, as opposed to filling in a form."

His dreaming sessions developed both new ideas and leaders. In these sessions, Wendt had the opportunity to personally coach his leaders on how to think about industries and exploiting opportunities. "When the time is right, you sit back and listen. I just get in awe, almost, as to how some people think, and it makes me feel very proud. I feel a lot more like a leader when I get done, than a manager."[66]

Just as we all "swim in a sea of air," we swim in a sea of information and ideas as well. They are everywhere around us, and there are millions of ways to use them, but most of us don't pay attention. And that's why so many of us miss so many opportunities. Winning leaders miss opportunities as well, because there are too many to take advantage of. But they miss a lot fewer than other people because they are always searching, and they are searching everywhere. Leaders are learners who get ideas from everywhere and encourage others to do the same. That's what keeps them ahead of other people.

Finally, leaders are never satisfied with their ideas; they are constantly looking for the next big one. As PepsiCo's Enrico says, "As soon as everyone is on board with one idea and you are in the shoot 'em up phase, the leader's job is to find the next one, to find that next growth platform. It may take a few years, which is scary, but you've got to find it."[67]

Values—Speaking with Words and Action

Winning Organizations Have Strong Values

- These values define desirable behaviors
- They support the organization's central goals

Winning Leaders Live the Values—Privately and Publicly

- Their personal conduct embodies the values
- Their actions reinforce the values in others

Values Are a Key Competitive Tool

- They are the fabric of the corporate culture
- They provide the "instinctive" grounding for smart actions

In the course of an idle conversation at Ameritech's former headquarters in Chicago late one afternoon, Mike Lach, a general manager of network operations, happened to mention to his boss that he had heard that Ameritech's CEO and chairman Dick Notebaert was going to visit a switching site where a major customer outage was occurring. "I called the team," Lach told Bob Knowling, then Vice President of Network Operations, "and let everybody know he was coming out." The conversation continued for about five more minutes and then Knowling got ready to head back to his office. As he started away, he turned and asked matter-of-factly, "Michael, any particular reason why you saw a need to call the troops and let them know that Dick was coming out?" Lach said that he didn't want them to be surprised, and wanted to make sure they remained focused on their efforts to restore service. Knowling, who had known Lach for many years but only recently hired him as one of his senior managers, replied seriously, "Mike, let me take a moment to just offer some observations for you. That's the way that you do it in a bureaucratic society. Dick ought to be able to walk out through our work environment, unannounced, and see that . . . we never have to prepare or practice because the general's in town. What you just demonstrated to the organization is that we need to make sure that we are on our Ps and Qs only when the chairman is around."[1] The next day, Lach sent an e-mail to all his direct reports, recounting the incident and saying, "I appreciated the coaching, and I want you guys to make sure that you don't see that kind of behavior out of me. If you do, call it out."

"Values" is such an overused term that I wouldn't bring it up if it weren't really important. But if I am going to talk about the difference between winners and losers, I have to talk about values. Just about every big organization in the world has a formal ethics or values statement hanging on the wall somewhere. So it's not saying anything special to note that winning companies have them as well. But unlike run-of-the-mill companies and outright losers, winners actually pay attention to their values. They think about them, *and* they live by them.

Many companies, although they probably won't admit it, use values statements largely as public relations tools. Having a values statement is good for a company's image in general. Corporate chiefs often turn to them when the company is under fire and say, "Look, we don't take advantage of suppliers or ship faulty products. It's here in our values statement." In fact, most executives do know intellectually that having good values is a good business practice, and most people don't deliberately lie, cheat, steal or otherwise behave dishonorably. But although they may talk about their values and even sincerely believe that their organizations are living by them, they rarely reflect on them or go very far out of their way to apply them to their everyday activities.

Winning organizations, on the other hand, are deeply concerned about their values. For the most part, the values espoused by winning organizations are no different from those of other well-intentioned but not-so-winning groups. You would be hard-pressed to find a responsible person anywhere who wouldn't tell you that he or she values honesty and fairness. However, as in the Ameritech example above, winners apply these values more rigorously than losers. Further, winning leaders are keenly aware of the importance that values play in shaping people's behavior. They see values as a competitive tool that allows their organizations to respond quickly and appropriately. So they invest huge amounts of time nurturing not only the big, immutable values of honesty and integrity, but also day-to-day values—such as teamwork, risk-taking or satisfying customers—that help the organization achieve its goals. Like missionaries, winning leaders constantly think about and preach their organizations' values. They embody them with their own actions. And they teach others to be leaders by constantly encouraging them also to examine the values and wrestle with their application in everyday situations.

In the last chapter, I discussed how ideas provide people with a common purpose and a clear understanding of their mission that allows them to work independently toward achieving it. The ideas unify them with a shared vision of "what" they are trying to accomplish, so they can each develop their own ideas and take the actions necessary to get the organization where it wants to be. Values provide a similar shared understanding that allows people to act independently, by addressing the "how." Values enable people to design their own actions by defining the rules of behavior and establishing the forms of conduct that will be rewarded, or not tolerated. Winning leaders reflect on values, and work on establishing them, just as seriously as they do ideas.

Great leaders have always known that morals and values are the cornerstones of society. Moses brought the Ten Commandments down to the Israelites who had lost their way, not only in the desert, but in their relationships with God and with each other. Jesus, Gandhi, Martin Luther King Jr. and the authors of the Declaration of Independence all focused on values as much as ideas. Shared values allow people to live and work together. They create a sense of community without which we would all be alone, pitted against everyone else in the world. Even commerce would be impossible without shared understandings about the sanctity of an agreement and the delivery of goods or services and remuneration.

Every organization has its own culture that reflects its values. For many decades in the steel and auto industries, for example, the overriding culture was one of distrust and animosity between unionized hourly workers and management. In slower times, before computers and high-tech telecommunications sped up the pace of global competition, companies could afford the layers of supervisors and managers needed to police the workers. The negotiated agreement between the companies and the workers was a "day's work for a day's pay," and supervisors were on the spot to ensure that the workers followed orders and kept their part of the bargain. But when the competitive landscape shifted in the 1970s and 1980s, costly and cumbersome bureaucracies became a liability. By the early 1980s for example, the product development cycle for the Japanese car companies was far below that of their counterparts in the U.S. That's when many executives began disassembling their bureaucracies, only to discover that taking cogs out of the wheels made the machinery run even more poorly. They needed to build new machines that didn't require so many cogs. And for these new machines to work, they needed to change the values and behaviors of the people operating them.

U S WEST, for example, undertook a costly reengineering effort in the early 1990s to cut operating expenses and prepare itself to compete in the new fast-paced telecommunications industry. It took out layers of people and revised its work processes, but it neglected to change the values of its workers. In fact, it continued to reward the old ones. So people continued to hang on to their bureaucratic mindsets and plodding, uncompetitive behaviors.[2] "My first week on the job it was immediately apparent that nobody had been accountable for the reengineering effort," says Bob Knowling, who joined the company in 1996 from Ameritech. "No one was accountable for meeting customers' expectations or adhering to a cost structure. . . . Service was in the tank, we were overspending our budgets by more than $100 million. Yet people weren't losing their jobs, and they still got all or some of their bonuses."[3]

From the start, some leaders, such as Marion Wade and his successors at ServiceMaster, understood that values have the power to guide and motivate workers just as well as or better than an army of supervisors. ServiceMaster, a highly successful facilities management company, focuses all of its activities around a simple four-line values statement that I will talk about below. Other winning leaders have turned to emphasizing values for purely practical reasons. A typical GE manager in the early 1980s, for example, supervised an average of seven subordinates. Today that number is fifteen to twenty and sometimes more.[4] The point is simple: When you can't control, dictate or monitor, the only thing you can do is trust. And that means leaders have to be sure that the people they are trusting have values that are going to elicit the decisions and actions that they want.

So, whether through inherent wisdom or smart learning, winning leaders recognize the importance of having corporate values that support the organization's goals, and of making sure that everyone in the organization understands and lives by them. In order to do this, I have observed, winning leaders deliberately and consciously do five things:

1. They clearly articulate a set of values for the entire organization or team
2. They continually reflect on the values to make sure that they are appropriate to achieving the desired goals
3. They embody the values with their own behavior
4. They encourage others to apply the values in their own decisions and actions
5. They aggressively confront and deal with pockets of ignorance and resistance

These five activities allow leaders to develop other leaders who share their values and who can teach them to other people in their companies. And when the values are straight and people who believe in them are in place, leaders make sure those values are reflected and reinforced in every decision and action, from compensation and appraisal systems to customer service practices.

While most successful organizations are careful about their values, few have made values as central to their day-to-day operations as ServiceMaster. The company has grown from a mom-and-pop Chicago-area mothproofing business into a $4.9 billion[5] facilities management conglomerate, in large part because it has been consistently guided by a set of strong and clearly stated values emanating from the very top of the organization. This is essential: Whether they are aware of it or not, leaders always establish the values—productive or counterproductive—by which their organizations operate. Therefore, to build a winning organization, a leader must clearly articulate, embody and encourage productive values.

The company that eventually became ServiceMaster was founded in 1929[6] by Marion Wade, a deeply religious man whose goal in life was to serve other people. He wanted to run his own business so he could live his values during the week as well as on the weekends. Over the years, the values that Wade taught have been adapted, but they remain at the core of everything ServiceMaster does.

When most organizations talk about serving people, they are usually referring to their clients or customers. But Wade's idea was that he would serve his workers, and he would do that by providing them with stable, secure, honorable employment. A crucial test of his determination came early on. At the time, ServiceMaster's primary business was mothproofing. Even though most of his employees were what might be called "menial" workers, Wade had always encouraged them to consider themselves partners in the business and to look for growth opportunities. So when they reported to him that homeowners were increasingly installing wall-to-wall carpet, he set out to find an efficient way to clean carpets. With the help of some chemist friends, he developed a compound that could clean carpets quickly with minimum inconvenience for the homeowner. Then he was faced with a choice. He could simply start selling the product, or he could go into the carpet-cleaning business. He chose the carpet-cleaning business because "his focus was on service, because service involved people and he wanted to relate to people," explains Bill Pollard, the current chairman of ServiceMaster. "He believed people were important; created in God's image with value and worth. And he wanted to relate his faith in how he treated people."

Wade didn't just believe that workers should think like partners; he believed that they should actually share in the risks and rewards of their work. "Wade had a practice, as soon as we were incorporated, of selling stock to the employees even though there wasn't any official system for that," says Pollard. "He'd loan them the money, and they'd buy the stock from him. And he used to go through the whole company and sell stock that way. Today over 20% of ServiceMaster is owned by employees."[7]

When you walk into ServiceMaster's headquarters in Downers Grove, Illinois, one of the first things you see is a marble slab engraved with its values:

1. To honor God in all we do
2. To help people develop
3. To pursue excellence
4. To grow profitably

But the important thing about ServiceMaster is not that the words are engraved in the lobby, but that these values are engraved in the hearts and minds of everyone who works for ServiceMaster—whether as an officer at headquarters, as a janitor mopping floors at a hospital, or as a specialist from its Chemlawn unit killing weeds in your front yard. They know the values, they believe in them and they live by them.

For many people who don't know the folks at ServiceMaster, the stated value of "To honor God in all we do" is troubling. Before we went to visit them, one of my colleagues suggested that their religious orientation might make them unsuitable as models for more "normal" organizations. But the truth is that, whether motivated by God or not, it's very good business to seek excellence, pay attention to profits and care about your workers. And when you get to know the people who work at ServiceMaster, you quickly see that there are no traces of ethereal otherworldliness about them. They are serious businesspeople firmly focused on winning. In Pollard's recent book, *The Soul of the Firm,* he talks about the link between God and profits. "Profit is a means in God's world to be used and invested, not an end to be worshipped. Profit is a legitimate measurement of the value of our effort. . . . God and business do mix, and profit is a standard for determining the effectiveness of our combined efforts."[8]

In addition to the four values engraved in the lobby, ServiceMaster also has a twenty-one-statement list of "ServiceMaster's Leadership Principles." It does say (No. 21): "We have all been created in God's image and the results of our leadership will be measured beyond the workplace. The story will be told in the changed lives of people." And it high-mindedly states that (No. 12) "We pay based on performance and promote based on potential, not belief, tenure, gender, race or friendships." But it also says: (No. 14) "We make and beat budgets"; (No. 2) "We are value driven and performance oriented"; and (No. 10) "There are no friendly competitors." There's nothing sentimental or squishy about that. The people at ServiceMaster aim to provide excellent service so the business will grow, and they work as efficiently as possible to generate profits. (They also understand the logic that ties them together—that God is honored by helping people develop, that the funds and opportunities to develop people come from profitable growth and that profitable growth comes from excellent work.)

ServiceMaster's portfolio of businesses includes cleaning hospitals, plants, and schools, food service programs, Terminix pest control services, Chemlawn lawn maintenance, Merry Maids home maid service, and American Home Shield, which services home appliances. Most companies find it hard to get workers enthusiastic about doing some of the grungy work these businesses involve. But at ServiceMaster, it's not a problem. Because everyone at ServiceMaster believes in the sanctity of the work (even those who aren't explicitly religious), and because they believe so firmly in profits, in serving people and in excellence, motivation is practically guaranteed. In his book, Pollard cites Shirley, a housekeeper in a 250-bed community hospital, as one example. Seeing herself in a key support role in the hospital, she once told Pollard, "If we don't clean with a quality effort, we can't keep the doctors and nurses in business; we can't accommodate patients. This place would be closed if we didn't have housekeeping."[9]

ServiceMaster has achieved such adherence to its values not only because it uses them as a litmus test in its hiring, but also because everyone from Bill Pollard and Carlos Cantu on down works at making them an everyday reality. One of the twenty-one leadership principles says (No. 6), "If you don't live it, you don't believe it." And they really mean it. Service permeates all the way to the highest level of the company. All ServiceMaster senior executives have worked in field operations—either starting as cleaners or other service technicians, or managing operations that do the hands-on physical work. And no matter how senior they become, each spends at least one day a year performing front-line service work. This keeps them in touch with the needs of the workers and emphasizes the importance of the front-line people's contributions. Bill Dowdy, president of ServiceMaster's health care business in the United States, visits about two customers a week and personally speaks with every one of his 2,500 managers at least once a year. When any one of them marks an anniversary of five, ten, fifteen or twenty years at ServiceMaster, Dowdy is on the phone that day to "thank them for their years. . . . Let them know we don't take the years for granted, we appreciate what they're doing."[10]

At ServiceMaster this commitment to the values is woven into every aspect of the business. How executives like Dowdy and Pollard spend their time is one sign of this commitment. Another is that workers' evaluations and compensation explicitly take into account how well their decisions and actions reflect the company's values. Work plans are designed to respect the dignity of workers and to support solid family lives. And because it cares about the health of its workers, the company actively invests in developing tools to make their jobs less strenuous. Eight hours of mopping floors, washing walls or cleaning hospital rooms can be grueling, so ServiceMaster invests significant resources every year to develop things like a specially treated dry mop to eliminate the unnecessary task of both wet-mopping and dry-mopping hallways, a new disinfectant mop dispenser to facilitate the sanitation process, window scrubbers for hard-to-reach places so that windows can be cleaned less laboriously and color-coded cleaning materials for illiterate employees.[11]

But weaving the company's values into the fabric goes far beyond these periodic reinforcements. In its hiring decisions, ServiceMaster looks for people with moral convictions and strong work ethics. Then it nurtures and tests them in small and large ways every day. ServiceMaster has a four-step methodology for teaching: (1) Prepare the learner. (2) Show the learner. (3) Have the learner show you. (4) Coach. It applies to values as well as skills. The leaders who thoroughly understand and believe in the values not only tell them to newcomers, but demonstrate them and quickly put the learners in real-life situations where they need to apply them. Then the teachers help the learners improve their performance. It's a powerful teaching tool that helps assure that the values permeate the organization from top to bottom.

Phil Myers was working nights as a janitor in an operating room in Indianapolis when his meticulous work attracted the attention of his supervisor, Chris Kinman. Kinman, who worked for ServiceMaster although Myers did not, began to give Myers more responsibility. Then one night he gave Myers the Service-Master manager's manual and asked him to read it. Myers, who still seems hyperactive after twenty-one years at ServiceMaster, wasn't much of a reader, so he just skimmed it. But Kinman urged him to dig in deeper and to think about it. Because he worked the night shift from 10:00 P.M. until 6:00 A.M., Myers only saw Kinman and the other ServiceMaster managers for one hour each day, before they went home at 11:00 P.M., but Kinman sought him out and made the most of the limited time. "Chris and I got to know each other," says Myers. "He would ask things like, 'What do you want to be when you grow up?' Six or seven months after that, I had the opportunity to become an evening supervisor for him." The opportunity frightened Myers because "I was a twenty-one-year-old kid about to step into a role of people who were old enough to be my parents if not my grand-parents. I had no formal education. I had taken some college classes and was going to college, but had no degree. . . . I was scared to death. I had led some people my own age in the Air Force, but now I was going to lead twenty people." But Kinman encouraged him. "I can remember that feeling [of fear]. But Chris put confidence in me. 'You tell me that you want to suc-ceed, I'll see to it that you do not fail. Just keep trying, and you will not fail,'" Kinman told Myers.

Shortly after he became a supervisor, Myers was put to the test. He discovered that a friend had left his shift fifteen minutes early but signed out at the normal time. "Now I had my first major, major situation," says Myers. "Number one, I had some-body here who was breaking a major time compliance rule. And, I had a person that I worked with for a year, who was my friend, and now . . . he was reporting to me." Myers turned to Kinman, who coached and tested but never directed him. "[Kinman's coaching] was to 'just be firm, fair and friendly.' He was not saying, 'Go terminate him. That's what you have to do.' Chris became a mirror to me, he held it up, and I had to say 'What's the right thing to do?' ... He took me through a process of review of what were my options and what was the right thing to do. And when I decided, Chris said, 'Go for it. If you need any help let me know. If you need me to be with you, let me know.'" Myers met with the employee alone, and after reviewing the event with him, decided he had to let him go because it was a serious violation of ServiceMaster's values of honesty and the sanctity of work.

While confronting a values transgression in one service worker may seem like a small deal, interactions like this are where the rubber meets the road. Values are only as good as their embodiment by every employee all the time. And it is people like Phil Myers handling situations like this every day that make the difference at ServiceMaster. On the front lines, these decisions can be even tougher than in the executive suite. When a top executive such as Bill Pollard fires another executive, he knows that the person is probably going to get eighteen months' salary as severance and is sitting on millions in stock. Supervisors like Myers are dealing with people in much more tenuous circumstances. Of his experience with the worker in Indianapolis, Myers, who now manages a ServiceMaster account at a hospital on Chicago's West Side, remarks, "I think it set the structure for discipline in my career. It was one of the major things because it was so serious. My thoughts were, 'Sam may no longer have an income.' But it was the fairest thing to do."

Myers has faced many more tests in leading three turnaround situations, two of which involved the pending loss of a big customer. In these situations, Myers says he has relied heavily on the ServiceMaster values to bring in the business result. The key to each of his successful turnarounds, he says, was honesty, teaching and respect for the workers. The workers are usually scared, says Myers, "that you're going to come in and all of a sudden people are going to get hatcheted. . . . [So] you go through the course of nurturing with people to get them to trust you, to have confidence in you and to give them some of our mission and corporate culture."

The cultural values that Myers works on are enthusiasm for the work, eagerness to find ways to do it better and respect for people. "If somebody's enthusiastic, that overrides a tremendous amount of weakness, in my opinion. Enthusiasm is about wanting to be someone." Myers says he also encourages people to be dependable and reliable and to "think on their own." But above all, he says, he works on "How do they treat other people? They can be all those other things, but if they're demeaning when they talk to somebody [it doesn't work]."

Myers spends a lot of time with his workers, teaching and encouraging them. He also reminds them that he appreciates their work. "Hey . . . I've been in the ranks. I know what it's like to be a housekeeper," he tells them. But he never forgets another ServiceMaster value, which is that nonexcellent work and failure to live up to values is unacceptable. In all three turnaround situations, he has let people go. His approach, he says, is to confront the negative people and allow them a chance to change; then if they don't change, he terminates them. He says he has to do this to allow the other people to flourish.[12]

Because it is low-tech, ServiceMaster is a particularly good example of a company where winning values make the difference. Of course, it does have expertise. After millions of hours of mopping floors, it has figured out a pretty effective and efficient way to do that. But in most of its businesses, it doesn't do anything that its customers couldn't readily do for themselves. So its key to success isn't "what" it does, but "how" it does it—reliably and well. Its workers value excellence, profits and human dignity, so they work with integrity, fairness and efficiency.

Changing Values

When most people talk about values, they mean the big immutable ones such as honesty and integrity. But there are many other values that leaders not only can but should periodically update and change. These are what I call "operational values," the ones that relate directly to an organization's business or its marketplace. Just as winning leaders use ideas and strategies to move their companies ahead, they also understand that having the right values can make a big difference. So when the marketplace changes, they develop new values along with new ideas. This is not a negative sign indicating that winning leaders sacrifice their morals to the grubby demands of commerce. Rather, it is a positive sign that they really do appreciate the role that values play in shaping behavior.

The late John Gardner, former Secretary of Health, Education and Welfare, founder of Common Cause and formerly a scholar in residence at Stanford University, described the role of leaders in renewing and changing values as:

- To renew and reinterpret values that have been encrusted with hypocrisy, corroded by cynicism or simply abandoned; and to generate new values when needed
- To liberate energies that have been imprisoned by outmoded procedures and habits of thought[13]

One of the biggest transformations in values and behavior that I know of was carried out in the mid-1990s at Ameritech. For many decades, Ameritech and the six[14] other operating companies created in the AT&T breakup were regulated monopolies that ran local telephone companies. Government rules set their profits, defined their markets and locked out competition. Since competition wasn't an issue, the values of Ameritech workers tended toward lifetime employment, consensus and stability. As the former head of Indiana Bell and former Ameritech CEO Dick Notebaert remarks, "How good did I have to be to run a monopoly? I didn't. How good did I have to be to make my rate of return? I didn't. It was guaranteed."[15]

These values translated into very plodding, slow-footed behavior at every level of the company. But amazingly, even though they themselves were lifers in the environment, both Notebaert and his predecessor as CEO, Bill Weiss, saw this. "The old culture went as follows," Weiss remarked dryly to me one day. "The five- or six-person management committee would meet. It was the most civil, disinteresting, unconstructive kind of meeting you could have. You did not get varying points of view. You had a constant waiting to find out where the boss stood so you could kind of move ahead with that. And if you didn't like what the boss wanted to do, you sat on your hands. That was the easiest way to confront it. You didn't really confront it directly, you just didn't do it with your heart, so nothing really got done very well."[16]

Notebaert describes the culture this way: "We had rules and procedures for every eventuality. We knew how to look and how to act and how to work within a hierarchy set in stone. . . . My proper role would have been to listen and maybe nod once in a while. But I was in a battle with the system and the system was winning. I wanted funding for a project I was convinced would improve customer service, but all my reports and cost analyses were bogged down in the chain of command. I took the risk and brought it up to Weiss [who was several levels above him at the time]. One by one, he asked my supervisors the status of the project, and each passed the buck up to the next level. . . . Believe me, I paid for that audacious behavior, but my project went through." The system was so slow that it took Weiss, who was vice president of operations at the time, to expedite a basic project proposal.[17] At lower levels of the company, workers were focused almost entirely on pleasing the regulators and making things easy for themselves. As a result, they would double- and triple-check every piece of paper before letting it out of their hands, lest there be the tiniest aberration that might disturb the regulators. And Ameritech would institute irritating self-serving little rules like not allowing customers to put covers on phone books, because Ameritech collected those phone books after one year, and it was easier to recycle them with no covers. And of course there was the classic, customer-be-damned practice of promising only that the service technician would arrive "sometime between eight and five on Wednesday."

Then along came the telecommunications revolution, and Ameritech found itself in a highly competitive marketplace where profits depend on speed and agility, and the old values were seriously getting in the way. In the new world, says Notebaert, "The only differentiator you have in the marketplace is speed of action. Better to take the action and make a mistake."[18] So Weiss, and later Notebaert, faced the enormous task of changing not only Ameritech's central business ideas, but also its culture. They set out new central strategies for the company to provide more services to current customers, to provide services to new customers and to invest domestically and overseas. They then assembled a team of more than 100 top managers to set out a new set of corporate values to support these ideas. They came up with the following list of core values:

1) Customers are paramount
2) We are members of one team—Team Ameritech
3) We will grow profitably[19]

A little later in this chapter, I will talk more about how Weiss and Notebaert implemented these new values—by personally embodying them, by getting others to wrestle with the values and figure out how to apply them in their own work situations and by aggressively confronting resistance—but right now the essential point I want to make is that winning companies don't just adopt a set of values and leave them in place. In the last chapter, I said that winning leaders are always testing and challenging their ideas, even the ones that are highly successful at the moment. The same is true for values. Winning leaders know that values, like ideas, must be continually reexamined, and must be changed when they lose their vitality or get out of step with the organization's goals.

Even if an organization doesn't have a clear need for new values, winning leaders still review them periodically. At Johnson

& Johnson, former chairman James E. Burke credits such a review with saving the company. In 1982, authorities traced the deaths of seven people to cyanide-filled capsules in bottles of Johnson & Johnson's bestselling pain reliever Tylenol. The tampering affected only a few bottles, and it occurred after the product had left the company's hands. Nonetheless, Johnson & Johnson immediately removed all thirty-one million bottles from store shelves and took returns from customers. The recall cost Johnson & Johnson more than $100 million.[20] But as a result of Johnson & Johnson's obvious concern for its customers and its prompt response, it not only gained stature in the marketplace, it emerged even stronger and healthier than before. Only three months after the crisis, Tylenol had reclaimed 95% of its previously top-selling market share.[21]

Burke says Johnson & Johnson's executives were able to respond so quickly to the crisis because they had a firm grasp of their values, thanks to a thorough review they had made of the company's ethics statement, or Credo, just a few years before. In the mid-1970s, when the company was enjoying an incredible growth streak, Burke had written a letter to Johnson & Johnson's leaders saying that "one of the most important elements of Johnson & Johnson's success over the years has been our ability to make our business decisions within the framework afforded us by our Credo. It has enabled us to operate in and prosper from a highly decentralized managerial style, while not having to forfeit our basic beliefs as a corporation." Burke went on to say that he knew, nonetheless, that the Credo, which hadn't been revised since 1948, needed revitalization if it was to continue to add value. "Today, in view of the rapid and far-reaching technological and social changes occurring within our society, it is more important than ever that our basic tenets or parameters of conduct be reflective of our beliefs and needs as a corporation."[22] He then convened a series of meetings with hundreds of executives and managers to go over the Credo line by line. The only ground rules were that at the end the participants had to decide to keep, reject or change the Credo. The discussions and debates ranged over topics such as the Credo's viability as a philosophical guide for day-to-day operations and how the company's daily operations reflected or did not reflect the Credo.[23]

At the end of the many-month process, the only changes they made were to update a bit of the language. But the effort had revitalized everyone's understanding of and commitment to the document's contents. Hundreds of employees now felt that they had played a direct role in shaping the company's philosophy and values. The discussions in the meetings had encouraged similar open discussions throughout the company about how well Johnson & Johnson's daily actions reflected its stated values. And because the leaders had so thoroughly examined and debated the document, they were better able, and more likely, to use it in their daily work. Johnson & Johnson's quick response to the Tylenol crisis was a direct result of this exercise, says Burke. "We could not have done what we did with Tylenol if we hadn't gone through the process of challenging ourselves and committing ourselves to the Credo," he later remarked.[24] I suspect he was right.[25]

Some executives never think seriously about values, so the possibility of modifying or updating them never crosses their mind. Others understand the role of values and the need to have appropriate ones, but in the crush of day-to-day business, they just don't get around to doing anything about it. On any given day, other things seem more important. However, it's often the case that people who don't examine their values don't live them either. Or if they do live them, they run the great risk that their unexamined values are like Plato's unexamined lives: "not worth living."

IBM learned this lesson too late. Its inwardly focused management team continued to perpetuate a culture of conformity in an era when the need for agility would have been better served by diversity. As a result, it forced out the curious types who might have seen and taken advantage of opportunities sooner. Similarly, while its business model fell into the dustbin of history, IBM hung on to a lifetime employment policy. When reality finally came crashing down in 1991, the result was the layoff of nearly 125,000 workers in three years and the demoralization of everyone else. The action also had the effect of debasing all the other values that Tom Watson Sr. had set for the company, which besides respect for employees, included the pursuit of excellence and outstanding customer service.[26] By the time Lou Gerstner was brought in to take over Big Blue, the focus had shifted from recapturing values to saving a dying patient by any means necessary. A serious examination of their values would not only have resulted in a more responsive culture, but would have also forced IBM's management to face the new realities in the marketplace.

Living the Values

As important as it is for leaders to espouse good values, what really matters is getting people to live by them. And this is where winning leaders and winning organizations clearly outclass the losers. They do it because they back up their words with actions. Winning leaders embody the values in their own lives, and they make sure that others do the same. Whether they are charged with keeping old values vital, as at ServiceMaster and Johnson & Johnson, or with changing them, as at Ameritech, winning leaders set the tone by clearly embracing the values themselves, openly wrestling with how to apply them in day-to-day operations and living by them, even in situations when it might be easier to do otherwise.

"I believe most people are very perceptive," said Dick Notebaert when he was CEO of Ameritech. "Over a period of time, if I have a false facade, people will tell me, 'You're lying.' . . . I have 60,000 employees, and they'll nail me right to the wall." The truth is that the leader gets nailed to the wall for failing to live the values only if he or she has created an open and honest shop. More often, people simply become demoralized and ignore the values just as the leader does. As ServiceMaster's leadership principle No. 6 says, "If you don't live it, you don't believe it."

In 1991, when Bill Weiss set out to transform Ameritech, he knew that "changing the culture" of the company would be wrenching to everyone—including, and perhaps especially, the old-timers in the executive suite. He also knew he had to drive the changes home by acting firmly and decisively himself. So as one of his first acts, he appointed four people to be his "Lead Team." In doing so, he skipped over the most obvious choices and selected four people lower down in the organization who were relative outsiders to senior management: Dick Notebaert (who later succeeded Weiss as CEO), Dick Brown, Gary Drook and Barry Allen. Notebaert, who was running Indiana Bell at the time, had been involved in building many of Ameritech's growth businesses, such as cellular communications. At 45, he was known for being a headstrong, shoot-from-the-hip leader. He told me once that "I would occasionally be asked to leave meetings because of my behavior."[27] Likewise Dick Brown, then president of Illinois Bell, Barry Allen, president of Wisconsin Bell, and Gary Drook, head of Ameritech publishing, all in their mid-forties, were misfits in their own rights. Like many other Ameritech managers, they were bright and knowledgeable, but they were also energetic, gutsy and aggressive enough to take on unexpected challenges.

In selecting the four unusual members of the Lead Team, Weiss sent a strong message that what worked in the past would not work in the future. People who were successful in the old culture would not necessarily succeed in the new. In shaking up the senior ranks, Weiss wasn't just acting as a chess player moving the pawns around. He was personally embodying the values and forcing himself to change. He was putting Team Ameritech first, regardless of tradition and personal relationships. Even though it was difficult for him, he persisted.

In 1991, Weiss was the only chairman Ameritech had known since it was created by the breakup of AT&T in 1984. At 62, he had spent his entire career in the Bell System. Three years before mandatory retirement, no one expected him to launch a major shakeup of the company. Balding and courtly, he played the part of CEO very well. His statements, always clear and precise, connoted his authority in the business and the predictability the organization strove for. His move to dramatically overhaul the company was the first embodiment of the new values of Ameritech. As Weiss talks about the early days of the transformation, you can watch him struggle. His usual clarity gives way to an occasional hesitation. Slowly he recounts the pain that senior people felt regarding the direction of the business. "We had people actually in torment about whether we could drive this business up to a higher growth trajectory. They just didn't believe it was possible without sacrificing so many things from the past that we weren't going to do it." When pressed on what this means, he struggles again. He is searching for the words to express the difficulty he faced in making the necessary decisions, his respect for the dignity of these individuals, as well as his overriding concern for the business. He settles for: "We have separated them on the most kindly terms possible."[28]

To make the values come alive, the Lead Team also took on the internal metrics that had guided Ameritech in the past. They changed evaluation systems and put new criteria in place, and they held up each of their own decisions and actions for public examination in the light of three simple questions: Does it help the customers? Does it build or reflect teamwork? Will it help the company grow profitably? Notebaert, with Weiss's authority, even killed a planned $1 billion investment in a new billing system because "we weren't trying to see the world through the eyes of the customer. We were trying to see the world through the eyes of the bureaucrats. And we were going to spend a billion dollars for the billing system [that] didn't do a damn thing for the customer."[29] In making an abrupt about-face on such a huge project, Notebaert and Weiss risked being tagged as erratic and indecisive, but they decided that the risk was worth the reward of demonstrating their willingness to live the organization's new values.

Wrestling with the Applications

When James Burke ordered the review of Johnson & Johnson's Credo in the mid-1970s, he did it because he wanted to make sure that the company's values were appropriate to the current business environment, but the process yielded another important benefit: It forced everyone in the company to look closely at the values and to wrestle with their application in daily life. And it was the executives' resulting familiarity and deep understanding of how the values played out that allowed them to respond so quickly and effectively to the Tylenol crisis. Because they had thought about the issues and tested the values in real-life terms, they didn't need to rethink their responses when the crisis came.

Like Burke, the other winning leaders I have met push people not just to memorize the organization's values but to wrestle with them, to internalize them and to use them. And they do it through both day-to-day activities and formal programs. Like preachers, they hold revivals and then revisit the same values day after day and week after week in daily real-life situations.

To symbolize the importance not only of having values but of using them, General Wayne Downing, former head of the Special Operations Forces, had a little stack of plasticized cards called "Reinventing Licenses" that he used to hand out to particularly enterprising individuals. On one side, the licenses, made up to look like driver's licenses, said:

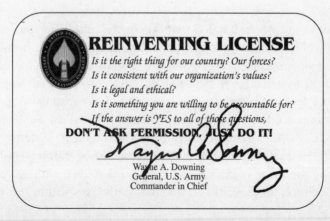

REINVENTING LICENSE

Is it the right thing for our country? Our forces?
Is it consistent with our organization's values?
Is it legal and ethical?
Is it something you are willing to be accountable for?
If the answer is YES to all of those questions,
DON'T ASK PERMISSION, JUST DO IT!

Wayne A. Downing
General, U.S. Army
Commander in Chief

On the other side, it listed the Special Operations mission and values:

> ## UNITED STATES
> ## SPECIAL OPERATIONS COMMAND
>
> *MISSION: Prepare Special Operations Forces to successfully conduct worldwide special operations, civil affairs, and psychological operations in peace and war in support of the Regional Combatant Commanders, American Ambassadors and their Country Teams, and other government agencies.*
>
> *WE VALUE: Our people, creativity, competence,*
> *courage, and integrity.*

The Reinventing Licenses are particularly interesting because, like the rest of the military, the Special Operations Forces has a culture that strongly values following orders, and General Downing is a man deeply steeped in that culture. So, coming from him, the license is an especially powerful symbol, because what it essentially says to his troops is that the world is full of paradoxes, and that the way they will succeed is by learning to live with them. The best members of the Special Operations Forces follow orders—except when their other values tell them to do something else.

Early in this book, I stated that one of the jobs of leaders is to face reality as it really is, and one of the realities of life is that it is full of paradoxes. Therefore, when John Trani, head of GE Medical Systems from 1986 to 1997 and now CEO of Stanley Works, faced the challenge of merging two companies—French Thomson–CGR[30] and Japanese Yokogowa Medical Systems— with GE's U.S.-based General Electric Medical Systems, he faced the reality not only that there would be culture clashes among the three organizations, but also that even within a unified culture, there would be inherent paradoxes within the values. So one of the first tasks he set himself was to deal with this reality and to help his people do so as well.

Clashes in corporate cultures and values are one of the biggest reasons that mergers don't work. Although each organization may have values and a culture that led it to success, there's usually some conflict when the separate workforces are put to work side by side. Sometimes the new organization grinds nearly to a halt before the values problem is, or can be, effectively dealt with. Even winning leaders sometimes lose the race against time. However, because they are aware of the importance of values and address them openly, winning leaders like Trani often succeed where others would fail.

Trani's task was complicated by the fact that the companies had not only separate corporate cultures, but also diverse regional and national cultures. Further, GE wanted to run a global business that combined the strengths of all three previously independent units, so to give precedence to the culture of one would debase and demoralize the others. But rather than ignore or sidestep this potential problem by keeping people from the different offices apart, Trani tackled the problem by going out of his way to put them together.

Soon after the merger, Trani set up a series of teams from the three offices. Their purpose was to discuss ideas and strategy and to develop a new set of values and operating rules based on the strengths of each of their previously separate organizations. And, as Burke did at Johnson & Johnson, he asked them to look at each of the values, explain why it was important and identify the behaviors on their own teams that were consistent or inconsistent with the values.

But Trani, who is an avuncular man with a down-to-earth manner, did not stop there. He next did something that marked him as a real winning leader. He led the executives to explore the paradoxes and conflicts inherent in the values they had selected. For example, the value of speed worked against the value of high quality. The value of teamwork appeared to be contradicted by the fact that they rewarded individual initiative.

And while they wanted improved customer service, at the same time they were telling managers to serve more customers with lower budgets and fewer people. Like politicians, many executives tend to ignore such paradoxes. They try to act as if each value is separate and equally important unto itself. But the world doesn't work that way. So, after they had agreed on a unified set of values, Trani called sixty of his top managers together, broke them into small groups and had them spend two and a half days going over them item by item, discussing not only how they would apply in specific day-to-day situations but also examining the places where conflicts among the values might arise. At the end, the paradoxes weren't eliminated, but the blinders were off. And because the executives had grappled with the paradoxes themselves, they were better able to help the people who worked for them to do the same.[31]

Fighting Ignorance and Resistance

At GE Medical Systems, the need for addressing and changing values became obvious as soon as Trani put the people from Tokyo, Paris and Wisconsin together in the same room and told them to work together. But at Ameritech, Weiss and his Lead Team faced a different situation. The company was full of long-time employees who were used to working together and comfortable with the old culture. And as far as most of them knew, the business was running well. So when the Lead Team began to talk informally about making big changes, the response from employees, even in the senior ranks, was generally, "Why? Don't mess things up. Just leave well enough alone."

But all was not well enough, and Weiss, Notebaert and their top colleagues knew that they couldn't afford to leave it alone. So they set about getting that message out to everyone else. "I got my wake-up call in two doses," says Bob Knowling, who was a general manager at Indiana Bell at the time. "The first was, we had a meeting that started on a Saturday morning, which meant we had to fly in on a Friday night—unprecedented in our business. We didn't do stuff on weekends. That was a tremendous signal that told me, 'Boy, this must be bigger than a bread basket—something is wrong.' You just didn't do that. So that was my first sign that something was different." Then, on the first day of the meeting, experts from inside and outside the company gave detailed reports about the telecommunications industry and the current state of Ameritech. They gave out data on revenue growth and return on assets and other specifics that Knowling had never had access to, even though he was a general manager. These discussions and this information, he says, sounded the alarm clearly for him. All of a sudden, he says, he realized, "Holy smoke, we've been dying of cancer and I didn't even know we were sick."[32]

Over the following months after that unusual weekend meeting, Weiss and the four young executives he had picked for his Lead Team spent hundreds of hours on efforts to change the company and the values of its managers so that Ameritech's employees and its customers would feel the difference. This was crucial because the company had decided to give up its regulated monopoly. In exchange for the right to offer long distance and other services, Ameritech would begin urging regulators to open its own local market to competition. If this happened—which it did in 1996—Ameritech's proprietary strength, its monopoly on service to over twenty million customers, would no longer be guaranteed. Customers would have to be delighted rather than despised, teams would have to come together to offer superior products faster than others and people would have to cut costs in order to stay competitive with new rivals. As Dick Notebaert would say later, "This is like we are taking off on a plane to Europe. Midway over the Atlantic we're told that the runway on the other side is too small. We are going to have to change the wings, and we can't drop a single customer in the process."[33]

No matter what they did, Weiss, Notebaert and their colleagues knew, the initial resistance would be massive. The changes were too great, the old ways were too ingrained and the company was too large for the changes to go down easily. Therefore, they adopted a three-pronged strategy. First, they would actively demonstrate their own commitment to the effort. Then they would teach others and give them an opportunity to get on board and, finally, they would get rid of the people who continued to balk. Over the next two years, nearly 5,000[34] people would leave Ameritech. Streamlining and downsizing would eliminate some jobs, but the decisions on who would leave were definitely related to various individuals' attitudes.

The development program started with the Group of 120, the leaders who had already received the Saturday morning wake-up call. As recognized leaders, the members of this group were clearly committed to Ameritech, so loyalty was not an issue. But because they cared so much and had big personal stakes in Ameritech's future, many were sincerely concerned that the changes were unnecessary or misguided. Others who agreed with the changes still found themselves resisting because the process was so threatening.[35]

The Lead Team had decided that the only way people could seriously change their attitudes and values was if they clearly understood what those old attitudes and values were. Chris Argyris, the social psychologist, has long had a concept about "espoused theories" and "theories in use." He argues that all of us operate with frameworks or theories about how things work and get done in the world. But there is often a gap between what we say is our theory and how we actually behave. I see this in organizations all the time where a manager espouses empower-ment and then in practice is a tyrant. This is true of values as well. People may think, for example, that they value openness and honesty, and then in their daily behavior withhold informa-tion and shade the truth.[36] At Ameritech, to help make the Group of 120 aware of how others perceived their actions (i.e., theories in use), the Lead Team arranged for groups of people who had been working together to rank their teammates on a number of criteria. Then each person would be given his or her score, along with coaching to help them improve.

From the start, Bob Knowling, the general manager from Indiana Bell, was dead set against the plan because he thought that it would destroy the teams and kill the transformation effort. But he didn't say much about it until the night before the scheduled sessions. Then, as participants gathered in the hotel bar for a nightcap, Knowling, an ordained minister and a 6'3" former Wabash College football player, began working the crowd. Individually and in small groups, he played on the same fears everyone had about the group evaluations. Soon a revolt had taken hold. "I can remember one night in a bar," says Notebaert, "we were going to do appraisals, and this huge guy named Bob Knowling, an All-American end, a huge guy, is in my face saying he's not going to do this appraisal stuff the next day."

The ferocity of Knowling's resistance unnerved the Lead Team and forced them to reconsider. They hastily assembled and asked themselves: Had they pushed too far too fast, as Knowling had said? Were they going to break the company apart? Should they call off the evaluations? In the end, they decided to stick to their guns. So Notebaert went to Knowling and said, "Look, I'm not sure this will be good either. I, like you, have never done it before. But the difference between me and you is that I'm going to try it. If I don't like it, I won't do it again, but I am going to try."[37] What could Knowling do? If Notebaert had the guts to take the risk, he would, too.

After the sessions, Knowling made an impromptu speech in front of the entire 120 people, in which he did something that Ameritech people rarely did. He said: "I was wrong." He went on to say that his feedback, while difficult to work through, was helpful. Further, he declared that his opposition was really resistance to the transformation. Looking at himself in the mirror, he said, he realized that he was supposed to be a change agent, but he was resisting instead. And he vowed to stop. He ended the speech by reaffirming his commitment to Ameritech and by asking others to examine their own motives and make the same commitment. Later, Knowling would be named the first head of the Ameritech Institute, a center where managers and leaders at all levels would be asked to grapple with values and issues and be given tools to help them do their jobs better.

After working with the Group of 120, the Lead Team, under Weiss's direction, launched a process to change the culture of the other 65,000 employees. Named Breakthrough, it was designed to communicate the new values, deal with the ignorance and resistance and embed the values as a new way of life at Ameritech. It followed the three-pronged approach. Ignorance would be treated respectfully, with explanations and encouragement to play through and see what happened, as Knowling had. Resistance would also get initial respect, supported by cajoling to join in. And, finally, the people who continued to resist would be terminated.

The Breakthrough process was set up on the "each one, teach one" principle. A thousand managers from across the company were convened fifty at a time for four-day workshops. Senior leaders explained the direction they were taking the company—from the changes in strategy to the new structure of the company to the new values. They presented the values as "Here's what more than one hundred people who came together have said the values would be. Now, you wrestle with them and see what they mean for you." Then the one thousand managers were sent out to teach the people who worked for them. As part of the exercise, each of the one thousand teams had to develop a project that would move the company closer to its new goals, and then carry it out using the new values. To make sure they didn't fall back into old habits, teams and team members periodically evaluated each other on the use of the new values. By the end of the effort in 1994, the projects in the Breakthrough program had not only given people hands-on experience with the new values, but had also given Ameritech a $700 million[38] benefit from the cost savings and revenue enhancements that resulted from the projects.

The last phase of the change effort took place in dozens of other initiatives. Having now taught the values to several thousand people and made them teach the values to others, the senior leaders at Ameritech took other important steps to instill and reinforce the values. For example, compensation systems were changed to reflect the new values. Layers of management were stripped out, which not only reduced expenses, but also forced responsibility to lower levels of the workforce. And the company was restructured to give more power to the people dealing with customers and less to the bureaucrats.

Ameritech is by no means perfect today. It still stumbles as it tries to get its footing in a highly competitive marketplace. But the fact that it is surviving and doing well is a testimony to the determination and success of its leaders in overcoming resistance and radically changing the values of more than 60,000 people. In fact while other Baby Bells have made huge "bet the company" wagers on mergers and acquisitions, Ameritech has been called by industry observers "definitely the best of the Regional Bell Operating Companies because of its management."[39]

Changing people's values is even harder than changing their ideas, but in the long run it is probably more important. Businesses may be divested or acquired. New markets may be explored. But these maneuvers are about 10% of the battle. For change to be effective, leaders must rewrite the software—the values that guide people's actions. That's why people like Bill Weiss, Dick Notebaert and Bob Knowling are so valuable. They can see the big picture, change their minds and mindsets and help others do the same.

Making It Happen

Getting Energy Out of Everyone

Winning Leaders Are High-Energy People

- They are focused and determined
- They like challenges and enjoy their work

Winning Leaders Create Energy in Others

- They motivate with their enthusiasm and actions
- Stretch goals inspire ambitious effort

Times of Transition = Teachable Moments

- The leader's specialty: Turning negative energy to positive uses
- If they don't have a problem to be fixed, they create one

One day in April 1992 at 6:00 A.M., forty manufacturing workers climbed aboard a bus at General Electric's range-building plant at Appliance Park in Louisville, Kentucky, and headed for the annual Kitchen and Bath Show in Atlanta. They were setting out on a crucial reconnaissance mission. Appliance Park, a sprawling old 1,100-acre complex, had once employed more than 23,000[1] workers. By 1992, the company had closed down one of its six large production buildings and stopped making room air conditioners and microwave ovens. Employment at Appliance Park had dwindled to 9,000.[2] The range line was losing $10 million a year, and the jobs of everyone on the bus were in jeopardy.[3]

The trip was the brainchild of Tom Tiller, who had arrived ten months earlier to take over as manager of the range plant. The plant had a history of antagonism between management and the union. At 29, Tiller was one of the company's youngest plant managers, and within two weeks of his arrival, he had laid off 400 people. "The building was in a fair bit of trouble," says Tiller, putting it mildly. Even worse, it seemed unlikely to Tiller that anyone outside of Appliance Park was going to do anything to make it better. GE wasn't investing in the business, it hadn't produced a new generation of products in twenty years and Jack Welch, GE's hard-charging CEO, was not known for his fondness for money-losing operations.

"The bus ride," says Tiller, "came from a sense of 'Somebody's got to do something here, and we can either wait for them to take care of it, or we can do it ourselves.'" The trip was both a signal to the workers about how serious Tiller considered the problem to be, and a concrete first step toward solving it. "We had to figure out how we were going to turn this business around. So we got on a bus and we rode down to the Kitchen and Bath Show in Atlanta," explains Tiller. "For a lot of them, it was the first time they were together . . . design engineers and people off the shop floor and so forth. We played some cards, we drank some beer and got people kind of comfortable together," says Tiller. Then "we went through every product that was offered down there, and we said, 'Well, we could take this idea, we could take that idea.'" By the time the trip was over, says Tiller, "There was a very clear sense of, 'We've got to do something. We've got to do it fast. We don't have 142 years to do it, and we're going to do it.'" And they did.

Within eighteen months, the people on the bus had spearheaded an effort that had three new products designed, built and delivered to the market. The plant went from a $10 million loss in 1992 to a $35 million profit in 1994. "There are two new production lines over there as a result of that bus ride, which is a big deal for the people in that building," Tiller told me four years later. "It's the difference between that building staying open and closing." Even today, he says, "Everybody knows what the bus ride was, where we went, why we went there and what came out of it."[4]

In the previous chapters, I talked about how winning leaders use ideas and values to promote leadership at all levels of their organizations. Ideas and values unify people and allow them to act independently in ways that effectively move the organization toward a common goal. The ideas and values are themselves strong motivators. In fact, one of the reasons they are so important to winning leaders is that they inspire people to action. However, ideas and values alone can't carry the day. Winning organizations do their jobs better than others. And in a highly competitive world, this means that they work faster and with greater energy. Therefore, winning leaders not only encourage people to have good ideas and develop strong values, but they also take deliberate actions to generate energy and to channel it to productive uses.

All organizations inherently have energy because they are made up of people, and people have energy. But in winning organizations, people seem to have more energy, and they certainly use it more productively. While the losers waste their energy on negative activities such as internal politics and resisting changes demanded by the marketplace, the winners use theirs positively to overcome problems and meet new challenges. They do this because their top leaders understand that positive energy produces positive results. They use energy, like ideas and values, as a competitive tool. And they consciously work at creating positive energy in everyone else in the organization.

In the course of this chapter, I will talk about how winning leaders use their own enormous energy to work longer, harder and more effectively than non-winners. I will discuss a number of methodologies and resources that winning leaders use to create positive energy in others. These include everything from personal face-to-face interactions that inspire confidence and determination to designing processes that encourage independent action to eliminating bureaucracies and time-wasting activities that foster inaction. But most importantly, I will talk about how winning leaders transform negative energy into positive energy, how they harness the energy that is generated in times of distress so that their organizations not only survive difficulties that destroy other institutions, but emerge stronger for the experience.

The GE example above is a perfect illustration of this phenomenon. Before Tom Tiller arrived at Appliance Park, the jobs at the range plant were in jeopardy, so the workers had plenty of stress-induced energy, but they were investing it in bickering, bemoaning their fate and resisting the cost-cutting efforts of the plant's managers. What Tiller did was rechannel that energy into fixing the problem. In short, by getting them to take responsibility for their own fate and by giving them confidence and hope, he transformed them from being a group of self-perceived "victims" and forged them into a team of take-charge winners.

It may sound like circular logic, but the truth is that one of the primary reasons that winners win is that they think they *can* win.[5] The possibility of achieving a desirable goal is the very ingredient that generates the energy required to achieve that goal and to tackle new ones. Therefore, one of the most valuable things that winning leaders do is build the determination and self-confidence in others to help them become leaders as well. Later in this chapter, I'll show you how they systematically do that.

Winning Leaders Are Highly Energized Themselves

Before I talk about how winning leaders create energy in others, it is important to note how extraordinarily energetic they are themselves. One of the first things I always notice when I talk to winning leaders or watch them in action is that they throw themselves wholeheartedly into everything they do. Good enough is never good enough for them. They care deeply about their work.

They believe that it has value and is important, and they approach it with a determination that just isn't found in people who are motivated by simple career aspirations. One way to describe winning leaders might be just to say that they are highly competitive, but there is a special kind of fire in them, one that pushes them not toward personal aggrandizement but toward the successful completion of a "mission." Leaders see everything in life as an opportunity to change and grow. As a result, they work longer and harder than most people can even imagine. Slowing down is not a thought that ever occurs to them.

To an observer, it often seems that leaders sacrifice themselves and their personal lives in order to be successful. And it's true that their long hours and concentrated focus do keep them from doing a lot of other things. But winning leaders don't see their hard work as a sacrifice. They are aware that they don't have time for other things, but in their eyes, that's not because of what the job demands but rather because of what they have chosen to give. In other words, they work hard not because they *have* to, but because they *want* to. They find it hugely rewarding, and they love doing it.

In fact, "fun" is a word that often crops up in conversations with leaders. When I asked Dick Notebaert, the hard-charging CEO of Ameritech, how he kept up his energy to keep working so hard day after day, he said simply: "Because it's fun." Later, when we had moved on to an entirely new topic, he said it again. "I don't understand how people . . . can do something that's not fun."[6] Wes Lucas, a vice president at AlliedSignal, brought up the topic of fun as well. He says he has a motto that he has borrowed from Fred Poses, his boss, which is: "Be safe. Do great things. Have fun." Lucas says he also understands that the people working for him will do a better job if they are having fun, too. "I look at my children and they are having fun playing 'house' and 'work,' and I keep saying how do I get my organization to do the necessary mundane tasks with that same excitement?"[7]

Where does this delight in tackling the difficult and this single-minded devotion come from? I don't have a perfect answer to that. But I have observed that these two characteristics are usually accompanied in winning leaders by enormous self-confidence. The winning leaders I have met are not all Horatio Algers, but they have all constructed from their experiences the firm conviction that if they diligently apply themselves, they can make a difference. This is, of course, true for everyone. We can all make a difference if we try, but winning leaders seem to have learned that lesson better than other people. Think back to the people whose stories I talked about in Chapter 4. All of them, even the younger ones like Tom Tiller and Debra Dunn, have no doubt that their work can make a difference. It is perhaps this confidence in themselves that accounts for their close attention to building confidence in others.

Many winning leaders display their energy physically. That they are action-oriented people shows not only in their decisions but also in their physical presence. Phil Myers, the ServiceMaster account manager I described in the last chapter, is almost hyperactive. He asked my colleague and me to wear running shoes to our interview so we could follow him during the day as he raced around the hospital on Chicago's West Side. Dick Notebaert awakes every day at 5:00 A.M. and goes jogging. Then, still dripping with sweat, he sits down to answer his e-mail. Because he uses e-mail as an electronic forum for any Ameritech employee who wants to write him, he receives and replies to more than fifty messages a day.[8] And I've seen Jack Welch white-hot with intensity for hours as he paced the stage talking to and answering questions from GE workers. Retired General Wayne Downing, the former commander of the Special Operations Forces, completed West Point, served two tours in Vietnam in airborne units and has completed two ultra marathons with lungs scarred so badly from childhood asthma that he only has half the lung capacity of normal humans. And the late Rear Admiral Chuck LeMoyne, Downing's deputy commander, continued to run three miles a day and swim while undergoing radiation and chemotherapy after the removal of his larynx. After the cancer

surgery in September 1995, he stayed on the job as deputy commander right up until his retirement in May 1996 rather than
accept less strenuous duty.

The enormous physical energy of these leaders excites and
energizes everyone around them. They set a pace that brings
others up to speed. Still, as impressive as their physical energy is,
it is their emotional energy, and their ability to evoke emotional
energy in others, that truly marks them as a breed apart. How
they display it isn't so important as the simple fact that they are
supremely engaged by their work, and it shows. A winning
leader can turn even the most mundane of meetings into an
exciting, fire-in-the-gut-building encounter.

Carlos Cantu, the soft-spoken former CEO of ServiceMaster,
is one of the quietest and most intensely energizing people I
know. Cantu is a fatherly gentleman of sixty-one years[9] who has
lived in both Mexico and the U.S. He retains a courtly, unhurried
manner not often found in major executive suites. When you are
with him, he acts as if he had all the time in the world. He sits
quietly, never interrupts and thinks before he speaks. But the
intensity with which he listens and the deliberation with which
he responds raises the commitment and energy level of everyone
he meets. "There's a contrast in my style and Carlos's style," says
Bill Pollard, ServiceMaster's chairman and Cantu's predecessor
as CEO. "One of my weaknesses [was] getting so involved in
something . . . that I may not have allowed the people who were
part of that particular project to fully express themselves.
. . . Whereas Carlos's leadership brings out the best. He has a
kind of very quiet style that people aspire to really perform so
that they don't disappoint him."[10] After a conversation with Carlos Cantu, you know that you have been heard, your comments
have been digested, he has responded with respectful consideration *and* he expects something to happen as a result. I, for one,
would hate to disappoint him.

One of the ways that Cantu brings out the best in others is by
demanding the best of himself. Everyone who has ever worked
with him knows that his intentions are sincere and honorable,

and that he doesn't give up until he has done everything possible to help them succeed. "I think the response that I get and the enthusiasm that I sense . . . is reflective of whether or not they believe that my interest and my inquiries are really [meant to be] productive . . . as opposed to just being a nit-picker," he says. Further, when Cantu feels that he has not given his best, or not succeeded in communicating, he will always give it another shot. "At the end of the day, I feel, every single person has got to come away [from a meeting with me] with something positive. . . . That is an absolute goal that I have. There are times when I do not feel that I have achieved the objective. [So, after a meeting,] I go back and try to touch those people. . . . I will get up from my desk and I'll be back in somebody's office that afternoon or I'll be back in that somebody's office the following day. And, I'll just say, 'Now, let's revisit these issues. How could we do this better?' . . . My goal is that at every single session I want to feel, first of all, that I'll accomplish the objective of the people who are responsible to me feeling that they've gained something from the experience. And I want to feel that I've learned something from the experience."[11] Cantu finds energy from knowing that he is making a difference to other people, and he evokes energy by the way he uses it.

Operating Mechanisms

At the same time that they are intensely competitive, good leaders like Tom Tiller and Carlos Cantu are much better than bad leaders at working with other people and building teams. That may sound like a paradox, but it's not. Highly competitive people are often loners, but in winning leaders, it is their very competitiveness that drives them to work so hard at energizing and coaching other people. This is because they are determined that their organizations succeed, and they know that they can't do everything themselves. They understand strategically that they need everyone in the organization giving his or her best efforts. So they work very hard to make that happen.

One way that leaders do this is through the operating mechanisms or routine processes that they use to run the business. Winning leaders instinctively realize that every meeting and every activity has the potential to create or destroy positive emotional energy. So they deliberately develop an operating style and design management processes with an eye to their effect on people's energy levels. For example, as I described in the chapter on ideas, Gary Wendt, former CEO of GE Capital, has inverted the strategic planning process so that his business leaders meet with him at the beginning of the process. This allows for a free-wheeling discussion of needs, ideas and possibilities that spurs everyone's imaginations at a time when no one is yet constrained by having invested in a specific desired result. Out of one such meeting, for example, came the idea for GE Capital to stop focusing on seeking a larger share of the existing truck leasing market and instead go after expanding the market by taking over fleets that companies were managing for themselves. "They came in thinking they were doing great, going to grow 20%," says Wendt. "They left knowing they could get two times that if they only got a small piece of the [larger] market."[12]

Too often, leaders who are not effective are victims of stale old processes that end up sucking energy from the organization. Some companies have this art form down to such detail that the strategy-setting process becomes almost ritualized Kabuki theater. The presenters carefully prepare their pitches. Meanwhile, the staff prepares the manager in charge with zinger questions that will make him or her look smart when he or she asks them. On the budgeting side, it's a constant game of sandbagging, where people set low expectations. Or they put anything in their budget just so they can be left alone. At one company I studied, the budget process had no validity at all. A manager reported that he had submitted a budget and then left for vacation. He returned to find that his revenue goal had been increased by 50% and his head count reduced. There was no discussion; this was the budget he had to work with.

Winning leaders, on the other hand, design their management processes so that fresh ideas bubble to the surface and people are energized. They do this by ensuring that people feel that the process is worthwhile, that timely and conclusive decisions are reached and that those decisions do, in fact, get carried out. To do this, leaders create operating mechanisms through which they assure that people are adequately prepared to make decisions, that the meetings—most decisions are made in face-to-face encounters—where decisions are made are substantive and that there is systematic follow-up to make sure the decision is implemented. One client of mine who rated his strategy, budget and personnel review processes on a scale of one to ten, for example, came up with a nine for strategy preparation, but the face-to-face meetings were a two. It turned out that the bad meetings were his fault because he included the wrong people and ran them poorly.

When Dick Notebaert took over at Ameritech from Bill Weiss, he very carefully designed all the operating mechanisms at his disposal. As I described in the last chapter, at most meetings at Ameritech people simply waited for the senior person to stake out a position and then went along. As a result, no one actually prepared before a meeting by researching relevant issues or forming a point of view. When Notebaert took over, he made it clear that people coming to meetings had better come ready to play. Early in his tenure as CEO, he stopped a meeting and asked an executive, "Hey, did you bother reading this stuff? Are you involved? Why are you here? Why are you wasting our time by participating?" He has never had to do that again, because the message was clear.

In return for demanding preparation and the full attention of his executives at meetings, Notebaert goes out of his way to make sure that the meetings focus on things that really matter. Previously, operating reviews at Ameritech often focused on internal politics. At these meetings, "You watch people's body language. Their shoulders go in, they kind of look down and they don't make eye contact, and it's depressing." But if you deal with substance, if "you start talking about competitors, you talk about customers and growing this business, people start to light up," he says.[13]

Larry Bossidy, CEO of Honeywell is the master of the follow-up. Bossidy holds meetings with each of his managers three times a year to discuss strategy, review operations and talk about personnel. At these meetings he listens, discusses and coaches the managers until they have mutually agreed on how to proceed with the business. Then, after each meeting, Bossidy personally writes a letter to the manager that reviews the meeting and says, in plain, straightforward English: "Here is what I liked about your plan. Here is what I didn't like, and here is what we agreed you would do about those concerns." If the manager concurs with the contents of the letter, he or she proceeds with the plan. If the manager doesn't, he or she gets back to Bossidy immediately to iron things out. Bossidy says that the meetings and the letters increase both his and the manager's energy by creating personal contracts that put them on one team working to deliver specific results.

Team-Building and Symbols

Phil Myers, the ServiceMaster hospital account manager, builds teamwork and keeps up his people's energy by constantly reminding them how deeply he respects them and their work. As a former janitor himself, he says that he knows what it feels like for people to say, "Who's that? Well, that's just the housekeeper." So he makes a point of noticing them, touching them on the shoulder as he passes by and letting them know that he recognizes them. He says these passing encounters work as a "lever for motivating people," because it gives them "instant value in the sense that they know I care about [them]." Further, Myers ferociously defends them against any slights or demeaning actions on the part of the various doctors, nurses and administrators around the hospital. After only two weeks on one job, Myers stormed into the office of the powerful director of the surgery department to announce that he was pulling all twenty-one of his people out of the operating room because she had "used foul language" and "talked to them like dogs." "If you want to clean this room with your orderlies, if you want to talk to your people like this, you feel free to do that," he told her. "But these people are my people. If you've got a problem, you yell at me. Don't yell at them. No one deserves to be talked to that way."[14] Need I say more about what this does for energy and morale?

Other leaders use a myriad of symbols, gestures and actions to unify and energize their workers. Eckhard Pfeiffer once ended a rally of Compaq workers by having himself, dressed in lederhosen, lifted to the rafters of the Houston Summit Arena to symbolize the heights to which the company would climb. Tom Tiller keeps a photograph in his office that is also displayed throughout the range building. There is a problem with a lot of ranges, he explains, which is that the door handles often get broken during installation. It's irritating to customers to come into a brand new house or buy an appliance that needs to be fixed before they use it. So the people in Tiller's building took it upon themselves to design a range with an unbreakable door handle. The picture is of Tiller and the president of the union, arm in arm, beneath a new GE range that is suspended from a crane by its door handle. It is not only a testament to the faith he has in his people and their product, but an acknowledgment of the need for management and the union to stand together if GE Appliances is going to move forward.

The list could go on forever. As in every other area of endeavor, winning leaders creatively use every available opportunity to further their goal of boosting energy in the organization. They cajole and coach. They use symbols such as giving awards and creating slogans that capture the challenges and excitement in their businesses. And they take actions of substance such as Jack Welch disassembling the mammoth GE bureaucracy because its petty regulations ate up people's time and sapped their energy.

In my mind, however, the most interesting and impressive thing about how winning leaders handle energy is their incredible ability to systematically harness the energy produced by stressful situations and put it to positive uses. It's a transformational process that has double value because it not only gets people to start doing things that solve problems and improve the situation, but it also gets them to stop doing things that harm themselves and divert the organization from its desired goals. As a result, winning organizations often emerge from times of stress stronger and more effective than they were before the problems hit.

Creative Transitions

When it comes to performing this almost alchemical transformation of negative energy into positive energy, there are two clear standout masters in my mind: Bill Cunningham and Eleanor Josaitis, who founded a nearly thirty-year-old organization in Detroit called Focus: HOPE. Unlike for-profit businesses that harness the energy of workers to improve and strengthen the organization, Focus: HOPE channels the energy of its poor inner-city clients into transforming their own lives. But while the use of the positive energy is not directed specifically at the organization, the methods Cunningham and Josaitis use to create it provide a textbook example of how winning leaders overcome defeatism and turn victims into victors. Thanks to Focus: HOPE, thousands of people who might otherwise be unemployed or in dead-end jobs have solid well-paying careers and hope for the future.

Father William Cunningham was a young Jesuit priest teaching English at Sacred Heart Seminary in Detroit when that city's race riots broke out in 1967 and army airborne units were sent in to restore order. Looking around him, Cunningham saw the poverty, rage and despair in the city's black neighborhoods and decided, "I can't keep teaching Beowulf and Shakespeare and English composition[15] . . . with the choppers coming and the half-tracks and the 50-caliber machine guns turned on the side of buildings, and the encampment of Central High School . . . [I felt] we had to do something." So, with Eleanor Josaitis, a suburban housewife at whose parish he had been a weekend pastor, he started Focus: HOPE.

Initially, Focus: HOPE set out to provide food for mothers and infants. Studies showed that malnourished babies lose a significant portion of their brain capacity during their first three years of life.[16] So Cunningham and Josaitis, operating on the theory that there can never be equal opportunity without equal capability, decided that they would try to level the playing field by providing nutrition. But they quickly saw that the feeding program was just a finger in the dike. The children were hungry because their parents didn't have jobs. If they really wanted to have a long-term impact, they needed to help the adults acquire the skills to find work.

Since the biggest employer in Detroit was the auto industry and some of the best-paying and most stable jobs were as machinists, Cunningham and Josaitis decided that they would teach inner-city workers not only to be machinists, but to be some of the best machinists in the world. Focus: HOPE graduates would get and keep jobs not because socially conscious employers pitied them but because they would be solid, reliable workers with skills that the employers needed.

Considering that many people in the inner city, even high school graduates, lack basic reading and math skills, this was an enormous challenge. But Focus: HOPE is doing just what it set out to do. It has an intensive Fast Track remedial program that raises students' math and language skills by an average of a remarkable 25% in just seven weeks. Some students take those skills out into the market to get clerical jobs, but most continue into the year-long Machinists Training Institute (MTI) program.[17] Not only has it placed more than 1,000 graduates in private-sector jobs, but it also operates a for-profit machine shop where its own graduates and volunteer retired machinists train others. In 1995, the shop sold $10 million of precision-machined parts to the auto industry and its suppliers.[18] One of its customers is Detroit Diesel, a leading manufacturer of engines. Detroit Diesel's president, Ludwig Koci, says he buys from Focus: HOPE because, while the pulleys he buys "may look like a simple little piece of metal, they are a highly machined and highly accurate piece of metal. And Focus: HOPE is doing a terrific job for us there."[19]

In 1990,[20] Focus: HOPE also opened the Center for Advanced Technologies in conjunction with six universities, five manufacturers and the Society of Mechanical Engineers to provide advanced degrees in industrial and manufacturing engineering. The curriculum includes not only sophisticated design and engineering courses, but also business administration and language training. Graduates of the six-year master's program will be fluent in German and Japanese and hold degrees from the participating universities, which include the University of Michigan and Lehigh University.

As Cunningham describes it, "We've got to knock down the last vestige of racist mentality: that black men and women are not suited, not fitted for, not capable of, the highest positions of contribution to our society."[21]

One of the biggest obstacles to achieving this goal, however, was that many of the black inner-city men and women themselves thought that they were "not suited, not fitted for, not capable of, the highest positions" of contribution to society. After years of failures and frustrations, they were locked in despair. During the riots they had shown that they literally had energy to burn. But they were using it to destroy their lives and the meager possessions that they had. The challenge that faced Cunningham and Josaitis was to get them to let go of the dismal past and take control of their futures. In the mid-1990s, as Americans struggle with getting people off the welfare rolls and into the workforce as mandated by the various welfare reform measures, Focus: HOPE is a model of success.[22]

William Bridges, a highly regarded executive development consultant who has studied personal and professional changes for over twenty years, has a theoretical framework that says that all successful transformations, or transitions, involve three distinct phases. There is the "ending" phase, when people disengage from the past and "the way things were." There is a neutral zone, which he calls the "transition" phase, when people have let go of the old but haven't yet figured out how to live with the new. And finally, there is a "new beginning" period during which people learn to feel at home with the new identity and to be productive with the new way of doing things. Bridges also draws a distinction between a "change" and a "transition." He explains it this way: "A change is a shift in the world around us. A transition is the internal process we go through in response to that shift. Changes are events and situations; transitions are experiences. . . . [Each change] will put the people it affects into transition."[23] Bridges concludes that many organizational change efforts fail not because people fear the change itself, but because they resist the unpleasant process of transitioning. Even though they may not know it explicitly, winning leaders inherently understand the psychodynamics of transitions as described by Bridges and are able to help others through them. This ability to capitalize on transitions and use them to create productive, positive energy is one of the keys of winning leadership.[24]

Building on Bridges's excellent theoretical work, I have identified five specific conditions that must be created in order for successful and energizing transitions to take place. Winning leaders don't necessarily have to create all of these conditions. In the case of Focus: HOPE, for example, every client who walks in the door already feels an urgent need. Otherwise he or she wouldn't have taken the first step. But *all* of the conditions must exist, and winning leaders make sure that they do. They are:

- A sense of urgent need that is clear and palpable to everyone in the organization
- A mission that is inspiring and clearly worth achieving
- Goals that stretch people's abilities

- A spirit of teamwork—a sense that "We're all in this together"
- A realistic expectation that the team members can meet the goals

A Sense of Urgency

For Focus: HOPE's clients, living in the depressed inner-city ghettos of Detroit clearly creates an urgent need. And in coming to its various programs, they are expressing a desire to break with the past. But that need and the desire are just the beginning. Leveraging off of those to evoke the productive energy the students need to succeed is the monumental challenge that Focus: HOPE faces. Cunningham, Josaitis and the rest of the Focus: HOPE staff do that by setting stretch goals, inspiring students' self-confidence by showing their own confidence in them and offering them resources. There is an old business school formula that says that to get people to change, you must have D + V + F > I. In other words, change occurs when (D)issatisfaction, plus (V)ision, plus a concrete (F)irst step is greater than (I)nertia. The clients at Focus: HOPE bring the dissatisfaction. Father Cunningham and Ms. Josaitis provide the vision and the first steps, plus an added ingredient: hope.

An Inspiring Mission

The second element that is essential to getting people to change is to offer them an attractive goal or mission. Because the prospect of change is so frightening, people need not only an urgent need to leave the past but the prospect of an unquestionably better future. And the stronger the attraction of the future, the greater will be the energy people exert to work toward it. At Focus: HOPE, the mission as articulated by Cunningham and Josaitis is to get people out of the cycle of poverty and into stable jobs where they can support their families and build better lives. The mission could be stated more narrowly as giving people the skills to find new employment. But Cunningham, with his preacher's flair and missionary zeal, knows that stating it more boldly and ambitiously produces more energetic effort.

The development of this action-oriented mission was critical in the evolution of Focus: HOPE from an agency that offered handouts into an organization that truly transforms lives. As a feeding program, its mission was a worthwhile one that inspired donors to give funds. But the clients were offered only the opportunity to be passive—albeit grateful—recipients of charity. It didn't incite or excite them to action because it offered them nothing to work for.

Stretch Goals[25]

The idea of using stretch goals to raise energy and get people to work harder is not a new one. It's one of the basic principles taught in Management 101. Winning leaders, however, stretch the concept and the goals much further than other people. In Father Cunningham's eyes, and mine as well, one of the key reasons for the phenomenal success of Focus: HOPE as an organization and of its students as individuals is the very audacity of their goals. Focus: HOPE doesn't aim to train workers, but to change the balance of economic power in the world. Its students don't just want jobs or just to be machinists. They are planning to become world-renowned as "renaissance engineers," a term coined by Cunningham. The first group of candidates to enter the Center for Advanced Technologies wrote and signed a pledge to "Accept the challenge. The gauntlet has been cast . . . to make Made in America mean THE STANDARD to which all nations must strive to achieve. . . . [We] accept the challenge of serious work and study hours, of sacrificing the short-term gain for the long-term goal. This is our commitment."

In the spring of 1996, Cunningham explained his philosophy of bold action to a group of visiting Ford Motor executives. "As leaders we do not set the goals high enough for our people," he said. "The exact synonym for consensus is mediocrity. . . . Leadership is salesmanship. Getting people to say, c'mon we can do this."[26]

Their high goals have helped Cunningham and Josaitis mobilize an incredible network of people. Former vice chairman of General Motors Lloyd Reuss was drafted by the duo to play the crucial role of Executive Dean for the Center for Advanced Technologies (CAT). He in turn immediately recruited four more retired auto executives to join Focus: HOPE's ranks.[27] He continues to draft Big Three retirees today. "For 38 years I worked at shaping steel, now I'm shaping lives,"[28] a proud Reuss states. Josaitis and Cunningham also energized corporations to provide funding. And they inspired Carl Levin, the Michigan senator who sits on the Armed Services Committee, to help arrange a $60 million Defense Department special industrial grant to build the CAT. "To witness what is going on here is simply breathtaking," Levin told the crowd at the center's dedication.[29]

Most important, though, the enormous challenge offered by Focus: HOPE has energized its inner-city clients. And with Cunningham and Josaitis as role models, they have even begun setting their own stretch goals. George Smith, a typical CAT candidate, says his end goal is a master's degree in Engineering and his own business. "Nobody owes you anything. If you want something, you have to work for it," he says.[30]

To watch Cunningham and Josaitis at work is a study in how leaders use sticks and carrots to energize people through stretch. At one minute, they express the highest of expectations. For example, students at Fast Track must be in class and logged onto their computers by 8:00 A.M. and not a second later. This policy is strictly enforced by Thomas Murphy, the ex-military sergeant at the helm, whose goal is to emulate real-world circumstances. "Companies don't tolerate tardy employees and we don't either."[31] At the next moment, Cunningham and Josaitis are expressing incredible admiration for and confidence in their students. After describing the profile of a CAT student, Cunningham once proudly asked an audience, "Where do they come from, these gems? Are they imported from Japan? Do we bring them in from Germany? Or do we even bring them in from

MIT? They come from the streets of Detroit. They labored through the Fast Track program, they pushed their way through the Machinist Training Institute, they held a job, and now they're starting at the CAT. There's nothing like them in the world."[32] The results are incredible energy and the dedication to do what they, and the rest of the world, thought they could not do.

Like Cunningham and Josaitis, all leaders who seek to use stretch as an energizer must walk a fine line. The goals must be high enough to inspire extraordinary effort, but they can't appear so unreasonable or unattainable as to discourage people from reaching for them. One way to make sure the goals appear attainable would be to limit the aspirations. But this would also limit the results, because lower goals usually evoke lower effort. As GE's Jack Welch put it in reviewing his company's very strong 1995 results: "As strong as the year was, we did not achieve two of what we call 'stretch' performance targets: operating margins and inventory turns. Over the last three decades, our highest corporate operating margin hovered around 10%, and our inventory turns around five, so in 1991 we set two 'stretch' targets for 1995: 15% operating margin and ten turns. 1995 has come and gone, and despite a heroic effort by our 222,000 employees, we fell short on both measures, achieving a 14.4% operating margin and almost seven turns. But in stretching for these 'impossible' targets, we learned to do things faster than we would have going after 'doable' goals."[33] A year earlier, in his annual letter to shareholders, he had explained that a "stretch atmosphere replaces a grim, heads-down determination to be as good as you *have* to be, and asks, instead, how good *can* you be?" (His emphasis.)

Teamwork and Hope for Success

As an alternative to lowering their sights, winning leaders make their goals seem attainable by building up the players' confidence and determination. One of the best ways to do that is by acknowledging the difficulties and creating "we're all in this together" teamwork. Where single individuals may despair of accomplishing a monumental task, teams nurture, support and inspire each other.

One of the ways that Focus: HOPE teams up with its clients is by alleviating some of the personal and family stresses that poor people face when they enter the workforce. For example, it runs a fully certified, well-staffed, up-to-date day care center for the children of its students. The 26,000-square-foot center provides infant care, toddler care, a Montessori school program and a before/after school program. A single mother of three, 24-year-old Denecia Harvey says that the facility took away her best excuse for not completing her education or starting a career. "I was always saying what I couldn't do. 'Oh, I can't do this because of my children.' Or, 'I don't have this for my children. I can't do this.' 'I don't have a babysitter.' I made an excuse for everything." Now she is studying to be a machinist, while her children are enrolled at Focus: HOPE's Center for Children.[34] To offer other kinds of support, Focus: HOPE has also recruited hundreds of professional engineers to serve as mentors and morale-builders for its students.

Although each student at Focus: HOPE is working to improve his or her own life, the common struggle serves to unite them as a team. They know that the program requires enormous effort from each student, and they draw strength from knowing that other people have chosen to make the commitment as well. They wear the dark blue Focus: HOPE aprons, which are part of each student's uniform during the day, like badges of honor throughout their communities at night. Instead of taking the aprons off as they walk out the door, students wear them home and to do their errands. Like the gang uniforms that so many of their neighbors wear, the Focus: HOPE aprons are a symbol that they have made a commitment and are part of a community.

Cunningham and Josaitis are also very clear about their own personal commitment and the fact that they are working with their clients in the struggle. As the students work to prepare themselves for self-sufficiency, Cunningham and Josaitis work alongside them, energetically raising funds and spreading the Focus: HOPE message. Their days start well before 8:00 A.M. and often stretch into the evening when they attend a dinner or banquet, deliver a speech or present an award for community involvement.

Cunningham's and Josaitis's respect for their students is further evidenced by the physical space they have created for them to work in. They take meticulous care in all aspects of the environment, from the striking gardens and trees to the clean graffiti-free retrofitted buildings making up the Focus: HOPE complex in inner-city Detroit. The once bombed-out and abandoned buildings have been totally modernized. The Center for Children is high-tech, with computers for the kids as well as a clean modern interior. At the same time, however, neither Cunningham nor Josaitis has an office. Their desks, like everyone else's, are situated in the open work space of Focus: HOPE's main building.

The new CAT center is designed as a total learning experience. It is important that the architecture symbolize and practically operate as a "work of the future," says Cunningham, who refuses to have "hand-me-down" computers or manufacturing equipment because he wants to energize and stretch his students and prepare them for the twenty-first century. There is a world-class electronic information center for computer-based instruction with links to the Internet, where every student is expected to complete a certain number of hours of work each week. They have even set up an executive-style dining room for the students to learn how to interact socially in business settings. There is a chef who prepares meals of different national origins, and the students are taught to set the tables properly, manners for different cultures, and how to carry on an appropriate business conversation.

With all this attention to detail and their hard work, Cunningham, Josaitis and the rest of the staff show their confidence in the students, and that helps the students develop confidence in themselves. Andre Reynolds, a CAT student who graduated from the Machinist Training Institute and now works in the organization's machine shop, plans to be a globe-trotting engineering troubleshooter. "So if they have a problem, let's just say, in Germany or in Japan," he explains, "they would say, 'Well, who can we get to solve this problem?' 'We'll call Andre Reynolds.' 'Where is he?' 'Well, the last I heard, he was in Washington.' They'll call me up and I'll fly to Japan and I won't need a translator because I already know the language myself."[35]

For tax purposes, Focus: HOPE may qualify as a charity, but it is run according to serious no-nonsense business principles. Like winning corporations, Focus: HOPE provides its clients/workers with a clear strategy; in this case, it's for attaining economic self-sufficiency. It provides them with the necessary skills, both the job-specific ones needed to be a good machinist and the personal ones related to attendance, attire and the demeanor needed to be a good employee. And it creates the energy to reach its lofty goals by supporting and encouraging those who have the determination to make it.

In the for-profit world, the mission may be stated differently. It may be adding shareholder value or, as Dick Stonesifer, former CEO of GE Appliances puts it, becoming "one team better and faster than anybody else in the world." But no matter what the mission or the field, success depends on getting the maximum possible energy out of everyone in the organization and channeling that energy to achieve positive results. All the winning leaders I have met are experts at that.

Masters of the Transition

In the Focus: HOPE and GE Appliances examples above, I described how Tom Tiller, Bill Cunningham and Eleanor Josaitis create the enormous amounts of positive energy needed to achieve seemingly impossible goals by drawing off of and rechanneling negative energy that already exists around them. But what about leaders who don't have a ready-made supply of negative energy to transform? What if their businesses are running well, their workers are happy and they don't have any monumental problems? How do they jump-start their organizations and energize them to keep moving ahead of the competition?

The answer is that they do it in much the same way as the leaders who do have obvious problems. The only difference is that they generate the stress themselves by raising their goals or otherwise creating a sense of urgency. Then they channel the energy it evokes using the same methods as Tiller, Cunningham and Josaitis. In other words, leaders of winning organizations not only use energy to effect transitions, but they use transitions to create energy.

I don't mean to suggest that good leaders go around causing trouble and menacing people just to get their energy levels up. But it is a significant characteristic of winning leaders that they sound alarms when other people think the seas are calm. Sometimes winning leaders see the warning signs sooner and more clearly than others, and sometimes it's simply that winning leaders are never satisfied. They always want things to be even better than they already are. So if the marketplace or other external forces don't create problems or opportunities, the leaders do it themselves by breaking down comfortable old structures, setting stretch goals and challenging people to rise to a new level of expectations. They do this because winning leaders understand that times of transition are "teachable moments," when people are most likely to respond because they feel that they must. So they create "burning platforms," and then help people figure out where and how to jump.

At Ameritech, after four years of having the "we-must-change-to-survive" message pounded into the core of the every process, operation, structure and individual, everyone took the idea as a given truth. But that was not always the case. In 1991, when Bill Weiss first came to visit me, no one at Ameritech but him seemed to understand the massive changes that were necessary. The old Ameritech was a methodical, bureaucratic elephant that would now be competing in a road race with cheetahs. The ideas, attitudes and behaviors that had allowed it to thrive as a regulated local telephone monopoly would doom it as a competitor in the global telecommunications industry that it was entering. In a few years, this undeniable truth would become painfully apparent to everyone, but Weiss knew that he couldn't afford to wait for that time. So, like the winning leader he is, he sent out the alarm. He first forced top management to analyze the company's situation, promoting those who embraced the need for change and getting rid of those who didn't. And, with a new executive team in place, he set about fanning the flames until everyone could see that the platform was on fire. Ameritech's success today is a testimony to the ability of Weiss and his successor, Dick Notebaert, to manage the transition and truly bring the company into a new competitive era.

At General Electric, Jack Welch did the same thing. In fact, his challenge was perhaps tougher than Weiss's, because GE had no apparent problems when he took over. While the breakup of AT&T and the deregulation of the telephone industry had at least signaled significant, although not necessarily fatal, problems for Ameritech, no such similar problems were apparent at GE. The mood, according to Welch's predecessor, Reg Jones, in his 1980 annual report letter, was one that simply required "self-renewal." With net income up 9% to nearly $1.7 billion in 1981, only nine other *FORTUNE* 500 companies boasted earnings this large. Shareholders didn't expect a rapidly appreciating stock—they were happy to collect approximately half of GE's earnings in dividends. GE's biggest strength was its stability; it had been growing in tune with the GNP for years. But Welch knew that given its recent dependence on back-logged orders for nearly one-third of annual revenues, GE would have to raise that mark to almost twice the GNP and expand its presence in overseas markets if it wanted to survive the 1980s. So instead of concentrating on self-renewal, GE's new head had to foment a revolution.[36]

Even winning leaders who don't feel the need for massive shake-ups like Weiss and Welch did still use smaller transitions and the elements of the transitional framework to build and maintain energy. Lew Platt, former CEO of Hewlett-Packard, once told me that his primary job in meetings is to create a sense of anxiety. He says that he is constantly pressing the people working in the company. "I've learned that you need to literally go around, and . . . to create some anxiety in the organization. You do that by playing out things that might change that would jeopardize your position, and by staying very attuned to competition. . . . We use our imagination a lot around here. And I encourage that."[37] The restlessness this fosters cascades throughout HP, resulting in the company's track record of constantly being ahead of its competitors.

Likewise, Gary Wendt, former CEO of GE Capital, says he believes that "any change, any place, any where, requires a crisis to make it. So, sometimes, I find it very helpful to—to use an unfortunate phrase—'Create the crisis.' . . . I can remember when I first came here in the mid-seventies saying: 'Okay, I know we're doing better now, but holy cow, you can't believe how terrible it's going to be in the next year.' . . . You just have to have people understand that there's a reason for [changing]."

Under Wendt's prodding, for example, GE Capital has revolutionized the equipment leasing business. It no longer merely provides financing, but offers the additional service of managing the equipment, making sure it gets where it needs to be and repairing it when it breaks. When GE Capital bids against banks or other financial services companies on leasing, it has these other avenues to make additional money. And the people at GE Capital often know their clients better, because they are involved in their operations.[38] Wendt could have framed the move into equipment management as an opportunity for GE to be a smart player and to jump ahead of the competition. But instead, he took the tack that the change was inevitable and GE was about to fall behind. "We could have gone along at 5%, 6%, and everybody would have been happy. But instead, we saw an opportunity and made a crisis out of it," he explains. "I said 'Oh, my God, the whole equipment and leasing business is going to change, we have to do something.' And that's what created the opportunity. . . . The consolidation that's taking place in the financial services industry helps me create a crisis for us every day. And I've just played it and played it and played it."[39]

While winning leaders like Welch, Platt and Wendt often create the need for transitions just to increase the energy levels in already thriving organizations, losers not only do not create inessential transitions, they also fail to take their companies through essential ones. I see this every day. Leaders allow people to hang on to the past, referring to departments by their old names or refusing to work with a joint venture or merger partner. More seriously, they let them hang on to old practices and behaviors at the expense of customers or a new vision for the company.

In my mind, the recent problems at Apple Computer are the clear result of a failed transition that started out right, but didn't finally take hold. When Michael Spindler became CEO at Apple in 1990,[40] the company clearly was having difficulties. It still had powerful assets, mainly in the form of the best and most user-friendly PC technology and an incredibly loyal following of customers and programmers. But it had begun to lose its technological edge. In 1994, the company introduced its Power line of computers, which should have solved some of its problems. It appeared, briefly, that the company might be back on the road to victory. The rollout was the smoothest in the company's history. The products were technically excellent and received well by customers. Unfortunately, within a year, the company was in trouble again. It missed shipments due to poor execution.[41] At the same time, Intel's new chips were hitting the market and matching the performance of Apple's. Apple had no answer to move ahead again. Before long, Apple's share of the market was sliding again and its financial performance continued its erratic pattern.[42]

The problem was that while they had gotten their energy up to overcome their earlier problems, the people who worked at Apple had not successfully transitioned to a new way of thinking and operating. After the Power PC's initial success, they assumed that it was time to return to the good old days. They believed that Apple's business model of proprietary design was still correct, that the best technology would always win and that Apple had the best technology. They failed to find the breakthrough ideas and thinking that would keep them ahead of the competition. The severity of the earlier problems had motivated them to action, but Spindler had failed to manage a real transition in the organizational mindset. He had failed to make a clear break with the past and get the Apple culture to embrace the new behaviors necessary to keep pleasing customers and survive in the future. When he resigned amid mounting losses in the spring of 1996, I can remember meeting Apple people who were still saying, "We're not worried, Apple is a company that always comes up and down. That's the way it is."

Spindler's successor Gil Amelio didn't fare much better in changing the Apple mindset. Throughout 1996, he took such drastic steps as announcing layoffs and restructurings that slashed payroll expense by 22% at the company.[43] As a last-ditch effort, and something of a slap in the face of Apple's own engineers, he finally spent $400 million to buy Next Computer.[44] This desperation play to give Apple a new operating system should have sent a strong message, but Apple's famously arrogant culture continued to look inside rather than outside. In February 1997, an industry observer wrote, "[Apple] executives still talk about how impossible it is to predict what will happen at Apple—and how hard it is to get employees to go along with the program."[45]

After yet another restructuring announcement in March 1997 that would trim the workforce by nearly another 30%,[46] Apple's Senior Vice President of Marketing, Guerino DeLuca, made a telling remark. DeLuca, perhaps not even aware of the irony of his statement, reported that this latest round of layoffs had brought "an urgency to Apple I have not seen before."[47] If that's true, it was about time. Later in the year Amelio was ousted by the board, most of whom later resigned. A new board was put in place, and, in what would have been sacrilege, Microsoft entered the picture with an investment in Apple topping $150 million.

The future of Apple is still uncertain. In the meantime, the jokes around Silicon Valley are that Apple stands for "Arrogance Produces Profit-Losing Entity."

In short, winning leaders are masters of transitions. They are people who relish change. They personally draw energy from transitions, and using transitions to create productive energy in others is one of their most powerful tools as leaders. Winning leaders are comfortable with transitions because they understand them and know how to use them. They may not have a theoretical framework like William Bridges does, but instinctively they create clean breaks with the past, inspire people with a vision of a worthwhile future and help them with the painful work of changing their mindsets and actions. As Larry Bossidy of AlliedSignal said in the remark that opened Chapter 2, "Show me a great company, and I'll show you one that has radically changed itself and is looking forward to the opportunity to do so again."

Edge

The Courage to See Reality
and Act on It

Winning Leaders Never Take the Easy Way Out

- They face the hard facts and make the tough calls
- Risk and pain don't deter them

Categories of Edge

- Portfolio—Pursuing new businesses and abandoning old ones
- People—Promoting risk-takers and confronting failures

Edge Isn't Cruel, It's Honest

- Winning leaders pursue the truth and can explain it to others
- Without edge, expedience wins over necessity

The best way I know to get people to accept the need for change is to not give them a choice. The organization has to know that there is a leader at the top who has made up his mind, that he is surrounded by leaders who have made up their minds, and that they're going to drive forward no matter what.[1]

—BILL WEISS, RETIRED CHAIRMAN AND CEO, AMERITECH

I can't help but wonder why leaders are so often hesitant to lead. I guess it takes a lot of conviction and trusting your gut to get ahead of your peers, your staff and your employ-

ees while they are still squabbling about which path to take, and set an unhesitating, unequivocal course whose rightness or wrongness will not be known for years. Such a decision really tests the mettle of the leaders. By contrast, it doesn't take much self-confidence to downsize a company—after all, how can you go wrong by shuttering factories and laying people off if the benefits of such actions are going to show up in tomorrow's bottom line and will be applauded by the financial community?[2]

—ANDY GROVE, CHAIRMAN OF INTEL

Bill Weiss and Andy Grove have both walked the talk by making tough decisions. Weiss started a revolution at his 65,000-person company. He unequivocally, and early on almost unilaterally, launched the company onto its transformation path. For three years, he personally embodied that transformation—by spending hundreds of days on issues of changing the company's structure and culture, by passing over his likely successors to find change agents in the company and by demanding that ten thousand people be engaged in the transformation in a twelve-month period.

Every two years, Andy Grove plunks down about $2.5 billion to build a plant to produce a new type of microchip.[3] This is essentially a bet on the future of Intel's new technology. So far, the bets have paid off big for Intel. Is Grove lucky, or a great gambler? Hardly. Grove is a great leader who looks for opportunities to change his company before the market changes ahead of it, and then makes it very clear to people what mountain they are about to climb.

Both of these leaders have displayed a leadership quality that I have come to call "edge": the ability to make tough decisions and the willingness to sacrifice the security of today for the sake of a better future. Dante once wrote that "the hottest places in hell are reserved for those who, in a time of great moral crisis, maintain their neutrality." Few leaders ever encounter times of great moral crisis on a societal level. But they all are called upon every day to face hard realities, to cut through conflicting currents and ambiguities and to stake out clear positions. And the people who succeed, the winners, are the ones who have edge.

This direct, take-no-prisoners style of action is one that I have often noticed in winning leaders over the years, but it was Jack Welch, the ultimate Mr. Edge, who put the name on it for me. In early 1996, my colleague Ram Charan and I were in Welch's office to discuss our ideas about leadership. I was sure that my three-pronged model with ideas, values and energy would be a hit with Welch, so I had eagerly looked forward to rolling it out for him. But it took Jack only a nanosecond to knock me flat. "You forgot something," he told me. "A leader's got to have edge. Without that, nothing else matters."[4] Welch started to come alive. His suit jacket already off, the pace of his speech quickened. He gestured with his hands, as if that would bring the words out quicker. "A lot of people have good ideas, and good values, and they can even energize others. But for some reason they are not able to make the tough calls. That is what separates, for me, whether or not someone can lead a business."

In the last chapter, I cited Father Bill Cunningham and Eleanor Josaitis of Focus: HOPE in Detroit as two masters at creating positive energy. I talked about how, through a carefully calibrated combination of stretch goals, support and team-building, they are able to lead their inner-city clients to turn negative energy to the positive purpose of acquiring job skills and careers. But Cunningham's and Josaitis's ability to create positive energy is only one of the reasons that Focus: HOPE and its clients succeed so well. Another is that Cunningham and Josaitis have edge, and by their example are able to inspire it in others.

Focus: HOPE's leaders display their edge in a number of ways. The most obvious one is in how they run their training programs. They strictly demand that students show up for class and do their work, and they dismiss those who don't. The dismissals are always painful, but Cunningham and Josaitis are unrelenting, because, as Cunningham explains, Focus: HOPE is helping people fight a war in which they are already disadvantaged. "We tell them that it's just like the real world. You come in late on your job, you get fired. . . . We are not in the business of saving souls. We are in the business of building competitive people. If they are not ready for that, that can't be our problem."[5]

The edge that Cunningham and Josaitis display in dismissing truant students is fairly straightforward and easy to grasp. It is painful for them and for the individual students who are dismissed, but they do it because they firmly believe that to do otherwise would diminish the program and its effectiveness. The dismissals serve the important goals of teaching the students a valuable lesson about responsibility and of making room for others who will take more seriously the opportunity to better their lives.[6]

The key element in exercising edge, however, isn't that it hurts, but rather that it is courageous. Edge is a complex combination of two factors. The first is an incredible drive to seek the truth, to find reality and base decisions on it. The second is the courage to act on this truth and make tough calls. And it is in the management of Focus: HOPE as an organization and the design of its programs that Cunningham and Josaitis have displayed their edge even more sharply.

At Focus: HOPE, from the very beginning Father Cunningham and Ms. Josaitis have shown edge not only in their willingness to face an unpopular reality but in their defiance of conventional wisdom in responding to it. The unpopular reality is that poor people don't fail just because society is unjust but also because they themselves are ill-equipped to succeed. In its mission statement, Focus: HOPE describes itself as a "civil rights" organization. But, in an era when "civil rights" meant "political action," they decided that "equal opportunity" meant "equal capability." So, rather than stage marches and lobby the statehouse, they resolved to take direct action by setting up a feeding program. To the critics who claimed that such "charity" would simply rob people of the incentive to change society, they replied that the program would help bring about change by making sure that young children didn't lose their mental abilities to malnutrition before they ever had a chance to become effective citizens. Their decision was startling and controversial in an environment where the mood was confrontational. Most people would have opted for quicker fixes, but Cunningham and Josaitis pursued their course of action because they felt that their vision of reality demanded it. On a couple of occasions, Focus: HOPE has filed lawsuits charging large employers with discriminating against minorities in hiring practices. But most of its efforts have been directed not at changing the outside environment, but at enabling its clients to compete in it.

Cunningham and Josaitis displayed edge once again when they had what was considered a model food program up and running, and decided to branch out by creating the Machinists Training Institute. Later they would add the remedial math and language skills program and then the Center for Advanced Technologies to provide bachelor's- and master's-level training in engineering. In retrospect, the success of Focus: HOPE's educational programs makes these expansions seem part of a natural progression. Thanks to Focus: HOPE training, more than one thousand people are now employed as machinists, in well-paying jobs that allow them to buy nutritious food for their families and educate their children themselves. Further, Focus: HOPE earns $10 million a year in revenue[7] to support its work by selling precision-machined parts produced by its graduates and machinists-in-training. But at each step along the way, Cunningham and Josaitis refused to back down in the face of ambiguity and resistance. "You'll never break into the auto industry," said social activists when they proposed the Machinists Training Institute. "You will spread your resources too thin," supporters of the food program complained when they started the remedial program. "You're reaching too high," said almost everyone when they began to talk about the Center for Advanced Technologies. Nonetheless, they pushed ahead, because, to paraphrase the old Barry Goldwater slogan from his 1964 presidential campaign, in their hearts they knew they were right.[8]

At each juncture, Cunningham and Josaitis could have decided to just stick to their knitting, to keep doing what they had been doing. And as each new effort diverted resources, they risked the future of their other, already highly effective programs. In the summer of 1996, Eckhard Pfeiffer showed edge when he dared to reshape Compaq at a time when it was enjoying record profits and a high stock price. He did it, however, because he believed the changes would ultimately be necessary and that the company's long-term survival was at stake. Cunningham and Josaitis, on the other hand, took risks and bet the farm when there was no such threat. They could have just continued to feed people, or to help them acquire skills that would allow them to get jobs. But they refused to settle for anything less than their very best shot at helping people be not just survivors but winners. I like to quote Harvey Hornstein, a professor at Columbia University, who wrote that "innovative change must involve the expression of an idea that is somewhat or wholly inconsistent with existing practice."[9] It is this spirit that drives Cunningham and Josaitis. It is the epitome of edge.

When I think about Father Cunningham and Ms. Josaitis and the enormous success of Focus: HOPE, I am drawn by the contrast between them and the generations of management that have all but destroyed their across-town neighbor General Motors. GM, with sales of $170 billion, is No. 1 on the *FORTUNE* 1000.[10] It was, unfortunately, No. 998 on *FORTUNE*'s annual ranking of Market Value Added (MVA) for 1996.[11] MVA measures how much wealth corporations are creating for their investors. It is the difference between total market value—what shareholders can take out—and invested capital, the money they put in. Corporations with a positive MVA have made money, while those with negative MVAs have been burning it. Over its lifespan, General Motors has destroyed $17.8 billion in stockholder wealth, more than any other company.[12]

There are several reasons for this, but one of the biggest, in my opinion, is that in GM's genetic code for leadership, there is a lack of edge. I am not sure how or where this developed, but I have seen it in generations of GM managers.

My first realization of this came in 1987, when Ram Charan and I met with Bob Stempel. Stempel had just been named president of GM, and was the heir apparent to Roger Smith, the company's chairman. I had worked briefly in 1984 and 1985 with Stempel, Alex Cunningham, the former executive vice president who ran GM's North American Auto Operations, and Lloyd Reuss, then a division head in North American Auto Operations.[13] When we met in 1987, I had just finished running General Electric's Crotonville executive training center for two years, and had agreed to sit down with Stempel to discuss leading transformations based on what I had learned from Welch at GE.

Bob Stempel is a wonderful human being—a true car guy who grew up around automobiles and was captivated by them at an early age. We met on the formal, dark-wood-paneled fourteenth floor of GM's headquarters building in downtown Detroit, surrounded by car memorabilia. Stempel believed deeply in General Motors and its people, and he wanted the company to succeed. A man with great values, he talked openly of the need to change GM.

But the lack of edge that has become characteristic of leadership at GM became clear at the end of the meeting. Stempel, who was now in line to take over the world's biggest company, should have been one of the world's most energized people at that time. His final comments spelled his own doom. Looking glum, his brow furrowed, he said, "Being at the top of GM is like being at the end of a long railroad track with decisions coming at you. Except the decisions never get to you, because there are a hundred people who have switches to pull that divert the train from ever reaching me." Stempel saw himself as a victim; eventually he would be named CEO but he never got control of the company.

In 1993, Stempel was removed in a board coup led by outside director John Smale. Smale, who distinguished himself with an excellent track record while CEO of Procter & Gamble, thought that Stempel was moving too slowly to change GM. He wanted fast action, he wanted edge and he convinced other board members (most likely correctly) that Stempel did not have what it took to lead GM. Smale temporarily assumed the chairmanship of GM's board and promoted several younger executives. But this shock has not been enough to break the heritage of inaction at GM.

In July 1996, GM announced a major realignment of its vehicle lines. But instead of taking outside advice to reduce the number of models it produces or get rid of some marketing divisions entirely, GM just tinkered.[14] It cut a few of the least popular cars, redesigned others that weren't selling and introduced several all-new models.

Maryann Keller, a prominent auto analyst at Furman Selz, an investment bank, told the *New York Times* that GM's fall program was "crazy—it makes absolutely no economic sense." Harry Pearce, the company's vice chairman, responded to such criticisms by saying that "in an organization as large and as complex as GM, it's naive to think you can make changes [quickly]. We're making what I would call consistent, steady progress."

"Consistent, steady progress." Toward what? Nine years after Bob Stempel had called me in to talk about transformation, the company still had a confusing array of 82 models of cars and trucks, a workforce of 700,000 and market share that had declined to under 32% of the U.S. car and light truck market from over 44% in 1980 and 35% in 1987.[15] Can you imagine Winston Churchill saying it would be naive to try to mobilize the United Kingdom quickly, "given our size and complexity"?[16]

Don't We Already Have Too Much Edge in the World?

Sometimes it may seem that there is too much edge in the world. There have certainly been a lot of people sacked for the sake of corporate profits lately. The painful restructurings are not limited to the United States. Daimler Benz, the pillar of German industry, recently turned its back on several loss-making divisions.[17] Japanese companies have challenged lifetime employment and laid off workers as they have begun to move manufacturing jobs offshore to take advantage of cheaper labor. Some of these harsh decisions do demonstrate leadership edge that is based on sound principles and solid business judgment. But others are the desperate acts of wimps who have avoided reality for a long time and are looking for the quickest way out of the corners they are in. And in the worst cases, they are the actions of greedy bullies who are propping up earnings at the expense of others.

It may be hard to detect the difference at first. But if you look deeper, you can see it. Essentially, edge is having the courage of one's convictions. It is the willingness of a leader to make a decision and to take principled actions when others would do nothing—make excuses and let things slide—or when they would pursue another course. Edge is the refusal (I'm tempted to say the "inability") to let difficulty stand in the way of acting on one's deeply held ideas and values. But in order to have edge, a leader must have deeply held ideas and values. It's true that without edge, ideas, values and teachable points of view might as well not exist. At the same time, however, a leader who doesn't have ideas, values or a teachable point of view cannot have edge. A person may make tough, unpopular decisions, but unless those decisions are based on firmly held convictions about the organization's purpose and values, they are simply arbitrary, and often cruel and stupid. A leader who shoots from the hip is exercising arrogance, not edge. Edge is about having principles and then following through on them.

Slash and burn leaders may be mistakenly believed to be leaders with edge. But they aren't, because they only tear down companies rather than building them up. The difference between leaders with edge and bullies is that leaders are motivated to set a good example for others and improve their organizations rather than to get more money for themselves or save their own jobs. They are drawn by a vision of organizational success rather than pushed by a fear of personal unemployment or distress. In fact, one of the hallmarks of winning leaders is that they display edge even when it causes them personal distress.

I recently witnessed an interesting debate by a client of mine. The debate was sparked by my last book, *Control Your Destiny or Someone Else Will: How Jack Welch Is Making GE the World's Most Competitive Company,* which I cowrote with Stratford Sherman. We opened the book with a scenario I encountered while I was at GE's Crotonville training center. Late one night in 1985, I happened upon one of the many breakout rooms there. In it was a group of young engineers and businesspeople, new hires to the company. Around the table with sleeves rolled up and food wrappers and dirty plates littering the room, they were feverishly debating two flip charts. One said, "Jack Welch is the greatest CEO GE has ever had." The other said, "Jack Welch is an asshole."

When I related this to the new client's people, many were shocked at the openness of the culture at GE. Others quickly internalized the debate. What followed was a fifteen-minute discussion which, like the one I described at GE, sprang up totally spontaneously. Most of the new client's people came to the conclusion that leadership in their culture had always been about building consensus. Mavericks were shunned. Leaders were the ones you could count on. They were good "company men" or "company women." Some people thought that this culture had gone too far. They believed that this had led to a culture and to leadership constrained by consensus and incrementalism. Others believed that you can't be both an asshole and a good leader.

I take the view that to some extent, every good leader is an asshole. I won't take that to the extreme and suggest that leadership be called assholeship. But I will point out that great leaders are often hated and despised precisely because they take risks and show edge. They have a perception of reality that others don't, and in trying to show us why their reality is right and why we should follow them, they run the risk of pissing some people off. Jesus Christ, Gandhi and Martin Luther King Jr., to name a few, were even killed by people who didn't like the realities that they saw or what they were trying to do about them. But winning leaders know that life isn't a popularity contest. So they do whatever they believe to be right, however painful or difficult it may be.

Truth and Courage

One way to tell if a leader really has edge is if he or she is willing to publicly admit his or her own mistakes. It's easy to overlook this telltale sign because it usually doesn't cause pain for anyone except the leader. But for the leader, it's the ultimate test of facing reality, the reality that he or she was wrong. It is also a positive sign that the leader will accept the honest mistakes of others as well.

Norm Mitchell, the former head of the Electrical Workers Union at General Electric's Appliance Park in Louisville, Kentucky, is one leader who doesn't mind admitting when he is wrong, and has done so, on more than one occasion, in quite spectacular fashion. Mitchell defines one of these instances as a highlight of his career.

It was in 1988, when he was a lieutenant at the union in Louisville. In the waning hours of the union's national contract with General Electric, the president of the local in Louisville fell ill. He called Mitchell and said, "Look, I'm sick, I've got to go to the hospital. You're the guy now." He told Mitchell, "You've got to go to New York. You've got to vote, and you've got to present it [the contract] to the membership."

Mitchell arrived late, shortly before the delegates were to vote. The union's chief negotiator was for the company's final offer, while other members of the union's negotiating committee were against the contract. In the end, the delegates in New York voted against the contract. Mitchell, having arrived late and having little information, also voted against it. This vote didn't bind the union, but it served as the national delegates' recommendation to the union members across the country about how they should vote when their chance came. If the membership voted "no," tens of thousands of workers would go on strike.

After the meeting, Mitchell went to the airport and boarded the plane back to Louisville. Fighting management came naturally to Mitchell, so he was braced for another walkout. Settling into his seat on the plane, he opened the thick draft of the contract and read it. Then he thought to himself, "Wait, this is crazy. This is a good contract. I don't know what happened up there, but this is a good contract."

When Mitchell got off the plane in Louisville, he had changed his mind. Over the next few days, both the company's unions relations person, Mark Krivoruchka, and Mitchell would present their cases to the union membership on passage of the contract. Krivoruchka expected that he would be lobbying the union to approve the contract, while Mitchell would be lobbying the union to reject it. But Mitchell surprised him. "Mark," he said, "I voted against the contract, but it's a good contract. . . . You stay out of this and I'll sell it." Krivoruchka was leery, but despite the protests of some plant managers, he agreed, and Mitchell began working vigorously. He assembled a team to talk to union members in Louisville about the contract. "We started selling the contract. We started putting it out; presenting it. Talking to the membership." Before long, word of Mitchell's campaign to educate and lobby on behalf of the contract spread throughout the country. "People around the country began calling saying, 'Are you all going to buy the contract?'" Mitchell would tell them, "It's a good contract. Read it." The final result of Mitchell's actions: "In 1988 the people of Louisville and the country voted to accept that contract [with] 75% [in favor]."[18] In this case, Mitchell faced the reality of the situation and was willing to take necessary risks to further the common good. That's edge.

Categories of Edge

Edge is something that leaders exercise every day. It's not a quality that just appears once a year at annual review time. It runs through a winning leader's veins like every other element of his or her teachable point of view.

There are basically two major categories of edge, or scenarios in which a leader's edge is tested. The first involves what I call portfolio decisions. These are often decisions about where to invest time, money and resources. The other involves people decisions, facing reality and making tough decisions about people. At Focus: HOPE, Bill Cunningham and Eleanor Josaitis have demonstrated portfolio edge in taking on new projects in the face of resistance, and people edge in cutting out the slackers who don't come to school on time. Winning leaders must have both kinds.

Portfolio decisions involve getting out of businesses as well as getting into new ones, and the decisions to disengage are most often the more difficult ones to make. Professor Larry Selden of Columbia University has a great framework to classify businesses that is helpful in thinking through portfolio edge. Selden has traced the performance of companies in the S&P 500 and discovered a correlation between stock performance and key financial metrics. More than any other variables, revenue growth and return on assets correlate best with stock price performance. The implication is clear—if a business wants better stock performance, it needs to have high revenue growth and a good return on the assets it uses to run its business. Selden notes that the top quartile S&P companies average 12% revenue growth and 16% operating return on assets.

When working with a multi-business company, Selden charts each of its businesses on a 2 x 2 matrix with revenue growth on the y axis and operating return on assets on the x axis. The best businesses, according to Selden, are the ones in the northeast quadrant. It is here that businesses maximize their contribution to shareholder value. A leader's job is to evaluate the ones that aren't in the northeast quadrant and decide if they are making a sufficient contribution to the company or if they should be changed or killed.[19]

Not every leader has the option of killing or adding businesses, but all leaders have to make "portfolio" decisions. At AlliedSignal, Mary Petrovich isn't free to decide that the St. Clair

Shores, Michigan, safety-restraint plant that she manages is going to stop making seatbelts and start making something else, but she can, and must, decide which programs and processes add the most value when it does make them. Likewise, ServiceMaster's Phil Myers can't decide to stop cleaning the medical center and start performing brain surgery instead, but he does have to decide which activities and cleaning procedures provide the most value for ServiceMaster and its customer. What Selden's framework does is allow leaders to look at each individual business or process and pinpoint those that are unproductive and inefficient. The question then is: Does the leader have the edge to take the actions necessary to fix or eliminate underperforming businesses?

Debra Dunn was a general manager in Hewlett-Packard's Test and Measurement business. The business was one of the company's oldest, making oscilloscopes, audio oscillators, electronic testing equipment and other products that trace their roots directly to the ones produced by Bill Hewlett and David Packard in their garage workshop in 1938.[20] But the business was seeking to branch out into the higher-growth areas, and Dunn's assignment was to come up with new products for high-tech communications networks. "We are called the video communications division, but we really should be called the venture capital division," she says.

In a cutting-edge business like this one, you can't ask consumers how to improve their cable modems or wireless interactive technology, because no one has them. But the price of waiting for perfect information is extinction. So, leaders like Dunn have to face reality and place their bets about where to go. The video communications division is actually a portfolio of four different businesses, all of which represent the next "big thing," all of which require resources and all of which have a loyal following of engineers and marketers who believe it should be the division's top priority. It's up to Dunn to sort this portfolio out and, within the portfolio, sort out which technologies to invest in developing.

"We've been having a lot of discussions about this," she told me one day. "We frame it like this: You have to build a very strong case for why it makes sense to invest in this business. We have to work on why this is the best place to invest. . . . We all own stock at HP, [so] we don't want HP investing in things that aren't well justified. Sure, you experiment in your labs, but your investments need to be based on really good plans."

Each of the products in the portfolio that Dunn inherited was based on just that—really solid plans. Speaking of one line of products, she says, "The market clearly exists for these products. There is a set of customers who have a set of challenges. These products solve those challenges. The customers know they have the challenge, and they know they need to solve it. So it appeared to be lower risk," she says.

As Dunn began to lead the video communications division into the business, however, it became clear that there were other elements that they hadn't foreseen. Among them was the fact that the network of existing customers and suppliers was tighter than anticipated. HP found a partner that could help them enter the market. But that partner fell apart, and as it crumbled, so did HP's strategy.

At this point, the strong HP culture kicked in. "There are plenty of people who get into the 'We just have to believe and work hard, and we can make it work' [mode]. And I think there are a lot of markets where that works for us," says Dunn. "We've got smart people. They're really good, and they tend to . . . plow through any brick wall you put in front of them." This can be a real asset "if the wall is two inches thick," she added, but in this case, it was more like two feet.

So Dunn made the tough decision to get out of the business and refocus her efforts elsewhere. "I had been involved in building the business [for two years]. . . . I had spent lots of time with . . . all of our key customers, and I liked this business. When you invest a lot [of personal energy] it's very painful to walk away from. . . . I didn't like the conclusion. But that didn't cause me to deny it or hide from it or pretend that reality is different than it is. . . . It was very difficult, but it's what I had to do."

When I asked her later about it, she answered me in almost the very words I would have chosen to describe a person who exercises edge: "I always find that I muster the energy and the conviction to do what I know to be the right thing to do." Then she explained, "If you just envision continuing in the path that you're on, you see that it's really unfair to the people who are invested and committed. I think I need to lead these people to success. And, if we're not on a path that can be successful, then I have to get us on a different path. . . . I have to be willing to say, 'You know, I appreciate your endurance and I empathize with your emotional investment in this business, but this doesn't make sense. Here is why it doesn't make sense. And we're not doing it anymore.'"[21]

Time and again, people show "portfolio" edge in fields as far apart as medicine, business and civil rights. In each, the dots on the 2 x 2 matrix may be different, but the principle is the same. Leaders strip out everything that does not help create their vision, which means first facing reality, often alone and against the stinging scorn of those they work with. It means having the courage to act, even if it means venturing into the unknown or cutting so sharply it bleeds.

People Edge

It isn't enough to set direction by making portfolio decisions and then hoping that people in the organization will have the desire or ability to get there. In fact, where a lot of leaders stumble is in not having edge about people, because it involves giving tough face-to-face feedback and sometimes firing people.

Leaders have got to look realistically at the ideas and values of those in the organization, compare them with where the organization is going and make sure the people in place are going to help and not hinder. People edge is about giving people tough feedback about their performance or their values. It means being open and honest about what the organization needs from each and every person, and listening to help people, but finally making a yes-or-no decision about whether or not a person stays or goes.

Leaders like Father Cunningham, Eleanor Josaitis and Jack Welch are clear—people who are helping the organization and its people reach their full potential stay, and others must leave. The difficult part is deciding at what point to make that call. I know how tough this is because I had to make several of these calls while at GE and while running a rural health care delivery system in the Appalachian region of Kentucky.

Jack Welch has a useful framework for thinking about this at GE. For Welch, people who are going to help the organization reach its potential have to be able to both provide performance improvements and live within the company's values. He created a device to help him think through some of his tougher calls on people issues. Welch described this tool in his 1991 annual report. He puts people into one of four cells on another simple 2 x 2 matrix with values and performances as its axes. Welch described the type of manager who goes in each cell.

> The first is one who delivers on commitments—financial or otherwise—and shares the values of our Company. His or her future is an easy call. Onward and upward.
>
> The second type of leader is one who does not meet commitments and does not share our values. Not as pleasant a call, but equally easy.
>
> The third is one who misses commitments but shares the values. He or she usually gets a second chance, preferably in a different environment.
>
> Then there's the fourth type—the most difficult for many of us to deal with. That leader delivers on commitments, makes all the numbers, but doesn't share the values we must have. This is the individual who typically forces performance out of people rather than inspires it: the autocrat, the big shot, the tyrant. Too often, all of us have looked the other way—tolerated these "type 4" managers because "they always deliver"—at least in the short term.

In the future, he said, these type 4 people would have to go.

Mary Petrovich, the young manager of AlliedSignal's safety-restraint plant in St. Clair Shores, Michigan, is another leader who has used edge about people to send a message to the organization. When Petrovich came to the plant, it had just been acquired. She knew that there was a huge need to improve performance, and she quickly discovered that the plant's woes were related to the values of the people working there. As we sat down to talk, she told me, "Many of the key operations folks never left the office to go on the floor. . . . And so there was terrible communication, there were terrible relationships and poor respect for mutual contributions. . . . Having that sort of eye-opener coming into it wasn't what I had expected to find."

When Petrovich arrived, the differences between the values of some of these managers and AlliedSignal's were dramatic. "There was a lock between the shop floor and the management area," she told me. "A lot of these managers did not have respect for people on the line. An hourly worker never came into this office area."

At the same time, she faced incredible performance pressures to make up for a loss of half a million dollars per month. This is the toughest time to exhibit people edge. New to her environment and under the gun, it would have been tempting to "make the numbers" and wait to fix the values-related issues. But, like Welch, Petrovich knew that she could not fundamentally improve the plant if she didn't tackle the issue of values. For example, the finance and accounting functions in the plant were known to be either invisible or, when visible, unhelpful. The quality advisers, similarly, enjoyed their status as expert gurus so much that they never left their department. Rather, people were expected to come to them as a person goes to a confessional: "Forgive me, Father, for I have created poor-quality parts today." So within one year, Petrovich replaced ten of twelve of the people reporting to her, getting rid of managers who were unwilling to team with production, purchasing and other departments. She took a risk: It was her first time running a plant, her first time as a general manager, and she was getting rid of people who supposedly knew the operation. This is edge: facing reality and having the courage to act, all to build for the future.

Petrovich began to create a new team of leaders to come together and turn around the plant. To do this, she is coaching each of these people. "I'm really trying to set the expectation and put the plan in place that we will be a management team. I tell people, 'You've got to get out of that mindset that says you are just responsible for your function.' I asked one staff person to grab a part from the plant so we could look at it. She didn't even know what it was. I said, 'We've all got to be able to do that to be effective.'" Her changes did not just involve top management. Very quickly, Petrovich and her team reconfigured everything from how the plant handled customer complaints to how it measured quality to how work teams were structured.

The changes in leadership have had a big impact, and there has been a remarkable improvement at the St. Clair Shores plant. In a short time, the financial performance has gone from a $500,000 loss each month to a $200,000 profit each month.[22]

Even at ServiceMaster, whose founding principles include providing stable growth and development for its workers, having people edge is a management essential. Bob Hutchins, ServiceMaster's account manager at a hospital north of Chicago, is responsible for more than 150 people comprised of employees from the hospital and ServiceMaster. Hutchins knows that if he lets them go, they may have trouble finding other work. He also knows that for many of them, the loss of their job may unravel other parts of their lives. Nonetheless, Hutchins is clear that his job is to put the good of the organization ahead of the interests of any individual. He cannot keep people who don't perform. If the company doesn't prosper, thousands of jobs will be at stake. Hutchins tries to soften the blows and help people land on their feet, but at the end of the day, he says, his responsibility is to balance his concerns and come up with the best result.

Throughout his career, Hutchins has found ways to face reality and make tough calls about people while treating them with dignity and respect. One of his favorite sayings is: "People don't care how much you know until they know how much you care." Hutchins recounted for me a couple of instances when he had the unpleasant task of easing out workers who could not handle the physical requirements of their jobs. In one instance Hutchins brought the family of a worker to the hospital to make sure they had enough of an understanding of the demands of her job. "I brought the kids in, and I let them know." Hutchins told them, "We need to do something about your mom. She physically can't keep up with the job, and it's a tough job. She's standing on her feet eight hours a day, bending, lifting. . . . Picture this. Your mom pushes this cart that weighs about thirty-five to fifty pounds, mops, bends over, picks up twenty pounds worth of garbage. What job do you have? Are you tired at the end of the day? Try doing her job all day."[23] Hutchins says that he can't keep workers who are unable to fulfill their duties, but he works with the families to find a solution so that when they leave they have a place to live and a strategy for surviving on less income.

Leading with Edge

Every so often, *FORTUNE* or some other publication produces an article listing the "Toughest Bosses in Business." Some of them are great leaders who have edge, who are tough because they know that they have to be for the good of the organization. Others are simply incompetents or jerks who substitute tyranny for leadership. The difference between them is that leaders are firmly focused on seeing reality, they respect other people and they go to great lengths to explain their actions and help others understand the difference between cruelty and edge. In company after company, leaders with true edge are valued not just by superiors but by the people working for them as well, because edge is something people want their leaders to show.

Brian Oxley, president and chief operating officer of Health Care and Management Services at ServiceMaster, once told me,

"Executives in business are like kids. They want to see if it's real or not."[24] I couldn't agree more. Everyone watches a leader very closely when a tough decision is getting made, in part because people in the organization often know that the decision needs to get made long before it even hits a leader's radar screen. By the time a leader is deciding, everyone else is waiting, watching to see what he or she will do.

Andy Grove is very clear about his responsibility to make decisions:

> Most companies don't die because they are wrong; most die because they don't commit themselves. They fritter away their momentum and their valuable resources while attempting to make a decision. The greatest danger is standing still. . . . When a company is meandering, its management staff is demoralized. When the management staff is demoralized, nothing works. Every employee feels paralyzed. This is exactly when you need to have a strong leader setting a direction. And it doesn't even have to be the best direction— just a strong, clear one.[25]

Eckhard Pfeiffer is a leader who energizes people with his edge. Pfeiffer, born in Germany and trained in finance, is not the portrait of what people consider traditionally charismatic. His speech is quiet and measured, and quite often comes out in a monotone. But he has repeatedly demonstrated edge through his quick shifting of Compaq's key strategies. He is able to do this because he is logical and fair. The result is that people are attracted to Pfeiffer, and they don't fear his decisions. Reviews and meetings with him are joint explorations. While he is known to be piercing in his investigation of issues, people who know him well cite his eagerness to learn, and they look forward to Pfeiffer's intellectual contributions. Further, when a decision is made, there is no doubt about it—Pfeiffer's resolve is legendary, which helps to create a culture of decisiveness throughout Compaq.

As tough and unpleasant as many "edge-ful" decisions are, good leaders are often able to win others over while teaching them to develop their own edge, by leading them to reach the same conclusion. At Hewlett-Packard, when Debra Dunn decided to get out of one of her businesses, she held a series of meetings. "The objective was to convey the path I was going down," she says.

> At the first meeting, I got up and took out the strategy statement from a year ago and began comparing its assumptions to the current reality. I said: "Let's revisit this. Here's the strategy we're pursuing. Here are the assumptions we're making. Here's what the market size was. What do you think the market size is now?" We felt we had to have a major partner to be successful in this business. So I asked, "Do we have any reason to think that isn't the case now? Do we have a major partner now? Do we see a major partner who we might have now?" So, we walked through every element of the strategy. I asked, what are the options here. People started saying, "Well, maybe we could partner with these guys. . . . We've got to study this more. We don't know enough."

Finally Dunn said:

> "Guys, I think if we're honest with ourselves, we know enough today to assess, with very high probability, what the likelihood of partnerships with each and every one of these people is, and none of them looks probable. . . . I know some of you think the right thing to do is to continue spending time on this. But, I am simply deciding that we are not going to do this, because we don't have time and we cannot afford to go down every theoretical path. We've got to apply some intuitive judgment here."[26]

Dunn says that half to three-quarters of the group was comfortable with her decision. The remainder really thought it was a mistake or that she wasn't committed enough to the business. So she went to talk with those people. "I said, 'You know, if you see something that I don't see, if there's information or data that you have that I don't have, then you need to give it to me. This is not a fun path to go down, but based on the world as I see it, it's what I have to do. So, help me here.'" In the end, says Dunn, there has at least "been some relief that I will just decide. There's been some, 'I don't agree with you, but I can live with you making decisions. That's your job and I'm glad you're doing it.'"[27]

Bob Hutchins at ServiceMaster is another leader who uses moments that demand edge to build teamwork and energize his people. As competitive forces struck the health care industry and cost pressures mounted early in the 1990s, it became apparent that ServiceMaster would have to become much more efficient to maintain its contract with the hospital where he was account manager. So Hutchins met with his entire staff of 150 workers and explained to them honestly, "We're going to change, and you need to change with us. And if you can't change, then we need to find another place that you'll feel comfortable in, because it's coming. I can't stop the change." He explained the economics of their situation, and pointed out that it was painful for him as well. "Look at my team. You used to see thirteen managers, now you see eight. I have the same frustrations [as you do],"[28] he told them. Then he asked for their help. The result was enough suggestions from his workers to reduce costs by 20% while increasing quality and service levels. Hutchins's honest articulation of the need for change broke down barriers. The trust and respect he showed for his workers energized them. Normally a situation like Hutchins's casts a pall over a place, with people wandering around feeling as if they had targets on their chests walking among a field of snipers. But Hutchins turned the gravity of the situation into a feeling that as a team they could meet the challenge.

Developing Edge

Edge is a key component in why companies win instead of lose in the marketplace, because more people with edge give an organization speed, boldness and energy. It is a complicated quality, though, and it must be taught carefully. This is because edge contributes to success only to the extent that it is used to carry out sound ideas, and in a way that reflects productive values. If people are encouraged to be tough indiscriminately, without regard to the validity of the purpose or the human impact, the disastrous result can be lots of people quickly, boldly and energetically making bad decisions and taking destructive actions.

Edge is a trait that is developed in the trenches throughout one's life. Leadership scholars, including Abraham Zaleznik, Eric Ericson, John Gardner and James MacGregor Burns, all have written about the importance of early childhood experiences and hardships in shaping character. Having suffered and recovered gives people a self-confidence and self-reliance that allows them to be unencumbered by the need to bend to popular will. It is this freedom that gives them the ability to make decisions based on reality, even though they may be unpopular or contrary to conventional wisdom. Debra Dunn's traumatic loss of her father and Roberto Goizueta's sudden trip from riches to rags courtesy of Castro's revolution certainly gave them a bias toward self-determination.

This doesn't mean, however, that you can't teach edge to mature adults. Perhaps to a greater extent than with the other qualities of winning leadership, an individual's personality and disposition play an important role in determining how much edge they will succeed in developing. But, like the other traits of leadership, edge can be taught or improved in just about everyone. The best way to do this is to put people in progressively more difficult situations where they have to make decisions, and then give them feedback and support. I once worked with someone who never made any decisions. He would always come to me and say, "Here are the three ways people on the team suggest doing this." So I started handing the decisions back to him. I would ask him what he thought we should do. Then I would lead him through an exploration of why his choice might or might not be the best choice. After a while, as he began to trust his own judgment and to see the positive results of his small decisions, he began making larger ones. Most organizations consciously expand people's job skills through promotions and transfers that build on their previous skills and give them an opportunity to add new ones. Winning organizations systematically develop edge in the very same way.

A good example of this is how the medical field develops its staff in emergency rooms. Triage is the basic concept that governs decisionmaking in a busy emergency room. When there are more patients than medical resources to serve them, the question is, Who gets helped and when? I did some team-building in 1976 with the staff of the Harlem Hospital emergency room in New York City. Part of my preparation was to learn about how the place operated. It turned out to be quite simple. The triage nurse is the key. She, or he, is the one who prioritizes which patients are seen when. It is the triage nurse who decides who waits in pain—mild or severe—while the staff treats heart attacks, gunshot wounds and other more serious conditions immediately. In extreme cases of war, triage nurses have to occasionally decide not to treat terminal patients in order to devote resources to people who might live. Triage only works if clear yes/no decisions are made. ER teams work with nurses closely in an apprenticeship mode. Triage nurses work first under supervision with a safety net—more experienced nurses and doctors who can correct any wrong decisions before it is too late. As the nurses are developed, they are coached on both the analytic process of making decisions and how to deal with the emotions of denying immediate care to people. As they demonstrate more and more edge, the safety nets are taken away.

In the business world, there are fewer opportunities to provide safety nets without creating bureaucratic controls. Nonetheless, businesses basically develop leaders with edge by giving people experience, coaching and then more experience. The companies I have seen do this well first take leaders and put them in positions where decisions have to be made, where success depends on setting a clear direction early. Debra Dunn, Mary Petrovich and Tom Tiller were all put in situations where they had to make decisions and redirect resources to assure the survival of their organizations. Once people are in these positions, winning companies give them a relatively long leash to make decisions and try things. When they succeed, they are given new jobs, with more responsibility and bigger tests. And when they mess up, they are given coaching and support.

A crucial element in this process is that winning leaders and winning companies use mistakes as coaching opportunities rather than causes for punishment. Treating mistakes as learning experiences, in fact, is one of the ways in which winning leaders encourage others to develop edge and take the risk of making tough decisions. The assurance that a single error, even a big one, isn't going to end their careers gives people the confidence to keep on making decisions. Of course, someone who is wrong more often than right is going to get pushed out of decisionmaking roles for everyone's good. A healthy acceptance of mistakes, however, helps would-be leaders learn not only that all decisions don't have to be right, but also that not making a decision is often worse than making a bad one.

Jack Welch says that he is a firm believer in the value of mistakes because he has made so many of them. In one instance in his early career in plastics, a Welch mistake actually resulted in the destruction of a plant (luckily, no one was hurt). But instead of firing him, GE required him to work through the consequences. Then, when Welch had learned from the experience, he was given new assignments. Welch continues to make and admit mistakes such as the purchase of Kidder Peabody, investing in factory automation and not attacking layers of bureaucracy at the company sooner. But he has a clear philosophy that such mistakes are an important learning experience. He once told several hundred of GE's most important leaders, "The idea that we were wrong is okay. ... What we have to be able to do is adapt and move and change ourselves."[29]

Edge is a difficult quality to judge from the outside because only the individual knows at the moment if he or she has a firm grasp of reality and is sincerely acting for the good of the organization. Over time, the rightness or wrongness, the pettiness or nobility, of a leader's actions will become apparent. But at the time when the decisions are made, it isn't always easy to tell the smooth-talking gamblers and charlatans from the gifted leaders. Only the individuals know for sure—which is one of the reasons that having values is so integral to having edge. The final test of edge is whether the leader can in total honesty say, "I acted when I should have. I've had the courage of my convictions."

Tying It All Together

Writing Your Leadership Story

Winning Leaders Portray the Future as an Unfolding Drama

- They tell stories that engage followers emotionally and rationally
- The stories weave together ideas, values and modes of behavior

Winners' Stories Create Scenarios for Success

- They build the case for organizational change
- They describe a winning future

Leaders' Stories Are Dynamic and Motivating

- They cast workers as protagonists who make change happen
- They guide participants to identify their own roles

Whoever authors your story authorizes your actions.[1]

—*SAM KEEN, AUTHOR AND CONTRIBUTING EDITOR TO* PSYCHOLOGY TODAY

The classic business story is much like the classic human story. There is rise and fall; the overcoming of great odds, the upholding of principles despite the cost, questions of rivalry and succession, and even the possibility of descent into madness.[2]

—*MARK HELPRIN, AUTHOR AND MEMBER OF THE BOARD OF EDITORS AT THE* WALL STREET JOURNAL

In the previous chapters, I've talked about six characteristics that define winning leaders—teaching and learning, ideas and values, energy and edge. Now it's time to wrap them all together. This brings me to what I believe is the ultimate hallmark of world-class champion leaders, which is the ability to weave all the other elements together into vibrant stories that lead their organizations into the future.

Leaders who have stories about the future are not simply leaders who have vision. Lots of management consultants have thriving businesses these days helping leaders develop "corporate visions" and holding "visioning workshops." These are valuable because an organization needs to know where it wants to be in order to act in a reasonably efficient manner to get there. But having a vision isn't enough for an organization to be a true winner, because being "reasonably efficient" is no longer enough. To be a real winner, to consistently stay ahead in today's rapidly changing world, organizations need to act quickly and decisively. This means that leaders must offer more than a vision, or a static snapshot, of where they want to be. They must also provide motivation and plans of action. Winning leaders do this by creating stories.

In his book *Leading Minds,* Howard Gardner, the noted Harvard psychologist, points out that as early as the age of five, humans understand the world through dramatic stories. Children relate to stories such as *Jack and the Beanstalk* and *The Little Engine That Could* because they feature protagonists with whom they can identify, and portray dramas of life that reflect the world around them. As people mature, their views become more complex. Nonetheless, he says, "adults never lose their sensitivity to these basic narratives." Therefore, the leader "who can draw on or exploit the universal sensitivity" to the classic storylines is the one who most often "succeeds in convincing an audience of the merits of his or her program, policy, or plan."[3]

I agree with Gardner's point that leaders who create and tell engaging human stories are better communicators than those who can't or don't. I would state even further, that the ability to create and tell certain kinds of dramatic stories is not only a useful tool, but an essential prerequisite to being a first-class winning leader.

Over the years, I have noted that there are three basic types of stories that leaders use to engage and energize others. The first of these are "who I am" stories. These are the personal stories that I talked about in Chapter 4. Leaders use these stories to describe to themselves and others their fundamental views about the world and to explain how they developed those views. These stories serve as vehicles to both communicate the leader's views and build an understanding between the leader and his or her would-be followers.

The second type of story is the "who we are" story. These stories are similar to the leader's "who I am" story, except instead of being about the personal experiences and frame of mind of the leader, they are about the joint experiences and attitudes of the people within the organization and their shared beliefs. At Nike, for example, the "who we are" stories revolve around being people who "just do it." The people at Nike see themselves as a rebel force acting more quickly and decisively than their stodgy competitors in the sportswear industry. Another group of rebels with a very different "who we are" story is the team at Southwest Airlines. Led by fun-loving Herb Kelleher, they identify themselves as people who "make travel fun and affordable." The message at both Nike and Southwest Airlines is that the people who work there are special people who have a shared history of success, and who can and will attain greater victories in the future by following their traditions. "Who we are" stories are one of the basic building blocks for creating teamwork and energizing individuals to contribute to the ongoing success of an organization.

Lots of leaders have "who I am" stories, and even more organizations have "who we are" stories. Both are essential to communicating ideas and values, and they help create the energy necessary for organizations to succeed in the competitive marketplace. But there is a third kind of story that in my experience is uniquely found among winning leaders and in winning organizations. These are what I call "future stories." Tied together, these three stories are what I call a leader's storyline. The storyline represents a consistent collection of themes. The themes start from the "who I am story." These are embodied by the leader and their followers in the "who we are" and future stories. It is this consistency that runs from a leader's personal story to the story of the future they are telling and embodying that gives the leader legitimacy.

Leadership is about change, about taking an organization or a group of people from where they are now to where they need to be. And the best way to get humans to venture into unknown terrain is to make that terrain familiar and desirable by taking them there first in their imaginations. Winning leaders create and use future stories to help people break away from the familiar present and venture boldly ahead to create a better future. They not only describe the future in terms that are personal and compelling, but they help others understand why and what they must do to get there. Without being able to do that, would-be leaders never get the sustained effort required to move toward their goal.

The winning leaders I have profiled in this book all lead through stories. Their organizations are facing different challenges, and they all have diverse cultures, but they are essentially doing the same thing, which is using their words and actions to lead others on a journey into the future. They are doing it by telling dynamic stories that cast the people in their organization as the protagonists, and then engaging them to act out those stories with a constant stream of examples, anecdotes and concrete actions.

In the previous chapters, I have repeatedly made the point that great leaders must have teachable points of view, and that they must have them in the areas of teaching, learning, generating ideas, promoting values, creating energy and displaying edge. These points of view set the direction and provide the guiding principles for the organization. But these points of view can't be just dry intellectual concepts. To be effective, leaders must bring them alive so that followers can and will act on them. This means that they must make them understood not just rationally, but emotionally. And they do this by weaving them into personal stories. The stories and the points of view are intertwined. Without the stories, the points of view are often just arid concepts. However, the stories must be solidly based in the leader's point of view. Otherwise, they are just idle entertainment that amuses and engages, but doesn't lead anyone anywhere.

Winston Churchill motivated and directed millions of people to make the enormous sacrifices necessary to win World War II by telling them stories to which they could relate personally. He definitely had teachable points of view about why Britain and the Allies had to win the war, and how they would do it strategically. But they wouldn't have been effective if he hadn't been able to drive them into the hearts of the people whose toil and sacrifice would be needed to win. So, instead of talking about geopolitical balances and military budgets, he talked about the antagonist in the story, "the German dictator . . . snatching the victuals from the table."[4] And he described Hitler as "a monster of wickedness, insatiable in his lust for blood and plunder."[5] More importantly, he told stories that depicted the painful actions that had to be taken, and that glorified the people who would take them. "We shall defend our island, whatever the cost may be. We shall fight on the beaches . . . we shall fight in the fields and in the streets. . . . "[6] "For each and for all, . . . the watchword should be, 'Carry on and dread nought,'"[7] so that "'Not in vain' may be the pride of those who have survived and the epitaph of those who fell."[8] While the oratory may seem florid to our ears today, at the time and in context, it served the very specific and important purpose of leading the British people into the future. It personalized the enemy and graphically described the consequences of inaction. It laid out courses of action that the British would need to take and behaviors they would have to display in order to defeat that enemy. And it painted them not only as victors, but as the heroes of an epic battle. In other words, Winston Churchill talked the

British people into a victorious future by telling them stories about how they could and would make the sacrifices to get there. Thanks to Winston Churchill, the British people "never, never, never, never" gave in.[9]

Martin Luther King Jr. similarly used stories of heroic future actions to engage tens of thousands of people in the struggle to attain equal rights and equal justice for black Americans. And, like Churchill, he did it by recounting the pains of the past, offering his dream of a much better future and describing how it would be achieved through the nonviolent actions of dedicated individuals. Early in the Montgomery bus boycott, King was arrested, and shortly after he was released his home was bombed. A lesser leader might have backed off at that point, but King galvanized the movement by proclaiming to the world: "I did not start this boycott. . . . I want it to be known the length and breadth of the land that if I am stopped, this movement will not stop. . . . Kill me, but know that if you do, you have fifty thousand more to kill."[10] And, he was right. When he was killed thirteen years later, the struggle continued, re-energized by the desire to fulfill the fallen leader's dream.

In business, leaders don't need heroic efforts on the order of those that Churchill and King required, but the principle is the same: They have to get people to do things that are unfamiliar and scary. And the way they do this is by dramatizing the reasons and the rewards as well as the behaviors necessary to achieve their goals.

As a student of corporate transformations and as a consultant, I have observed that all winning leaders do this, and there is a classical pattern to their stories. Some leaders deliberately map them out, while others just instinctively create them. In any event, they always cover three essential elements:

- The case for change
- Where we are going
- How we will get there

Leaders deliver these three messages through their words and their deeds. To describe this in fuller detail, I'll show you how two leaders have used stories to help transform their organizations.

Jack Welch's transformation at GE is an excellent example of a leader creating a story for the future of the organization based on the elements of his own "who am I" story. Welch loves to compete. As a child, he organized games with other kids in Salem, Massachusetts. He was captain of his hockey team in high school, ran entrepreneurial businesses within GE and continues to compete aggressively, even in his leisure time. He speaks proudly of winning the golf championship at the Sankety Head Golf Club on Nantucket. Welch is a fierce competitor. He knows what it's like to win and to lose, and he likes winning better. So in 1981, when he became CEO, he began to craft a story about making GE a winner.

From the very start, one of Welch's core business ideas was that the bloated structure GE had built over a hundred years was out of shape to deal with increasing competition. He saw that the 1980s and 1990s would be the most brutally competitive decades in business history. Emerging technologies, globalization, deregulation and other changes were stripping away any protections lumbering giants had enjoyed.

Out of this point of view, Welch began to articulate a number of core values for GE. First and foremost, he wanted a company that valued honesty and speed above procedure and bureaucracy. Having grown up in an entrepreneurial environment in GE's plastics business, Welch abhorred GE's complex systems that encouraged people only to play the system rather than play against competitors.

Welch also had a point of view about how to energize people. It was pretty simple: Winning energizes people. For that reason, he wanted to give people ownership of their businesses, and then differentiate rewards based on performance.

His point of view on edge was straightforward: Leaders get paid to make yes-or-no decisions. For Welch, that meant making unpleasant decisions about which businesses would go and which would stay. But he was clear that other leaders had to make equally tough decisions in their businesses.

Welch passionately believed all of these things, but to engage—if not arouse the passion of—GE's thousands of workers, he knew that he had to take these teachable points of view and craft a story they could buy into. When Welch became CEO, GE was a massively complex conglomerate of dozens of businesses. Revenues and earnings could be expected to grow at a very predictable 1% to 2% a year. And most people thought of this complexity and stability as a virtue. Business schools probably taught about GE more than any other company. The paradigm was that rational scientific management, devoid of passionate leadership, was the key to success.

But Welch took on this very same renowned system and used it to craft a story about why GE had to change. He explained that the complex machinery that ran GE was slowing it down. He described competitors—global and entrepreneurial—who were eating GE's lunch, because they didn't have so many controls and layers between decisionmakers and customers or suppliers. He pointed to other companies that had been successful but had now fallen on hard times, and he predicted that the same thing would happen to GE.

In telling his story, he picked apart GE's businesses and revealed weaknesses others did not see. Many businesses were living off huge order backlogs. When those ran out, where would they be? Other businesses had practically no productivity growth and no growth in new orders. To meet their operating income targets, these units were raising prices. The higher prices were causing a slow erosion of market share. When the slow erosion turned into a landslide, where would these businesses be?

Having described in graphic terms why GE had to change, Welch moved on to describing a new future for GE. It would be one in which GE would be the winningest company in the world because it would be "No. 1 or No. 2" in each of its businesses. On the emotional side, he described a new GE that would be a very different place to work. GE would be "the world's most exciting enterprise. Where ideas win. Where people flourish and grow. Where the excitement of their work lives is transferred to their whole lives." He talked about speed not just as a competitive weapon, but as an "organizational energy giver. People love speed. Think about fast cars, fast boats, fast planes. People get excited by speed. I want us to have that excitement," he said.[11]

This glorious new future, however, he told them, would require that they sacrifice the stability of the past in order to reach for the opportunities of the future. He summed up GE's competitive strategy in a one-line storyline: No. 1 or No. 2—fix, close or sell. This was revolutionary in 1981, when he first articulated it. In those days, companies were still clinging to diversification models in which they balanced the business cycle by having a number of businesses. The game was how many businesses you could have. The more you had, the more you covered the risk of the business cycle. The quality of the businesses was secondary. This old game, Welch told his people, was one that GE would no longer play.

Almost from the day he started as CEO, Welch began telling his story in actions as well as words. It would have been nice to wait for people to understand, but Welch knew he could not. Part of making people understand his story and helping them change would be to let them experience what it would be like to live in the new GE. So he took immediate actions to start transforming GE's business portfolio. In the first two years of his tenure, he bought and sold $8.5 billion worth of businesses. To simplify GE's labyrinthine bureaucracy, he created thirteen[12] global businesses. And he dismantled GE's corporate planning staff, which had engineered its complex system of reviews and appraisals. In its place, he held quarterly sessions with his business heads in order to share best practices and drive initiatives across the company.

As time went on, Welch's sophistication in describing the future became more refined. By 1985, he had a description of GE's business model that reduced the complex behemoth to one page. Using that page, Welch has described to thousands of people how the pieces of GE fit together to form a "Growth Engine" that can grow revenue and earnings at double-digit rates (unheard of for most industrial companies). The Growth Engine story became so well understood that the leaders of GE's once-antagonistic unions now use it in speeches to their memberships.

In describing how GE would get to this vision, Welch also focused on the "soft" side. For GE to be the world's most exciting enterprise, the behavior of every person in the company had to change. Welch articulated four values that he wanted to guide behavior at GE—speed, simplicity, self-confidence and stretch. He coined the term *boundarylessness,* to which many companies now aspire. And he took specific actions to bring about changes in people's behavior. GE began rating leaders on adherence to the values. These leaders were given 360-degree evaluations by bosses, peers and subordinates to measure their behavior against the values.

Welch also attacked elements of GE's bureaucracy further down in the organization. He demanded that businesses take out layers of managers. Welch knew that if GE were to succeed, it would have to use the hearts and minds of all of its employees. The best way to do that was to take complexity and layers out of the company, so that everyone could experience how the new, leaner GE would operate. He also abolished GE's uniform pay scale, so that it could pay the best and brightest people for the best and brightest performance. At every point, he explained his actions and tied them back into his basic storyline for making the company a winner.

In dismantling GE's bureaucracy, Welch created a new company, one that gets the most out of people by allowing them to create their own ideas and act on them. Welch doesn't have the same degree of control over GE that his predecessors did. But his influence is even greater, because he has developed hundreds of leaders who believe in the story for GE and are creating their own stories for where their units are going.

Welch set out to make GE the world's most competitive and exciting enterprise. Those are subjective measures that are almost impossible to judge. Objectively, however, GE is far and away the world's most valuable enterprise, with a market value in excess of $230 billion.[13] Even more compelling evidence of the effectiveness of Welch's story is the speed and nimbleness with which his gargantuan organization changes.

When Jack Welch took over at General Electric, he was like Chicken Little with a thick New England accent. But through his articulation of a consistent, credible and understandable story—and his actions to back it up—he set GE on a winning new path.

One of the most powerful things that leaders do with their stories is to give people a clear picture of what their lives will be like as the future unfolds so that they will take the actions necessary to get to the desired goal. They do this by crafting stories that feature members of the audience as the protagonists in an unfolding drama. They not only describe the organization's future, they give the audience an understanding of how they must behave and what they must do to participate in creating that future.

These stories are what Howard Gardner calls "identity stories." "Stories of identity—narratives that help individuals think about and feel who they are, where they come from, and where they are headed," says Gardner, "constitute the single most powerful weapon in the leader's arsenal."[14]

One of the best leaders I've ever met at putting individuals at the center of his story for the future is General Wayne Downing. As head of the U.S. Special Operations Forces, Downing transformed the organization, and he did it, in large part, by using vivid stories that not only explained the realities of changing world politics, but also the actions that would have to be taken by the members of his command.

Historically, the Special Operations Forces have been America's most fearsome and effective warriors. The Special Operations Command is a fairly new entity, formed as an inter-service unit in 1987 after poor administrative controls doomed a multi-service effort to rescue American hostages held by Iran.[15] But its predecessor organizations—and current subsidiary units—pro-

duced the world-famous fighters, demolition experts and sabo-
teurs of the Green Berets, the Army Rangers, the Navy SEALs
and the Delta Force anti-terrorist group. They were (mostly)
men who prided themselves as wild and fearless combatants.

By the early 1990s, however, wild and fearless combatants
were not what the U.S. needed. The world had changed abruptly.
"The gospel I preach, both internally and externally, is that the
world has changed. The Berlin Wall has gone down. . . . Everything is different, relationships are different, the needs for the
U.S. military are entirely different. We've got to change to meet
those needs," says Downing.[16] The fall of the Soviet Union and
the decline of the Eastern Bloc meant a shift in America's international position from facing a monolithic threat to facing many
regional and ethnic ones. A potentially serious war or civil upris-
ing could occur anywhere in the world, at any time and in any
form. This meant that the need for traditional military operations was diminishing, while America's international policy was
becoming increasingly complicated. The need in the future
would be for a military that could play a much wider variety of
roles in implementing American foreign policy. General Downing's job was still to produce fearsome warriors, but ones who
could serve as peacekeepers, policemen and on-the-spot diplo-
mats. At the same time, American society was becoming increasingly reluctant to tolerate the reckless, out-of-bounds personal
behavior for which many members of the Special Operations
Forces were notorious. Like corporations suddenly faced with
fierce global competition, the U.S. Special Operations Forces had
to rebuild itself to meet new demands.

To drive home the need for change, General Downing began
an intensive internal campaign. He needed to convince a corps
of historically lone-wolf Rambo types that there would be
diminishing demand in the future for people whose primary
skills were swimming, shooting, hand-to-hand combat and pur-
portedly biting the heads off snakes. The U.S. could not afford to
lose its fighting capability, but unless the Special Operations
Forces showed a more functional day-to-day utility, they would

lose resources and eventually fall into mediocrity. Like Welch, Downing took concrete actions to change things at SOF, from its training procedures to its criteria for appraising officers to the way it interacted with other government agencies. Downing, however, focused most of his energy on reaching the hearts and minds of his troops. To do that, he translated his message into graphic images and stories that no one could miss.

The future that General Downing painted for the Special Operations Forces was one in which its members would be "quiet professionals," prepared to further American policies overseas whenever, wherever and however necessary. And he brought it to life with stories about challenges that the members of the Special Operations Forces could, would and must meet. He talked in broad terms of the national interest, and how the Special Operations Forces could not fail the American people. And he talked about specific assignments in which SOF had already risen to these challenges. He talked about Haiti, where Special Operations Forces essentially administered and policed eight hundred towns for six months. "We had twelve Special Forces guys in a town of 70,000. And they made it all work," he told me admiringly. Or he would cite the peacekeeping mission in Bosnia, where U.S. Special Forces were able to work successfully with Russian paratroopers because they had "language and cultural skills, they knew all the Russian weapons, they knew how to establish rapport, they knew what the objectives of the international forces were and the rules of engagement."

The point, he told them repeatedly, was that the only thing certain about the future would be its unpredictability. There may be another conventional war someday, so the U.S. must be prepared, he told his troops. But the more likely scenarios would be confusion, uncertainty and volatile regional unrest. In these circumstances, the U.S. Special Operations Forces must be prepared to meet whatever challenges arise. They must constantly innovate in their thinking and in their training, and be ready to do whatever might be needed to carry out U.S. policy. In short, they had to be prepared to change and to change again, and to act as "'quiet professionals.' We don't want to be people who go around telling people how big and tough and bad we are," he told them. "Instead, we will just go out and do it, and people will look at us and say, 'Hey, those guys really, really are good. They can really do what they're talking about.' That is the highest form of praise."

For General Downing, the biggest challenge was helping the people of SOF figure out what their own roles would be and how to model their behavior for the future. He did this with a constant stream of stories designed to give them an image of the vital and diverse assignments they would be asked to fulfill. His message was that every member of the Special Operations Forces must be prepared to respond quickly and effectively to the unpredictable.

To bring a sense of identity, Downing insisted that every person in the command and in forward deployed units understand the unique role that Special Operations Forces play and how each of them contributes to its fulfillment. We wanted it "so a guy down there on a Special Forces A-Team could see who he was and how he fit in this [network] of organizations that was going to achieve our organizational goals. And, of course, what we wanted to get was a correlation between his personal goals, his unit goal, and our goals for the command."

Downing's stories at once excited and challenged. He would share with the troops, "We've got an essential role to play in U.S. national strategy. We do things that nobody else can do. People have extremely high expectations from us. We cannot fail. . . . The stakes are too high. Our reputations are on the line. All the hard work that's gone to getting us to where we are today can be entirely lost by one team going out and taking some rash action." But he also provided support and placed the individual SOF soldier squarely in the stories' starring roles. "It's vital to the United States that we do this. We're going to have to sacrifice. We're going to have to work together. And, oh, by the way, you guys and gals are the greatest people on the face of the earth. And this is why you are."

To explain why these troops were the best, he had story after story after story. He picked them up as he traveled the world and he told them in far-flung locales, from makeshift camps in jungles to the halls of Washington. Each story highlighted the key roles that individuals played and drove a sense of pride in being associated with SOF. They furthered his storyline that SOF could accomplish its important mission only through the actions of extraordinary individuals. The stories always drove home "the importance of their mission. And, number two, the vital role that they play in the accomplishment of that mission. You know, whether you are a captain, or you're a sergeant, or you're a corporal, what you do is important, and what you do contributes significantly."

Like Welch, Downing would tailor individual stories for each purpose and each audience. To explain to troops that Special Operations Forces are ". . . no matter where you're at or what the context is, you're an instrument of national policy," Downing would tell the story of a Special Operations Forces unit working in Africa during the summer of 1994. The fighting in Rwanda had reached a crucial point, and thousands of refugees were dying of starvation. Any rescue operations would have to be staged out of Uganda, but the Ugandan President was inclined not to get involved because of the instability it might cause in his country. At the request of the American ambassador, a Green Beret team left a joint training exercise with the Ugandan military and drove eight hours to meet him in Entebbe. The ambassador told the Green Beret commander to expect to get nowhere with the President. "Then," says Downing, "this Caucasian twenty-eight-year-old Special Forces captain walks in and greets the President of Uganda in his native tongue, tells him how happy he is to see him again [because the President has been to the training site] and immediately establishes a rapport." After some negotiation, the President agreed to help the airlift of rescue supplies through his country. Downing says proudly, "Sometimes the only access the ambassadors get with the national leadership is through our guys."

And as General Downing finished telling me this story, he launched into another and another. One of his favorites, which he says emphasizes the vital roles played by enlisted men, is about the SOF patrols that infiltrated Iraqi lines during the Gulf War. The most tense time of the Gulf War was during the Iraqi Scud missile attacks on Israel. "It was intolerable to Israel. They were going to have to do something to retaliate. They were talking about going into Iraq to stop the firings. If that happened, it probably would have fractured the coalition before the ground war had started," says Downing. The solution was small units of SOF who infiltrated behind enemy lines into western Iraq and scouted the desert, revealing the positions of mobile Scud launchers to Air Force bombers. Their work took an excruciating toll on the Iraqi Scud capability and helped convince Israel to stay out of the conflict, preserving the coalition.

A picture of one squad sits under the glass top of General Downing's desk. He often shows it to people, describing it in detail. Downing's deputy, Admiral LeMoyne, once used the photo in congressional testimony on the role of Special Operations Forces to emphasize that people are more important than hardware, and that it doesn't matter what their rank is.

The testimony brought the crowded hearing room to silence. As the lights dimmed, the image of the patrol was projected onto a screen for the Senate panel and spectators to see. Admiral LeMoyne began telling the story of the picture of this squad behind enemy lines.

There are 11 men on that patrol. . . . They are some 200 miles from the nearest friendly positions. . . . They are heavily clothed, because it is cold in Iraq in January. That patrol was our most successful reconnaissance patrol. It was behind Iraqi lines for 22 days. It gave us invaluable information on Iraqi strategic launching systems, on their lines of communication, on the disposition of their forces. The Iraqis knew they were there, and the Iraqis actively looked for them. At one point they were within 1900 meters of the patrol, but the patrol was never found. The patrol never fired a weapon. They were successfully extracted and brought back home.

The point, the patrol leader . . . was an army sergeant major. It was a patrol of sergeants [with no commissioned officers]. They are emblematic of what Special Operations is today. They are professional. They are dedicated. They are people of integrity and great determination. They best represent our motto for Special Operations—"Quiet Professionals."[17]

Downing's stories are diverse, but like Welch's, they all serve the same goal of taking people into the future by describing it in a way that is clear, consistent and emotionally engaging. Leaders sometimes have seemingly zany visions, and often set impossible targets and demand incredible performance. But in order to win, organizations must take risks and be willing to break with the past and undergo wrenching change. Therefore, leaders must offer people a sense of why and how they will get from where they are to where they need to be in the future. And the best ones do it by telling, in both words and actions, interesting, engaging, inspiring stories.

Crafting a Leadership Story

At GE and SOF, Jack Welch and General Downing created stories to bring about transformations that they had already mapped out conceptually in their own minds. At Royal Dutch/Shell, the company's leaders are approaching the process from the other end. They are using the creation of the story as a means for designing the transformation.

The Anglo-Dutch oil and chemical producer has long been one of the largest and most powerful companies in the world. In 1994, however, its leadership team saw several signs that the company needed to make some serious changes. While Royal Dutch/Shell's profits of $6.2 billion and market value of more than $100 billion ranked number one in the world, its return on assets was a meager 6.53%.[18] It was not making the cost of capital on many of its investments. And competitors such as Exxon were getting better margins in a number of key businesses.

Royal Dutch/Shell's management structure is unusual in that instead of a CEO, it has a Committee of Managing Directors (CMD), four in 1995, five in 1997. So the formulation of the transformation plan and story had to be a group process. But, in fact, all good organizations are run through teamwork. So the story-creation/transformation planning process that Royal Dutch/Shell used is one that can be put to good use by many other companies as well.

The first problem that faced the CMD was that while they knew they needed to change, they had no clear handle on where they wanted to get, and certainly no plan for getting there. So, with a team of consultants, they set out in 1995 to essentially write themselves into the future. They would create a future story for Royal Dutch/Shell, and in the process design a transformation. The team of consultants included me; Michael Brimm, a professor from the Institute for European Business Administration (INSEAD) in Fontainebleau, France; and Patricia Stacey and Phil Mirvis, two independent consultants. The four members of the CMD at the time were Cor Herkstroter, John Jennings, Mark Moody-Stuart and Maartin van den Berg.

At the first meeting, we spent a day and a half analyzing the company, strategically, financially and culturally. Then, on the second afternoon, I handed each of them a mocked-up cover of the *Economist* magazine dated four years in the future—July 1999. The title proclaimed in bold color, "The Transformed Shell." Inside were blank pages. I asked each of the CMD members to spend an hour writing his version of the story of Shell's journey from 1995 to 1999. I gave them a list of topics that their stories should cover. What would Shell look like in 1999? What would be its sales, net income and market value? What businesses would it be in, and what businesses would it have divested? What would the culture be like? How would employees and others perceive the company? And how would the changes have come about? At the end of the hour, the CMD members read the articles out loud to each other. They had each focused on different things, but they also had many things in common. They had a beginning.

The case for change was the clearest element of the story. Each of them noted the company's sluggish performance relative to competitors on margins and return on capital. Several also noted that Shell's culture seemed to have gone awry. The company was proud of its technical accomplishments such as deep-sea oil exploration, but it paid little attention to commercial opportunities. It wasn't generating innovative new business ideas. A company that had once embodied the spirit of pioneering and daring entrepreneurs was now driven by a civil service entitlement mentality.

The story of the future was fuzzier. The CMD members knew they wanted Shell to regain its commercial, entrepreneurial spirit. They wanted it to be known not just for technology but also for superior leadership and management throughout the company. They could describe in some detail how big they wanted the company to be, and what businesses it should be in. However, describing exactly how Shell would get there proved harder. After several hours of dissecting the articles, the CMD came up with a list of common themes and a list of disagreements. They also decided that while they worked out the details of the story, they would also start involving other people.

Over the next several months, the CMD members met individually with several hundred other leaders throughout the company. They tried out the story, telling it, listening to others' responses and refining it. Then, in October 1995, the CMD called together fifty of Royal Dutch/Shell's top leaders in an old church that had been converted to a conference facility. The customary beginning to a meeting like this at Shell is for Herkstroter to give a speech. This time, however, he did something different. He stood up and instructed each of the fifty people to take out a piece of paper and write a letter resigning from the "Old Shell." Each letter, which would detail what was wrong with the "old" company, would help build the storyline from the past to the future. The exercise also prodded each of these key executives—many of them twenty-five-year veterans who had helped build the company—to come to grips with the urgent need to change. At the end of twenty minutes, they divided into four groups and read the letters out loud.

During the next three days, the fifty leaders worked on fleshing out the case for change, designing the "New Shell" and figuring out how the company would get there. They created a series of catchphrases, including "breakthrough performance," "top performer of first choice," "energized leadership" and "unleashing talent at all levels." Then, for each of these phrases, they filled in the details of what it meant and how it would be achieved. They described, among other things, how behaviors of individuals at the company would have to change from a painstaking focus on consensus to one of individual initiative.

With the story of the New Shell taking shape, the CMD and its senior leadership began to enroll more and more people. In 1996 and 1997, they created a portfolio of action learning programs to drive the Shell transformation. In one of the programs, called "Value Creation," the CMD identified key strategic initiatives for the company and then assigned younger managers to help solve the problems. Over a six-month period, these young leaders would meet with the CMD and then come up with real, implementable solutions. The issues they faced included such things as how to reposition the Shell brand worldwide and achieving cost leadership in the industry.

In order to push the story deeper into the organization, the CMD also named ten highly regarded young executives to form a Leadership and Performance (LEAP) team. Under the leadership of Mac MacDonald, their assignment was to develop leaders throughout Shell—to give them the financial, managerial and leadership skills to reinvent their businesses in line with a new Shell Business Framework that had been designed with the help of Professor Larry Selden of the Columbia University Business School.

The LEAP team chose as their vehicle helping leaders to develop stories. The LEAP team puts people through an intense process of examining their own experiences and teachable points of view. As a model for fashioning their own stories, CMD member Steve Miller (who was added as a fifth member in 1996) appears at every workshop to talk about his experiences and points of view. Then they help people marry their own learning to the Shell business framework to come up with stories and action plans for transforming their units.

As part of this process, the managers are then sent back to their work units to tell their story and launch projects to make it come alive and produce results. In Argentina, for example, a team resegmented the customer base, and then initiated a plan to offer totally new services such as fleet management services for taxi companies. They also began focusing on new product offerings and improving their marketing of snacks and beverages. Through this process, 20,000 people will be actively engaged in living out the new Shell story.

Herkstroter is clear that the Shell story is still being crafted and revised and that there is a long way to go, but he feels that it is the key to transforming the company. The story, according to Herkstroter, "reflects aspirations we know we may not currently live up to in every case, but which we feel certain we should be aiming towards. Where we fall short, I recognize the temptation to dismiss the messages, but I believe people in Shell will want to respond constructively and work together to close the gaps."[19] Even though the transformation is still in its early stages, the story of the New Shell has been a powerful way to mobilize action.

Stories are a powerful tool for engaging people emotionally and intellectually and for leading them into the future. And the best leaders use them to do exactly that. As I have stated repeatedly in earlier chapters, successful leaders must have teachable points of view about ideas, values, energy and edge. It is through stories, however, that they tie them together and teach and energize others to move from the present into a winning future.

Conclusion

Leading into the Future

Winning Leadership Is About Building for the Future

- In the short term, leaders prepare organizations to respond to change
- For the long term, they create organizations that can sustain success

Success Is Achieved by Developing Other Leaders

- Companies with the most leaders are the most agile and effective
- The legacy of winning leaders is other winning leaders

The Best Leaders Know When It's Time to Leave

- They don't hang on when it's time for the next generation to take over
- They exit cleanly and let the new leaders lead

In a very real sense, the future is what winning leadership is really all about. It is about building an organization that responds to customers' demands today, and is able to do so again tomorrow and the next day. This means that winning leaders are constantly looking ahead. For the short term, they watch the horizon to spot impending changes in the marketplace so they can develop ideas and structures that will allow the organization to respond efficiently and effectively. More importantly, for the longer term, it means that they prepare their organizations to continue to thrive beyond the foreseeable future. Both of these activities require developing the leadership abilities of others.

The truth is that the world is changing so quickly that even though leaders may be able to spot and prepare for broad economic and industry shifts, responding efficiently to the nitty-gritty demands of the moment requires lots of people at all levels with the ideas, values, energy and edge to make decisions and to act quickly and appropriately. For the long term, it means preparing a next generation of leaders who will, in turn, develop the next generation. And ultimately, it means letting go and allowing those leaders to lead into the future.

What all of this boils down to is stewardship. Winning leaders understand that their job is to take the human capital, the most important asset of their institution, and make it more valuable for tomorrow's world. And they do this by teaching. They impart the content of their solid business ideas and strong values. They have teachable points of view that allow them to show people how to develop their own ideas and values, and to find the energy and edge to implement them. And they engender in others the desire and the ability to develop other people who will have ideas, values, energy and edge.

After a leader has left the organization, Wall Street and other outside observers may remember him or her for whether he or she made or lost $1 billion or quintupled the stock price. But profits and stock prices are just the measurement of a job done well or poorly. The core competence for sustained excellent performance is developing the leadership skills and talents of others. Larry Bossidy had it exactly right when he said that if you are a winning leader, "what you will remember is how many people you developed."[1]

There are some companies where coaching, mentoring and leadership development is deeply embedded in their genetic code. These include such "academy" companies as Procter & Gamble, Hewlett-Packard, Intel and GE, whose "graduates" routinely go on to other companies, carrying the genetic material with them. Glenn Hiner, John Trani and Larry Bossidy have taken their General Electric genes and begun replicating them at Owens Corning, Stanley Works and AlliedSignal. Many of the founders and leaders at Silicon Valley start-ups are replicating the development processes sired at Hewlett-Packard and Intel. These academy companies make a proven ability to develop others an explicit part of the promotions process. These are in contrast to the losing companies where I have met CEOs who can't name a single leader they have developed.

Creating an Organization Where Leaders Develop Leaders

While some executives don't develop leaders, I believe that most can. It requires, however, a strong commitment. A leader who aspires to be a winning teacher organizes every meeting, makes every decision and designs every organizational structure with developing others in mind. For winning leaders, teaching is not a now-and-then or sideline activity. It is *how* they lead and at the heart of everything they do.

There are no cookie-cutter rules for building a company where leaders develop leaders, but there are some general guidelines that I have developed from watching organizations that have done it well. If you think of these organizations as consisting of the technical, political and cultural systems that I described in Chapter 2, you can spot the elements.

Technically, leaders create systems that encourage, reward and support leaders developing leaders at all levels. It's why Larry Bossidy at AlliedSignal and Gary Wendt at GE Capital developed corporate structures that give lots of people responsibility for running their own businesses, and why the Special Operations Forces turns its best and brightest into instructors.

Politically, it means making sure the guns are pointed out. Many executives have trouble turning the competitiveness of their teams toward competitors. But to have leaders develop leaders, people can't see life as a zero-sum game. Senior leaders have to convince people that developing leaders is good for them in the short and long term. They do this first of all by developing a teachable point of view about why a system of leaders developing leaders is good for the company. Without this, no one will believe their commitment, and any attempts to energize the rest of the organization will seem like "flavor-of-the-month" cheerleading events. Developing leaders requires the energy and the determination of everyone in the organization. So, the first task of the leader is to motivate and excite them to join in the effort. And then the leader must back up his or her words with actions that reward people based on the totality of their contribution, not just their quarterly results. At GE, many people ignored Jack Welch's message about the need to develop others until he started stripping power from those who did not do so. At Intel, Andy Grove makes the point by including developing others in the criteria for managers' bonuses.

In the cultural arena, winning leaders create norms that make developing other leaders an essential part of everyone's job. They do this by personally role-modeling it, as Roger Enrico and Admiral Ray Smith do, and by holding up others who do so as models. At HP, for example, the founders, Bill Hewlett and Dave Packard, are remembered in corporate lore more for being great teachers than for being savvy businessmen and engineers. Building such a culture creates a mindset that developing others is what leaders do.

Finally, winning leaders actively use their companies' human resource management systems to promote the development of leaders. At many companies, the human resources department is relegated to the role of just a bothersome necessity. But the leaders of winning companies such as GE, and PepsiCo have created human resources departments with the specific assignment of designing and implementing a leadership development strategy. Headed by a respected member of senior management, these departments are charged with maintaining pipelines of leaders from new hires to the CEO. These detailed development plans not only assure that the company has the leaders it needs at every level, but that employees are given assignments and opportunities that will expand their leadership abilities.

Paradox of Short Term/Long Term

It is important to note that all of this focus on the future takes no pressure off of winning today. Mastery of the paradox of short term versus long term is essential to winning leadership. The Andy Groves, Roberto Goizuetas and Jack Welches of the world laugh at as naive the debates among business academics and journalists who often bemoan the short-sighted quarterly earnings focus of Wall Street. Welch dealt with the issue at a Harvard Business School gathering in 1986 by responding: "That argument is nonsense. As leaders, we get paid to win in the short term and make sure that we are stronger in the long term." He went on to talk about investing for the future, and about GE's Crotonville Executive Training Institute, whose leadership development activities he sees as an important twenty-first-century strength builder. This is why leaders whose only tool is cutting jobs do not make it as leaders in my book. They are not long-term generators of value. They clearly are short-term, run-the-stock-price-up-by-slashing-and-burning, non-world-class opportunists.

This long-term/short-term paradox manifests itself in a number of ways, including its requirement that leaders let go of some of their own ego needs to allow others to grow and ultimately take over the reins of the organization. While winning leaders must have strong ideas and solid values, and the energy and edge to pursue them relentlessly, they must also be able to teach, to listen to others and to let them lead as well. This requires that they be strong and vulnerable at the same time. They must have strong beliefs, but they must hold them loosely. They must be strong enough to not fear vulnerability. They must be willing to take the risks of pursuing their firmly held beliefs, understanding that they will not always be on the mark, and will sometimes fail. And if they want to be truly effective teachers, they must be willing to share their struggles and doubts, in order to impart a real understanding of leadership to their students and followers. In other words, they not only have to be able to get others to let go of the present in order to get to a winning future, but they must also be able to do it themselves. They risk their own images of strength and infallibility in order to help others develop their own strengths.

Let me remind readers of the courageous behavior of the late Michael Walsh of Tenneco, who died of a brain tumor. He told me once that when he was diagnosed he "could have sat on a rock and died," but that as he reflected, "I realized that I viewed myself as a CEO, the company was in a radical transformation being led by me, and that I was still functioning well."[2] So he decided to openly share everything with the board. He told them he wanted to continue to lead as long as they saw that he was fit, and that his doctors would share everything with the board to help them monitor the situation. He then used his remaining years to reintensify his efforts at developing others, using his own impending death as a lever for action.

The need to be vulnerable presents a huge psychological problem for most people. To invest in the generative—and generous—process of developing others while living in a competitive world requires a well-balanced person without a lot of ego problems, unresolved power needs and conflicted feelings about his or her own competence. For the psychologically challenged, success is tied to self-aggrandizement, power for the sake of power and stepping on others as a means to an end. For our psychologically fit winners, it means being comfortable with admitting and addressing inadequacies as well as capitalizing on strengths.

No Time-Outs: Simultaneous Transformation and Succession

Now that we have entered the twenty-first century, it is clear that to be winners, companies must master revolutionary change with enthusiasm. CEO leadership changes have taken place at GE,

IBM, 3M, HomeDepot, Honeywell, Coca-Cola, and PepsiCo as well as scores of other companies. These transitions have not all been smooth because of a failure to build a leadership engine in many of these supposed blue chip companies. For Merck, Kodak, HP, 3M, Home Depot, AT&T, and IBM to have all had to hire outside CEO's is the ultimate measure of a failed leadership pipeline. Some, like GE, PepsiCo, and Wal Mart, clearly had strong leadership pipelines and were able to transition to new leadership without slowing the momentum of continuous transformation.

Succession is not just a CEO concern. Leaders at all levels of the organization live in a world of constant change. They have no "time-outs" to stop changing while they groom other leaders. They must figure out how to use constant change to simultaneously develop other leaders. Our leaders in the middle of the organization must be taught to both lead change and groom other leaders. It is the responsibility of the top group of leadership to teach and reward both successful transformation and successful development of leaders.

Bill Weiss has perhaps set the standard for simultaneous transformation and succession. In his last three years as CEO of Ameritech, he undertook to radically transform the company from a regulated telephone monopoly into a competitive telecommunications provider, and at the same time he developed and selected his successor. In fact, he used the transformation as a vehicle to select and groom the successor.

Transitions: Continuity Through Letting Go

The ultimate test of a leader's commitment to the future comes at the end of his or her career, when it is time to retire and get out of the way. They may have spent a lifetime developing others to be leaders, but when the time comes to move on and let others lead, can they do it? Do they have the edge to make the tough call that takes them out of the game? The winners do. They care enough about the future and have sufficient confidence in the success of their teaching that they step aside and let the next generation of leaders take over.

This letting go in succession is very difficult for most leaders. But they must do it. It's the final paradox that in order to remain winners, organizations must improve continuously, and the only way they can do that is by having smooth, clean transitions from one generation of leaders to the next. If the new leader has to worry about pleasing and being second-guessed by the old one, he or she isn't free to lead by his or her own best instincts. So the strongest and best leaders, the ones most committed to the future of the organization, leave it when their time is up. This is why Bill Weiss left the Ameritech board when he stepped down as CEO in 1994. The new CEO, Dick Notebaert, was only forty-seven years old and the company was undergoing massive changes. But Weiss knew that in order for those changes to continue, they would have to be made according to Notebaert's script. Weiss had coached Notebaert, mentored him and taught him everything he could. Now he had to get out of the way and entrust the future to Notebaert.

The companies that compromise and don't make clean transitions have huge leadership problems as a result. IBM's decline under John Akers was not all his fault. How could he make the necessary changes and cast aside the structures and practices held dear by previous leaders when his board included retired CEOs John Opel, Frank Cary and Tom Watson Jr. Roger Smith's presence on the GM board likewise added to Bob Stempel's woes. The only exception that comes to mind, where a retired CEO has actually added value, is at ServiceMaster, where Bill Pollard remained as chairman and a supportive partner to CEO Carlos Cantu.

Jack Welch framed this issue for himself and GE at an annual general managers' meeting by saying his biggest challenge as a leader was "helping make GE younger every day while [he and others] get older."[3] He knew that his assignment in the next three years was to coach and select his successor while continuing the transformation of GE. The good news at GE is that its governance process mandates that retiring CEOs leave the board.

Welch turned GE over to now CEO Jeff Immelt, who won out over Jim McNerney, who became CEO of 3M, and Bob Nardelli, who became CEO of Home Depot. Not only did GE have an internal successor, but three finalists from a pool of as many as ten at the beginning of the decade prior to Welch's retirement. GE's emphasis on leaders at all levels developing other leaders not only provided the bench strength for GE but has provided the pool of CEO talent for many other companies. Tom Tiller left GE to become CEO of Polaris, and Gary Wendt is CEO of Conseco, to name two of our leaders in this book.

In short, as the subtitle of this book states, winning leaders build winning organizations by developing other leaders. It is only by combining the strengths of everyone in the organization and helping them to work to his or her best ability that organizations can win in the marketplace today. And it is only by teaching them to, in turn, develop other leaders that success can be sustained into the future.

I started this book with a story about Roger Enrico and how he shaped the future of PepsiCo by personally teaching others in the company to be leaders. He successfully turned over the CEO role to Steve Reinemund. In the later chapters, I focused on other winning leaders to illustrate specific traits of winning leadership. I talked about how Tom Tiller and Gary Wendt of GE, Roberto Goizueta of Coca-Cola and Debra Dunn of Hewlett-Packard have incorporated lessons from their pasts into teachable points of view about leadership. I used Larry Bossidy of AlliedSignal (now Honeywell) as the lead example in the chapter about the importance of having clear business ideas. Marion Wade and Bill Pollard of ServiceMaster were the role models in the chapter on building organizations with strong values. To illustrate how winning leaders turn negative energy into positive energy, I again talked about GE's Tom Tiller (now CEO of Polaris), and I introduced Father Bill Cunningham and Eleanor Josaitis of Focus: HOPE, who also served as the exemplars in the edge chapter. Throughout, I have cited examples of a number of other winning leaders, including Bill Weiss and Dick Notebaert, formerly of Ameritech (Notebaert is now CEO of Tellabs), Jack Welch of GE, Eckhard Pfeiffer of Compaq, Lew Platt at Hewlett-Packard, Andy Grove at Intel and Bob Knowling at U S WEST (now CEO of Internet Access, Technologies).

None of these people is the perfect leader. They are all take-charge individuals who on occasion step in and do things themselves when it might be better to let someone else learn from the experience. They are not always instantly clear and totally articulate about what they are doing and why they are doing it. Sometimes they're even too nice and gentle to people in situations when exercising edge and kicking ass might be more appropriate. They all have their stronger and weaker points. But they are all winning leaders because they understand the complex demands of their jobs and take all of them seriously. They have strong business ideas and operate their organizations according to deeply held values. They consciously build and channel the energy of their employees. They face reality and are willing to make tough decisions. And, most importantly, they are conscientious learners and teachers, dedicated to developing everyone in their organizations to be learners and teachers as well.

The Leadership Engine: A Teachable Point of View

A Leader's Teachable Point of View

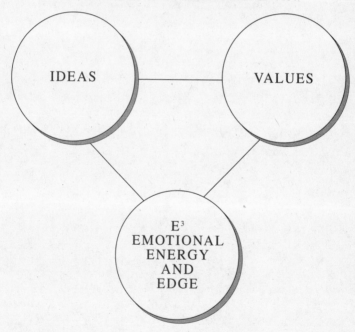

Introduction

The Leadership Engine: A Teachable Point of View

Organizations that have a Leadership Engine win because they have leaders at every level who teach others to be leaders. Teaching and learning are at the heart of these organizations.

In *The Leadership Engine: How Winning Companies Build Leaders at Every Level*, I have described the basic building blocks of leadership. Leaders have these building blocks and they teach others so that they have them too.

- Learn from experience;
- Develop teachable points of view about both how to build and run a business and how to develop other leaders;
- Generate sound ideas for how the business will add value and succeed in the marketplace;
- Instill values that help the organization reach its goals;
- Create positive emotional energy;
- Make tough decisions; and
- Pull all the other elements together into vibrant stories that motivate others to reach for a better future.

There are no simple recipes for teaching or learning any of these abilities. In this handbook, however, you will find some assessment tools, practical exercises and methodologies that can help you improve your own leadership abilities, teach others to

*We are grateful for the important substantive contributions of Chris DeRose to this handbook.

improve theirs and build a Leadership Engine that will put your organization on the road to a winning future.

I have worked with many executives who have found these exercises useful. After you work with them, you may want to have your team do the same thing, either in a group or individually. This handbook is not going to provide the answers. It will help you to better develop your point of view and the leadership needed to make your company a winner.

The Pinnacle: Profound Teaching Requires Commitment

True learning takes place when the leader/teacher invests the time and the emotional energy to engage those around him or her in a dialogue that produces mutual understanding. Autocrats can command behaviors by issuing orders. But developing an organization of genuine leaders who will continue to teach others requires a serious commitment to teaching.

Figure 1 presents my way of thinking about the importance of leaders teaching leadership. It is the basis of long-term organizational success because it ensures that a company will have a supply of leaders who have developed their points of view and are ready to act on them. By forcing new leaders to constantly teach and learn, this way of teaching leadership renews a company. There are four critical factors to consider:

1: Depth of Learning
The depth of learning that occurs both for the leader and the follower varies significantly depending upon the leader's approach. At the most superficial level, a command-and-control leader does not create much learning for him/herself or the follower. At the other end of the spectrum, both the leaders and the followers learn from each other.

2: Commitment
Commitment is another critical factor. Teaching entails a serious commitment on the part of the leader to nurture individuals and a serious commitment on the part of the followers to wrestle with the teacher's point of view and develop their own.

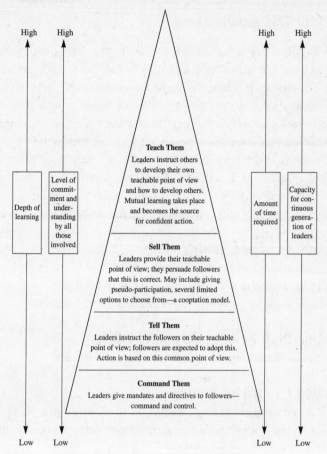

Figure 1: Approaches to Leading and Teaching

3: Time

It takes little time to command and much time to teach.

4: Continuous Generation of Leaders

When there is genuine teaching, a positive cycle is created. Learners have developed their own points of view and are energized to help others as they have been helped. They consequently make good teachers. By contrast, the command model launches cycles that range from blind obedience to open revolt.

Plan for This Handbook

This handbook is aimed at getting you to the top of the pyramid and helping you develop a Leadership Engine in your organization. The first step is to develop your own teachable point of view and work to improve your own leadership abilities. After that, you have to work to develop others and make sure that they are, in turn, developing even more people in your organization.

Sections II through IX of this book will help you assess and improve your own leadership. Sections X and XI will help you think about how you will teach other leaders. The last section encourages you to take a first step and move forward.

Section II: Facing Reality
- Look at the hand you have been dealt
- Ground your teachable point of view in reality
- Evaluate your own capacity as a leader and teacher

Section III: A Point of View Isn't Enough
- Provide a baseline of your teachable point of view

Section IV: Past as Prologue
- Recognize the learning that has occurred over your lifetime
- Use your experiences consciously as opportunities to build your teachable point of view
- Focus on lessons from the experiences that had the greatest impact on you—those that had an emotional effect

Section V: Winning Ideas
- Recognize the requirements for leaders to bring central ideas to their business
- Analyze the shift needed in the central ideas for your business
- Translate these ideas into actions
- Summarize your teachable point of view on ideas

Section VI: Values in Action

- Understand the connection between values and ideas
- Articulate the values that reinforce and support the business ideas
- Practice delivering your own message about what values it will take to win

Section VII: Energizing the Organization

- Establish the role of energy in leadership
- Develop a framework for maintaining your own energy and energizing others

Section VIII: Edge

- Understand the role of edge in leadership
- Examine the difficult people and portfolio decisions facing your business
- Develop your point of view on when and how to make the tough calls

Section IX: Creating Your Storyline

- Use personalized stories to communicate your teachable point of view
- Write the storyline for where your organization is going and how it will change

Section X: Encouraging Leaders to Develop Others

- Examine the systems that can be used to encourage leaders developing leaders

Section XI: Building the Teaching Organization

- Examine your organization's pipeline for developing future leaders
- Assess the tools that can be used for development
- Create a personalized process to lead and teach your own people

Section XII: It's Up to You

- Demonstrate your commitment by taking the first step

Facing Reality

Objectives:

- Look at the hand you have been dealt
- Ground your teachable point of view in reality
- Evaluate your own capacity as a leader and teacher

The first step to becoming a better leader and building a better organization is facing the reality of where you and the organization are now.

You may think that you already know. At General Electric, when Jack Welch became CEO in 1981, it appeared to many people that the company was doing well. It was the toast of management pundits. Reg Jones, Welch's predecessor as CEO, was one of the world's most respected businessmen. The company had dozens of Harvard Business School cases written about it. It had a strong balance sheet, and healthy earnings that could be expected to grow predictably for as long as anyone cared to think about. But when Welch took an unblinking look, the reality turned out to be much more grim. While many GE units were shipping lots of products out the door, they were running on backlogs. A significant number of its businesses were mired in mediocrity. And the ones in a position to become strong winners were being stifled by the bureaucracy. From this reality, Welch was able to draw up a plan for making GE a much stronger organization.

At Compaq in 1991, Eckhard Pfeiffer similarly assessed his

company's strategic situation and decided that immediate action was needed at a time when many others believed that gradual change would solve the company's problems. Because he was willing to face the hard cold facts about the company's dire position, he was able to take the necessary actions in time to save the day.

To start out, therefore, you must make an honest assessment of reality. Start with the hard issues—How is the company performing financially? Should investors be happy, sad or indifferent to own the company? Then look at the softer issues—How does leadership function in the company? How prepared are you to lead and to teach?

The realities for each person and each organization will be different, and the assessment won't provide any immediate answers about what to do. You must, however, make sure that you know where the starting line is if you want to be in the race.

Reality #1: Performance

For publicly traded companies, the capital markets provide an excellent yardstick. A stock price that is rising faster than other comparable companies indicates not only that you are doing well, but that investors believe that you will continue to do well. A stock price that is sagging or rising slower than competitors indicates the opposite, that investors are losing faith in you. Fashions and fads can sweep Wall Street, but over time, the market will give you the most objective evaluation of your performance.

Wall Street is really a reflection of future expectations. Based on your past performance and your plans for the future, analysts and investors assign a value to your stock. If your company demonstrates the ability to increase future earnings or pay more in dividends, your stock price rises, and investors benefit. This drives total return, the profits that investors make by owning your stock. Investors want companies capable of creating long-term value, and companies do this by growing and by being operationally efficient.

YOUR PERFORMANCE REALITY

Take a moment to record the total return to your investors over the last five years. Compare it to some indices such as an index of your competitors, the Dow Jones, and the Standard & Poor's 500 (smaller companies can use the Russell 2000) index. If you don't have the information, many sources such as Bloomberg Financial Markets and S&P have these statistics, and *Business Week* prints annual performance rankings that may help. All of these are available at most public and company libraries.

Total Shareholder Return	1992	1993	1994	1995	1996	Total 5-Year Return
Your company						
Dow Jones Industrial Average	7.41%	16.90%	5.05%	36.72%	28.62%	84.73%
S&P 500 Index	7.61%	10.02%	1.36%	37.45%	22.90%	71.21%

Notes: Total Return includes dividends reinvested. Source: Bloomberg Financial Markets, Total Return Analysis.

What are the implications for your company?

_____

_____

_____

_____

To understand why your stock has performed the way it has, look deeper into your historical and projected performance. Growth in your "top line," revenue from sales, shows that customers are increasingly valuing your products or that you are selling to more people. But many companies grow their costs as quickly as their sales, so they don't profit. Growth in your "bottom line," or net income, reflects your operational efficiency. What are the trends in both your top- and bottom-line growth?

	1995	1996	(projected) 1997	(projected) 1998	(projected) 1999	(projected) 2000
Top line (Sales)						
Bottom line (Net income)						

What are the implications for your company?

_____

_____

_____

_____

Reality #2: The Organization

While Wall Street and the outside world look at results, it's the leader's job to ensure that those results keep improving. The keys to delivering hard performance are soft issues. How well people can face reality, how well people learn, how willing they are to make decisions and how energized they are to act are all determinants of how well a company will do in the marketplace. These "soft" items come from the leadership of the company, which sets the tone and influences behavior.

For a company to develop the soft elements of a winner, it must have leaders with proven track records develop other leaders. This requires a serious commitment from both learners and teachers. I find that most companies, even when they can identify star performers with great track records, do not do enough to encourage them to teach others. The companies that have a Leadership Engine make teaching an explicit part of leadership. Everything at the company is geared to building leaders at all levels. Those leaders then drive results.

Figure 2 shows the human resource systems that can be strategically utilized to encourage leader development. Traditionally, these HR systems have been used only to develop and

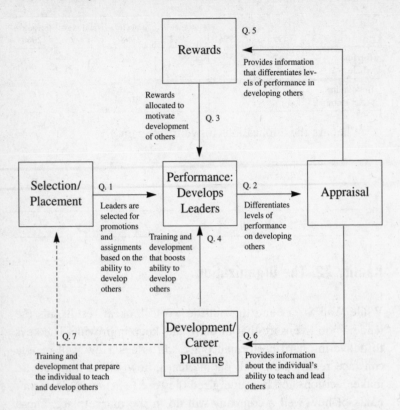

Source: Steward Friedman, Noel Tichy, and Dave Ulrich, "Strategic Human Resource Management at Honeywell, Inc." in *Strategic Human Resource Management* (New York: Wiley, 1984).

Figure 2: Encouraging Leaders to Develop Others

motivate individual performance and development. By tying these to how well people in a company develop others, an organization can provide large-scale systems for leader development and build consistency in organizational beliefs, norms and values.

YOUR ORGANIZATION'S LEADERSHIP REALITY

Take a moment to assess how well your organization encourages leaders developing leaders. In the space below, I have recorded the various elements that can encourage leaders to develop others. Circle the score that shows how often your organization encourages leaders to develop other leaders.

		Never		Sometimes		Always
1. Selection/ Placement	In our company, leaders are selected for promotions and assignments based on their ability to develop others	1	2	3 4		5
2. Appraisal	We assess and differentiate levels of performance for how well people develop other leaders	1	2	3 4		5
3. Rewards	Rewards are allocated to motivate people to develop other leaders	1	2	3 4		5
4. Development/ Career planning	Training and development boosts people's ability to develop other leaders	1	2	3 4		5
5. Development/ Career planning	Our development and career planning provides information about an individual's ability to teach and lead others	1	2	3 4		5
6. Transition to new roles	When people are selected for a new position, they receive training and development that prepares them to teach and lead in their new role	1	2	3 4		5

If you circled 1's for each of these questions, you are not in a company where leaders develop other leaders—or if they do, they do so in spite of the company. In the past, some successful companies such as IBM or Westinghouse have lost focus on how to develop leaders. So they decided to outsource the development of their leaders to consultants and executive programs. If you scored a 5, you are probably in an organization with a Leadership Engine—where leadership at all levels is valued and leaders make it an important part of their mission to develop other leaders. Companies like GE and Intel and the United States Special Operations Forces are great examples. In these organizations, leaders are encouraged to teach and are rewarded for it.

Consider your scores and write the implications for your organization below.

_____

_____

_____

_____

_____

Preparing to Teach Others

Whatever the organizational forces might be, you still have to assess your own personal readiness to teach other leaders. To do this requires, in my opinion, several characteristics. One is having a teachable point of view—beliefs in what will make you win today and the principles for running and growing a business into tomorrow—that can be clearly communicated. The other requirements are an intense commitment to development, the willingness to be a vulnerable role model and the ability to personally coach and mentor. Consider the case of Jack Welch of GE.

Welch is lauded for his business principles, his financial acumen and his clear, succinct story of where GE was going. But what people don't realize is that Welch is a great teacher. He coached dozens of GE's most important executives in his everyday interactions with them. He went to GE's Crotonville Executive Development Center every two weeks and didn't miss a session in his many years as chairman.

When Welch was there he was the epitome of a leader who developed other leaders. He got into free-ranging discussions. He jousted with participants and tested their thinking. And he was vulnerable enough to show that he did not have all the answers. All this led to a great learning environment where everyone, including Welch, was excited about learning from each other.

Below is a note that Welch sent to participants in GE's Executive Development Course in September 1996. If you read the letter, you'll see that Welch is straightforward about his intent for the discussion he is about to have with a group of employees—he wants to have a fun, exciting session, talking about the important issues at GE. He is going to expose them to a level of thinking that gets them ready to move to the next level of leadership at GE: thinking about the whole business; what values and performance make for great, good, and average employees; and challenging them to think about what they would do differently if they were CEO. An observer once described Welch at these sessions as more of a Phil Donahue character than a senior executive because he runs around with the microphone, whipping up people's emotions and facilitating their discussion. I couldn't agree more.

```
                                    September 26, 1996
        EDC—
        I'm looking forward to an exciting time with
   you tomorrow. I've included here a few thoughts for
   you to think about prior to our session.

        As a Group (perhaps 3 groups)
        Situation -
        Tomorrow you are appointed CEO of GE.
        - What would you do in first 30 days?
        - Do you have a current "vision" of what to
          do?
          - How would you go about developing one?
          - Present your best shot at a vision.
        - How would you go about "selling" the
          vision?
        - What foundations would you build on?
        - What current practices would you jettison?

        Individually--
          I. Please be prepared to describe a
             leadership dilemma that you have faced
             in the past 12 months, i.e., plant
             closing, work transfer, HR, buy or sell
             a business, etc.
```

II. Think about what you would recommend to accelerate the Quality drive across the company.

IIIa. I'll be talking about "A, B & C" players. What are your thoughts on just what makes up such a player?

IIIb. I'll also be talking about energy / energizing / edge as key characteristics of today's leaders. Do you agree? Would you broaden this? How?

I'm looking forward to a fun time, and I know I'll leave a lot smarter than when I arrived.

Jack

YOUR LEADERSHIP TEST

As you ponder the Welch example, consider how ready you are to develop other leaders based on the following criteria.

		Never	Sometimes	Always
1. Focus	When coaching others you focus on the total picture of leadership—both hard, analytic issues and soft issues such as how you energize people and how you make decisions.	1	2 3 4	5
2. Teachable point of view	You have a clear articulated point of view on the ideas, values, energy and edge required to be a winning leader in your company.	1	2 3 4	5
3. Commitment	You personally see developing others as an important part of your leadership. Opportunities to develop other leaders are not limited to formal teaching programs.	1	2 3 4	5
4. Role model	When you teach others you are open to learning. You can readily name things that you learned from others who you are coaching. People feel open to express their own viewpoints, debate them with you and come out with a different perspective.	1	2 3 4	5

about ideas, values, energy and edge and how to engender them in others. So it may seem premature to ask you to articulate yours now. But I have found in workshops that having participants test out the concept at a very early stage is the best way to demonstrate its power and importance.

THE TELEVISION INTERVIEW

Imagine that you are about to be interviewed. NBC's Tom Brokaw is doing a documentary on leaders who are building great organizations by developing other leaders. He wants to document you as a leader and get your teachable point of view on tape. In sixty seconds, the camera is going to come on. At that point, the interviewer will ask you: "Please tell me your teachable point of view on leadership—what ideas you have for your business and how you get those, what values will make those ideas work, how you energize people and how you exhibit edge to make the tough calls."

Think of how you would respond in this interview:

_____

_____

_____

_____

_____

_____

_____

_____

_____

_____

I would encourage you to actually share your response with someone else or record it and review it. How did it feel? The important thing here isn't what you said, but that you probably have some strong opinions on these issues, but may not be able to articulate them as well as you would like. This comes with practice. The rest of this handbook is designed to stimulate your thinking and then give you practice.

Past as Prologue— Your Own Leadership Lessons

Objectives:

- Recognize the learning that has occurred over your lifetime
- Use your experiences consciously as opportunities to build your teachable point of view
- Focus on lessons from the experiences that had the greatest impact on you—those that had an emotional effect

One of the reasons that winning leaders are great teachers is that they are great learners. Before you can teach, you must learn. Most leaders have teachable points of view because they have reflected on their own lives and experiences. They not only know what they know, but they can tell you where they learned it.

Tom Tiller, the former head of GE's silicone business, for example, says he learned to take risks and the power of human potential from growing up around his grandfather. Debra Dunn, a senior vice president at Hewlett-Packard, says she learned about trusting her own abilities and taking responsibility after her father died when she was a young teenager. And Gary Wendt, former CEO of GE Capital, will tell you that he learned about setting prices and running a business from working for a former used car salesman in Texas.

This section will ask you to examine the important leadership and learning events in your life. This will help you to begin to bring to the surface some of your tacit knowledge—the lessons that you carry around with you—and make them explicit. Take each exercise in turn. At the end, you'll be asked to record some elements from your teachable point of view that have grown from your life experiences.

YOUR PROUDEST LEADERSHIP MOMENT

One of the most important leadership lessons you can learn is that we have all learned about leadership. With reflection and constant learning, you can improve your leadership abilities. Everyone has enjoyed leadership success at some point. At some time, whether in high school or college, on the athletic field, in a community or church group or at work, we have all made things happen through other people that otherwise would not have occurred. We have all been leaders. Looking back over your life, what is the moment that you are *most* proud of as a leader? Use the space below to capture the details of that moment:

_____

_____

_____

_____

_____

_____

_____

_____

YOUR WORST LEADERSHIP MOMENT

Similarly, just as all of us have enjoyed success, we've also experienced the pain of leadership failure. Learning to be a leader requires looking back and learning from past mistakes so that you don't repeat errors in judgment or mistreat people. As you review your life, what was your most disappointing experience as a leader?

_____

_____

_____

_____

_____

_____

_____

_____

Using Past Experiences

One of the characteristics of winning leaders is that they consciously think about their experiences. They roll them over in their minds, analyze them and tie them together into teachable points of view. They constantly update and refine these views as they acquire new knowledge and experience. And they store them in the form of stories that they use not only for guiding their own decisions and actions, but also for teaching and leading others.

Abraham Zaleznik, Erik Erikson, James MacGregor Burns and a host of other respected psychologists and historians have noted that much of leadership is formed by early life experiences—the time you learned about responsibility while caring for a sick grandparent, or the time you learned about business when your lemonade stand went bust. The most important lessons are the ones that have a big emotional impact—the ones that made you feel elated or downtrodden, proud or ashamed. As you progress through life, the lessons can be just as important and jarring. The important thing is to soak up all you can from them.

In order to help people think about how their personal and professional life experiences have shaped them as leaders, I share some of my experiences. One that takes me back to when I was eleven years old in Meriden, Connecticut, is my first business venture. I was elated one July afternoon when a representative of the local newspaper, the *Meriden Record,* offered me the opportunity to have my own paper route. I said yes after consulting my parents. The high emotional energy began to wane after a while. The good news was I had a business and was making money; the bad news was that it was a morning paper route in a rural setting, requiring me to ride my bike three miles to deliver thirty-four papers at 5:30 A.M., rain or shine, right through winter. I lasted two years and then bailed out of my first business to start a new one at thirteen.

At this ripe age, I became a chicken farmer, long before Frank Perdue. As with Frank, I figured that there was a market for high-quality roasters. I had observed one of our neighbors in Meriden who sold eggs and roasters. I decided to just raise roasters so I went to the chicken hatchery in Wallingford, Connecticut, and bought fifty little, several-day-old chicks. I raised them to be young roasters, which I methodically prepared for sale, killing and plucking the feathers. I then learned a painful lesson in business: products without markets spell trouble. I had the roasters, but no market. I had no customers or distribution channels. Panicked, I called friends and family, but I only sold a few. I was stuck with a huge inventory of roasters, forty to be exact. I went bankrupt giving them away. As funny as these stories are, they do begin shaping how one approaches business.

As a new professor at Columbia University, I spent time in rural Appalachia, helping the Hazard Family Health Services survive when its parent organization temporarily went bankrupt. The year turned out to be a leadership test. Rather than acting as a consultant and expert, I had to step in and run the clinic. The financial crisis that erupted the week I arrived meant the hospital did not meet its payroll. This led to some health crises and serious unemployment issues for members of the staff. I tell how that experience provided the intellectual and emotional foundation for working at GE in the mid-1980s. I was running Crotonville at the time, and GE was downsizing by over one hundred thousand people. I had to deal with managers caught up in this downsizing numerous times at Crotonville. Having dealt with job loss and its effects in small communities in Hazard, Kentucky, I had a teachable point of view on the role of corporations in society, employment, social responsibility, etc.

I share my own stories to illustrate the type of material that individuals need to explore over their lifetimes. You need to identify the actual experiences, the impact they had on you at the time and what you have learned from them that shapes your teachable point of view.

LIFELONG LEADERSHIP LESSONS

Review your life as a series of emotional learning experiences. Take a few minutes to consider the lessons you have learned in the past. Start with whatever is your first important leadership experience, whether as a child, young adult or businessperson. Then, after you have brought yourself to the present, record some of your major lessons.

Experience	Leadership Lessons I Learned
1.	
2.	
3.	
4.	

The distillation of ideas, values, edge and methods for energizing others you've just completed form the beginning of your teachable point of view. These are the lessons that you've drawn from your experiences that you can articulate and teach to others. The following sections will help you to further define each of these as you prepare your teachable point of view.

Winning Ideas

Objectives

- Recognize the requirements for leaders to bring central ideas to their business
- Analyze the shift needed in the central ideas for your business
- Translate these ideas into actions
- Summarize your teachable point of view on ideas

Ideas are the underpinning for every human endeavor. They are the organizing principles within organizations, and it is the leader's job to make sure that they are well founded and appropriate. Companies need ideas that fall into two categories: "quantum" ideas that define how the company will add value and compete in the marketplace, and "incremental" ideas about how to implement the quantum ideas and continuously improve performance. Leaders must make sure that their organizations have both by articulating clear quantum ideas and by developing others to come up with good incremental ideas, and eventually to be able to formulate their own quantum ideas. Because all businesses are in a never-ending cycle of obsolescence, this means that while leaders must be clear about their ideas, they must also constantly reevaluate them, scrap the ones that are no longer appropriate and develop new ones that will keep them ahead of the competition.

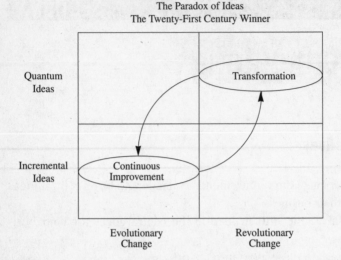

Figure 3: Quantum and Incremental Ideas

Quantum Ideas

All businesses are built around ideas. Entrepreneurs build their organizations on a central idea. Theodore Vail, for example, grew AT&T on the idea of "universal service" and created the world's largest regulated monopoly by striving to provide telephone service for every person in the U.S. (an idea that came to the end of its life cycle with the breakup of AT&T in 1984). Henry Ford founded Ford Motor Company on the idea of mass production of cars, a radical idea at the turn of the century. Ray Kroc, founder of McDonald's, stole Ford's mass production idea and invented the fast food industry. Tom Monahan, founder of Domino's Pizza, built his business around the idea of home delivery. And Bill Gates's central idea of controlling the operating system for personal computers built Microsoft, one of the world's most valuable enterprises. At some point in the life of most businesses, though, the original founding idea is no longer appropriate and a new one must supplant it.

Leaders have the responsibility for generating a business's central idea. The idea must provide the intellectual catalyst for action. In the case of GE, when Welch took over he had to supplant the original "general" electric idea (meaning GE should enter all electricity businesses, regardless of GE's competitiveness) with the concept that GE must be No. 1 or No. 2 in all of the industries in which it participated. If not, the businesses in question had to be fixed, closed or sold. Eckhard Pfeiffer had to challenge Compaq's central idea of building over-engineered machines and selling them at high prices. He had to do this because new segments of the market were taking shape. Further, microprocessor and software technology were creating standards that lowered barriers to entry and gave most personal computers the same functionality in the eyes of the bulk of consumers. Pfeiffer's new central idea was that Compaq would identify specific segments of customers. It would define their requirements in functionality, quality and price. And then it would engineer and build those machines and deliver them to customers at those prices. Prior to that, all computer companies had built the machines they wanted to and then tacked on a margin to arrive at their product offering.

YOUR QUANTUM IDEA

Whether you are the CEO or the head of a small group in an organization, you need ideas to succeed. These ideas need to help you establish a competitive position for your business in the external environment and marketplace, create valuable services or products, find innovative ways to distribute your goods and find the market segments that will make you money. In order to help you generate ideas and build your teachable point of view, here are some questions to answer:

1. What are the key changes in your external environment?

   CUSTOMER NEEDS:

   TECHNOLOGY:

GOVERNMENT/REGULATION:

COMPETITORS:

OTHER:

2. How do your current core competencies match up to this changing environment?
3. To succeed in the future, what change is required from the old central idea? What is the transformation that is required?
4. How are you monitoring the environment to constantly pick up new ideas?

Here is how Eckhard Pfeiffer would have answered these questions for Compaq in 1991.

1. What are the key changes in your external environment?

CUSTOMER NEEDS:

A wider set of people are becoming customers for PCs. The PC is no longer just something to have on a desktop for engineers and analysts. Now universities want them for students, companies want them for all employees, parents want them for young children.

TECHNOLOGY:

Microsoft and Intel have teamed up to provide open standards for operating systems. This lowers barriers to entry for competitors and levels the playing field between technologically advanced PC makers and those with less advanced technology.

COMPETITORS:

Competitors are coming into the market based on the expanding customer base and open standards for technology. Many are now offering sufficiently functional PCs at much lower prices than ever.

2. How do your current core competencies match up to this changing environment?

Compaq's current core competencies lie in building over-engineered machines that could be dropped off the table repeatedly and plugged in and still work.

Other than design, Compaq has few core competencies. It is not a strong marketer or distributor. Its manufacturing is based on an over-engineering zeal, not efficiency.

This locks Compaq into a position as a high cost, high price competitor.

3. What is the change from the old quantum idea? What is the transformation that is required?

The current quantum idea is to design and deliver the best PC designs and the absolute highest level of quality.

This quantum idea limits our ability to reach many expanding markets of the PC industry, because it prices our products out of reach.

The new quantum idea is to define segments in the PC market. Each one has their own needs in functionality and quality. They also each have their own price points.

While other computer companies make the machines they are good at making, Compaq will start with the customer. Compaq will define their needs and design machines to meet those. Then, Compaq will engineer and produce the machines to deliver them to customers at their price points while we make a profit.

Compaq's distribution will go from a few hundred select marketing partners to thousands who can reach a variety of customer segments.

Compaq will redesign everything about its manufacturing

operations to reduce cost as it delivers the right machines to the right markets. Finally, Compaq will expand capacity as it goes after many more segments than it did previously.

4. How are you monitoring the environment constantly to pick up new ideas?

Compaq's senior team will operate in a flat, team-oriented environment. Because markets move fast the team will meet frequently to discuss new trends and adjust our ideas.

Finally, periodically, teams of senior executives will be charged with coming up with ideas to reinvent the company based on changes in technology, customers and competitors.

Note that it was this approach that led to Compaq's major reorganization in 1996. Compaq did this when its stock was at an all-time high. But having lived through one crisis in 1991, Pfeiffer did not want to let the company become outdated again. It changed before it had to, by having senior executives look for new ideas. As many people thought the PC would be supplanted by worldwide networks, the new quantum idea for Compaq is to think of computing as a communication process rather than a computational process. As a result it has launched brand-new products aimed at the Internet and networking, and it reorganized itself to attack new segments again. One year after the reorganization, Compaq's stock continued to rise to higher and higher levels.

Now answer the four questions for your business:

Business Ideas

---

1. What are the key changes in your external environment?

---

2. How do your current core competencies match up to this changing environment?

---

3. What is the change from the old quantum idea? What is the transformation that is required?

---

4. How are you monitoring the environment constantly to pick up new ideas?

Building Systems to Support Your Ideas

Now that you have thought about the quantum ideas shaping your business, you have to consider how to build an organization that is going to operate in the changing environment you are facing. It is essential to rework the fabric of the company at the most fundamental levels.

I like to think of a company as comprised of technical, political and cultural systems. The technical system organizes how people, capital and technology come together to produce goods or services for the marketplace. The political system influences power, career opportunities and reward allocation. And the cultural system creates a shared set of norms, beliefs and attitudes for people in the company.

Strong central ideas become ingrained into each of these systems. When Jack Welch took over at GE in 1981, for example, the company was in multiple businesses doing countless things, all of them generically related to "electricity." This was the quantum idea: do anything and everything electric. The technical system was composed of sophisticated strategy and finance tools that welded the company together. In the political arena, GE's leaders wished to exert stringent controls on the people in GE's disparate businesses. So there was a strong central staff that determined the uniform pay scale across all of GE's hundreds of operating businesses. Business leaders had to come to headquarters to ask for permission on even the most simple issues. And a myriad of other tools were designed to control behavior at a company this diverse. Culturally, the company looked for "GE people" who were strongly rooted in this bureaucratic mode. They had to take pride in keeping a well-tuned machine running predictably.

As Figure 4 shows, GE's technical, political and cultural systems developed in line with the central ideas for the business. Each of these systems manifested itself in three ways—strategy, organization structure and human resource management.

	Strategy	Organization Structure	Human Resource Management
Technical	• Diversify • Religious devotion to budgets • Grow high-tech businesses • Strategic planning	• Decentralize • Systematic structuring	• Engineer-dominated professional recruit • One pay system • Formal appraisals; work goals
Political	• CEO as constitutionalist • Banker role	• Hierarchical • Functional boundaries • Political centralization	• Succession very formal; systematic • Rewards similar; lock-step • Approvals boss down
Cultural	• "Scientific management" • Decentralized philosophy; centralized behavior • Oligopolistic • Stewardship	• GE "way of doing things" • Core business culture dominance	• GE recruits screened for culture • Development used to shape culture • Appraisal and rewards "GE way" driven

Figure 4: General Electric's Old Technical, Political and Cultural Systems

When Welch arrived, he had different ideas based on his own teachable point of view. He saw the 1980s and 1990s as a brutally competitive time. He saw GE's idea of being a general electric company as a colossal waste of shareholder capital and management energy. He wanted to match the tough market conditions against his best and brightest to win. So he started to refocus GE.

He also knew that to win, GE's operating companies would need to be free from the bureaucratic centralization that made operations predictable but glacially slow. So he took away many controls from the past system, like the uniform pay scales and the finance mafia. He replaced them with a supportive staff who assisted businesses. In one example, he eliminated almost all of GE's corporate strategic planning staff, well over one hundred people. In their place, he instituted a system of open dialogue between himself and thirteen global business leaders. These people would present their strategies in an honest, straightforward way and Welch would react. Together they would determine the answers.

Take a look at GE's Technical-Political-Cultural (TPC) matrix in Figure 5 to see how these systems are linked to Welch's basic business ideas.

	Strategy	Organization Structure	Human Resource Management
Technical	• No. 1 or No. 2 in all of our industries • High-growth businesses only	• Thirteen businesses • Share best practices • Boundarylessness	• Multiple pay systems • New staffing systems • Development as a continuous process
Political	• Integrated diversity	• No "wedding cake" hierarchies • Cross-functional teamwork • Empowerment, decisionmaking pushed to lower levels	• Rewards very flexible • Approvals from below as well as above
Cultural	• Speed, simplicity and self-confidence • Ownership • Share best practices • Work-out	• Shared values • Many cultures • Common vision	• Human resource systems shape and mold boundarylessness • New staffing and support values

Figure 5: General Electric's Technical, Political and Cultural Systems

INGRAINING YOUR BUSINESS IDEAS

Take the opportunity to record how you can translate your business ideas into action. Fill out the TPC matrices for your company as they are now and as they should be to support your new business ideas.

Today: Existing Business Ideas ⟶ Existing Technical, Political and Cultural Systems		
Strategy	**Organization Structure**	**Human Resource Management**
Technical		
_____	_____	_____
_____	_____	_____
_____	_____	_____
_____	_____	_____
_____		_____
Political		
_____	_____	_____
_____	_____	_____
_____	_____	_____
_____	_____	_____
Cultural		
_____	_____	_____
_____	_____	_____
_____	_____	_____
_____	_____	_____

PULLING IT TOGETHER

Take the opportunity now to pull together your teachable point of view on ideas. Create a presentation to some important stakeholders—the financial analysts who follow your stock, your Board of Directors or your employees.

	Strategy	Organization Structure	Human Resource Management
Tomorrow: New Business Ideas ⟶ New Technical, Political and Cultural Systems			
Technical			
Political			

Tomorrow: New Business Ideas ⟶ New Technical, Political and Cultural Systems		
Strategy	**Organization Structure**	**Human Resource Management**
Cultural		

Create a few slides that detail your new business ideas and what you are doing to make them a reality. This is your teachable point of view on ideas.

Headline: _____

Headline: _____

Headline: _____

Headline: _____

Values in Action

Objectives:

- Understand the connection between values and ideas
- Articulate values that reinforce and support the business ideas
- Practice delivering your own message about what values it will take to win

---

Just as ideas determine the results that a company wants and the processes it will use to attain them, values determine how people in a company behave and interact with each other and with the outside world. Values can, like ideas, be an important competitive tool. Organizations that value independent action, for example, are likely to resolve customer complaints faster than ones that require layers and layers of approvals. And ones that value respect for front-line workers are more likely to get good performance and good ideas bubbling up from them than companies that operate simply by the rule of a day's pay for a day's work.

All organizations have values, whether they are explicitly stated or not. In winning organizations, however, values are not only explicitly stated, but are periodically examined and evaluated to make sure that they in fact support behaviors that will achieve the desired goals. It is the role of a leader to make sure that everyone understands not only the values, but how they are linked to the organization's goals and actions. Values are not a statement of behavioral aspirations but a guide and an important part of how work is done every day.

When Marion Wade started ServiceMaster, he had strong religious values about wanting to give people a sense of worth and dignity. This has translated into ServiceMaster's business ideas. The company has a lean organization because it wants to have people exercise drive and initiative. A ServiceMaster manager once explained to me how the company's values and ideas are linked:

> At ServiceMaster we believe in the dignity of every individual and the best thing we can do is give people opportunities to grow and achieve their maximum potential. Everyone at ServiceMaster understands that. For the chairman that means he is always looking for new businesses to enter. For me, it means always trying to expand the services at existing accounts and to find new customers. If I am constantly giving my people opportunities to grow and I want to do that for more and more people, the only way I can do both is to grow this company.

ServiceMaster's business idea, to focus on growth, is a direct outgrowth of its mission and values. Growth is part of the determination for every manager's compensation, as is whether or not they treat people with dignity and respect.

At GE, Jack Welch has married ideas and values in a different way. Welch started with the ideas and then began to shape a set of values for the company. Welch's business ideas focused on what he saw as the brutally competitive 1980s and 1990s. Formal, bloated companies like GE wouldn't make it, he said in 1981, long before this became a fashionable statement. With these ideas, he started to craft a set of organizational values. Welch started with speed. GE employees would be those who wanted to do things faster and faster. He moved to self-confidence. Welch wanted employees who were self-confident enough to let others do their work, were focused on only the important tasks and didn't build bureaucracy to control people. The way to get speed was through simplicity. Finally, in the mid-1980s, he settled on *boundarylessness*. Boundarylessness means that people value forming ad hoc teams to get things done, that they are flexible and that they are focused on pleasing customers, not satisfying internal requirements.

Whether you start with the values, as at ServiceMaster, or with the ideas, as at GE, the important thing is that as a leader you make sure that the two are consistent. The values are well communicated and reinforced in many ways throughout the organization. This section of the handbook will help you do both.

Ideas and Values Together

When Jack Welch took over at GE, there was both an ingrained set of ideas and an ingrained set of values, and they complemented each other. GE's business idea was to be in every business it could, regardless of the company's performance in that business or its profit potential. GE was after coverage and uniformity. The values of the people at the company were aligned with this. People generally valued stability. They upheld a complicated bureaucratic system. Power and control were very important. In fact, when you first met a manager at GE and were invited into his or her office, you would often spend the first several minutes of the meeting looking at the ceiling. You weren't looking for divine inspiration, you were counting the tiles in the ceiling. The more tiles, the bigger the office. And the bigger the office, the more power and status the person you were visiting held. This determined your behavior.

When Welch took over, his new ideas required new values. He saw the world as too brutal to go on being in all those businesses where GE was uncompetitive. So he wanted GE to be No. 1 or No. 2 in every industry in which GE participated. If not, he was going to fix, close or sell the business. This meant that GE had to go from values that sent conflict under the table to values that brought it out in order to openly confront reality and decide how to respond. Welch thought speed was the key to success. So he wanted to throw out bureaucratic controls. This meant that GE people had to value their autonomy and had to take more initiative.

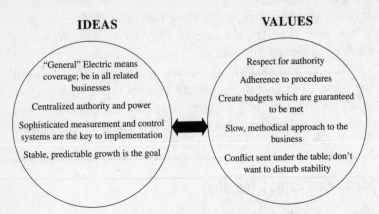

Figure 6: GE's Old Ideas and Values

Below I've tried to capture the GE ideas and values as Welch usually described them. As you can see, they were nothing like the old, but they fit together.

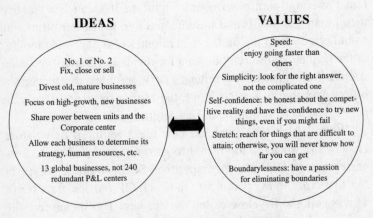

Figure 7: Connecting GE's Ideas and Values

YOUR VALUES

Take a few minutes to build on the work you did to articulate your ideas in the preceding section. Think about how the values system of your company can reinforce your central business ideas. In the next exercise, you'll work on articulating the connection between the ideas and values.

Step 1: Write your new ideas in the bubble on the left.

Step 2: Write the values that will support these ideas in the bubble on the right.

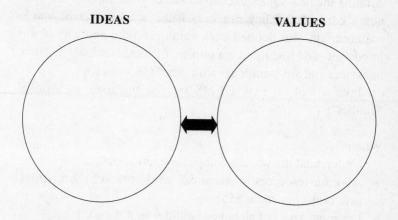

IDEAS   VALUES

Teaching Values

Ingraining a set of values in an organization—large or small—is hard work. The best leaders do this by articulating a set of values, and then having individuals wrestle with the details of what those values will mean in their daily lives. The next exercise will take you through a group of important questions that everyone in your organization should be able to answer: What are the values? Why are they important? What are some examples of behaviors that support the values and some that go against those that are needed? How do these values overlap or conflict with each other? Take the time to complete the exercise by carefully answering these questions yourself. Then discuss them with the people who work for you so they can answer them as well.

When GE acquired the medical systems business of France's Thomson group and Japan's Yokogawa Medical Systems and began to combine them with its own U.S.-based General Electric

Medical Systems unit, John Trani, the former president of GEMS, faced the challenge of bringing together three very diverse cultures. Trani immediately recognized that he needed to create a shared mindset and organization-wide understanding of the values required to support the new business theory. So Trani took GEMS's top managers through an integrative process of defining the new values needed to succeed and support the business's core ideas. They not only listed a broad set of values required, but also defined each value carefully and why it was important and explored examples of positive and negative behaviors and any paradoxes with other GE values.

Take a look at how GEMS tackled the issue of "Global Mindset":

What:
- Understand the world's competitive environment
- Allocate resources to maximize world market share (products, projects, people, $$$)
- Leverage assets of global capabilities to win locally
- Success is measured on global and local results
- Cultural understanding necessary to assess behaviors

Why:
- Mission is to be No. 1 worldwide
- Participation in global markets is required for GEMS growth
- Achieve real competitive advantage by leveraging global expertise
- Global activity will affect you

Positive Behavior:
- Attendance and participation in global task forces, etc. (language, culture)
- Sharing best practices

Negative Behavior:

- Unfinished products shipped to other poles
- Focusing on local measurement (i.e., P&L) vs. supporting total business goals
- Business decisions based on contribution margin derived from transfer price
- Artificially making one global market look better than others through distorted transfer pricing

Paradoxes:

- Global resource allocation vs. Jobs/Security/Pride
- Measurements/Accountability/Operating Mechanisms: Do they support local goals & issues?
- Soft values vs. Hard results

ARTICULATING VALUES

Conduct the same exercise for your own critical values. As you can see, ideas and values must be mutually supportive. Take some time here to articulate how your ideas and values are connected in an everyday context.

Value	Why Is It Important?	Positive Behavior	Negative Behavior	Paradoxes
1.				
2.				

3.				
4.				
5.				

CONNECTING YOUR POINT OF VIEW ON IDEAS AND VALUES

Step 1: Imagine that you are going to give a speech to a group of employees. This could be a group of new hires or experienced managers. Your assignment is to explain the values of your company. You are successful if they have a clear sense of why these are the values and how they are applied.

Step 2: On the lines below, outline what you would say in your speech.

Step 3: Practice. I recommend trying to give this speech. Give it to friends, colleagues, employees, your spouse. Ask for feedback. Keep working on it. It took Jack Welch nearly five years to come up with the term *boundarylessness*. Be patient and keep working.

_____

_____

_____

_____

_____

_____

_____

_____

_____

_____

_____

_____

_____

Energizing the Organization

Objectives

- Establish the role of energy in leadership
- Teach a framework for maintaining your own energy and energizing others

In the past, we used to reward the lone rangers in the corner offices because their achievements were brilliant even though their behavior was destructive. That day is gone. We need people who are better at persuading than at barking orders, who know how to coach and build consensus. Today, managers add value by brokering with people, not by presiding over empires. Competition is tough, and it takes brains to win. But today we look for smart people with an added dimension: they have an interest in other people and derive psychic satisfaction from working with them.

—LARRY BOSSIDY, FORMER CHAIRMAN AND CEO, ALLIEDSIGNAL

Like the people Bossidy describes, all of the winning leaders I've studied share a passion for people. They draw their energy from helping others get excited about improving their businesses. And they energize their people at every opportunity with stimulating ideas and values.

Equally important, leaders model the intensity and energy that it takes to stay ahead competitively and meet ever more ambitious goals. In part, they do this because they love what they do. They also know how to keep themselves engaged in what they are doing at the moment. Leaders focus on how they make people feel after each interaction. Carlos Cantu, the former CEO of ServiceMaster, may have summarized this best when he said, "At the end of the day, I feel, every single person has got to come away with something positive [from one of his meetings]."

This doesn't mean that leaders aren't truthful. As I discussed earlier, they are brutally honest about their business's competitive realities, and they don't sugar-coat their views. But they provide equal parts sobering reality and inspiring exuberance. They offer people self-confidence to pursue the opportunities that change offers.

Being a winning leader means tapping a deep reservoir of emotional energy. This drive and motivation mixes needs for accomplishment, power and, most importantly, institutional legacy. This is the essence of what James MacGregor Burns means by transformational leadership; namely, leaders are energized not just by the goals of the team or the organization, but by transforming and coaching individuals to be leaders themselves.

Simply put, a leader's job is to energize others. Notice that I don't say it's part of their job; it *is* their job. There is no "time off" when a leader isn't responsible for energizing others. Every interaction a leader has is either going to positively energize those around them or negatively energize them. When Larry Bossidy went to an AlliedSignal factory, he had a skip-level breakfast in which he met alone with mid-level managers and front-line people. Then he held a town hall meeting with hundreds of workers. People there were not going to be neutral. They were going to say either, "He's a dynamic guy, excited about the future of the company" or "He's a dud." Similarly, when Andy Grove delivers a keynote address at a technology conference, he has a few short minutes to energize people with the idea that Intel has a handle on the future of technology and is going to continue its industry leadership. He either energizes or doesn't. Winning leaders use the power of ideas and values to energize people. They don't always win every time, but they have a very high percentage of success and they consciously work at getting better.

PERSONAL ENERGY

As a leader, you must first start with self-awareness of your own sources of emotional energy. What are the activities that energize you most, and which activities strip you of your emotional energy and leave you feeling angry, frustrated, bored or tired?

What energizes you the most? (Specify activities.)

_____

_____

_____

What deenergizes you the most? (Specify activities.)

_____

_____

_____

After reflecting on these activities, think about ways in which you can either enhance energizers or remove blockages to unleash more positive emotional energy.

How I Can Raise My Level of Positive Emotional Energy:

_____

_____

_____

_____

_____

Balancing Energy in One's Life Space

Leaders need to be able to monitor their energy and have ways of renewing themselves. In today's fast-paced world, there is increasing talk of burnout and lack of balance between work, family and personal time. Our winning leaders struggle with this as much as, if not more than, anybody else. But they still find ways to energize others. The challenge for all of us is to find sources of renewal. They can range from physical exercise to hobbies to spiritual activities. I find that one of my important sources of renewal is running, something I have done for over thirty years. Andy Grove is an avid cyclist, Jack Welch a golfer, Dick Notebaert a skier and scuba diver.

I have a simple philosophy: Everything in life can be energizing if I take control of it. An important step in dealing with energy is understanding how it flows in one's life space. Edgar Schein in his book _Career Dynamics_ starts off with a very useful framework for examining one's life space. He focuses on the three major domains of our lives: (1) Ourselves—the biosocial self, (2) our family—parents, siblings, children and extended family, and (3) our work. He argues that all of our life activities and energies can be categorized in these three areas. For each of us the amount of time and energy devoted to each domain varies, as does the degree to which each is positively energizing and the degree of either conflict or synergy between the three domains.

Energy in Your Personal Life Space

Examine your life space by drawing three circles: one for self, one for work and one for family. Let the size of each circle represent relative investment of time in that activity, let's say over a typical week. Overlap the circles to the extent that the activities do or do not overlap. For example, the drawing below represents a family business where the individual is working with family members and doing things with the family and work colleagues of a recreational nature as well. What the drawing does not tell us is whether or not this is energizing or deenergizing. A dysfunctional family may be sucking energy from all domains of their members' lives.

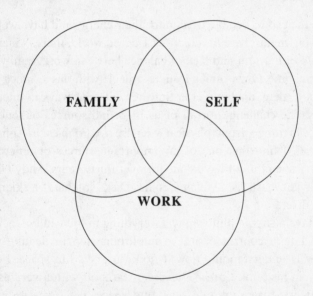

Figure 8: Life Balance in a Family Business

The second example is from a young consultant who shared an illustration of his life space in a workshop. Basically, his life is dominated by work, with a little time spent on his own recreation and friendships and almost no time for his family (a wife who is also a consultant, no children).

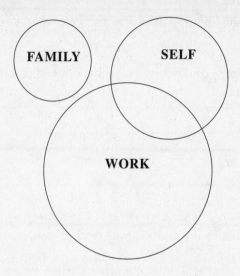

Figure 9: Another Life Balance Example

YOUR LIFE SPACE

Using the examples above, draw three circles to show how much overlap exists between your personal, family and work activities. Use the size of the circles to represent the relative amount of time you spend in each area.

Now examine the effects of how you balance your energy and time:

1. Identify energy conflicts (work/family, self/work, self/family).

_____

_____

_____

_____

2. Identify energy synergies (self-renewal through work-related activities, family involvement with work groups, etc.).

_____

_____

_____

_____

How I Can Enhance Energy in My Life Space:

_____

_____

_____

_____

The Leader Developing Leaders Challenge

It is not enough to work on your own life space. As a leader, you need to help and coach others to do the same. The life space exercise you just completed is a great activity to build into either individual coaching or workshop settings. It legitimates people taking ownership and control of how they spend their time. Your challenge as a leader is to be a listener and learner, to help others deal with these issues as you grapple with them yourself.

Leaders Energize Others Through Transitions

The balance of life issue is one way to help each individual deal with personal energy. The bigger challenge is getting a large group of people energized around the future, which always means change. In today's world, this is radical, revolutionary change.

Change unleashes a lot of mixed emotions: fear, hope, anxiety, uncertainty, elation, sadness, excitement, and so forth. The key for leaders is to ultimately deal with emotional energy in a positive way while recognizing the reality of the struggle. They do more than give inspiring speeches and pep talks. They help people to see the opportunities that lie before them and create an environment that supports fulfillment of the group's mission. The most critical part is leading people through transitions laden with deeply mixed emotions.

Leaders channel these mixed emotions into a positive force. When the Detroit riots broke out in 1967, many of the inner-city inhabitants proved they had energy (literally) to burn. They destroyed buildings and set the city ablaze. Father William Cunningham and Eleanor Josaitis founded Focus: HOPE, a nonprofit civil rights organization, one year later and set up headquarters in the location that had seen the most gruesome rioting. Cunningham and Josaitis had a simple thesis—equal opportunity meant nothing without equal capability—so they set about building an organization that fed inner-city babies who were losing their brain capacity due to malnourishment. Eventually, Cunningham and Josaitis founded day care centers, remedial educational programs and training institutes for kids off the street to learn high-tech manufacturing skills. The same energy that people had directed toward burning their city is now directed toward bettering their lives.

Tom Tiller faced a crisis situation on a smaller scale in 1992.

At the age of only 29, he had been named to lead the kitchen range plant at GE Appliances' sprawling Appliance Park facility in Louisville, Kentucky. The kitchen range manufacturing operation was in trouble. It had not released new products in years and was losing money. Appliance Park had seen its employment dwindle from 23,000 in its halcyon years to just over 9,000. There was a pall in the kitchen range building.

Tiller, the plant manager at the time, had to lay off 400 people in his first several months. Sensing that reactive leadership would send the Range Division straight into the grave, Tiller decided that he needed to create a positive, proactive experience for his organization. He needed to take a road trip. He put forty people—from manufacturing, engineering, design and others—onto a rented bus and headed for the Atlanta Kitchen and Bath Show. The group's charge was simple: Find new products that would keep the plant alive. People were infused with Tiller's energy and urgency. They sensed that "we've got to do something before something gets done to us." At the Kitchen and Bath Show, Tiller's team combed through every display. They meticulously studied competitors' products and came up with new ideas of their own. When they returned to GE's Louisville plant, their energy didn't wane. Within eighteen months the division had generated three new products. The plant stayed open, going from a loss to a $10 million profit.

The bus trip is a perfect metaphor for what leaders do to create energy. All of the doubts about the future of the range plant had led to negative energy for its workers and managers. Tiller took the people, brought them together as a team and gave them a sense that they had to and could do something. The energy went from negative to positive, and with hard work, they won.

Leaders make people want to be a part of change. Slogans and cotton-candy sugar highs don't do it, because change inevitably is somewhat painful. To help people get through the turmoil, leaders must understand the psychological dynamics of change for every individual.

Bridges's Teachable Point of View

William Bridges's transitions framework helps us understand the challenge of continuous change. Bridges argues that life has many emotional transitions, from childhood changes, to the death of loved ones, to children growing up and moving on, to job and community changes. How we handle these predictable emotional transitions is the key to growth and healthy emotional energy in life.

Bridges has one very simple premise: If we do not properly end things in life, we cannot create opportunities for self-renewal and move on to new beginnings. There are some very predictable psychodynamics of transitions, which successful leaders must master for themselves and help others master. The ending is a process of "creative destruction." It is triggered by an action or event. For example, dealing with death creates what Bridges calls *disengagement* in which people begin to separate from the past—you literally realize things are different. This then leads to a more complex psychological task in dealing with the death of someone close, what he calls *disidentification*. This refers to the untangling of old identities. One example of this phenomenon is when a spouse dies and the surviving one keeps using the pronoun "we." It takes time to "dis-identify." You must come to grips with the fact that you yourself have been changed. It is a form of facing reality and accepting it, no matter how painful, so that life can move on.

Disenchantment is where people most often get stuck. Many people react to life's difficult transitions by trying to re-create the "good old days" and repeat habits that no longer match their new situation. This is often the case with multiple divorces where the psychological profile of the new partner is similar to the old's, or a series of job mistakes that all share the same source. Another equally destructive process is *disillusionment,* becoming a victim of the ending. A very clear medical fact is that when one partner of an older couple dies, holding all medical indicators constant, the likelihood of death in the next two years increases for the survivor. The only plausible explanation is psychological;

in Bridges's terms, disillusionment. In other spheres of life, for example, the perpetual victimization felt by someone who loses a job and can't get up the energy to seek new employment appears as disillusionment.

Bridges argues that we must first cognitively understand the dynamics of transitions and then have both individual and institutional means for coping. This framing is at the core of how leaders deal with emotional energy.

To move from endings to new beginnings, Bridges argues, requires dealing effectively with the transition phase, a period when psychological forces pull and tug in conflicting directions. On the one hand, people feel remorse and pain over their loss. On the other hand, unable to change the situation, they may want to move on and put the past behind them.

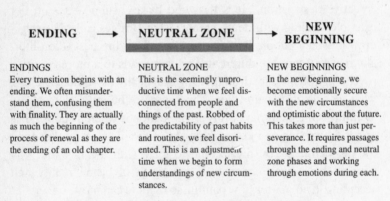

ENDING →	NEUTRAL ZONE	→ NEW BEGINNING
ENDINGS	**NEUTRAL ZONE**	**NEW BEGINNINGS**
Every transition begins with an ending. We often misunderstand them, confusing them with finality. They are actually as much the beginning of the process of renewal as they are the ending of an old chapter.	This is the seemingly unproductive time when we feel disconnected from people and things of the past. Robbed of the predictability of past habits and routines, we feel disoriented. This is an adjustment time when we begin to form understandings of new circumstances.	In the new beginning, we become emotionally secure with the new circumstances and optimistic about the future. This takes more than just perseverance. It requires passages through the ending and neutral zone phases and working through emotions during each.

Figure 10: William Bridges's Transition Framework

Take the example of an executive I knew who had worked at a company that had been very successful. A new chief executive arrived and announced a new strategy. This was assumed to be a mere rumbling until the new chief executive took action. The result was a flurry of acquisitions that brought about a new business sector. The executive I knew had worked in the company's traditional businesses. He now saw himself relegated to what was viewed as an unimportant part of the company. The new business sector had a different culture than the old company, and the chief executive made it clear that this was the culture he wanted the whole company to adopt. Here are the emotions I witnessed in the executive:

ENDINGS	NEUTRAL ZONE	NEW BEGINNINGS
After a period of denial, the executive realized that things would be different—his traditional sources of power were gone. Rather than being a role model, he now had to learn a new culture and new ways of doing things. His emotions were as follows: • Disengagement: He began to see himself in the context of the new organization, fighting for his role as opposed to enjoying high prestige. • Disidentification: He no longer identified himself with the company. Rather, he put the term "old" in front of it. "I'm a vice president from the old company," he would say. • Disenchantment: He realized that what he liked about the past—the title he had earned, the clout he carried were things of the past. • Disillusionment: He felt like a victim. He felt he had no control over what had happened or what would happen.	The executive struggled between his emotions of endings and finding a new beginning. Specifically, he had these emotions: • Confusion: He would constantly say, "I don't know what to do to get along" and would find himself being upstaged by executives new to the company. • Resolution: He resolved not to just stick it out but to adjust and become productive again. • Bipolar reactions: "At one moment you may find yourself hopeful about the future and at another moment wondering about where you are going."	He adjusted to the new way of life. His emotions here included: • Understanding: He crafted a new sense for his role—to maximize the value from the mature part of the company. • Acceptance: He accepted the need to work hard to fulfill his new role. • Hope: He looked forward to the future again. • Fondness: He remembered the past extremely fondly (even the bad elements).

Figure 11: A Transition Example

These emotions are fundamental to human nature, and societies across the globe have created mechanisms for dealing with transition. Take death as an example. It is not by accident that worldwide, across religions, cultures and history, societies have invented a set of social processes that share striking similarities for dealing with the pain of loss. In most cases, there is first a recognition that this is a traumatic emotional time for those who were close to the deceased. Support is provided through the gathering of family and friends and through the ceremony of religious rituals. There is a focus on the ending (the viewing of the body, a eulogy or other ceremonies of closure) to generate acceptance that the loss is real and permanent. And, in many cases, a celebration is held to honor the loved one and to help the family positively remember the past while moving on to a new beginning.

These same principles underlie the well-handled outplacement of individuals in companies. Organizations around the world generally handle outplacement with an intuitive recognition of Bridges's framework. They honestly deal with the individual and "disengage" them from the job by letting them know they no longer have a position. They then provide both financial and counseling support (outplacement counseling) to help handle the ending, the transition and the new beginning. Former employees are counseled on their past accomplishments, strengths and weaknesses and helped to mobilize their energy for a new beginning. When this is done well, many people move on to exciting new beginnings.

For leaders, who must continuously renew and transform their organizations, this framework is the underlying conceptual road map. Tom Tiller's bus trip was a great transition vehicle that became a metaphor to help energize thousands of people. The use of the trip is similar to the rites of passage that Bridges notes have been used by leaders throughout history to mark times of great change. Tiller created a transition journey that bonded a group of diverse people to a search for a new beginning. The socializing ("We played cards together, drank together, and learned together") built teamwork and generated energy around a new beginning for the business. The trip was focused on ideas. It reinvented the range line by going to the Kitchen and Bath Show, studying the competition and then coming up with better ideas to beat them. More important, the trip taught everyone teamwork and the value of controlling the organization's destiny to win, lessons that remain deeply entrenched five years later.

How Leaders Sustain Emotional Energy

It is out of the ebb and flow of emotion that leaders generate positive energy. Jesus Christ, Martin Luther King and other historical leaders all faced monumental emotional challenges. It is precisely because of this ebb and flow that they were made stronger. Trauma, crisis and failure are the sources of new emotional energy if the leader is a dedicated learner with clear ideas, values and vision.

The leader must continuously face Bridges's transition framework and find new personal beginnings before being able to lead others. Bill Weiss and Dick Notebaert at Ameritech had to "kill the old 'Bellhead' mentality" and create a competitive telecommunications company. They were part of that old culture, so they had to break out of it themselves first before they could lead others.

ENDINGS	NEUTRAL ZONE	NEW BEGINNINGS
• React to an ending; acknowledge it and don't deny it. • Realize you are headed for the neutral zone; prepare for confusion. Find some new source of stability and guidance that will help you through.	• Find a regular time and place to reflect. • Review your life; you can't move on without putting the past in context. • Symbolically mark your passage from the old to the new. Many societies use a vigil for this experience in which a young person is sent away to survive for a time on their own. When they return they are a mature member of the community. • Use sources of support and guidance to help you make sense of your transition and sort out your understanding of the new world.	• Take bold new actions; test your adjustment and expect some failures. • Help others; the process of assisting others who are struggling with the transition will put your emotions in context.

Renewal is a core skill of the leader. Structures, processes and possibilities are always in flux and must be continuously altered. For Bill Cunningham, the Focus: HOPE credo of "daring to go where no one has gone before" kept driving him to energize his organization. He took the central idea of "equal capability" to confront racism, expand his operations from basic food distribution and run one of the world's most advanced integrated manufacturing engineering programs. He kept renewing himself with new stretch targets, which in turn helped him and his partner, Eleanor Josaitis, energize their organization.

Each phase of transition is predictable. There are many things you can and should do to respond to them.

FACING THE EMOTIONAL REALITY

Understanding where people are in a transition is the first step toward helping them get to a new beginning. Think for a moment about where you are in whatever transition your organization is facing now. Then think about your team and the organization as a whole. Give each one a rating on the scales below.

Everyone faces unique circumstances, and therefore there will

	Ending/ Have not dealt with end		In Transition		New Beginning/ Emotionally reenergized
You	1	2	3	4	5
Your Team	1	2	3	4	5
Your Organization	1	2	3	4	5

be unique implications from doing this exercise. When Eckhard Pfeiffer assessed his top team at Compaq in 1996, he found that some had fully dealt with Compaq's transition from being a PC company to a group of new businesses based on the revolution in digital communications and entertainment. These people he promoted. Those who were partway there, he tried to help. And those who could never make it, he let go.

That was his answer. Maybe you are in the opposite situation. Maybe you are still holding on to the good old days more than those around you. Think for a few minutes about the numbers you circled and then record your thoughts on the implications of these numbers below.

Implications:

Energizing People Through Transitions

Whatever the implications, a leader has the job of helping others master transitions. Leaders constantly diagnose themselves, their teams, their organizations and others along the dimensions above. They understand how people are dealing with transitions so they can help channel their energy into positive behaviors.

In thinking about Bridges's work and watching leaders, I've identified five things leaders do to help people through transition:

1. Create a sense of urgency
2. Define a mission that is inspiring and worth achieving
3. Set goals that stretch people's abilities
4. Build a spirit of teamwork
5. Create the expectation that goals can be met

To energize people, leaders think through how they will do each one of these things. Gary Wendt ran GE Capital, one of the world's most successful companies and one of its largest financial institutions. According to Wendt, one thing he had to constantly do was give people a sense of urgency by "creating a crisis." It was Wendt's way of making people uncomfortable with what they have. One team of managers came to Wendt very pleased with its projections for double-digit growth. Wendt quickly dismissed the forecast. He wanted the company to double in just a few years. The result of such behaviors is that people at GE Capital realized that yesterday's performance is never good enough for tomorrow and that they had to focus on getting better all of the time.

Once Wendt had to instill a sense of urgency in his discussions, he went about doing the other things he had to do to get his team on board. Below I have provided some examples of how leaders create energy. Take a look at the descriptions and then record thoughts on how you can help your organization change.

	Example	Generic Principles
Urgency	Gary Wendt created a crisis by talking about how drastically competitors and markets were changing ahead of GE Capital.	• External threats and opportunities • Technologies which are causing quantum changes in your business • Customers or suppliers which are concentrating or integrating • Competitors which are growing in strength and aggressiveness
	Other leaders take important symbolic steps. To wake up his organization, Bill Weiss (Ameritech) called meetings of senior executives on weekends and made them look at the performance of the company in new ways.	
Mission	Father Cunningham of Focus: HOPE reinforced his organization's important mission at several levels. First, he aimed candidates in Focus: HOPE'S training programs toward self-sufficiency. Not content to leave it there, he placed these same people at the forefront of the civil rights movement. According to Cunningham, civil rights will never be achieved until people can see "young black men and women in the highest positions of productivity in our society." Suddenly, the candidates struggling to make ends meet while they study to be machinists aren't just thinking about getting a paycheck, they are thinking about serving as community role models.	• Playing to win vs. playing not to lose • Building something special • Epic struggle of good vs. evil • Making a difference in customers' and employees' lives • Put people in the company in the roles of protagonists

	Example	Generic Principles
Mission	Robert Goizueta, former chairman at Coca-Cola, made an inspiring mission out of selling a 100-year-old product. Rather than celebrate Coca-Cola's meteoric growth, Goizueta focused on the vast opportunity ahead. The human body needs 64 fluid ounces a day to survive. Coca-Cola currently only provides two to the average person. The message to his troops—Let's go get the rest! In framing Coca-Cola's mission this way, Goizueta ensured there would always be something to strive for, new heights to climb. He highlighted the key roles of Coca-Cola's people worldwide in getting there. "We need people who see opportunities where others don't. People who walk into a room and see where Coca-Cola isn't, not where it is."	• Playing to win vs. playing not to lose • Building something special • Epic struggle of good vs. evil • Making a difference in customers' and employees' lives • Put people in the company in the roles of protagonists
Stretch	Jack Welch set stretch targets for performance at GE. The company won't reach its mission of being the world's most competitive enterprise unless it actually reaches levels of performance that people thought were impossible. So Welch set stretch goals of achieving ten inventory turns and a 15% operating margin by 1995. For the last thirty years, GE's inventory turns have hovered at around 5% and operating margins at around 10%. In stretching for these "impossible" targets, the company learned to do things faster and better than if it were going after doable goals.	• Setting objectives that seem out of reach • Moving farther and faster than people think you can
Teamwork	Dick Stonesifer, who ran GE Appliances, used the phrase "One team, better and faster than anybody in the world" to show he wanted the company to work. And Stonesifer, or Stoney as he was called, would make himself a full member of the team. He personally would receive feedback from his team, share it with 20 people at a time, and then ask for help. The message was clear, "We're in this together, I need your help to get better."	• Providing people with the support they need to contribute • Rewarding people for helping each other • Assigning work to ensure interdependency • Making yourself a vulnerable member of the team
Confidence	Tom Tiller, who organized the bus trip when he was at GE Appliances, was the master at showing his confidence in people. The bus trip was a perfect example—rather than hire consultants Tiller arranged the bus trip to show that his group of people could save its own plant.	• Showing confidence in people • Having a positive attitude—the leader must show he or she is confident the team will get things done • Physically demonstrable and tangible acts

Figure 12: Examples of Energizing People Through Transitions

ENERGIZING PEOPLE THROUGH CHANGE

Take a few minutes to think through how you will use each of the five elements above to energize people about change.

Urgency

How will you give people a sense of urgency? Think of competitive threats and opportunities. Think of drawing the dire consequences of inaction in a verbal picture people will immediately understand.

_____

_____

_____

_____

_____

Mission

How will you craft an inspiring mission? How will you connect your mission to people on a level that is important to them individually without being so vague that it loses meaning?

_____

_____

_____

_____

_____

_____

Stretch

What goals and objectives will you set? How will you make your stretch goals seem worthy of striving for?

_____

_____

_____

_____

_____

Teamwork

How will you instill a sense that you are all (including yourself) preparing for change?

_____

_____

_____

_____

_____

Confidence

How will you give people the confidence that can help them overcome their fears?

_____

_____

_____

_____

ENERGIZING INDIVIDUALS

As a leader working with and developing others, you need to think about how the combination of the five factors above affects people. Each individual deals with change and emotions differently. The goal is to use whatever combination of these factors each person needs to help them work through transition. Think about each individual on your team. Record what you will do with that person individually in order to energize him or her.

Team Member	Urgency	Mission	Stretch Goals	Teamwork	Confidence

Mobilizing Energy Throughout the Organization

The leader must create ways of generating emotional energy in the organization both through face-to-face activities and large-scale system-wide means.

There is absolutely no single best way to do this. The style and personality of each leader are different and so is the organizational context. This requires leaders to discover their own repertoire of ways to energize people face-to-face. Winning leaders rarely miss an opportunity to energize their people. The now infamous MBWA (management by walking around), when done correctly, is an obvious, simple mechanism for staying in touch, listening and energizing people. When done poorly, it is a source of cynical jokes about the leader.

This section of the handbook provides you with a catalogue of best practice examples to stimulate your creativity as a leader. You may already be doing many of these or have others that you use. The challenge is to keep improving.

Leader	Example	Warning!
	PERFORMANCE TRIPS	
Gary Wendt, former CEO of GE Capital	Annually, the top several hundred performers were given a several-week trip to some exotic part of the world such as China, India or Russia with their spouses. Gary Wendt personally led the delegation. He picked the destination very carefully—it was some area of the world he wanted these leaders to be focused on for growth opportunities. During the trip, Wendt made sure people were exposed to ideas and relationships they could use. The result was not simply a celebration but also a learning event which built a long-term perspective and gave a window to the future.	Not done right, these types of trips can turn into hoopla drinking and playing boondoggles.
	SKIP LEVEL MEETINGS	
Larry Bossidy, former CEO of AlliedSignal	Larry Bossidy religiously held skip level meetings at least once a week over breakfast with about ten people. They were open, candid, very interactive sessions. He listened, learned and taught.	One CEO deenergizes his managers at every skip level meeting by being overly formal and intimidating. These sessions feel more like an inquisition than a mutual exchange.

Leader	Example	Warning!

TOWN HALL MEETINGS

Andy Grove, Chairman of Intel

Andy Grove makes sure that he gathers all the people possible at a site, a factory for example, to have a no-holds-barred, question and answer session. He deals with several hundred people at a time. He answers every single question and gets back to people when he can't. They are a great opportunity to learn about employees' ideas, and about how Intel is performing in its customer and market segments. These are also great opportunities for Grove to teach how he thinks about the business and his outlook on its prospects.

Overly controlled town hall meetings with staff people filtering or planting questions will create frustration, not positive energy. Also, the leader needs a teachable point of view or they will not be able to handle grilling from front-line employees without sacrificing credibility.

NEW MANAGER ASSIMILATION PROCESS

Tom Tiller, former head of GE Silicones

Each time Tom Tiller was transferred, he had one of the human resource staff members interview his new direct reports to prepare for a session where they could discuss anything they wanted to know about the "new boss." The discussions ranged from their hopes and fears, expectations for his role, what they intend to do to support the transition and what he wants from them. He prepares a very clear document for everyone that explains his impressions of the organization, his expectations, his plan for the organization, his personal career plan and his last 360 feedback report. The straightforward articulation of who Tom is strips away all the insecurities people have about changing leaders. He turns their negative energy into a promise for the future.

The new manager assimilation process is powerful, but if given too little time, or not run in a totally open fashion, it can dig the new leader a negative energy hole.

ATTENDING LEARNING EVENTS

Dick Notebaert, former CEO of Ameritech

Dick Notebaert went to the Ameritech Institute for numerous programs to hold no-holds-barred dialogue. He gathered all the program participants, usually about 50 to 100 people, into the "pit" of a large tiered classroom and spent an hour or two of highly charged dialogue and teaching. He used the opportunity to talk with employees about their views on customers and growing the company. The participants provided written feedback to him, a one-pager from everyone: 1) Issues that were resolved for me. 2) What still troubles me. 3) My number one takeaway from the session.

When I ran GE's Crotonville in the 1980s, the defensive "come and preach" leaders got nailed. The participants ended up being deenergized and cynical about the leader.

Leader	Example	Warning!

COACHING SESSIONS

| Dick Stonesifer, retired CEO of GE Appliances | One-on-one coaching which combines written and interactive dialogue and problem solving is a world-class skill of Dick Stonesifer's. He had regular candid "tough love" sessions with each of his people, where he always helped them establish a clear personal development plan. Stonesifer himself is very open about his own development needs. | Not having things in writing is a big mistake. The higher up people are in the hierarchy the more distortion takes place—people do not recall what was said six months ago or may leave a joint session with very different interpretations about expected changes in behavior. |

TRANSITION WORKSHOP

| Bob Knowling, former Vice President of Network Operations, US WEST | One of the most emotional events for a team is when their boss gets fired. Knowling had to remove several long-time managers as part of his transformation. He designed a transition process. He held a workshop with the departing boss's team, a session where he taught them Bridges's transition framework and then ran a workshop to get the emotions out on the table, to set expectations and to explain honestly why their boss was fired. He worked the team through the emotional transition and laid the groundwork for a new beginning. | This is truly world-class candor. Those who are not prepared to lay their case for change out in the open, and who do not have the self-confidence to deal with messy emotions are going to get clobbered. |

BENCHMARKING

| Jack Welch, former CEO of GE | Welch is an absolute nut about benchmarking. He brought CEOs and business outsiders to share at his Corporate Executive Council (20 or so most senior people at the company) meetings best practices. He also visited throughout the company and many other companies to make sure that his people were constantly sharing best practices. | Leaders do not delegate benchmarking. All too many companies have quasi-academic benchmarking groups and catalogues of cases. Benchmarking is an energizing learning event, especially when done with a team. |

Figure 13: Some Best Practice Examples for Creating Energy

DESIGNING YOUR PORTFOLIO OF ENERGIZING EVENTS

Consider what you can do to improve the energy level of your team and organization.

	What	When	With Whom
1.			
2.			
3.			
4.			
5.			
6.			

GENERATING A TPOV FOR EMOTIONAL ENERGY

Leaders pull together all of the currents of emotional energy running through their organizations. They understand what excites them personally and how to maximize their contributions to create positive emotional energy in their co-workers, team and organizations. Reflect on the exercises you've just completed and pull together your succinct, articulate point of view on emotional energy. Summarize your thoughts on each of the following:

Personal Energy

1. What energizes me:

2. Energy conflicts and synergies in my life (work/family/self):

3. Energy through transitions—how I do this:

4. Face-to-face energizing:

Energizing a Team

1. How do I energize individual team members:

2. How do I mobilize energy throughout the organization:

SECTION VIII

Edge

Objectives:

- Understand the role of edge in leadership
- Examine the difficult people and portfolio decisions facing your business
- Develop your point of view on when and how to make the tough calls

---

If there's a shortage of leadership at some corporations, it's almost certainly equated with a lack of edge. Edge is the agent that converts ideas and values into action. In short, it is the ability to make tough decisions. It is having the courage of one's convictions and the willingness to take principled actions when others would do nothing.

Dante once wrote that "the hottest places in hell are reserved for those who, in times of great moral crisis, maintain their neutrality." While few leaders encounter "great moral crises," there are important decisions that a leader, and for that matter everyone, makes every day. More importantly, it is through the tough decisions that people's leadership is tested. It is through these decisions that people have to deny the pleasures and security of short-term gains in order to take a risk for long-term sustainability and growth. It is in these decisions that people weigh the trade-offs of living with principle versus immediate gain or comfort. These are the decisions that often determine the course of a team, department or company.

They also determine a leader's credibility. Long before a leader makes a tough decision, people are waiting for them to do it. Salespeople are the first to know a product isn't selling. They wait, and try hard to sell it or think of clever ways to make up for its shortcomings, while they wonder why the jerks at headquarters keep producing these things. They are waiting for a leader to make a decision and say, "We've always made this, but it's no longer a good product. We're going to fix it or stop making it." Leaders who make these decisions in a timely fashion build their credibility, while those who don't torpedo it.

Edge Is Honest, Not Brutal

Leaders with edge refuse to let difficulty stand in the way of acting on their deeply held ideas and values. Leaders with edge are driven by the desire to realize their vision for the organization. They cut through uncertainty and ambiguity to face reality, and they act decisively.

Unlike autocrats and bullies, leaders with edge are motivated by what is best for the organization, not by personal gain or indulgence in the exercise of power. And, unlike many weak-willed managers, they are insistent on a clear-minded adherence to the company's core ideas and values. They are good at saying "no" long before the marketplace has forced their hand and threatened an end-of-year bonus or long-term job security.

People Edge

The first front on which leaders exhibit edge is people. This is tough. It means honestly assessing people. It means looking them in the eye as you give them feedback. And it means letting go of some people. But to help their organizations and their people reach their full potential, leaders know they have to do this.

Jack Welch had a useful framework for reviewing people at

General Electric. In his 1991 annual report letter, he described four types of managers at GE:

1. The first is one who delivers on commitments—financial or otherwise—and shares the values of our Company. His or her future is an easy call. Onward and upward.
2. The second type of leader is one who does not meet commitments and does not share our values. Not as pleasant a call, but equally easy.
3. The third is one who misses commitments but shares the values. He or she usually gets a second chance, preferably in a different environment.
4. Then there's the fourth type—the most difficult for many of us to deal with. That leader delivers on commitments, makes all the numbers, but doesn't share the values we must have. This is the individual who typically forces performance out of people rather than inspires it: the autocrat, the big shot, the tyrant. Too often all of us have looked the other way. . . . But now these people must go.

> —JOHN F. WELCH JR., "LETTER TO SHAREHOLDERS,"
> 1991 GENERAL ELECTRIC COMPANY ANNUAL REPORT

A useful way to conceptualize *how* people are performing versus *how well* they perform is to look at the Performance/Values matrix. As Welch points out above, looking at performance alone is hopelessly short-sighted. Leaders embed values into an organization by behaving consistently with these beliefs on a daily basis. Those who don't measure up to the company's stated values are destructive and must be helped to improve or they must leave.

PERFORMANCE/VALUES MATRIX

Assess the people with whom you work closely on both the values and performance dimensions by placing them within the grid below.

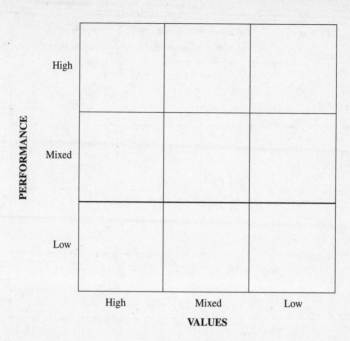

After assessing people, your role as a leader is to act on this reality. Those who have no hope of improving should be separated from the company. But many people will represent difficult dilemmas. Those who have good values but perform poorly, and those who perform well but have bad values represent the toughest choices. They are important choices, too, as everyone watches what a leader does with these people.

The first step is to give people feedback (you may wish to show them this grid). The next step is to work with each person on developing them in their needed areas.

Think through specific behaviors and incidents so that you can give direct feedback to the people you've rated above. Develop a plan for who you will work with and how you can assist each person.

	Person	Behaviors That Exemplify Need for Coaching	What I Can Do to Help
1.			
2.			
3.			
4.			
5.			
6.			

Business Edge

Leaders must also exercise edge on another basic front, their business portfolios. This means making decisions about which products to offer, which customers to serve and which businesses to enter. This often involves discontinuing activities or products and replacing them with others.

Andy Grove and Gordon Moore of Intel faced one such monumental decision in the mid-1980s. Their company's main product was computer memories. When the market began to shift, Grove and Moore struggled for two years with how to respond. Finally, they decided to exit the historically profitable segment of memories in order to compete aggressively in microprocessors. The computer world has never been the same. Intel has grown to dominate this industry with nearly a 90% market share.

On a smaller scale, leaders at all levels of companies make tough decisions every day. For example, Mary Petrovich, who ran a safety-restraint plant in AlliedSignal's automotive sector, faced a turnaround situation the day she started her job. She quickly had to decide which initiatives she would keep and which she would toss. When she took decisive action, people immediately sensed there was a new direction for the plant. She transformed a poorly performing plant that was losing $500,000 a month into a first-class operation that made $200,000 a month.

In short, challenges that require decisive action confront leaders across all aspects and all levels of their business: under-performing assets, poor product sales, unprofitable customers, inadequate supplier quality, new product extensions, new investments, and so forth.

FACING BUSINESS EDGE

This activity asks you to face reality about the decisions that you need to make. In order for your organization to win in the long run, you need to figure out what tough decisions need to be made. What will you do, and by when?

The Tough Edge Decisions I Need to Make

(Areas to consider: products, services, customers, suppliers, investments, etc.)

What I Will Do   By When

1. _____   _____

2. _____   _____

3. _____   _____

4. _____   _____

5. _____   _____

6. _____   _____

Developing Edge: Triage

Edge can be developed. The key is getting people to face increasing levels of complexity, stress and risk/reward consequences. An excellent example is how triage nurses are trained in emergency rooms. They start as understudies and then are given more responsibility, along with more stress. At every step, experienced doctors and nurses coach and mentor them. They help them work through technical issues as well as emotional ones. The point is to make sure they realize the importance of making balanced decisions and have the skills and courage to do so.

Winning companies do the same thing. They place leaders in situations where definite yes-or-no decisions are required. They coach them after they make the decisions. Those who do well move to bigger, tougher assignments. Those who don't do well don't move on. If you had to entrust your life to a triage nurse, you would do best to make sure he or she had successfully operated under fire in a big-city emergency room where they gained significant experience taking immediate action under stress.

Personally developing edge and developing it in others is often stressful but relatively straightforward. Put yourself and others in situations where such behavior is called for and then keep increasing the stakes. It never gets easy, and the goal is not to desensitize you to the pain that tough decisions can create for yourself and others. But practice in facing difficult decisions will give you the self-confidence to act on your beliefs and values, and it will test your conviction to those ideas and values.

ENHANCING YOUR EDGE DEVELOPMENT

Consider what you can do to improve your capacity for triage. What assignments and experiences would help you? Who would be a good mentor? Think of some creative ways of dramatically enhancing your triage capability.

_____

_____

_____

_____

_____

ENHANCING EDGE IN OTHERS

As a leader developing other leaders, what is your action plan for the key people on your team who need to develop more edge? How will you teach edge and triage? How will you give them difficult experiences that test them? How will you ensure that a failure does not irrevocably hurt the company, while you keep stress in the situation?

Key People	Edge-Enhancing Experiences
1.	
2.	
3.	
4.	
5.	
6.	

COMMUNICATING EDGE

Decisions are never made in a vacuum. Your decisions will impact how you feel about yourself and how others perceive you. But all of the winning leaders with whom I have worked constantly communicate their views on when edge is necessary and how to handle these challenging decisions with compassion.

Imagine that you have just made one of the difficult people or portfolio decisions you considered in the exercises above. If you were talking to a group of co-workers or employees, how would you explain it and communicate your perspective on edge? Use the space below to write down your teaching notes:

_____

_____

_____

_____

_____

Creating Your Storyline

Objectives:

- Use personalized stories to communicate your teachable point of view
- Write the storyline for where your organization is going and how it will change

---

Winning leadership is about creating the future, controlling your own destiny. In order to do this, leaders need a compelling story. Throughout *The Leadership Engine*, and throughout this handbook, I have made the point that leaders require a teachable point of view in order to express themselves clearly and teach others. But a leader also needs a dynamic story about where he or she is taking the organization. It is these stories that excite people about the future and spur them to act.

Leaders essentially tell three types of stories. The first is *Who I Am* stories. They describe what makes them tick, what kind of a person they are. The second is *Who We Are* stories, which provide some sense of identity for a group, either through common experiences or a common mission. And the last is the *Future Story*. In this story, a leader provides a description of why the group must change (that is, why they must leave a place), where they are going and how they will get there.

Tied together, these three stories are what I call a leader's storyline. The storyline represents a consistent collection of themes. The themes start from the "Who I Am Story." These are embodied by the leader and their followers in the "Who We Are" and future stories. It is this consistency that runs from a leader's personal story to the story of the future they are telling and embodying that gives the leader legitimacy. The story and the teachable point of view are inextricably linked. A teachable point of view can be a set of arid concepts, seemingly disconnected, until it is brought together in stories that help people make sense of the present and look forward to the future. At the same time, a story not grounded in a teachable point of view can be merely an amusing or intoxicating tale.

As an example, think about Martin Luther King Jr. King had been a student of politics and religion and received a doctorate. King could give his teachable point of view about why segregation and discrimination had to end on religious, social or political grounds. But he didn't attack the system solely on intellectual grounds. Instead, he told his story. The story was rooted in his personal development from having grown up in the South and having suffered the abuses of that society. His speeches told a compelling story of the future "where children would not be judged by the color of their skin, but by the content of their character."

Leaders and Stories: Howard Gardner's Concepts and Application

Howard Gardner, a noted educator based at Harvard University, wrote a wonderful book, *Leading Minds* (New York: Basic Books, 1995), in which he describes how leaders use stories. The following charts paraphrase some of his descriptions of how leaders do this.

The Story: Context and Impact

The story is the critical component of leadership. A leader must appreciate what constitutes a story, struggle personally to create a story and use the story to provide the organization's members with a sense of identity and values.

Gardner's Concepts	Implications for Your Story
Gardner uses the term "story" in a broad sense. Stories include narratives and invented accounts that serve as symbols. Further, stories include overt or propositional accounts communicated directly by the leader and the vision of life that is embodied in the actions and the life of the leader.	• The story can be manifested in a variety of forms. No matter their form, effective stories offer the audience a vision of life—a way to interpret the present and shape the future. • Leaders' actions form the story as much or more than their words.
"The story is a basic human cognitive form; the artful creation and articulation of stories constitutes a fundamental part of the leader's vocation. Stories speak to both parts of the human mind: its reason and emotion."	• The story must appeal to both people's rational and emotional desires.
"I deliberately use the terms story and narrative rather than message or theme. In speaking of stories, I want to call attention to the fact that leaders present a dynamic perspective to their followers: not just a headline or snapshot, but a drama that unfolds over time, in which they—the leaders and followers—are the principal characters or heroes."	• Building the storyline for a company is an ongoing process. • The audience should sense that this is the beginning of an ongoing journey to constantly revise and pursue its goals for what the company will be and how it will perform.

Gardner's Concepts	Implications for Your Story
"It is the particular burden of the leader to help other individuals determine their personal, social, and moral identities; more often than not, leaders inspire in part because of how they have resolved their own identity issues." "Typically, these identity stories have their roots in the personal experiences of the leader in the course of his own development. But it is characteristic of the effective leader that his stories can be transplanted to a larger canvas—that they make sense not only to members of his family and close circle, but to increasingly large institutions and, at an extreme, heterogeneously constituted political entities."	• The corporate storyline begins with its key leaders. • Senior leaders must struggle with their own identities: "What type of a leader am I? What do I want my legacy to be? What values do I want to ensure are embodied in my business." • The storyline must recognize several distinct groups in your business and give them an identity.

The Audience: Readiness and Receptivity

Leaders must appreciate several key aspects of an audience. Most importantly, leaders must understand that their stories are in competition with other stories for the attention and devotion of followers. This realization leads to several behaviors that can help leaders claim a "mindshare" of followers' attention.

Gardner's Concepts	Implications for Your Story
"The audience is not simply a blank slate, however, waiting for the first, or for the best, story to be etched on its virginal tablet. Rather, audience members come equipped with many stories that have already been told and retold in their homes, their societies, and their domains. The stories of the leader—be they traditional or novel—must compete with many other extant stories; and if the new stories are to succeed they must transplant, suppress, complement, or in some measure outweigh the earlier stories, as well as the contemporary oppositional 'counterstories.'"	• What is the legacy of stories that exist within the company? • How does the new story compare to the extant stories—what is different, what are variations on the core ideology of the company? Which elements of the story will people resist? Which elements will be new and serve to unlock people's potential?

Gardner's Concepts	Implications for Your Story
"The best chances for success lie in a steadfast concentration on the same core message, along with flexibility in how it is presented, and openness to the message being apprehended at a number of levels of sophistication."	• Senior leadership must walk the talk— all activities, signals, communications should be consistent with the storyline. • Senior leadership must be comfortable with the chaotic, messy process of unfreezing people's mindsets, using constructive conflict to generate new ideas, and using them to refine and re-create the new organization. Rapid clarification will stunt the healthy process of debate. • What, precisely, is your key message? • How consistently is this message communicated by each member of your leadership team? • Have the senior leaders—the carriers of the new story—planned how to adapt the message to various audiences without compromising its underlying principles?

The Organization: The Ultimate Goal

The storyline should be crafted within the context of becoming institutionalized and reflected in the organization. The story can only be fulfilled if its lasting legacy is embodied in your business.

Gardner's Concepts	Implications for Your Story
"While a leader can sometimes speak directly to a large audience and achieve initial success via the perceived bond between himself and his auditors, enduring leadership ultimately depends on some kind of institutional or organizational basis. If the leader already belongs to an organization, it is his job to bring the organization along."	• The senior leadership's objective should be nothing less than a transformation of the entire company—from its structure and governance to the values and vision of life shared by its employees. • Without this complete transformation, the story is likely to become a temporary diversion from the company's current course. • Senior leaders need to be active leaders (instead of passive observers) to "bring the organization along."

The Embodiment: Walking the Talk

A key component of any leader's story is the reflection of that leader's actions. The embodiment of the leader's actions should further the storyline.

Gardner's Concepts	Implications for Your Story
"The creator must in some sense embody the story, although he need not be saintly. Indeed, the credibility of some leaders may actually be enhanced if they have had— and have come to terms with—a rocky or even counterstory past."	• Be honest and open regarding how each member of the senior leadership group arrived at their interpretation of the collective story. • By demonstrating vulnerability, senior leadership can make the story more compelling.
"If the leader seems to contradict the story by the facts of his existence, if he appears hypocritical, the story probably will not remain convincing over the long run."	• Consistency between words (or other conveyances) of the story and the current behavior of its creators is critical. • Every senior leader at the company should take the "mirror test." Those behaviors consistent with the new story should be encouraged. Inconsistent behaviors must be eliminated.
"The individual who does not embody his messages will eventually be found out, even as the inarticulate individual who leads the exemplary life may eventually come to be appreciated."	• The story should come from the heart. • Emotion and personal involvement are more important than slick communication. • Leaders need to show their vulnerability and deep commitment through face-to-face communication and demonstration of new behaviors.

Enduring Features of Leadership

- Understand your audience—who they are and what must change within them
- Appreciate the nature of the audiences, including its change-able features
- Invest your own (and others') energy in the building and maintenance of an organization
- Embody in your own life the principal themes of the story

Building off these basic themes from Gardner's and others' work, I believe these are the guidelines for creating an effective story.

- Speak to valued aspects of the past and honor timeless traditions
- Deal with new and complicating trends such as globalization, the proliferation of technical expertise, the shifting of economic power to new countries
- Define a winning future, in which the organization and its people are victorious
- Appeal to morals, ethical codes, examples of courage

Step 1: The Essence of Your Teachable Point of View

Before jumping into the creation of a full storyline, you need to have a basic sense of the plot: where you want to go and how you want to get there. For leaders, this is the ideas, values, emotional energy and edge that they bring to their organizations.

You've made some notes at the end of each section of this handbook on your teachable point of view. Take some time to identify how the elements fit together and summarize them on the chart below. You might imagine that you have to prepare an overhead to talk to new hires at your company. The example below is of a chart that Jack Welch could have used if he were presenting to a group of young GE managers at Crotonville, the company's Management Training and Development facility.

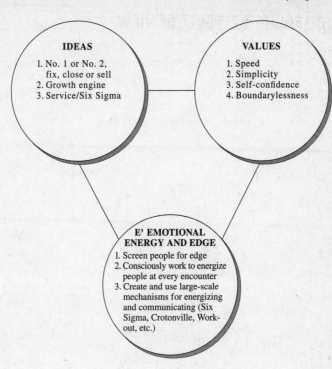

IDEAS

1. No. 1 or No. 2, fix, close or sell
2. Growth engine
3. Service/Six Sigma

VALUES

1. Speed
2. Simplicity
3. Self-confidence
4. Boundarylessness

E³ EMOTIONAL ENERGY AND EDGE

1. Screen people for edge
2. Consciously work to energize people at every encounter
3. Create and use large-scale mechanisms for energizing and communicating (Six Sigma, Crotonville, Work-out, etc.)

Figure 14: Welch's Teachable Point of View

YOUR TEACHABLE POINT OF VIEW

Fill in the chart below with the key elements of your teachable point of view as a leader.

A Leader's Teachable Point of View

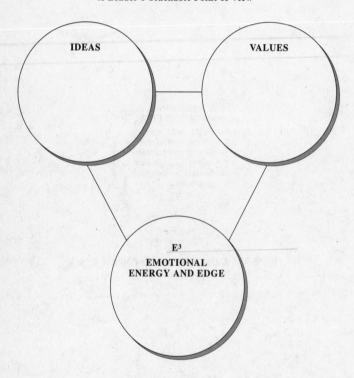

The next step is to do the same preparation for key elements of your storyline.

The *Who Am I* Storyline

Figure 15 includes some examples of these stories and how leaders use them to communicate their individuality, vulnerability and teachable point of view.

Leader	Story	Leadership Theme
Andy Grove, Chairman of Intel	In a cover story in *FORTUNE* magazine, Grove tells of how he controlled his own destiny when faced with prostate cancer. The basic message was that he took control. He did his own homework by working with over a dozen doctors, learning all that he could. Then he put the pieces together to create his own treatment plan.	Control your own destiny.
Tom Tiller, former Head of GE Silicones	Told stories of his grandfather teaching him about stretch goals. Tiller's grandfather would give him impossible tasks like building a runway or let him run his own lumber business. Each time, Tom would have the frustrations of early failure and missteps but he answered the challenge.	Set seemingly impossible stretch goals to get the most out of yourself and others.
Eckhard Pfeiffer, former CEO of Compaq	As a 4-year-old in total poverty after WWII, he became a refugee with his mother and no worldly possessions. The feeling of absolute panic gave him an incredible will to succeed. His ability to rise from this taught him that he could survive anything, and that he should never be afraid to take risks.	Be willing to take risks and change everything.

Leader	Story	Leadership Theme
Gary Wendt, former CEO of GE Capital	For his first job after Harvard Business School, Wendt went to work in Houston, Texas, for a land developer who made him sell home building lots. Wendt had expected to go to this company and be a fancy MBA strategist and financial expert. But Harlan, the owner, said, "You have to prove to me you can sell before you do anything else in the business." Wendt says after several days of depression, wondering why he had invested all that time and money in an MBA when his first job was asking him to sell house lots, he decided he had no alternative and that he would. He then says that, after selling his first lot and going on to be a very successful salesperson, he learned a lesson GE could never have taught him: that business is two parties agreeing on price and value, whether a used car, a lot, or a jet engine. The second story from his days with Harlan was having the firm go bankrupt. Wendt had to try and keep it running without enough cash to pay people's salaries in order to pay suppliers.	Stay close to the customer and the guts of the business if you want to succeed.
Rogellio Robledo, President and CEO of Frito-Lay International	Rogellio was a rising star at PepsiCo's Frito Lay Division. His intensity was burning out his team. One of his mentors arranged for seats behind the coach at a basketball game. His assignment to Rogellio—watch the coach and then we'll talk about what he does. Says Rogellio, "That's when I learned I had to listen to how the team was doing before I spoke."	Let your people and your team express themselves.
Bill Pollard, Director of ServiceMaster	He tells a collection of stories that underscore the importance of learning about leadership from all facets of life. One story is battling a bleeding ulcer at age 33 while in a high pressure Chicago law firm. Realizing that his work was out of control, he became a college administrator and professor. Later his work in an Ecuadorean village helping them set up a communal water system and his trip to Eastern Europe during the cold war gave him ideas about giving people at ServiceMaster a greater sense of mission.	Leadership is about deep learning from a wide range of life experiences—leaders must keep putting themselves in new situations to learn.

Figure 15: Examples of Stories Leaders Tell

WRITING YOUR "WHO I AM" STORY

As you look at the elements of your teachable point of view, what are some personal stories that capture how your perspective was shaped?

Story   ## Leadership Theme

_____   _____

_____   _____

_____   _____

_____   _____

_____   _____

Step 2: Bringing It All Together

Who I Am stories are critically important because they give leaders credibility. They allow them to speak from experience, as someone who shares the joys and pains of life just as their followers do. But that alone is not enough. Leaders must also be able to take their story and their teachable point of view to create dynamic stories about the future of their organizations. These stories give people a sense for three things:

- Why things must change
- Where the organization is going
- How they will get there

Importantly, leaders put these stories in the frame of their audience. They talk about where they are going in the context of what it will take from followers to get there and what the payoff will be when they arrive. Coca-Cola's Roberto Goizueta provided an example of the power of these stories.

Goizueta's story tells of the world of opportunity awaiting people who work for Coke. In Goizueta's eyes, these opportunities were infinite. Most people would balk at what is perceivably an overstatement. After all, Coca-Cola is a hundred-year-old product with the most established brand perception in the entire world. It must be mature, the cynics say. But it doesn't seem so when Goizueta told of the 5.7 billion people around the world who drink sixty-four ounces of liquid each day just to survive. The refreshing, economical Coke soft drink, Goizueta continued, currently only accounted for an average two ounces per person. Capturing the remaining sixty-two ounces would provide people with an enjoyable drink while enriching Coca-Cola's shareholders, partners and employees.

Goizueta didn't stop with why the organization must change or the stretch goal it was trying to achieve. His narrative even included a description of the story's central protagonist, the answer to how the organization would achieve this remarkable feat. Goizueta described the ideal Coca-Cola managers as those with the uncanny ability to walk into a room and see where Coke is not, rather than where it is.

WRITING YOUR STORY

The best storylines include a message about who the people in the organization are as a group, the community that they form. Most importantly, you should lay out a clear road map of where the organization is going that includes:

- Your case for change
- Where we are going as an organization
- How we will get there

Use the space below to draft an outline of your thoughts, and then write the complete story separately.

_____

_____

_____

_____

_____

_____

_____

_____

_____

_____

Step 3: Taking Your Story Off-Broadway

One of Roger Enrico's key tenets is to take an idea "Off-Broadway," to test it and then recraft it. Leaders all have multiple constituencies, whether you are a twenty-nine-year-old Tom Tiller taking over the range line at GE Appliances having to deal with the union, managers and other departments; Jack Welch, whose constituents included suppliers and customers; or Eckhard Pfeiffer when he was at Compaq worrying about the institutional investors, a whole new set of joint venture partners and creating new customer stakeholders.

IDENTIFYING YOUR KEY STAKEHOLDERS

In the diagram below, lay out your key stakeholders, the ones you must enroll in your storyline to succeed. Then develop an action plan for taking your storyline Off-Broadway.

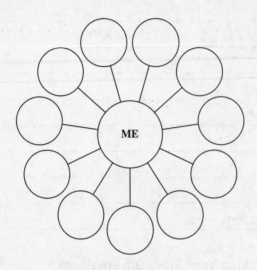

PREPARING TO GO OFF-BROADWAY

One of the best examples of taking a storyline Off-Broadway is what happened at Royal/Dutch Shell in the fall of 1995. The four senior leaders of the company each ran half-day workshops with their staffs to engage them in the storyline. They each presented the storyline to groups of twenty to thirty executives. It was not scripted by staff, but was crafted by them at a meeting earlier in the summer. It included the case for change, where they wanted to lead Shell into the future and how they were going to help Shell get there. They each practiced with their own stories and their own examples, and they each gave the storyline with as much emotional energy as possible. The results were mixed. Some stumbled a bit, but in all cases they engaged their staff in getting helpful feedback, and each ran the workshop so that each individual had to stand up in small groups and present his or her own version of the storyline to each other and get feedback. Thus, a process of enrollment was kick-started.

Consider how you can test your storyline with the various key stakeholders you have.

Stakeholder Group	How I Will Take It Off-Broadway
_____	_____
_____	_____
_____	_____
_____	_____
_____	_____
_____	_____
_____	_____
_____	_____
_____	_____

Encouraging Leaders to Develop Others

Objective:

- Examine the systems that can be used to encourage leaders developing leaders

Lots of companies, now, come as far as we've come. Some of them take the next step to preeminence. Others find the task too difficult, the road too long, too arduous and they fall back. In a sense we rationalize mediocrity. Let that not be us. We're going to be about action and passion because, without it, it is not to have lived. Remember what happens when we get where we want to go. We benefit our families and our employees—that's very close to us—but also our customers and our suppliers. We gain the respect for those people who choose to measure us. We justify our business careers. We just didn't come to work, we did something special.   —LARRY BOSSIDY, FORMER CHAIRMAN AND CEO, ALLIEDSIGNAL

Larry Bossidy kept reminding his leadership team at AlliedSignal of the legacy they all want to leave: a better company, a better institution, for the future.

Bossidy's challenge for each person to make a difference meant a leader needed to be focused on weaving his or her point of view into the fabric of the organization and develop other leaders. Some places have done this for years. Hewlett-Packard and Intel regularly produce leaders who are actively recruited by a host of other high-tech companies that feel fortunate to steal away just a few. GE, Procter & Gamble and McKinsey & Co. are also "academy" companies that produce leaders who are sought after to assume senior executive positions in other organizations.

Organizational Systems: Improving Leaders' Development of Others

These organizations have such a strong legacy of high-quality people because their leaders recognize the strength in having leaders develop others. They architect their companies to encourage and reward this. As I described in Section V, this means working on three levels—the technical, political and cultural. When done correctly, these are woven together to encourage and assist leaders to develop others.

TECHNICAL STRAND

—The strategy and systems within the company all demand that leaders assume responsibility and take initiative, regardless of their hierarchical position. Rewards are provided for those who develop other leaders.

POLITICAL STRAND

—Power is distributed so that people at all levels and in various parts of the company are able to provide coaching and development opportunities for others.

CULTURAL STRAND

—Developing other leaders is viewed as one of the highest forms of service that can be provided to the organization. Star performers proactively develop others.

For example, take a look at how GE's technical, political and cultural strategies encourage leaders to develop other leaders.

GE's strategy of being number one or two in all industries in which it competes demands a high level of performance from each business. Businesses need to be fast just to stay in GE's portfolio, calling for leaders at all levels. Welch's demand that GE delayer took the machinery of control away from its hierarchical bureaucrats. The company improved its human resource process to give each person the tools to access his or her development needs and create improvement plans.

TECHNICAL STRAND

Leaders who develop other leaders are celebrated at GE.

CULTURAL STRAND

Welch took power away from the centralized headquarters and gave it to the business units. Each business unit was made to recognize its responsibility to develop leaders. Corporate refused to assume the task of people development but strongly supported it by providing world-class resources such as the Crotonville Management Development Center.

POLITICAL STRAND

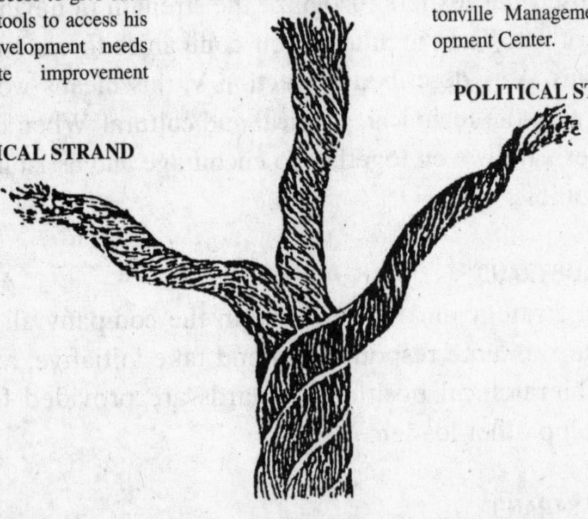

Figure 16: Using TPC to Improve Leadership Development Ability

Now work on how you can craft your own technical, political, and cultural systems to encourage leaders to develop other leaders. Consider the questions in the figure below before moving on to the exercise.

Technical:

1. Are leaders at all levels expected to understand the company strategy, define their own initiatives to support the central objectives and execute?
2. Is the organization structure decentralized enough to allow people to exercise leadership? Is it so decentralized or undefined that people can't understand the expectations for them as leaders?
3. Do pay systems reflect the value placed on leadership?

Political:

1. What is the relationship between the CEO and the rest of the company? Leaders will not develop if power is completely centralized.
2. How is political power shared? Do people have the power to act as leaders and influence the direction of the organization?
3. How is development handled in the context of succession? Is the development of others rewarded with promotions or new assignments?

Cultural:

1. How strong are the cultural messages within your company about the importance of leadership development?
2. Do people feel that they can shape the culture of their own unit?
3. How well do you screen new recruits for leadership?

Figure 17: TPC Analysis of Leadership Development

TPC FOR INCREASING LEADERS' DEVELOPMENT OF OTHERS

	Ways to Increase Leaders' Development of Others
Technical Systems	
Political Systems	
Cultural Systems	

Human Resources Systems: Enhancing Leaders' Development of Others

The aim of all human resource systems should be to drive the performance of the individual and thereby the organization. In Section II, you used the figure below to analyze the current state of how well your company's human resource systems are motivating leaders to develop others. Each human resource system can be constructed to encourage leaders to develop other leaders. It is a continuous process of screening for people who want to develop themselves and others, appraising them for their ability to do so, rewarding them for positive performance on this dimension and then helping them to further develop their skills through training and development or on-the-job experience.

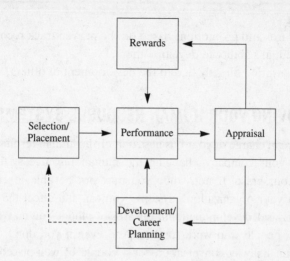

Figure 18: Human Resource Systems for Leaders to Develop Others

Selection

Does your organization select for leadership, not only technical skill?

How well does it use the following criteria for selection into the company and/or into positions of higher responsibility?

    The individual's articulated teachable point of view

    A track record of developing other leaders

    Specific evidence of effective teaching in the recent past

Appraisal

Is evidence of success at leadership development assessed?

Are the mentoring and coaching abilities of each person frequently surveyed?

Is there a continuous review of the leader's teachable point of view?

Development/Career Planning

Is there an emphasis on people understanding others' jobs so that they can provide assistance and coaching?

Are development processes at all levels designed for leaders to do the teaching?

Is there investment in finding new ways of developing leaders?

Rewards

Are rewards and promotions based on the proven track record of an individual's ability to develop others?

Is compensation directly tied to the development of others?

IMPROVING YOUR HUMAN RESOURCE SYSTEMS

If you are in charge of your business unit or the human resource systems in your company, changing the human resource systems is within your grasp. If not, while you may not be able to entirely redesign your organization's systems, you can still affect the selection, appraisal, development and rewards of others. You may have a group of people who work for you. And even if you don't, it's no secret that hallway conversations or a couple of well-placed comments can encourage others to examine how they perform.

Consider the most important thing you can do to improve each of your company's human resource systems.

	The Most Important Improvement I Can Make
Selection	
Appraisal	
Development/ Career Planning	
Rewards	

Building the Teaching Organization

Objectives:

- Examine your organization's pipeline for developing future leaders
- Assess the tools that can be used for development
- Create a personalized process to lead and teach your own people

In order to develop leaders at all levels of the organization, the total system needs to be geared toward two things: WINNING today and BUILDING for tomorrow. Winning companies are multitask organizations. They are like winning athletic franchises that are constantly recruiting and developing new talent as they seek the national or world championship. The leaders developing leaders agenda must be embedded in the organization from top to bottom. There must be a teachable point of view on how the leadership pipeline is structured, that is, what it takes to develop as a leader at this organization. Then there must be methodologies in place for teaching and development.

Architecting the Leadership Pipeline

In order to design a pipeline, you must carefully think through what leadership you will need in the future. The last thing you should do is fall victim to the rearview-mirror exercises that many consultants and human resource staff perform. These generally look at who succeeded in the past and how they got to be successful in order to build a competency model. As a result, your organization develops yesterday's leaders. Your challenge is much more creative and difficult. You have to take your best guess as to what the world will need tomorrow.

This was exactly the challenge given to myself and a group of others by Jack Welch in the mid-1980s. He recognized that how he got to be CEO at GE was irrelevant for how his successor would be developed. GE needed to take a total, clean-sheet look at how it was developing leaders for the twenty-first century. It then needed to have a leadership development framework and process to build leaders at all levels of the company.

After about eighteen months of working with Welch's most senior team, we turned out a white paper describing the necessary capabilities of leaders at different career levels at GE. It divided the leadership pipeline into five stages, and assigned learning and development tasks needed at each stage before further career progression. It also focused on the mechanisms for leadership development, including primary job assignments, enrichment opportunities, prospective broadening experiences, coaching development and formal educational opportunities.

A summary of the leadership development pipeline capabilities are included in the table below.

	Interpersonal Skills	Functional/ Product Skills	Organizational Skills
Individual Contributor	• Build effective communication and relationship skills • Effectively deal with personal strengths and weaknesses	• Develop specific functional skills • Learn roles and relationships within the functional/product unit • Develop work planning, program and performance assessment skills	• Synthesize personal values with organizational value system • Understand how his/her function and business relates to the entire company • Grasp the role of the company in the global marketplace • Learn about customers and suppliers

	Interpersonal Skills	Functional/ Product Skills	Organizational Skills
New Manager	• Learn to delegate work and get things done through other people • Learn to effectively appraise the performance of subordinates and secure their improved performance • Acquire and effectively apply team-building skills • Learn to share insights and values with others so that effect is multiplied	• Acquire basic managerial skills, such as budgeting or program planning	• Reconcile personal values with company's shared values • Learn to integrate work of unit with related units
Experienced Manager	• Develop negotiation skills and effectiveness in dealing with conflict situations • Gain executive communication skills required for broad-scale communications • Increase ability to deal with ambiguity, paradox and situations where there is not a single "right" answer	• Gain deep, well-rounded understanding of all related functional skills in area of prime assignment	• Develop strategic thinking skills and the capacity to use both inductive and deductive problem-solving • Learn how to effectively implement organizational change • Understand the difference between what is best for the customer and what is easiest for the business • Maximize understanding of global business dynamics and inter-functional relationships
General Manager	• Gain capacity to deal concurrently with multiple issues of increasing complexity and ambiguity • Develop a recognition that he/she cannot and should not try to solve all problems personally • Build skill in framing problems for others to solve • Understand how to maximize contributions of individual, team and staff • Develop a recognition that asking for help is a sign of maturity rather than a weakness • Develop the sensitivity to respond to the needs of others based on limited stimulus or cues		• Refine broad perspective that extends to the well-being of the entire organization • Sharpen analytical and critical thinking skills for organizational problem-solving • Play an active role in the development of the vision for his/her business

	Interpersonal Skills	Functional/ Product Skills	Organizational Skills
Business Leader	• Learn to effectively exercise power in making those decisions that only the leader can make • Develop projection and extrapolation skills to deal with situations where he/she has no first-hand knowledge • Develop sensitivity to the forces that motivate people to behave as they do		• Develop multifunctional integration skills to manage a business based on profit and loss basis • Develop and effectively articulate the vision for the business • Develop the capacity to conceive, not just adopt, change • Develop an effective understanding of the dynamics of the industry • Develop a balanced posture between leadership of the business and integration/cooperation among the functions or other business in the company • Develop the capacity to effectively manage community relations

Figure 19: GE's Leadership Development Pipeline

We also developed a series of tools and on-the-job experiences that would help people learn the skills required at each career stage.

As an example, I've provided the tools available to the thousands of young employees, primarily engineers entering from off-campus recruiting.

Primary Position Assignment	Enrichment Assignment Options	Perspective Broadening Experiences	Coaching Emphasis	Educational Options
• Entry-level trainee • Individual contributor assignment in function for which trained	• Cross functional assignment that broadens understanding of functions • Customer contact for technical people • Headquarters experience for field sales person • International exposure assignment • Audit staff non-financial worker	• Special assignment to stretch abilities and test creativity • Send on college recruiting assignments • Fill out EMS-3 for first time • Attend customer-centered event	• Short-cycle work planning for rapid feedback • Realistic performance appraisals • Interpersonal relationships • Career perspectives coaching by immediate supervisor, entry-level program manager or local HR personnel	• Entry-level functional training • Entry-level leadership conference • Intermediate functional training • Managerial skills course • Interpersonal communications workshop • Creative thinking workshop • Pre-supervisory skills training • University or other functional training

Figure 20: GE's Development Tools for Individual Contributors

ARCHITECTING THE PIPELINE FOR YOUR ORGANIZATION

Your current position and functional background determine the extent to which you can determine and change the leadership development systems in your organization. No matter your ability, you can personally improve your ability to develop other leaders by thinking through what leadership abilities they need.

If you are a business leader or human resources executive it would be useful to think through a framework very similar to the one we used at GE. This exercise will ask you to think through how you can better develop those people you directly work with.

Team Member	Career Phase (Individual Contributor, New Manager, Experienced Manager, General Manager, Business Leader)	Interpersonal Skills Required	Functional/ Product Skills Required	Organizational Skills Required
1.				
2.				
3.				
4.				
5.				
6.				

Now for each individual on the team, your challenge is to create development experiences that will benefit them and your business. The important thing is to consider the full range of development experiences, including those involved in fulfilling the person's primary assignment, giving them stretch/enrichment assignments, perspective broadening experiences, coaching and educational opportunities.

An example is provided below to help you.

Team Member	Preferred Developmental Experience	Opportunity to Provide the Experience	When
1. Jane Jones	• Cross-functional • Ability to energize team	• Special project team assignment on non-hierarchical team • Team skills course at corporate training facility	• Next month through the end of the year • Before promotion to mid-manager position
2.			
3.			
4.			
5.			

Leaders Teaching Leaders

The Leadership Engine has been about how leaders generate more leaders through teaching. After the leader has established some basic principles, it is up to him or her to design ways to teach others. The key to a teaching organization is that leaders are constantly challenged to have both a teachable point of view and a methodology for teaching. Then the litmus test of the leader's commitment is the amount of high-quality time the leader invests in developing others.

Step 1: Benchmark and Diagnosis

Roger Enrico set a world-class benchmark with his Building the Business program at PepsiCo. He ran ten programs in 1994 and 1995 while he was the vice chairman of the company. They each begin with a five-day off-site seminar led personally by Enrico. For the next ninety days, participants apply what they learn while simultaneously doing their regular jobs and keeping in close touch with Enrico. The program concludes with a three-day workshop in which everyone shares the insights and lessons of the prior three months. Because only nine or so people attend each seminar, it allows plenty of one-on-one time with Enrico.

The price of admission to Enrico's course is a business-building idea important enough to be one of the top three priorities of the participant's division. Otherwise, says Enrico, "There's no way to make it happen." He takes participants off-site to help them rethink their role in the company. The very first evening he knocks people off balance by telling the participants that "nobody in this room can look at the company's problems and blame the turkeys at the top. You're now one of them." During the workshop he uses short presentations, interviews with Pepsi executives and Socratic dialogue to challenge the students' fundamental approach to problem-solving. He constructs the seminar around his five leadership tenets.

YOUR LEADERSHIP DEVELOPMENT PROCESS AND MINDSET

Keeping the Enrico example in mind, assess your current approach to development. The crucial ingredients to build a world-class development process are listed below. Test yourself to see how you stack up from old way to new way.

Leader's Role		Old Way / Mixed / New Way	
1. Teachable point of view	Outside faculty and consultants' concepts	1 2 3 4 5	The leader has a personalized and teachable view on: a) leadership, b) running the business, c) creating change
2. Time commitment	Limited to less than a day	1 2 3 4 5	Full-time involvement
3. Vulnerable role model	One-way sharing by leader, minimal feedback and dialogue	1 2 3 4 5	Leader is a mutual learner, open to ideas, gives and receives feedback, admits mistakes and dialogues for improvement
4. Coaching role	Little or no coaching	1 2 3 4 5	Leader has a coaching mind set, creates the coaching setting and has the ability to implement

Participant's Role

1. Commitment	Perfunctory, go through the process with minimal emotional engagement	1 2 3 4 5	Emotionally engaged and willing to make the substantial time commitment both at the workshop and on the job
2. Risk	Low-risk, low-stress classroom environment	1 2 3 4 5	Moderate stress and risk due to high performance expectations and evaluation
3. Team/network involvement	Learning primarily as a personal experience	1 2 3 4 5	Not a solo development experience but requires teamwork and broader networking capacity
4. Implementation	New ideas are taught in the program—little on-the-job implementation	1 2 3 4 5	Implementing change is the core learning vehicle of the program—throughout the process leaders must apply learnings on the job, i.e., try things and get feedback

Design Parameters

Old Way   Mixed   New Way

1. Selective small group	Limited use of performance and future potential selection screens	1 2 3 4 5	Hand-picked, small groups of people with explicit performance and potential selection screens
2. Action learning projects development	Concepts and case studies	1 2 3 4 5	Real projects which allow practice of leading change and hard business results
3. Process over time	A single one- to four-week event	1 2 3 4 5	Multiple workshops spread over months with real application and projects between workshops
4. Blend the hard and the soft	Programs emphasize either people management or functional expertise but do not blend the two together	1 2 3 4 5	Holistic design—soft (leadership, teamwork, change) and hard (business strategy, financial results) tightly coupled in all learning, application and coaching activities

SCORE YOURSELF

Old way developer of leaders	24 points or less
Mixed; partway there	24–48 points
New way developer of leaders	48 points or better
The Gold Medalist	60 points

©1995, Noel Tichy, Chris DeRose

DESIGN A PROCESS FOR LEADERS TO DEVELOP OTHER LEADERS

Consider your score from above and think of the elements you can improve to get to a 5 on each element.

LEADER'S ROLE

My Role as a Leader	Specific Actions Required	By When
1. Teachable point of view		
2. Time commitment		
3. Vulnerable role model		
4. Coaching role		

PARTICIPANT'S ROLE

My Role as a Leader	Specific Actions Required	By When
1. Commitment		
2. Risk		
3. Team/network involvement		
4. Implementation		

DESIGN PARAMETERS

My Role as a Leader	Specific Actions Required	By When
1. Selective small group		
2. Action learning projects development		
3. Process over time		
4. Blending the hard and the soft		

It's Up to You

Objective:

- Demonstrate your commitment by taking the first step

After preparing your teachable point of view, your story and your teaching methodologies, the question is: Will you do it? There are two conditions necessary to accelerate your capacity to be a leader who develops others. The first is a continual capacity to improve yourself. The other is to provide significant emotional experiences for your organization. The last two activities in this handbook will help you meet these challenges.

Continuous Mirror Test: Dick Stonesifer's 360 Coaching

Dick Stonesifer was CEO of General Electric's Appliance business from 1991 to 1996. During that time, his business produced several officers for other businesses at GE. How did he do it? Through a relentless focus on developing leadership.

Stonesifer used every major business review as a coaching opportunity. He would take the time to work with every person on his eighteen-member Business Executive Council (BEC) and offer them coaching on all aspects of their leadership, from how they developed strategies to how they executed product launches to how they energized the unionized workforce at the plant.

Stonesifer was so effective not just because of his focus, but because of his role-modeling. He personally had an extensive list of what he thought were his development needs. He was totally open about the fact that he, like everyone else, had things to improve.

Stonesifer has always been focused on his own personal development. For years, he has developed and created a personal development priority list. After years of working with others and watching 360 feedback rise in popularity, Stonesifer had an epiphany. "I finally got sick and tired of having basket case leaders whose feedback said they were Machiavellian or incompetent stand up and say, 'I need to work on communication.' I had to get people to expose themselves and be vulnerable so that they could develop."

Stonesifer developed a process called 360 Coaching. At the annual off-site for Stonesifer's team, he would start the day by presenting to everyone the verbatim data he had received during his 360-degree assessment. This was the result of a survey asking each of the members of his Business Executive Council to describe what he did well or poorly. The praise he received was sincere, as the criticisms were brutally candid. But Stonesifer didn't edit a word. He would show the results of his survey on an overhead screen, talk about each and then ask his team for help to improve. He then asked them to break into groups of four and generate some suggestions for how he could improve, while he left the room to provide them with privacy. Stonesifer returned in an hour to listen to the feedback from the group and establish an action plan that he could use to implement their recommendations.

Stonesifer's recommendations gave him an opportunity to develop—he used the feedback to improve his leadership style—and he also role-modeled the vulnerability that a leader needs to have. Stonesifer asked each individual on his team to do the same. Immediately after giving Stonesifer their recommendations, the group broke into smaller groups of four. Each person shared their data with a smaller group of people to get feedback and assistance. His example created an environment of openness where this succeeded. People need to be vulnerable role models admitting their mistakes to get others to do so.

"In the end, this is the only way to get leaders to develop others. We all know what we do well or poorly. The issue is: Am I going to help or am I going to bitch about you over by the water cooler?" Thanks to Stonesifer, the water cooler is a lonely place to be at GE Appliances.

YOUR 360 COACHING EXPERIENCE

Plan your own coaching experience. In the space below, plan the ideal event for role-modeling your vulnerability and inspiring others to do the same:

1. How can I create an environment of trust and openness?

2. Where will I get data about my own performance?

3. Who will I involve in the discussion?

The Bus Trip

In Section VII, Tom Tiller's bus trip to the Atlanta Kitchen and Bath Show with his cross-functional team was described. The trip created an emotionally charged event that drew people together with the expectation of success. It was a first step toward transformation that built on the sense of urgency pulsing throughout the range division of GE's Appliances unit. It took people's fear of failure and layoffs and converted it into positive energy, stretching people to contribute every idea they had.

Tiller's willingness to take action and his clear sense of purpose—new products were needed to save the plant—provided people with confidence and emotional inspiration. He created the opportunity by allowing people to go, as a team, to the Kitchen and Bath Show. And he created the physical space—the bus—for people to interact and share their ideas.

YOUR BUS TRIP

What is your bus trip? What activity can you use that will simultaneously provide a first step toward achieving your business vision and emotionally energize your organization?

_____

Goal:

_____

Who needs to be involved:

_____

What I'll do to physically engage people:

_____

Why this will be emotionally exciting. How I will set the context and inspire teamwork:

_____

Conclusion

The challenge to develop other leaders is daunting. It means thinking more, doing more and risking more than pushing ahead as a great individual leader. But in the end, it is the true test of leadership and the ultimate route to sustained winning.

The Leadership Engine and this handbook have hopefully provided you with some concepts and, more important, some inspiring examples for you to develop your own leadership. I wish you the best on this important journey.

Notes

Introduction

1. The Building the Business Program run by Enrico produced immediate financial benefits for PepsiCo. The action projects resulted in new ideas and new revenues for the company. I estimate that over a five-year period, close to $2 billion in new revenue will be added. Note that several of these ideas will benefit the Restaurant Division, which is due to be spun off from PepsiCo in late 1997.

2. Gordon Moore, cofounder of Intel, pronounced his famous law in 1965. Known as Moore's law, it states that the number of transistors that can be packed onto a sliver of silicon would double every eighteen months. (Source: "Crossed Lines," *The Economist*, 29 March 1997, 88.) Moore is also credited with a second law that implies that eventually the cost of producing the ever more complicated chips will make their production uneconomical given the microprocessor industry's current structure. (Source: Philip E. Ross, "Moore's Second Law," *Forbes*, 25 March 1996, 116.)

3. Grove's interest in teaching goes beyond his work at Intel. He has also authored books such as *High Output Management* (New York: Random House, 1983); *One-on-One with Andy Grove: How to Manage Your Boss, Yourself, and Your Coworkers* (New York: G.P. Putnam's Sons, 1987); and most recently, *Only the Paranoid Survive: How to Exploit the Crisis Points That Challenge Every Company and Career* (New York: Doubleday, 1996). He also regularly teaches a course for MBA students at Stanford University's Graduate School of Business.

4. For a detailed description of Welch's development of and participation in the Crotonville program, see Noel M. Tichy and Stratford Sherman, *Control Your Destiny or Someone Else Will* (New York: Doubleday, 1993).

5. *CBS This Morning* segment on the Navy SEALs, April 29–May 3, 1996.

6. For a discussion of the long-standing debate on this subject, see Jay A. Conger's chapter "Leaders: Born or Bred?" in *Frontiers of Leadership: An Essential Reader*, ed. M. Syrett and C. Hogg (Oxford: Blackwell Publishers, 1992), 361–69.

Chapter 1: The Leader-Driven Organization

1. Bill Weiss, conversation with Noel Tichy and Patricia Stacey.

2. From December 31, 1992, to December 31, 1996, Ameritech's annual return including reinvested dividends was 19.0%. The Standard & Poor's Telephone Index (an index comprised of GTE, SBC Communications, Ameritech, U S WEST, NYNEX, Bellsouth, Alltel Corporation, Frontier Corporation. and Bell Atlantic) returned 13.9%. The S&P 500 during this time returned 17.2%. For the three years prior to this period (from December 1989 to December 1992), Ameritech's lead over its competitors was smaller. Ameritech returned 7.2% to the S&P Telephone Index's 4.0%. During this time, the S&P 500 returned 10.8% annually. All returns include reinvested dividends. (Source: Bloomberg Financial Markets, Total Return Analysis, for index returns; Ameritech data from Center for Research in Securities Market Index Database; and Bloomberg Financial Markets, Total Return Analysis, for all 1996 data.)

3. "The *Forbes* 500," 21 April 1997.

4. Bill Weiss, conversation with Noel Tichy.

5. Andrew S. Grove, "How (and Why) to Run a Meeting," *FORTUNE*, 11 July 1983, 132. Grove offers greater insights on the importance of maximizing returns on time in his book *High Output Management* (New York: Random House, 1983).

6. Letter to shareholders, ServiceMaster Annual Report, 1995.

7. Noel M. Tichy and Ram Charan, "The CEO as Coach," *Harvard Business Review,* May 1995, 69.

8. Lou Gerstner became CEO of IBM in 1993. He took immediate restructuring charges that caused the company to post an $8 billion loss in 1993. (Source: Bloomberg Financial Markets, Equity Financial Analysis). Beginning in 1993, IBM outperformed the Standard & Poor's Computer Systems Index each year except 1995. Its total annual return, including reinvested dividends from December 31, 1992, to December 31, 1996, was 34%. For the S&P Computer Systems Index it was 25%. (Sources: Center for Research in Securities Market Index Database; Bloomberg Financial Markets, Total Return Analysis, for 1996 data.) By the end of 1996, IBM's market value had increased about $50 billion to $77 billion, meaning Gerstner had returned it roughly to the level it was at when John Akers became CEO in 1984. (Source: Bloomberg Financial Markets, Equity Financial Analysis.)

9. Amal Kumar Naj, "Hennessy Is Retiring at AlliedSignal Inc., Sooner Than Expected," *Wall Street Journal,* 27 June 1991, A1.

10. CNN *Moneyline,* October 28, 1993.

11. In conducting this research, I chose the companies very carefully. I

wanted to find those companies that had a reputation for developing leaders. At the same time, I wished to avoid those companies that had built large leadership development bureaucracies and had no performance track record to show for their efforts. The companies I looked at were ones that had innovative practices in developing leaders at all levels. I cross-referenced this with their performance track records.

The following table is a simple analysis of the performance of some of the companies in this book. The first column states the company name. The second column shows the companies' annualized total return (including reinvested dividends) from the period December 31, 1991, to December 31, 1996. The third column shows annualized total return for a large basket of stocks representing the market as a whole. And the fourth column shows annualized total return for the most appropriate comparative index for each company. The right-hand set of columns provides the same comparisons over a ten-year period from December 31, 1986, to December 31, 1996.

As you can see, the companies I have studied have proven themselves against competitors, and investors have rewarded them. I would encourage readers to conduct the same type of due diligence as they benchmark other companies or hear of the latest fads sweeping management circles—it's simple and quickly separates the true value-adders from the slick packagers.

	Five-Year Analysis			Ten-Year Analysis			
Company	Annual Total Return	Market Comparison*	Industry Index	Annual Total Return	Market Comparison*	Industry Index	Specific Index
Intel	61.06%	15.20%	44.50%	106.92%	32.85%	53.63%	S&P Electronic Semiconductors Index
Compaq	53.27%	15.20%	12.18%	87.51%	32.85%	N/A	S&P Computer Systems Index
Hewlett-Packard	30.20%	15.20%	12.18%	39.44%	32.85%	N/A	S&P Computer Systems Index
Allied-Signal	27.20%	15.20%	12.64%	36.21%	32.85%	24.66%	S&P Diversified Manufacturers Index
General Electric	24.25%	15.20%	20.40%	43.69%	32.85%	27.57%	S&P Electrical Equipment Index
Service-Master	23.47%	11.32%*	11.58%	47.31%	20.21%*	21.15%	NYSE Industrials
Ameritech	19.17%	15.20%	13.04%	35.31%	32.85%	N/A	S&P Telephone Index
PepsiCo	13.36%	15.20%	19.71%	51.53%	32.85%	N/A	S&P Beverages/ Soft Drinks Index

It is clear that the only company to not outperform both the market basket of stocks and its index is PepsiCo. I would note that over a ten-year period, it did beat the market soundly. Further, I believe PepsiCo has brighter days ahead under Roger Enrico's leadership.

Notes:

* For each company, the market comparison is the Standard & Poor's 500 Index. ServiceMaster has a unique capital structure and is therefore compared to the NYSE Composite Index rather than the Standard & Poor's 500 Index.

* Ten-year comparisons against industry indices not available for Hewlett-Packard, Compaq, Ameritech and PepsiCo, as these industries weren't tracked as such by Standard & Poor's going back to 1986. (Source: Bloomberg Financial Markets, Total Return Analysis.)

12. The craze over Internet stocks resulted in incredible valuations for such young companies from 1994 to 1996. By 1997, however, this was drying up. Many initial public offerings were being delayed or pulled due to a leery feeling among investors. And the valuation of companies that had gone public had lost their lighter-than-air feeling among investors. In fact, of the 34 new public Internet companies tracked by multimedia research firm Digital Video Instruments, only three were trading above their initial offering price. The remaining 31 had lost half their value between when they began to trade and April 1997. (Source: Michael Meyer, "Rethinking High Tech," *Newsweek,* 28 April 1997, 56.) Additionally of the 16 start-ups on the American Stock Exchange's Interactive Week Index, 12 were trading below their initial offering price. (Source: C. Kinou Treiser, "Internet Stocks: Suffering a Terminal Illness?" *Investor's Business Daily,* 25 April 1997, A11.)

13. "Suddenly, Growth Is All the Rage," *Financial Times,* 24 August 1996, 2.

14. "Up with Upsizing," *Pittsburgh Post-Gazette,* 10 March 1996, E1. The article cited a study from the book *Grow to Be Great* (New York: The Free Press, 1975) by Dwight L. Gertz and Joao P. A. Baptista. The authors of the study divided *FORTUNE* 1000 companies into four groups and looked at their performance from 1988 to 1993. (Please note that prior to 1994, *FORTUNE* produced the *FORTUNE* 1000 list, which consisted of the 500 largest U.S. industrial corporations and a selection of 500 large service businesses. In 1994, *FORTUNE* began producing only the *FORTUNE* 500 list, which was a mixture of industrial and service businesses.) The four categories were: shrinkers (companies whose revenues and profits had grown more slowly than their industries), cost cutters (companies whose revenues grew more slowly than their industries, but whose profits had grown more rapidly), unprofitable growers (companies

whose revenues grew faster but profits slower than their industries) and profitable growers (companies that had increased both revenue and profits more rapidly than their industry). From 1988 to 1993, the compound annual growth rate in the market value of these companies was: shrinkers 5% unprofitable growers 8%, cost cutters 12% and profitable growers 19%.

15. The early divestitures included Utah International, Consumer Electronics, Housewares and Central Air Conditioning. Other divestitures brought the total to $14 billion between 1981 and 1992. (Source: Noel M. Tichy and Stratford Sherman, *Control Your Destiny or Someone Else Will* [New York: Doubleday, 1993], 29, 252, GE Timeline.)

16. GE's stock price reached 70³/₄ on July 30, 1997. With 3.27 billion shares outstanding, GE has a market value of over $230 billion. (Source for financial data: Bloomberg Financial Markets, Total Return Analysis.)

17. Leslie Cauley, "IBM Plans to Oust John Akers as Chief/Tradition Proves to Be His Undoing," *USA Today,* 27 January 1993, 1B. At the end of John Opel's tenure as CEO in late 1984, IBM's market value had reached $73 billion. By 1987, Akers, Opel's successor, had brought it to its peak of $106 billion. However, as of early 1993, market value had declined to roughly $30 billion, leading to Akers's ouster by the board.

18. Barbara Grady, "Kodak Replaces CEO over Turnaround Efforts," *Reuters Business Report,* 6 August 1993.

19. Suzanne Oliver, "The Battle of the Credit Cards," *Forbes,* 1 July 1996, 62.

20. Larry Bossidy, conversation with Noel Tichy.

21. Richard Notebaert, interview by Noel Tichy and Eli Cohen, March 1996.

22. James Kitfield, "New World Warriors," *Government Executive,* November 1995, 39.

23. Stratford Sherman and Noel M. Tichy, "A Master Class in Radical Change," *FORTUNE,* 13 December 1993, 82.

24. Patricia Asp, interview by Eli Cohen, January 1996.

Chapter 2: Why Are Leaders Important?

1. From *Mastering Revolutionary Change,* a *FORTUNE* video series by Noel M. Tichy and Stratford Sherman, Video Publishing House, 1994.

2. "Transformational leadership" is a term coined by James MacGregor Burns in his classic book *Leadership* (New York: Harper & Row, 1978). Burns describes three types of leadership: "The relations of

most leaders and followers are *transactional*—leaders approach followers with an eye to exchanging one thing for another: jobs for votes, or subsidies for campaign contributions. Such transactions comprise the bulk of the relationships among leaders and followers, especially in groups, legislatures and parties. *Transforming* leadership, while more complex, is more potent. The transforming leader recognizes and exploits an existing need or demand of a potential follower. But, beyond that the transforming leader looks for potential motives in followers, seeks to satisfy higher needs, and engages the full person of the follower. The result of transforming leadership is a relationship of mutual stimulation and elevation that converts followers into leaders and may convert leaders into moral agents. This last concept, *moral leadership,* concerns me the most. By this term I mean, first, that leaders and led have a relationship not only of power but of mutual needs, aspirations, and values; second, that in responding to leaders, followers have adequate knowledge of alternative leaders and programs and the capacity to choose among those alternatives; and, third, that leaders take responsibility for commitments—if they promise certain kinds of economic, social, and political change, they assume leadership in the bringing about of that change" (p. 4, paperback edition).

3. The authors of *In Search of Excellence* (New York: Harper & Row, 1982), Tom Peters and Robert Waterman, actually allude to the importance of leadership, despite their best efforts. They write, "We must admit that our bias at the beginning was to discount the role of leadership heavily. . . . Unfortunately, what we found was that associated with almost every excellent company was a strong leader (or two) who seemed to have had a lot to do with making the company excellent in the first place."

James C. Collins and Jerry I. Porras, in writing *Built to Last* (New York: HarperCollins, 1995), take their arguments about the importance of culture to an extreme. Regarding the success of Jack Welch, they argue that he was able to change General Electric because he had grown up in the company and was a product of its robust culture. Unfortunately, this is the wrong read from the Welch experience. As I discuss later in this chapter, Welch was not successful because he was a product of the GE culture. Rather, he had survived in spite of it. The first thing Welch did was dismantle the business portfolio the company had built over 100 years and scrap the internal bureaucracy.

4. Edgar H. Schein, *Organizational Culture and Leadership* (San Francisco: Jossey Bass Inc., 1992).

5. Bob Ortega, "Life Without Sam," *Wall Street Journal,* 4 January 1995, A1.

6. Judith Dobrzynski, "Rethinking IBM," Business Week, 4 October 1993, 86; and Amy Cortese and Ira Sager, "Lou Gerstner Unveils His Battle Plan," *Business Week,* 4 April 1994, 96.

Gerstner's executive team as of 1996 consisted of 13 people, six of whom came from the outside. These six people were: Senior Vice President for Human Resources J. Thomas Bouchard (joined IBM in October 1994), Senior Vice President of Strategy J. Bruce Harreld (joined IBM in September 1995), Senior Vice President and General Counsel Lawrence R. Ricciardi (joined IBM in May 1995), Senior Vice President and Chief Financial Officer G. Richard Thoman (joined IBM in late 1993), Vice President and Controller James M. Alice (joined IBM in June 1995), and Vice President and Treasurer Jeffrey D. Serkes (joined IBM in August 1993). Other executives beneath the executive team of 13 were also brought in to run important divisions, such as Jim Firestone, who runs the consumer division.

7. AlliedSignal's productivity grew at an average annual rate of 5.6% from 1991 to 1996. (Source: John S. McClenahen, "52 Fiefdoms No More," *Industry Week*, 20 January 1997, 58.

8. Richard Notebaert, interview by Noel Tichy and Eli Cohen, March 1996.

9. "Up with Upsizing," *Pittsburgh Post-Gazette*, 10 March 1996, E1.

10. Patrick Spain and James Talbot, *Hoover's Handbook of American Companies 1996* (Austin, Tex.: The Reference Press, 1996).

11. Compaq had sales of $1.2 billion in 1987. (Source: Spain and Talbot, *Hoover's Handbook of American Companies 1996*). This was the fastest company to reach this milestone. (Source: Grove, *Only the Paranoid Survive* [New York: Doubleday, 1996], 45).

12. Spain and Talbot in *Hoover's Handbook of American Companies 1996* note that Dell started his business selling computer components after enrolling at the University of Texas in 1983. By 1984, Dell's dorm-room business was bringing in $80,000 per month.

13. Grove, *Only the Paranoid Survive*, 49.

14. Grove, *Only the Paranoid Survive*, 47.

15. Paul Carroll, *Big Blues* (New York: Random House, 1993), 261–62.

16. David Kirkpatrick, "IBM Is Back with New PCs and a New Attitude," *FORTUNE*, 11 November 1996, 28.

17. Grove, *Only the Paranoid Survive*, 64.

18. Carol Loomis, "King John Wears an Uneasy Crown," *FORTUNE*, 11 January 1993, 44.

19. Leslie Cauley, "IBM Plans to Oust John Akers as Chief/Tradition Proves to Be His Undoing," *USA Today*, 27 January 1993, 1B.

20. Gary McWilliams, "Can DEC Beat the Big Blue Blues?" *Business Week*, 13 August 1990, 114.

21. Gary McWilliams, "Crunch Time at DEC," *Business Week*, 4 May 1992, 30.

22. McWilliams, "Can DEC Beat," 114.

23. Maria Shao, "Ken Olsen Resurfaces," *Boston Globe,* 24 March 1993, 1.

24. Under founder Ken Olsen, DEC did not weather the storm of the PC revolution well. DEC underwent three major reorganizations between 1988 and 1993. It flip-flopped on important strategies. It staked its future on developing a RISC chip in-house in 1987. It killed this program in 1988 and then revived it again later.

   Internal competition made managers more concerned with protecting their fiefs than operating the company successfully. In 1989, with cracks in the company clearly visible, DEC announced plans to reduce its workforce. However, after only three years, only 10,000 people had left the 126,000-employee company.

   All this resulted in a sliding market value that has gone from $26 billion in 1987 to $4.6 billion in July 1992, when Olsen was forced out. (Source: McWilliams, "Crunch Time at DEC," 30.) On December 31, 1996, DEC's market value was up to $5.6 billion, a far cry from the value added by other companies in its industry. (Source: Compact Disclosure database. Suhoch, Claude, Version 4.5F, October 1995, Digital Library Systems Incorporated.) In April 1997, it was trading at $26 a share, making it worth roughly one-third of its annual revenue. Compare that with Hewlett-Packard, which is worth 1.25 times its revenue. (Source: Rita Kosella, "Solving the DEC Puzzle," *Forbes,* 5 May 1997, 45.)

25. All Richard Notebaert quotes are from an interview by Noel Tichy and Eli Cohen, March 1996.

26. Andy Grove provides an excellent description of the changes occurring in the computer industry, which I have summarized here, in *Only the Paranoid Survive.*

27. Grove, *Only the Paranoid Survive,* 91.

28. Grove, *Only the Paranoid Survive,* 87.

29. Spain and Talbot, *Hoover's Handbook of American Companies 1996.*

30. Grove, *Only the Paranoid Survive,* 89.

31. The painful remaking of Intel took nearly two full years. The crisis in memory chips began for the company in the fall of 1984. In 1985 and 1986, the company took some steps to battle the situation. In mid–1985 the infamous discussion between Moore and Grove took place. The transformation of the company to its focus on microprocessors was completed by mid-1986. (Source: Grove, *Only the Paranoid Survive,* 88, 95.)

32. Grove, *Only the Paranoid Survive,* 142–43, 145.

33. The following chart captures Intel's profit and revenue growth from 1984 through 1996:

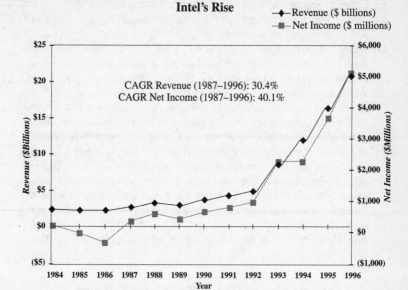

Intel's Rise

◆ Revenue ($ billions)
■ Net Income ($ millions)

CAGR Revenue (1987–1996): 30.4%
CAGR Net Income (1987–1996): 40.1%

Sources: S&P Stock Reports, Intel Annual Report (1989), Intel News Release 1997

34. Spain and Talbot, *Hoover's Handbook of American Companies 1996.* The scraps left over by Intel in the microprocessor market are picked up by AMD and Cyrix, with roughly 5% of the market, who make Intel-compatible chips. The next most formidable competitors are IBM and Motorola, who share the 3.3% of the market belonging to Power PC chips. (Source: Paul C. Judge, "Why the Fastest Chip Didn't Win," *Business Week,* 28 April 1997, 92.)

35. Grove, *Only the Paranoid Survive,* 97.

36. Noel M. Tichy and Stratford Sherman, *Control Your Destiny or Someone Else Will* (New York: Doubleday, 1993), 27, 29, 317, GE timeline. Acquisition and divestiture amounts reflect those from 1981 through 1996. (Source: General Electric Company Corporate Public Relations.)

37. Noel M. Tichy and Stratford Sherman, *Control Your Destiny or Someone Else Will* (New York: Doubleday, 1993), 65.

38. Welch simplified GE's structure by taking out layers between his office and the businesses. The new structures are depicted in the charts on pages 309 to 311. (Source: Noel M. Tichy and Stratford Sherman, *Control Your Destiny or Someone Else Will* [New York: Doubleday, 1993], 282–83.)

39. Letter to Shareholders, General Electric Annual Report, 1995.

40. John F. Welch Jr. (remarks at Operating Managers Conference, Boca Raton, Florida, January 1994).

41. Welch began the Quality program in 1995. He has stated that it will achieve Six Sigma quality (3.4 defects per million operations in manufacturing or service processes). In his 1996 annual report letter, Welch reported that GE's quality efforts had already paid for themselves and that the additional investment of $300 million in 1997 would bring in an additional $400-$500 million in savings. This focus on tangible results is a Welch hallmark from the days of Work-Out. If the Quality program succeeds at GE, it will be the biggest, fastest, most successful application of quality principles ever. The different results from this program versus quality programs that floundered at other companies are the result of the fact that it is being used by leaders at a company with a leadership heritage that can make quality work.

42. John F. Welch Jr., remarks at Operating Managers Conference, Boca Raton, Florida, 1994.

Chapter 3: Leadership and the Teachable Point of View

1. Larry Bossidy, speech at AlliedSignal's Senior Management Meeting, May 1994. Such conferences are held twice a year for the heads of AlliedSignal's businesses and senior staff executives.

2. Warren Bennis, "Learning to Lead," *Executive Excellence,* January 1996.

3. George Catlett Marshall. *United States Information Agency/The Marshall Plan* [on-line]. Available: http://www.usia.gov/topical/pol/marshall/mp-bio.htm [20 May 1997].

4. Bill Stewart, "Blazers Regroup After Injuries," United Press International, 3 May 1990.

5. Mike Mulligan, "Two Sides to Bulls' 'Triangle,'" *Chicago Sun-Times,* 17 December 1992, 99.

6. Ronald Rosenberg, "One by One, Corporate Giants Fall . . . " *Boston Globe,* 27 January 1993, 49.

7. IBM had exactly 256,207 employees at that time in 1993, according to Patrick Spain and James Talbot, *Hoover's Handbook of American Companies 1996* (Austin, Tex.: The Reference Press, 1996).

8. Although coercion and manipulation may be very effective in getting specific things done, these techniques do little to provide employees with an understanding of what is being done and why. Without that kind of understanding and acceptance, it becomes impossible to sustain the efforts of employees without continual monitoring, direction and more threats. Thus, in addition to ethical concerns, coercion is not practical or efficient as a long-term strategy.

9. General Electric Corporate Public Relations Department. These acquisitions and divestitures are for Welch's tenure from 1981 to 1996.

10. Andrew S. Grove, *Only the Paranoid Survive* (New York: Doubleday, 1996), 6–7.

11. Carol J. Loomis, "Dinosaurs?" *FORTUNE,* 22 February 1993, 36.

12. Grove, *Only the Paranoid Survive,* 120, 123.

13. Roger Enrico, interview by Noel Tichy, February 1995.

14. Cover, PepsiCo Annual Report, 1995.

15. Lori Bongiorno, "The Pepsi Regeneration," *Business Week,* 11 March 1996, 70.

16. Noel M. Tichy and Christopher DeRose, "Roger Enrico's Master Class," *FORTUNE,* 27 November 1995, 105.

17. Noel M. Tichy and Christopher DeRose, "The Pepsi Challenge," *Training & Development,* May 1996, 58.

18. Noel M. Tichy and Christopher DeRose, "Roger Enrico's Master Class," *FORTUNE,* 27 November 1995, 105. The idea of telling stories is an extremely important one. We address it in greater depth in Chapter 9.

19. Eli D. Cohen, Lynda St. Clair, and Noel M. Tichy, "Leadership Development as a Strategic Initiative," *Handbook for Business Strategy 1996* (New York: Faulkner & Gray, 1997), 151.

20. Tichy and DeRose, "The Pepsi Challenge," 58.

21. PepsiCo decided in late January 1997 to spin off its restaurant division, consisting of KFC (formerly Kentucky Fried Chicken), Taco Bell, Pizza Hut and some other smaller restaurant chains. The spin-off is expected to be completed by the end of 1997. (Source: Patricia Sellers, "Why Pepsi Needs to Become More Like Coke," *FORTUNE,* 3 March 1997, 26.)

22. Patricia Sellers, "How Coke Is Kicking Pepsi's Can," *FORTUNE,* 28 October 1996, 70. See also Robert F. Hartley, *Management Mistakes and Successes,* 5th ed. (New York: Wiley, 1991), for a description of Coke's decision to change its formula.

23. Roger Enrico, interview by Noel Tichy, February 1995.

24. United States Special Operations Command (USSOCOM) Fiscal Year 1996 Briefing presented to Noel Tichy and Eli Cohen, January 1996.

25. Each year the SOF is deployed on a variety of missions. The "operations tempo" or number of these missions has increased dramatically, rising 108% between 1992 and 1995. During this time SOF took part in over eight thousand deployments, nearly three thousand of which took place in 1995 alone. On average, they spend time in more than sixty countries each week. (Source: United States Special Operations Command Fiscal Year Briefing presented to Tichy and Cohen, January 1996.)

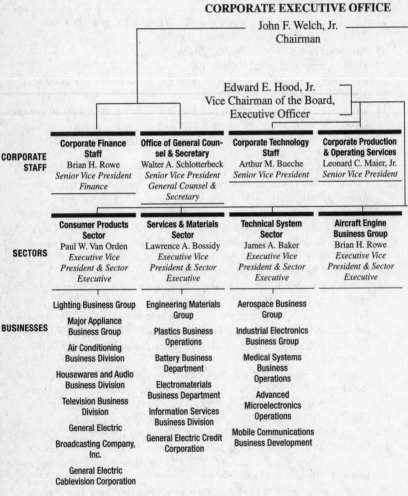

GE ORGANIZATION 1981
CORPORATE EXECUTIVE OFFICE

John F. Welch, Jr.
Chairman

Edward E. Hood, Jr.
Vice Chairman of the Board,
Executive Officer

CORPORATE STAFF	**Corporate Finance Staff** Brian H. Rowe *Senior Vice President Finance*	**Office of General Counsel & Secretary** Walter A. Schlotterbeck *Senior Vice President General Counsel & Secretary*	**Corporate Technology Staff** Arthur M. Bueche *Senior Vice President*	**Corporate Production & Operating Services** Leonard C. Maier, Jr. *Senior Vice President*

SECTORS	**Consumer Products Sector** Paul W. Van Orden *Executive Vice President & Sector Executive*	**Services & Materials Sector** Lawrence A. Bossidy *Executive Vice President & Sector Executive*	**Technical System Sector** James A. Baker *Executive Vice President & Sector Executive*	**Aircraft Engine Business Group** Brian H. Rowe *Executive Vice President & Sector Executive*

BUSINESSES	Lighting Business Group Major Appliance Business Group Air Conditioning Business Division Housewares and Audio Business Division Television Business Division General Electric Broadcasting Company, Inc. General Electric Cablevision Corporation	Engineering Materials Group Plastics Business Operations Battery Business Department Electromaterials Business Department Information Services Business Division General Electric Credit Corporation	Aerospace Business Group Industrial Electronics Business Group Medical Systems Business Operations Advanced Microelectronics Operations Mobile Communications Business Development

John F. Burlingame
Vice Chairman of the Board,
Executive Officer

Corporate Relations Staff	**Corporate Productivity & Quality Staff**	**Corporate Planning & Development Staff**	**Executive Manpower Staff**
Frank P. Doyle	Walter A. Schlotterbeck	Daniel J. Fink	Theodore P. LeVino
Senior Vice President	*Senior Vice President General Counsel & Secretary*	*Senior Vice President*	*Senior Vice President*

Industrial Products Sector	**International Sector**	**Power Systems Sector**	**Utah International Inc.**
Louis V. Tomasetti	Robert R. Fredrick	Herman R. Hill	Alexander M. Wilson
Executive Vice President & Sector Executive	*Executive Vice President & Sector Executive*	*Executive Vice President & Sector Executive*	*Chairman of the Board & Chief Executive Officer*

International Trading Operations	Tribune Construction & Engineering	Ladd Petroleum Corp.	
General Electric Espanola, S.A. Latin American	Nuclear Energy		
General Electric do Brasil, S.A.	Large Transformer		
Canadian General Electric Company Limited			

	Legal Staff	Business Development	Finance	Research & Development
CORPORATE STAFF	Benjamin W. Heirman *Senior Vice President General Counsel & Secretary*	Gary M. Reiner *Senior Vice President*	Dennis D. Dammerman *Senior Vice President*	Walter L. Ross *Senior Vice President*

SECTOR LAYERS TAKEN OUT

	GE Aircraft Engines	GE Financial Services	GE Areospace	GE Plastics
BUSINESSES	Brian H. Rowe *President & CEO*	Gary C. Wendt *Chairman, President & CEO*	Eugene F. Murphy *President & CEO*	Gary L. Rogers *President & CEO*

GE Appliances	GE Motors	GE Medical Systems	GE Electrical Distribution & Control
J. Richard Stonesifer *President & CEO*	James W. Rogers *President & CEO*	John M. Trani *President & CEO*	W. James C. McNerdy, Jr. *President & CEO*

GE ORGANIZATION 1992

CORPORATE EXECUTIVE OFFICE

John F. Welch, Jr.
Chairman

Edward E. Hood, Jr. Vice Chairman	Frank P. Doyle Executive Vice Chairman	John F. Burlingame Vice Chairman

External & Industrial Relations Frank P. Doyle *Executive Vice President*	**GE International** Paolo Fresco *Vice Chairman*	**Human Resources** Jack O. Peiffer *Senior Vice President*

GE Transportation Systems Robert L. Nardelli *President & CEO*	**GE Industrial & Power Systems** David C. Genever-Walting *President & CEO*	**NBC** Robert C. Wright *President & CEO*	**GE Lighting** John D. Opie *President & CEO*

GE Information Services
Helenen S. Runtagh
President

	Legal Staff	**Business Development**	**Finance**	**Research & Development**
CORPORATE STAFF	Benjamin W. Heirman *Senior Vice President* *General Counsel &* *Secretary*	Gary M. Reiner *Senior Vice President*	Dennis D. Dammerman *Senior Vice President*	Lewiss Edelheit *Senior Vice President*

SECTOR LAYERS TAKEN OUT

	GE Aircraft Engines	**GE Capital**	**GE Plastics**	**GE Transportation Systems**
BUSINESSES	Eugene Murphy *President & CEO*	Gary C. Wendt *Chairman, President &* *CEO*	Gary L. Rogers *President & CEO*	Robert L. Nardelli *President & CEO*

	GE Appliances	**GE Motors**	**GE Medical Systems**	**GE Distribution & Control**
	J. Richard Stonesifer *President & CEO*	James W. Rogers *President & CEO*	John M. Trani *President & CEO*	Lloyd G. Trotter *President & CEO*

GE ORGANIZATION 1993
CORPORATE EXECUTIVE OFFICE

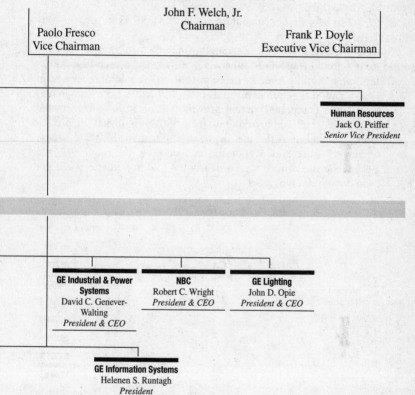

John F. Welch, Jr.
Chairman

Paolo Fresco
Vice Chairman

Frank P. Doyle
Executive Vice Chairman

Human Resources
Jack O. Peiffer
Senior Vice President

GE Industrial & Power Systems
David C. Genever-Walting
President & CEO

NBC
Robert C. Wright
President & CEO

GE Lighting
John D. Opie
President & CEO

GE Information Systems
Helenen S. Runtagh
President

26. Rear Admiral Irve C. LeMoyne, interview by Noel Tichy and Eli Cohen, January 1996.

27. *CBS This Morning* segment on the Navy SEALs, April 29–May 3, 1996.

28. Rear Admiral Irve C. LeMoyne, interview by Noel Tichy and Eli Cohen, January 1996; *CBS This M1orning* documentary on the Navy SEALs, April 29–May 3, 1996.

29. *CBS This Morning* documentary on the Navy SEALs, April 29–May 3, 1996.

30. Biography, Rear Admiral Ray Smith, United States Navy.

31. Rear Admiral Ray Smith, interview by Eli Cohen, March 1996.

32. Intel grew rapidly after its decision to focus on microprocessors. In 1987 it had $1.9 billion in revenue. In 1996, it had $20.8 billion in revenue for a compound annual growth rate of 30.46%. During the same time, Intel employees grew from 19,200 to 48,500 for a compound annual growth rate of 10.85%. Further, 16,000 of these employees were added after the end of 1994. Between 1987 and 1994, while the company grew nearly ten-fold in revenue, it did not even double its employees.

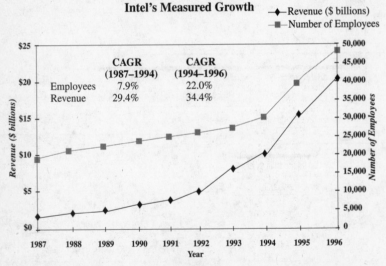

Intel's Measured Growth

Sources: For 1987–1995 data, Patrick Spain and James Talbot, *Hoover's Handbook of American Companies 1996* (Austin, Tex.: The Reference Press, 1996); for 1996 data, Intel news release, January 14, 1997.

Chapter 4: Past as Prologue—Learning from Experience

1. Gail Sheehy, *New Passages: Mapping Your Life Across Time* (New York: Random House, 1995), 169.

2. Bob Knowling, speech to the Michigan Business School, August 1996.

3. All Tom Tiller quotes are from an interview by Noel Tichy and Eli Cohen in May 1996.

4. Coca-Cola has had a remarkable run under Goizueta. In addition to the increase in profits, the stock market has increasingly grown to respect his leadership, increasing market value even faster.

Coca-Cola's Rise in Market Value

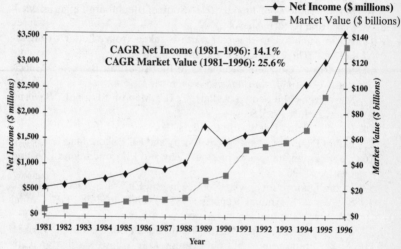

Note: "Income" is income after extraordinary items.

Sources: The Coca-Cola Company Annual Reports 1995 & 1991, 1996 net income is taken from "financial highlights" on http://www.cocacola.com and Compact Disclosure

5. Betsy Morris, "The Wealth Builders," *FORTUNE,* 11 December 1995, 80.

6. John Huey, "The World's Best Brand," *Time,* 31 May 1993, 44.

7. Betsy Morris, "The Wealth Builders," 80.

8. Economic Value Added, like MVA, was pioneered by Stern Stewart. EVA is a company's after-tax net operating profit minus its cost of capital (both borrowed and equity) that year. Studies have shown that a company that racks up positive EVA year after year will see its MVA soar, while negative EVA will drag down MVA as the market loses faith that the company can provide a return on invested capital. (Source: Ronald Lieber, "Who Are the Real Wealth Creators?" *FORTUNE,* 9 December 1996, 107.) In fact, *Investor's Business Daily* noted that from 1981 to 1995, Coke's stock price had increased 25% per year, while its EVA had increased 26% per year. Other measures

such as Return on Capital Employed did not yield such a tight correlation. (Source: "The Real Thing: Coke's Unbeatable Record," *Investor's Business Daily,* 19 May 1995, A3.)

Internally to Coke, Goizueta uses EVA to evaluate individual projects. Rather than use traditional measures, Coke managers all over the world are actually evaluated on their use of capital. Coke managers know how much capital they will use for given projects and how much they expect to make. If the project does not add economic value, it has little chance of surviving.

9. Betsy Morris, "The Wealth Builders," 80.
10. Market value as of June 6, 1997. (Source: Bloomberg Financial Markets, Total Return Analysis.)
11. All information in this paragraph is taken from "Letter to Shareholders," The Coca-Cola Company Annual Report, 1995.
12. Roberto C. Goizueta, "Remarks to the American Bankers Association," *The American Banker,* 5 November 1986, 4.
13. Marc Frons and Scott Scredon, "Coke's Man on the Spot," *Business Week,* 29 July 1985, 56.
14. Betsy Morris, "The Wealth Builders," 80.
15. Debra Dunn, interview by Noel Tichy and Eli Cohen, June 1996.
16. Debra Dunn, interviews by Noel Tichy and Eli Cohen, June 1996 and October 1996.
17. Debra Dunn, interview by Noel Tichy and Eli Cohen, October 1996.
18. Sources: GE Annual Reports, 1987 to 1996. In 1996, GE Capital delivered $2.817 billion in net income for GE.
19. Gary Wendt, interview by Noel Tichy and Eli Cohen, March 1996.
20. At $227 billion in assets, only Fannie Mae, Chase Manhattan, Citicorp and Bank America top GE Capital in size. According to the *Forbes* 500 Assets ranking for 1996, Fannie Mae has over $351 billion in assets, Chase Manhattan has over $336 billion, Citicorp has over $281 billion and Bank America has over $250 billion. (Source: "The *Forbes* 500," *Forbes,* 21 April 1997, 203.)
21. Gary Wendt, interview by Noel Tichy and Eli Cohen, March 1996.

Chapter 5: The Heart of Leadership—It Starts with Ideas

1. Jeanne Dugan, "The Best Performers," *Business Week,* 24 March 1997, 122. (Market value as of February 21, 1997.)
2. Patrick Spain and James Talbot, Hoover's *Handbook of American Companies 1996* (Austin, Tex.: The Reference Press, 1996).
3. Nike has recently been criticized for the use of low-wage labor in the production of its shoes around the world. Any such labor practices are carried out by Nike's subcontractors, and few if any of the workers are Nike employees. Nike has been making efforts to deal with this issue, but the debate will no doubt continue for some time. My asser-

tion about the motivation of Nike employees because of the clarity of Knight's ideas is valid as it applies to the company's executives, middle managers, salespeople, designers and others around the world.

4. Bill Pollard, interview by Noel Tichy and Eli Cohen, January 1996.

5. Lewis Platt, interview by Noel Tichy, June 1996.

6. "AlliedSignal's Transformational Story," handbook accompanying the *Mastering Revolutionary Change FORTUNE video series,* Video Publishing House, 1994, 7. In 1990, the year before Bossidy's arrival, AlliedSignal had net margins that had decreased to 3.7% from 5.9% three years earlier. Its cash flow was a net negative $143 million, down from a positive $156 million in 1987. Its debt to common equity ratio was over 75%. Allied's woes caused it a $273 million loss in 1991. In 1992, with Bossidy at the helm, the company took steps to face its problems. It took a huge restructuring charge, resulting in a $712 million loss for 1992. (Source: Bloomberg Financial Markets, SEC Filing.) AlliedSignal did post a loss in 1992 but by the end of 1993 had already turned it around. They haven't looked back since.

1992	Net Income:	$712,000,000
1993	Net Income:	$411,000,000
1994	Net Income:	$759,000,000
1995	Net Income:	$875,000,000
1996	Net Income:	$1,020,000,000

(Source: AlliedSignal 1996 Annual Report)

7. Noel Tichy and Stratford Sherman, *Mastering Revolutionary Change video series;* and John S. McClenahen, "'52 Fiefdoms' No More," *Industry Week,* 20 January 1997, 58.

8. Total return to investors is defined as the total return earned over the holding period by reinvesting all realized dividends back into the security on the ex-date of that dividend. To be exact, AlliedSignal returned 505.98% to its shareholders, while the Dow Jones returned 198.27%. These numbers were calculated over the period December 31, 1990, to March 31, 1997. (Source: Bloomberg Financial Markets, Comparative Analysis.)

9. Market value on December 31, 1991. (Source: Bloomberg Financial Markets, Financial Analysis.)

10. Bloomberg Financial Markets, Financial Analysis.

11. AlliedSignal Annual Report, 1992.

12. Bloomberg Financial Markets, Financial Analysis.

13. Spain and Talbot, *Hoover's Handbook of American Companies 1996.* Data calculated for five years prior to 1991 and 1991 to 1995. From 1991 to 1995, revenue grew from $11.8 billion to $14.3 billion. In 1996, revenues were $14.0 billion, reflecting the sale of AlliedSignal's antilock braking business in that year.

14. John Barter, interview by Charles Burck and Eli Cohen, February 1996.
15. While Toyota did have the leanest machine in the world, with efficiencies that every other car maker benchmarked, it had missed out on important breakthrough ideas. *The Economist* reported that in the marketplace, "For most of this decade Toyota has arguably been dozing." In Japan, its cars were dull. And while it was incrementalizing to get efficiencies at home, Toyota missed the other breakthrough in the industry—global manufacturing and supply systems. Abroad, Toyota had not built enough manufacturing capacity. When the yen soared, Toyota's cars, which had to be exported from Japan, were too expensive.

    By the latter half of the decade, this had turned around. Toyota launched eleven models in the Japanese market between 1996 and 1997. It ramped up important investments in the United States and Europe. Production outside of Japan, as a percentage of Toyota's total production, will rise to 65% in 1998 from 48% in 1994. (Source: "Toyota on the March," *The Economist,* 22 March 1997, 83.)

16. In the *Harvard Business Review,* James Womack, who chronicled the success of Japanese manufacturing techniques with the book *The Machine That Changed the World* (New York: HarperPerennial, 1991), wrote that "many western managers mistakenly believe [that success in manufacturing] is something one can only achieve gradually through *kaizen,* or continuous improvement. However, by first practicing *kaikaku,* or radical improvement" companies achieve in one day the changes others could never make. (Source: *Harvard Business Review,* September/October 1996, 140.)

17. ServiceMaster's customer level revenue for 1996 was $4.9 billion, with earned revenue at $3.5 billion. Customer level revenue includes revenue realized by ServiceMaster's franchises. (Source: ServiceMaster press release, "ServiceMaster Achieves 26th Consecutive Year of Growth in Revenues and Profits," January 23, 1997.)

18. This example was part of a powerful effort at Ameritech to create the company's "Growth Engine." As part of Ameritech's transformation, Dick Notebaert worked closely with Professor Larry Selden of the Columbia University Business School. Using Selden's framework, Notebaert worked numerous days over a six-month period to frame and modify the growth engine. This simple model, which could be displayed in a few pages, explained the interrelation of Ameritech's new business units and the key financial measures that would drive the company.

    The Growth Engine also created a linkage between the actions of individual employees at Ameritech and the company's financial performance. It did this by first determining which financial measures were the key to shareholder returns—revenue growth and return on assets. Then, for each business, the Growth Engine determined what were the value drivers—what operational measures would affect performance on these financial measures. For example, for people in the business of providing phone service to residential customers, a key operational measure was network utilization. The network represented a huge asset whose costs of maintenance were primarily fixed for wide levels of usage. If more calls were placed on the network (an increase in network utilization), more revenue would be brought in with little incremental cost, and the return on the asset would increase significantly.

With the new understanding from the Growth Engine, several projects were started to increase network utilization during the Breakthrough Leadership process. For example, one team discovered that most of Ameritech's homes that were technologically capable of receiving a second line didn't have a second line operating. This team immediately started an aggressive campaign to increase the number of second lines in these homes. This included aggressive advertising and special incentives for customers to start using a second line.

This may sound like a simple idea, and it is a simple idea. But it had never been used before. People at Ameritech weren't focused on return on assets, because the traditional regulatory environment did not require them to be. The Growth Engine gave people a simple framework with which to understand the business as a whole and their role in making it successful.

19. Letter to Shareholders, AlliedSignal Annual Report, 1995. AlliedSignal's overarching goals for each year following Bossidy's arrival in mid-1991 were:

  1992
  • Make Our Numbers
  • Make Total Quality a Reality, Not Just a Slogan
  • Make AlliedSignal a Unified Company
  (Source: Noel M. Tichy and Stratford Sherman, "A Master Class in Radical Change," *FORTUNE,* 13 December 1993.)

  1993
  • Make Our Numbers
  • Make Total Quality the Foundation of Our Performance
  • Make Growth Part of Our Commitment
  (Source: Larry Bossidy, remarks at senior management meeting, Morristown, New Jersey, November 12, 1992.)

  1994
  • Make Our Numbers
  • Make Quantum Improvements Through Total Quality
  • Make Growth Happen
  (Source: AlliedSignal Annual Report, 1993.)

1995
- Make Our Numbers
- Commit to Operational Excellence and Total Quality Leadership—Phase II
- Grow by Satisfying Customers

(Source: AlliedSignal Annual Report, 1994.)

1996
- Make Customer Satisfaction Our First Priority
- Drive Growth and Productivity Through Integrated World-Class Processes
- Make All of Our Commitments (Including Net Income and Cash Flow)

(Source: "AlliedSignal CEO Commentary: Larry Bossidy's Views on Topics of Interest to AlliedSignal Employees," December 1995.)

20. Mary Petrovich, interview by Charles Burck and Eli Cohen, February 1996.
21. Biography, Mary Petrovich, AlliedSignal.
22. Mary Petrovich, interview by Charles Burck and Eli Cohen, February 1996.
23. This was Clawson's position at the time of the interview. Since then he has moved on to a new position as President of Laminate Systems, AlliedSignal Engineered Materials Sector.
24. Curt Clawson, interview by Charles Burck and Eli Cohen, February 1996.
25. Peter Drucker, *Managing in a Time of Great Change* (New York: Truman Talley Books/Dutton, 1995), 22.
26. The previous section has been adapted from Peter Drucker's "Theory of the Business" chapter in *Managing in a Time of Great Change.*
27. Roger Enrico, interview by Noel Tichy, February 1995.
28. Kate Button, "King of Compaq," *Computer Weekly,* 30 September 1993, 28.
29. Spain and Talbot, Hoover's *Handbook of American Companies 1996.*
30. Bob Stearns, Senior Vice President for Technology and Corporate Development, conversation with Eli Cohen, May 1997.
31. Jerry Jasinowski and Robert Hamrin, *Making It in America* (New York: Simon & Schuster, 1995), 303.
32. "Compaq Computer Corporation," Harvard Business School Publishing 9-491-011, 1990 (revised 1991).
33. "Compaq Computer Corporation," Harvard Business School Publishing 9-491-011, 1990 (revised 1991).
34. Andrew S. Grove, *Only the Paranoid Survive* (New York: Doubleday, 1996), 45.
35. Spain and Talbot, *Hoover's Handbook of American Companies 1996.*

36. Bloomberg Financial Markets, Historical Analysis.
37. Jasinowski and Hamrin, *Making It in America,* 303.
38. Jasinowski and Hamrin, *Making It in America,* 303.
39. Kate Button, "King of Compaq," *Computer Weekly,* 30 September 1993, 28.
40. Jasinowski and Hamrin, *Making It in America,* 303.
41. David Kirkpatrick, "The Revolution at Compaq Computer," *FORTUNE,* 14 December 1992, 80.
42. Jasinowski and Hamrin, *Making It in America,* 306–7.
43. Compaq Public Affairs Department.
44. Compaq Annual Report, 1993.
45. Compaq Annual Report, 1993.
46. David Kirkpatrick, "The Revolution at Compaq Computer," *FORTUNE,* 14 December 1992, 80.

   Compaq's sales in 1992 were $4.1 billion. In 1993, they were $7.2 billion. Profits also rose over this same period from $213 million to $462 million. (Source: Compaq 10-K Report, 1996.)
47. Bloomberg Financial Markets, Financial History and Profitability Ratios.
48. The comparative stock price appreciations of Compaq versus the different indices were calculated by taking the simple return over the holding period due to the change in the equity's price. The period over which these numbers were calculated was from December 31, 1991, to December 31, 1996. Comparing total returns to investors including reinvested dividends, Compaq has returned 746% (it paid no dividends) vs. 103% for the S&P 500 and 78% for the S&P Computer Index from December 31, 1991, to December 31, 1996. The S&P Computer Index includes the following companies: EMC Corporation, Dell, Apple, Tandem, Digital Equipment Corporation, Silicon Graphics, Unisys, Data General Corporation, Intergraph Corporation, Amdahl Corporation, Seagate Tech, Compaq, Sun Microsystems, Hewlett-Packard and IBM. (Source: Bloomberg Financial Markets, Comparative Analysis.)
49. Letter to Shareholders, Compaq Annual Report, 1994.
50. Eckhard Pfeiffer, interview by Noel Tichy and Eli Cohen, March 1996.
51. Bob Stearns elaborated on the opportunities for Compaq: "I think there's tremendous opportunity there. It's a service opportunity and a content opportunity and a tremendous opportunity to add features to this box that were not part of the base line features of a PC." He put it very bluntly, saying, "The people who make computers, though, not just the component parts, [will be] the people who are really in touch with the market and what's happening. And the people whose name will be on the product when people think about how it

changed their lives will be Compaq. Do you want to make brake lin-
ings or do you want to make cars." (Source for both quotes: Bob
Stearns, interview by Noel Tichy and Eli Cohen, March 1996.)

52. Compaq now builds and configures PCs to order rather than according to forecasts. In 1996, that took inventories from 69 days to 30
days, contributing $1 billion to its cash hoard at year's end. It's fur-
ther shortening supply lines to take almost 20% out of its logistics
costs, saving over $300 million per year. (Source: Gary McWilliams,
"Compaq: There's No End to Its Drive," *Business Week,* 17 February
1997, 72.)

53. Compaq has reorganized into four customer-focused global product
groups: Enterprise Computing, PC Products, Communication Products and Consumer Products. It consolidated its five geographic sales
regions into a worldwide sales, market, service and support organization. Pfeiffer also added four new members to the senior management team, while some previous members of senior management left
the company.

   Additionally, Compaq has increased its partnerships with other
companies, which will help put the company at the center of conver-
gent technologies. For example, it collaborates with Intel and
Microsoft to create the servers that run networks. It is also cooperat-
ing with Intel and consumer electronics firms to create the standards
to produce a hybrid PC/TV. (Sources: Gary McWilliams, "Compaq:
There's No End to Its Drive," *Business Week,* 17 February 1997, 72;
and Dean Takahashi, "Intel, Compaq, and Others Join Forces . . ."
Wall Street Journal, 28 March 1997, B3.)

54. Compaq opened 1996 with a stock price of $40 a share. By mid-sum-
mer, during Pfeiffer's reorganization, it was trading at $59. (Source:
Bloomberg Financial Markets, Historical Price Graph.)

55. Donald Katz, *Just Do It* (New York: Random House, 1994), 68–69.

56. Drucker, *Managing in a Time of Great Change,* 32–33.

57. Kathy Rebello, "Inside Microsoft," *Business Week,* 15 July 1996, 56.

58. For much of 1994, Gates knew of the Internet, but openly disdained
it. As one observer pointed out, "[Gates's] view was the Internet was
free. There's no money to be made there. Why is that an interesting
business?" In 1995, Gates and Microsoft puzzled ploddingly through
the importance of the Internet while their energy was focused on
decidedly pre-Internet-era proj-ects such as the release of Windows
95 and creating the Microsoft Network, a proprietary on-line service
to rival America Online. (Source: Rebello, "Inside Microsoft," 56.)

   Finally, in the latter half of 1995, Gates got serious about the
Internet. He picked a date, December 7, 1995, as the day Microsoft
would cross the Rubicon. He immediately dispatched dozens of executives to craft the company's Internet strategy by then. On December 7, 1995, it became clear to the world that the sleeping giant had

awakened. The ideas for its Microsoft Network were changed (though it did eventually return as a proprietary on-line service). Microsoft would battle Netscape for browser market share, and create new software to help companies link their networks to the Internet. Virtually every piece of software created by the company now helps people link to the Internet or the worldwide web. And Microsoft, which had always created its own standards, gave up control over the standards for its ActiveX file-linking technology which it had spent over $100 million to develop over seven years. (Source: Bart Ziegler and Don Clark, "Microsoft Gives Technology Away to Beat Rival," *Wall Street Journal,* 2 October 1996, B1.)

59. Eckhard Pfeiffer, interview by Noel Tichy and Eli Cohen, March 1996.

60. "120 Years of Innovation," GE History [on-line]. Available at http://www.ge.com/ibhis0.htm [20 May 1997].

61. I have earlier noted that Welch created thirteen businesses in the new GE. Currently there are twelve, reflecting the sale of the Aerospace business in 1992.

62. GE Capital's growth record for the past few years is as follows:

Year	Net Income ($Millions)	Total Assets ($Billions)
1988	788	75
1989	927	58.7
1990	1094	70.4
1991	1275	80.5
1992	1499	92.6
1993	1807	117.9
1994	896	144.9
1995	2415	185
1996	2817	227
CAGR:	17.1%	21.5%

(Sources: General Electric Annual Reports, 1996, 1993, 1989.)

63. Gary Wendt, interview by Noel Tichy and Eli Cohen, March 1996.

64. Curt Clawson, interview by Charles Burck and Eli Cohen, February 1996.

65. Gary Wendt, interview by Noel Tichy, Ram Charan and Charles Burck, June 1996.

Gary Wendt has a clear teachable point of view about growth that he uses to teach others at GE Capital. On pages 322 to 327 are a set of slides he actually uses to relate that point of view to people at GE Capital in his teaching sessions.

66. Gary Wendt, interview by Noel Tichy and Eli Cohen, March 1996.

67. Roger Enrico, interview by Noel Tichy, February 1995.

MEETING THE
CHALLENGE OF

WENDT'S TOP 10 IDEAS FOR STIMULATING

GROWTH

But, No Matter What Else You Try…   **Tip #1**

GROWTH

SUCCESS   FORMULA

Give Business Development AT LEAST AS MUCH …

}

THOUGHT
+
ATTENTION
+
TIME & RESOURCE COMMITMENT
+
LEADERSHIP
+
INTENSITY

}

As You Do Anything Else in Your Business Universe

MAKE IT A PART OF YOUR CULTURE AND YOUR BEING!!

Necessary Element for Successful Growth Culture   Tip #2

...ALLOW...

STAR GAZING

—Innovating
—Experiementing
—DREAMING

Or, Do It His Way

"You can't

realize your

dream unless

you have one

to begin with."

—Thomas A. Edison

Many Aids Exist to Provide a Path, If You Wish

*"Branches of
the Growth Tree"*

```
                                                    ┌ Type/
                                                    │ Segment
                                      ┌ Customer    │
                                      │ Growth      ├ Place/
                                      │             │ Geography
                     ┌ Contributed    │             │
                     │ Value          │             └ Time/
                     │ Growth         │               Occasion        VALUE
                     │                │             ┌ Value            CREATION
                     │                │ Value Per   │
                     │                └ Customer    ├ Variety
Profitable           │                  Growth      │
Business ────────────┤                             └ Service
Growth               │
                     │                             ┌ Best Practice
                     │                             │ Transfer
                     │                ┌ Learning   │
                     │                │ Rate       ├ Process
                     │                │            │ Reengineering
                     └ Productivity   │            │
                       Growth         │            └ Smarts
                                      │            ┌ Organization
                                      │ Pace       │ Effectiveness    PRODUCTIVITY
                                      │ Of         │
                                      └ Execution  ├ People
                                                   │ Capabilities
                                                   │
                                                   └ Culture
```

Seizing Opportunity   Tip #4

Whenever Possible

ACQUIRE

We Have $ They Have
                                   Output Capability

We Have   They Have
Experience   Distribution

SPEED

In a Fast Changing World

Where to Look for Opportunity (Geographic)   Tip #5

Get

GLOBAL

We Have   They Have
Technology   2–3x Mkts

We (Must Have)   They (at Least Some)
Patience   Have Growth

PRESENCE

In an Ever Smaller World

Finding Opportunity (Close In)   Tip #6

DRUCKER'S RULE

"Successful Innovations Exploit
Changes That Have Already Happened."

DRUCKER FOLLOW ON

The Most Important Structural Trends Are Seen in the Distribution of
Consumers' Disposable Income.

Where to Look for (Conceptual)   Tip #7

Make Change the Opportunity (Not the Problem)

- Demographic *Changes*

- Technological *Changes*

- Political *Changes*

- Competitive *Changes*

- Value/Taste *Changes*

Practical, Proven Management Techniques
for Getting Broader Involvement in Growth   Tip #8

- Strategic Time Management
  —Plan Your Week

- "Innovation Councils"

- Establish a Separate Futures Budget

...And, Of Course...

- Reward *Forward* Movement

- "Stretch"
  —Keep the Challenge Meaningful

Who Should Focus Your Business Development Efforts   Tip #9

Wrong (Old) Way: Business Development Is
the Responsibility of the
Strategic Planning Department

Right Way: Business Development
Is Everyone's Responsibility!!!

Get the Proper Focus   Tip #10

"Don't Be Ashamed of Profits!"[a]

*(a) i.e., It Should Be the Focal Point for Why
You Need Business Expansion Activities*

Chapter 6: Values—Speaking with Words and Action

1. Robert Knowling, interview by Eli Cohen, December 1995.
2. In 1993 U S WEST announced a plan to reengineer its phone company by consolidating 560 service centers into 26 regional super centers, eliminating 5,000 jobs. It proceeded to do this but did not think through the new behaviors that would be required. The effort was a failure. U S WEST proceeded to shut down their old system before getting the new one up to speed, sending customer complaints through the roof. Regulators began fining the corporation for complaints in excess of the assigned ceiling, and customers began to file suits. One man in a Denver suburb waited three months to have a

phone line installed in his home. By the end of 1994 only 1,685 jobs had been eliminated and U S WEST was "taking a step back" from its reengineering effort by "reverting to the old way of doing things." (Sources: Kevin Maney, "Rocky Time at U S WEST/Phone Company Blazes Trails, Hits Potholes," *USA Today,* 27 October 1995; and Tom Locke, "U S WEST Retreating from Plan," *Denver Business Journal,* 9 December 1994.)

3. Noel M. Tichy, "Bob Knowling's Change Manual," *Fast Company,* April/May 1997, 97.

4. Noel M. Tichy and Stratford Sherman, *Control Your Destiny or Someone Else Will* (New York: Doubleday, 1993), 277.

5. ServiceMaster's customer-level revenue for 1996 was $4.9 billion, with earned revenue at $3.5 billion. Customer-level revenue includes revenue realized by ServiceMaster's franchises. (Source: ServiceMaster press release, "ServiceMaster Achieves 26th Consecutive Year of Growth in Revenues and Profits," January 23, 1997.)

6. ServiceMaster went public in 1962. (Source: Patrick Spain and James Talbot, *Hoover's Handbook of American Companies 1996* [Austin, Tex.: Reference Press, 1996].)

7. C. William Pollard, interview by Noel Tichy and Eli Cohen, January 1996.

8. C. William Pollard, *The Soul of the Firm,* (New York: Harper Business, 1996), 20.

9. C. William Pollard, *The Soul of the Firm,* 20, 47.

10. Bill Dowdy, interview by Eli Cohen, February 1996.

11. "ServiceMaster Industries Inc.," Harvard Business School Publishing 9-388-064, 1987 (revised 1988), 5.

12. Phil Myers, interview by Noel Tichy and Eli Cohen, June 1996.

13. John William Gardner, *On Leadership* (New York: Free Press, 1990), 122.

14. In addition to Ameritech, they are SBC Communications (formerly Southwestern Bell), BellSouth, Pacific Telesis, Bell Atlantic, U S WEST and NYNEX.

15. Richard Notebaert, interview by Noel Tichy and Eli Cohen, March 1996.

16. *Mastering Revolutionary Change,* a *FORTUNE* video series by Noel Tichy and Stratford Sherman, opening segment. Video Publishing House, 1994.

17. Richard C. Notebaert, "The New Rules of Telecommunications," speech to Young Executives Club, Chicago, Illinois, May 24, 1994.

18. Richard Notebaert, interview by Noel Tichy and Eli Cohen, March 1996.

19. Ameritech's leaders spelled out what each of these values meant in more detail. The statements below were a result of several hours of senior leaders wrestling with the new values and how they should apply.

Team Ameritech: Values for Winning

Ameritech is breaking through from a culture where we thought we were entitled to customers and profit, to a culture where we will have to earn both. Our values will drive this breakthrough. Therefore, as a corporation and as individuals, we will be guided by the following:

CUSTOMERS ARE PARAMOUNT: No matter how much or how fast the business changes, this one value will remain constant.

We will look at customers' desires as opportunities, and we will act to develop the marketplace to our best advantage.

We will deliver exactly what the customer wants. We will respond to customers quickly. Each of us will listen to customers and use their input to develop innovative solutions or add value to our products and services. In this way, we will earn our customers' loyalty and business.

We will measure our success against customer expectations. In doing so, we will strive for continuous quality improvement because every defect opens the door to our competitors.

We will succeed if our customers are saying, "Ameritech is our choice."

WE ARE MEMBERS OF ONE TEAM—TEAM AMERITECH: Teamwork will be the key to high performance. We will succeed as a team.

We will help and challenge each other to learn and excel, so each of us may reach our fullest potential. We will act with trust, respect, honesty and high ethical standards. We will value diversity. We will be obsessed with quality, work with facts, and move quickly to improve our processes. We will be results-oriented.

We will welcome changes, because the best way to do business today will be improved tomorrow—and every day thereafter.

WE WILL GROW PROFITABLY: World-class companies are built on profits and sustained growth. We are openly committed to financial excellence that will reward our employees and our investors by meeting customer desires.

We have a stake in our business and are accountable for excellent performance. We will take ownership and we will focus our energy on growing the business profitably by meeting our customers' needs. In this way, all the members of Team Ameritech will earn our future.

Ameritech Values in Action

For each of the Ameritech values, we want you to provide a concrete example of a behavior that illustrates consistent behavior (positive) and inconsistent behavior (negative). These examples are not to be hypothetical, but actual examples you see in your unit.

VALUE	EXAMPLE OF CONSISTENT BEHAVIOR	EXAMPLE OF INCON- SISTENT BEHAVIOR
Customers Are Paramount		
• Look at customers' desires as opportunities		
• Deliver exactly what customer wants		
• Listen to customers		
• Earn customers' loyalty and business		
• Measure success against customer expectations		
Teamwork		
• Help and challenge each other to learn and excel		
• Act with trust, respect, honesty, and high ethical standards		
• Value diverstiy		
• Move quickly to improve processes		
• Welcome change		
Profitable Growth		
• Committed to financial excellence		
• Reward employees and investors by meeting customer desires		
• Accountable for excellent performance		
• Take ownership for growth of business		

20. "Centennial Journal: Chicago's Poisoned Tylenol Scare, 1982," *Wall Street Journal,* 29 November 1989, B1.

21. *Moody's Handbook of Common Stocks* (New York: Moody's Investor Services, 1989).

22. James E. Burke, "Challenge," letter issued to Johnson & Johnson employees during meetings, December 8–10, 1975.

23. The version of the Credo as of 1997 reads as follows:

Our Credo

We believe our first responsibility is to the doctors, nurses and patients, to mothers and fathers and all others who use our products and services. In meeting their needs everything we do must be of high quality. We must constantly strive to reduce our costs in order to maintain reasonable prices. Customers' orders must be serviced promptly and accurately. Our suppliers and distributors must have an opportunity to make a fair profit.

We are responsible to our employees, the men and women who work with us throughout the world. Everyone must be considered as an individual. We must respect their dignity and recognize their merit. They must have a sense of security in their jobs. Compensation must be fair and adequate, and working conditions clean, orderly and safe. We must be mindful of ways to help our employees fulfill their family responsibilities. Employees must feel free to make suggestions and complaints. There must be equal opportunity for employment, development and advancement for those qualified. We must provide competent management, and their actions must be just and ethical.

We are responsible to the communities in which we live and work and to the world community as well. We must be good citizens—support good works and charities and bear our fair share of taxes. We must encourage civic improvements and better health and education. We must maintain in good order the property we are privileged to use, protecting the environment and natural resources.

Our final responsibility is to our stockholders. Business must make a sound profit. We must experiment with new ideas. Research must be carried on, innovative programs developed and mistakes paid for. New equipment must be purchased, new facilities provided and new products launched. Reserves must be created to provide for adverse times. When we operate according to these principles, the stockholders should realize a fair return.

One Johnson & Johnson Plaza, New Brunswick, New Jersey 08933
All contents copyright © 1996 Johnson & Johnson

24. From Francis J. Aguilar, "James Burke CEO Johnson & Johnson Philosophy and Culture (Abridged). A Question and Answer Session with Advanced Management Program Participants," Harvard Business School video.

25. Johnson & Johnson periodically holds such review and challenge sessions of the Credo. As a result, the Credo has evolved over time. New versions are periodically issued based on the debate of hundreds of key managers in challenge sessions. The core of the Credo has not changed, indicating that a large part of the benefit comes from the process of engagement and debate, which brings about understand-

ing of how values are to be applied. The Credo was originally written by General Robert Wood Johnson in 1943. Below are replicas of the letter Burke sent to kick off the challenge sessions mentioned in the text and the discussion guide used in those sessions.

Johnson & Johnson

JAMES E. BURKE
CHAIRMAN OF THE BOARD   NEW BRUNSWICK, NEW JERSEY

CHALLENGE

The challenge I would like to pose to you for consideration at this "Challenges" Seminar follows:

One of the most important elements of Johnson & Johnson's success over the years has been our ability to make our business decisions within the framework afforded us by our Credo. It has enabled us to operate in and prosper from a highly decentralized managerial style, while not having to forfeit our basic beliefs as a corporation.

Today, in view of the rapid and far-reaching technological and social changes occurring within our society, it is more important than ever that any basic tenets or parameters of conduct be reflective of our beliefs and needs as a corporation.

We believe, therefore, that one of the important challenges facing Johnson & Johnson in the coming year is to determine and accept a Corporate philosophy that can guide our decision making processes in all parts of our corporation in the future.

With this in mind, we would like to have a group of high-level executives from our companies and Corporate divisions review our Credo to question whether or not all or part of it is still applicable, what changes, if any, might be recommended, and most important, how to implement it in the management of our companies.

This should be an examination of the Credo in depth, both as to its total meaning and the significance of each of its parts.

J. E. Burke

(The above CHALLENGE was issued by J. E. Burke at the December 8–10, 1975 meeting)

CREDO CHALLENGE MEETING
Discussion Group Questions

The following questions may be useful in your discussions; however, feel free to discuss any othe Credo concerns you may have.*

I. Is the Credo, in its present form, a viable philosophical guide in the day-to-day operation of o business? Should it be changed or modified?

II. What is the intent of "Our Credo"?

   A. What does it mean in terms of our day-to-day operations?

      1. How is it implemented in our companies?

      2. How is the effectiveness of its implementation evaluated?

   B. Do the various levels of the organization understand and accept its intent?

   C. How can we best communicate its intent to our employees?

   D. How can we determine the actual level of understanding and acceptance?

   E. Is the order of priority accepted?

III. Does the *regular* reward system within Johnson & Johnson; that is, compensation, promotio recognition, etc., encourage management to actually carry out "Our Credo"?

   A. Do we, in fact, reward our management for accomplishing the fourth responsibility and on after that do we concern ourselves with their performance on the previous responsibilities?

   B. How can we reinforce all of our employees to perform in a manner supportive of the Cred philosophy?

IV. What roles do we ask our employees to play in carrying out the Credo?

   A. Is fulfillment of the Credo responsibilities mandatory for all levels of management?

      1. Are there different expectations for different levels? (For example: Do top level manag feel that sales and profit growth are the overriding consideration at the expense of the other paragraphs of the Credo?)

      2. Are there different expectations at the plant level?

      3. Do you feel that the Executive Committee and your company's Management Board op ates in accordance with and reinforces the Credo?

V. What specific plans would *you* design for yourselves and your companies that would make yo day-to-day operations *more supportive* of Our Credo?

   A. How would you attempt to implement each paragraph of Our Credo more effectively into your operations?

   B. Who would be responsible for reinforcing these plans?

   C. What time frames would be set for the establishment of each part of the plan?

   D. How do you intend to evaluate your new efforts in attempting to implement Our Credo on on-going basis?

---

*Each group should appoint a spokesperson who will report a summary of that group's opinions, suggestions and plans to J. E. Burke or D. R. Clare in the full group session.

26. Daniel Quinn Mills, *Broken Promises* (Boston: Harvard Business School Press, 1996), 12–13, 68.

27. Richard Notebaert, interview by Noel Tichy and Eli Cohen, March 1996.

28. Noel M. Tichy and Stratford Sherman, *Mastering Revolutionary Change, FORTUNE* video series.

29. Richard Notebaert, interview by Noel Tichy and Eli Cohen, March 1996.

30. Noel M. Tichy and Stratford Sherman, *Control Your Destiny or Someone Else Will* (New York: Doubleday, 1993), 261.

31. Readers interested in learning more about managing competing values in organizations should refer to work by Robert E. Quinn and his colleagues. Quinn's 1988 book, *Beyond Rational Management: Mastering the Paradoxes and Competing Demands of High Performance* (San Francisco: Jossey-Bass, 1988), focuses on competing values at the organizational level. *Becoming a Master Manager: A Competency Framework* (New York: Wiley, 1990) by Robert E. Quinn, Sue R. Faerman, Michael P. Thompson and Michael R. McGrath focuses on the individual level. It describes different skills that managers need to successfully manage competing values and provides exercises to help managers master those skills.

32. Robert Knowling, interview by Noel Tichy and Eli Cohen, December 1995.

33. Richard Notebaert, interviews for *Mastering Revolutionary Change* video series.

34. Ameritech introduction in the accompanying handbook to *Mastering Revolutionary Change* video series.

35. At subsequent meetings throughout 1992, 12 of the 120 leaders had to be removed for nonconformance to the effort to transform Ameritech's culture. (Source: Noel M. Tichy, "Simultaneous Transformation and CEO Succession," *Organizational Dynamics,* summer 1996, 45.)

36. Readers interested in a more in-depth discussion of this subject should consult Chris Argyris and Donald Schon, *Organizational Learning II: Theory, Method, and Practice* (Reading, Mass.: Addison-Wesley, 1996).

37. Richard Notebaert, interview by Noel Tichy and Eli Cohen, March 1996.

38. Tichy, "Simultaneous Transformation and CEO Succession."

39. Peter Elstrom, "Telecom's Pit Bull," *Business Week,* 1 July 1996, 71.

Chapter 7: Making It Happen—Getting Energy Out of Everyone

1. See *Save the Park,* an internal company video produced by General Electric Appliances.

2. Barbara Ettore, "GE Brings a New Washer to Life," *AMA Management Review,* September 1995, 33.

3. Data on losses taken from Tom Tiller interview by Noel Tichy and Eli Cohen, May 1996.

4. Data on yearly profits and quotations from Tom Tiller interview by Noel Tichy and Eli Cohen, May 1996.

5. In psychology, this phenomenon is referred to as the "self-fulfilling prophecy" or Pygmalion effect. For further information, see D. Eden, "Self-Fulfilling Prophecy as a Management Tool: Harnessing Pygmalion," *Academy of Management Review,* January 1984, 64–73; and D. Eden, "Leadership and Expectations: Pygmalion Effects and Other Self-Fulfilling Prophecies in Organizations," *Leadership Quarterly,* Winter 1992, 271–305.

6. Richard Notebaert, interview by Noel Tichy and Eli Cohen, March 1996.

7. Wes Lucas, interview by Eli Cohen and Charles Burck, February 1996.

8. Richard Notebaert, interview by Noel Tichy and Eli Cohen, March 1996.

9. Bloomberg Financial Markets, *Hoover's Handbook* electronic database.

10. C. William Pollard, interview by Noel Tichy and Eli Cohen, January 1996.

11. Carlos Cantu, interview by Noel Tichy and Eli Cohen, January 1996.

12. Gary Wendt, interview by Noel Tichy, Ram Charan and Charles Burck, June 1996.

13. Richard Notebaert, interview by Noel Tichy and Eli Cohen, March 1996.

14. Phil Myers, interview by Eli Cohen, June 1996.

15. *MacNeil-Lehrer News Hour* 1992 segment on Focus: HOPE; Father William Cunnigham, cofounder of Focus: HOPE, acceptance speech at the University of Michigan Business Leadership Awards, 1995.

16. Father William Cunningham, acceptance speech at the University of Michigan Business Leadership Awards, 1995.

17. Program information on Fast Track and MTI programs provided by Focus: HOPE.

18. Tom Henderson, "Tech Trek," *Corporate Detroit Magazine,* July 1995, 27.

19. Focus: HOPE's machine shops have become valued suppliers to the auto industry. They are the sole provider of the pulleys sent to Koci's Detroit Diesel. They also supply GM and Ford with aluminum intake manifolds in contracts approaching 100,000 parts per year. (Source for manifold information: Henderson, "Tech Trek.")

20. Henderson, "Tech Trek."

21. Father William Cunningham, acceptance speech at the University of Michigan Business Leadership Awards, 1995.

22. Focus: HOPE has been studied as a model to be replicated in other urban areas. The finance ministers of the world's richest countries (the so-called G–7) met at Focus: HOPE during their summit in Detroit in 1994. It has also been visited by President Clinton and members of his cabinet in March 1994.

23. William Bridges, *Jobshift* (Reading, MA: Addison-Wesley, 1994), front cover, 194–95.

24. William Bridges started his work on transitions in the 1970s. Bridges studied at Harvard, Columbia and Brown, where he earned his Ph.D. in American Civilization in 1963. Bridges was teaching literature at Mills College in California, when his own career change caused him to be keenly interested in how people deal with transitions.

He organized several discussion and support groups for people going through life transitions—those caused by career change, divorce and deaths of loved ones. It was in these groups that Bridges came to understand the basic elements of any human transition. Starting in the 1980s, he began to focus on how people transition through massive organizational changes. His work has been used by dozens of companies to help understand what their people go through during change.

In his extensive work, Bridges describes in depth the psychological processes that go on during each phase of transition. During each transition, people go through a period of disengagement, disidentification, disenchantment and disillusionment.

I have used his frameworks to teach thousands of executives about their own emotions and the emotions of those who work for them that arise due to organizational change. Surprisingly, very few executives think about how the emotions of transitions affect people's performance, including their own. After I described Bridges's framework, one executive remarked to me and thirty of his colleagues, "This explains why you can feel euphoric one day and like shit the next." The key for leaders is not to try to circumvent these emotions, but to understand them, deal openly with them and begin to channel the energy in a positive direction.

In developing his model for transitions, Bridges builds on the classic work of John Bowlby, *Loss,* vol. 3 of *Attachment and Loss,* (New York: Basic Books, 1980); and Elisabeth Kübler-Ross, *On Death and Dying* (New York: Macmillan Publishing Company, 1969).

25. The literature on goal-setting theory is extensive and supports the idea that difficult goals result in higher performance than do easy goals, as long as the goals are accepted. For additional information on goal-setting research, see G. P. Latham and G. A. Yukl, "A Review of Research on the Application of Goal Setting in Organizations," *Academy of Management Journal,* December 1975, 824–45; and E. A.

Locke and G. P. Latham, *A Theory of Goal Setting and Task Performance* (Englewood Cliffs, NJ: Prentice Hall, 1990).

26. Father William Cunningham, speech to executives for Ford Leadership Program, April 22, 1996.

27. Tom Henderson, "Engineering Change," *Corporate Detroit Magazine*, July 1995, 31.

28. Jon Pepper, "Ex-GM Chief Lloyd Reuss Now Devotes His Time to Shaping Lives Instead of Steel," *The Detroit News*, 24 December 1995, C1.

29. During this speech, Levin presented the second of three $20 million checks to Father Cunningham. (Source: *MacNeil-Lehrer News Hour* 1992 segment on Focus: HOPE.)

30. Tom Henderson, "Tech Trek," *Corporate Detroit Magazine*, July 1995.

31. Chris Kelley, "Detroit Program Tackles Inner-City Renewal From Within," *Dallas Morning News*, 5 December 1995, 13A.

32. Father William Cunningham, acceptance speech at the University of Michigan Business Leadership Awards, 1995.

33. John F. Welch Jr., letter to shareholders, General Electric Company 1995 Annual Report.

34. Henderson, "Tech Trek"; Denecia Harvey's quote from *MacNeil-Lehrer News Hour* 1992 segment on Focus: HOPE.

35. *MacNeil-Lehrer News Hour* 1992 segment on Focus: HOPE.

36. The source for this paragraph is Noel M. Tichy and Stratford Sherman, *Control Your Destiny or Someone Else Will* (New York: Doubleday, 1993), specifically, "self-renewal," 33; "stature," 87; "dividends," 35; "GNP for years," 16; and "survive the 1980s," 88–89.

37. Lewis Platt, interview by Noel Tichy, June 1996.

38. Gary Wendt, interview by Noel Tichy, Ram Charan, and Charles Burck, June 1996.

39. Gary Wendt, interview by Noel Tichy, Ram Charan, and Charles Burck, June 1996.

40. Nikhil Hutheesing, "David Amelio versus Goliath Gates," *Forbes*, 16 December 1996, 228.

41. David Einstein, "Apple Stopped Shipment of Faulty Laptops," *San Francisco Chronicle*, 15 September 1995, A1.

42. Apple's market share in PC computers slipped from 9.5% in 1991 to 9% in 1992. It spiked in 1993 to almost 9.5% before falling to beneath 8.5% in 1994 and falling slightly again in 1995. (Source: Brent Schlender, "Paradise Lost," *FORTUNE*, 19 February 1996, 64.) It is also interesting to note that Apple offered total returns to investors of – 50% in 1993, 34% in 1994, –23% in 1995 and –32.5% in 1996. (Source: Bloomberg Financial Markets, Total Return Analysis.) Meanwhile Compaq, Dell and IBM have been enriching investors.

43. Lee Gomes, "Herein Lies the Worm," *Wall Street Journal*, 18 October 1996, B4.

44. On August 8, 1996, Apple reported that its new operating system, Copland, would suffer further delays and was already a year behind schedule. Copland was Apple's hope to update the operating system of its Macintosh computers, which was essentially twelve years old by then. By August 1996, Amelio had redirected resources to focus on Copland. Unfortunately, this was not enough. By December of that year, the company had decided to purchase Next in order to acquire its operating system because it could not wait for Copland. The acquisition was expensive, costing over $400 million, and was largely panned by analysts and industry watchers. (Sources: Lee Gomes, "Delays in Programming Force Apple to Offer Copland Piecemeal on Internet," *Wall Street Journal,* 8 August 1996, B4; Stewart Alsop, "Apple's Next Move Misses the Mark," *FORTUNE,* 3 February 1997, 129.

45. Alsop, "Apple's Next Move Misses the Mark," 129.

46. Russ Britt, "Can a Newly Pared Apple Still Produce Hit Products?" *Investor's Business Daily,* 26 March 1997, A6.

47. Lee Gomes, "Apple's Latest Overhaul to Concentrate on Cutting Product Line, Bureaucracy," *Wall Street Journal,* 14 March 1997, B5.

Chapter 8: Edge—The Courage to See Reality *and* Act on It

1. Noel M. Tichy, "Simultaneous Transformation and CEO Succession," *Organizational Dynamics,* summer 1996, 45.

2. Andrew S. Grove, *Only the Paranoid Survive* (New York: Doubleday, 1996), 143.

3. Otis Port, et al., "The Silicon Age? It's Just Dawning," *Business Week,* 9 December 1996, 148.

4. Jack Welch, interview by Ram Charan and Noel Tichy, March 1996.

5. *MacNeil-Lehrer News Hour* 1992 segment on Focus: HOPE.

6. One in three of the candidates who enter Focus: HOPE's Machinist Training Institute do not finish due to the program's difficult and stringently applied codes on achievement and attendance. (Source: *MacNeil-Lehrer News Hour* 1992 segment on Focus: HOPE.)

7. Tom Henderson, "Tech Trek," *Corporate Detroit Magazine,* July 1995, 29.

8. Goldwater's slogan was "In your hearts you know he's right."

9. Hornstein wrote an excellent book entitled *Managerial Courage: Revitalizing Your Company Without Sacrificing Your Job* (New York: Wiley, 1986). It explores the emotional and intellectual reasons why some people feel compelled to engage in courageous acts. While Hornstein never used the term *edge,* his work is an outstanding framing of why leaders have edge and how they use it.

10. Based on 1995 sales from "The *FORTUNE* 500," *FORTUNE,* 29 April 1996, F43.

11. Ronald B. Lieber, "Who Are the Real Wealth Creators?" *FORTUNE,* 9 December 1996, 107.

12. "Creating Stockholder Wealth," *FORTUNE,* 11 December 1995, 116.

13. Noel M. Tichy and Mary Anne Devanna, *The Transformational Leader* (New York: Wiley, 1986).

14. The *New York Times* reported that more drastic proposals were indeed considered by outsiders and at least some GM executives. The reasons GM senior management did not make these moves was that "they are under pressure from dealers—and GM's own marketing divisions—to keep even slow moving cars alive." (Source: Rebecca Blumenstein and Gabriella Stern, "GM Decides to Reposition . . ." *New York Times,* 30 August 1996, A2.)

15. Keith Bradsher, "What's New at GM? Cars, for a Change," *New York Times,* 8 September 1996, 10.

16. I would note that GM did take on one very large innovative project. It started the Saturn car division in the early 1980s. However, even this investment was indicative of the company's lack of edge. In order to try new things and break from the mold, the company had to start a whole new division, rather than reshape its current ones. GM hoped to take the learnings from the Saturn division to the rest of GM. While some may have penetrated, they have come slowly. And most of GM remains as cumbersome as ever.

17. Daimler Benz in fact cut its payroll from 366,000 in 1993 to 290,000 in early 1997 as it closed Fokker, a Dutch-based aircraft manufacturer, and AEG, an electrical products subsidiary, among others. This was part of a broader restructuring in German industry. In all, profits from German business were expected to rise 25% to $45 billion from 1995 to 1996. And Deutsche Morgan Grenfell calculated that profits for the thirty biggest public companies in Germany would rise 37% in aggregate. While some of these gains were attributable to the depreciation of the Deutschemark and the recovery of the German economy, Deutsche Morgan Grenfell estimates that 75% of the increase in profits was due to the painful restructuring German companies have gone through. (Source: "Boom and Gloom in Germany," *The Economist,* 5 April 1997, 57.) In my opinion, the German industrial leaders are finally confronting the reality that their industrial model has become outdated. Some of these leaders no doubt were acting with edge—they had finally seen reality. Others, however, were acting out of fear and desperation. It is, unfortunately, difficult to determine how many there are in each camp.

18. Norm Mitchell, interview by Eli Cohen, June 1996.

19. Professor Larry Selden's framework can be applied to products, businesses and customers. Whatever the unit represented by the dots is, it should be applied in the context of the whole company. Businesses not in the northeast quadrant may add value in certain ways. Those in the

northwest quadrant may provide future revenue though they require extensive investment now. Those in the southeast quadrant may be providing cash to fuel investment in high-growth projects. Even businesses in the southwest quadrant may provide benefits in keeping important customers or enhancing an aspect of a company's reputation of offering a full product line. Further, the measurement of return on operating assets must be done very carefully. For example, some products may have a low return on assets if assets and costs are attributed in greater proportion than the marginal effects of offering this product indicate.

20. *Hoover's Handbook of American Companies 1996* (Austin, Tex.: The Reference Press, 1996).
21. Debra Dunn, interview by Eli Cohen, October 1996.
22. Mary Petrovich, interview by Charles Burck and Eli Cohen, February 1996.
23. Bob Hutchins, interview by Eli Cohen, June 1996.
24. Brian Oxley, interview by Eli Cohen, January 1996.
25. Grove, *Only the Paranoid Survive,* 152.
26. Debra Dunn, interview by Eli Cohen, October 1996.
27. Debra Dunn, interview by Eli Cohen, October 1996.
28. Bob Hutchins, interview by Eli Cohen, June 1996.
29. John F. Welch Jr. remarks at GE's Annual Operating Managers Conference, January 1991, Boca Raton, Florida.

Chapter 9: Tying It All Together—Writing Your Leadership Story

1. *Your Mythic Journey* (New York: Putnam, 1989), xiv. Sam Keen is the author of thirteen books, including *Fire in the Belly* (New York: Bantam Books, 1991) and most recently, *Hymns to an Unknown God* (New York: Bantam Books, 1994), and is a contributing editor for *Psychology Today.* He is a consultant at more than two hundred colleges, universities, clinics, institutes and corporations worldwide and he was a colleague of the late Joseph Campbell. (Sources: *Writer's Directory* [Gale Research Inc., 1996]; and Sam Keen, Putnam-Berkley [online]. Available: http://www.putnam.com/authors/sam_keen/author.html [1997, June 8].)
2. Edward O. Welles, "Why Every Company Needs a Story," *Inc.,* May 1996, 69.
3. Howard Gardner, *Leading Minds: An Anatomy of Leadership* (New York: Basic Books, 1996), 44.
4. Robert James Rhodes, "A Total and Unmitigated Defeat," speech to the House of Commons, October 5, 1938, *Winston Churchill His Complete Speeches 1897–1963,* vol. 4 (New York: Chelsea House, 1974), 6004.

5. Rhodes, "The German Invasion of Russia," radio broadcast, London, June 22, 1941, *Winston Churchill His Complete Speeches 1897–1963*, vol. 6, 6427.

6. Rhodes, "Wars Are Not Won by Evacuations," speech to the House of Commons, June 4, 1940, *Winston Churchill His Complete Speeches 1897–1963*, vol. 6, 6225.

7. Rhodes, "The War at Sea," speech to the House of Commons, December 6, 1939, *Winston Churchill His Complete Speeches 1897–1963*, vol. 6, 6175.

8. Rhodes, "The War Situation," speech to the House of Commons, September 28, 1944, *Winston Churchill His Complete Speeches 1897–1963*, vol. 7, 6990.

9. Rhodes, "These Are Great Days," speech at Harrow School, October 29, 1941, *Winston Churchill His Complete Speeches 1897–1963*, vol. 6, 6498.

10. Howard Gardner, *Leading Minds: An Anatomy of Leadership*, 207.

11. John F. Welch Jr., remarks at GE's Annual Operating Managers Conference, January 1991, Boca Raton, Florida.

12. Noel M. Tichy and Stratford Sherman, *Control Your Destiny or Someone Else Will* (New York: Doubleday, 1993), 317.

13. On July 30, 1996, GE's stock reached 70¾ with 3.27 billion shares outstanding; their approximate market value is over $230 billion. (Source: Bloomberg Financial Markets, Total Return Analysis.)

14. Howard Gardner, *Leading Minds: An Anatomy of Leadership*, 43.

15. The botched mission in Iran in 1980 was the impetus for trying to increase the effectiveness of America's forces that conducted these types of missions. The Special Operations Command was proposed to unify these forces from different branches of the armed services. Several of these same agencies and branches of the armed services resisted the joint command, which is why it was not formed until 1987.

16. All quotes from General Wayne Downing, are from an interview by Eli Cohen, July 1996.

17. Federal News Service, March 2, 1994.

18. Avenue International Company Profile—Financial Statement Analysis. Return on capital during this period was 10.4%. The market value information is taken from James Norman, "Slow Payoff," *Forbes*, 27 February 1995, 62.

19. "Shell Business Framework," Royal Dutch/Shell internal document.

Chapter 10: Conclusion—Leading into the Future

1. Larry Bossidy, remarks at AlliedSignal Senior Management Meeting, May 1994.

2. Michael Walsh, conversation with the author.

3. John F. Welch Jr., speech at Operating Managers Conference, January 1997, Boca Raton, Florida.

Sources

Interviews

Abrahamson, Colonel David, United States Special Operations Command. Two interviews by Eli Cohen, April 1996.

——. Interview by Eli Cohen, February 1997.

Abroscotto, Stephanie, Ameritech. Interview by Eli Cohen, February 1996.

Aldrich, David, ServiceMaster Inc. Interview by Eli Cohen, January 1996.

Alpuche, Charles, PepsiCo. Interview by Noel Tichy and Eli Cohen, April 1996.

Anderson, Colonel Dorian, Ranger Training Brigade, United States Army. Interview by Eli Cohen, February 1997.

Apperson, Michael, AlliedSignal. Interview by Charles Burck and Eli Cohen, February 1996.

Asp, Patricia, ServiceMaster Inc. Interview by Eli Cohen, January 1996.

Baltes, Thomas, PepsiCo. Two interviews by Eli Cohen, April 1996.

Barbas, Paul, GE Capital Computer Leasing Services. Two interviews by Eli Cohen, April 1996.

Barter, John, AlliedSignal. Two interviews by Charles Burck and Eli Cohen, February 1996.

Bastian, Edward, PepsiCo. Two interviews by Eli Cohen, April 1996.

Boll, Judy, Ameritech. Interview by Eli Cohen, February 1996.

Bossidy, Lawrence A., AlliedSignal. Interview by Noel Tichy and Ram Charan, November 1994.

Brinstin, Sergeant Jay A., 1st Battalion 75th Ranger Regiment United States Army. Interview by Eli Cohen, February 1997.

Burnham, Dan, AlliedSignal. Interview by Charles Burck and Eli Cohen, February 1996.

Cantu, Carlos, ServiceMaster Inc. Interview by Noel Tichy and Eli Cohen, January 1996.

Carabelli, Hank, Ameritech. Interview by Eli Cohen, February 1996.

Chittenden, Lesa, AlliedSignal. Interview by Charles Burck and Eli Cohen, February 1996.

Clawson, Curt, AlliedSignal. Interview by Charles Burck and Eli Cohen, February 1996.

Cole, Skeeter, GE Appliances. Interview by Eli Cohen, June 1996.

Cox, Kevin, PepsiCo. Interview by Noel Tichy and Eli Cohen, April 1996.

Dammerman, Dennis, GE Corporate. Interview by Noel Tichy and Eli Cohen, February 1996.

Dekker, Marijn, AlliedSignal. Interview by Charles Burck and Eli Cohen, February 1996.

Denny, Specialist Jason C., 1st Battalion 75th Ranger Regiment United States Army. Interview by Eli Cohen, February 1997.

Derickson, Sandra, GE Capital. Two interviews by Eli Cohen, April 1996.

Dowdy, Bill, ServiceMaster Inc. Interview by Eli Cohen, February 1996.

Downing, General Wayne, United States Special Operations Command (Retired). Interview by Eli Cohen, July 1996.

Dunn, Debra, Hewlett-Packard. Interview by Noel Tichy and Eli Cohen, June 1996.

——. Interview by Eli Cohen, October 1996.

——. Interview by Noel Tichy and Eli Cohen, October 1996.

Dur, Admiral Phil, United States Navy (Retired). Interview by Eli Cohen, January 1996.

Elliott, Sharon, Starbucks. Two interviews by Eli Cohen, January 1996.

Enrico, Roger, PepsiCo. Interview by Noel Tichy, February 1995.

Finn, Frank, PepsiCo. Interview by Noel Tichy and Eli Cohen, April 1996.

Fraizer, Michael, GE Capital. Interview by Noel Tichy and Eli Cohen, April 1996.

Fulkerson, John, PepsiCo. Interview by Noel Tichy and Eli Cohen, April 1996.

Gutsch, Hans, Compaq Computer. Interview by Eli Cohen, March 1996.

Hofmeister, John, AlliedSignal. Interview by Charles Burck and Eli Cohen, April 1996.

Hutchins, Robert, ServiceMaster Inc. Interview by Eli Cohen, June 1996.

Jeffries, Colonel Richard, United States Special Operations Command. Interview by Noel Tichy and Eli Cohen, April 1996.

Jensen, Colonel Harold, United States Special Operations Command. Interview by Noel Tichy and Eli Cohen, January 1996.

Johnston, Lawrence, GE Appliances. Interview by Noel Tichy and Eli Cohen, May 1996.

Knowling, Robert, Ameritech. Interview by Eli Cohen, February 1996.

——. Interview by Eli Cohen, December 1995.

——. Interview by Noel Tichy and Eli Cohen, December 1995.

Knowling, Robert, U S WEST. Two interviews by Chris DeRose, June 1996.

Lach, Michael, Ameritech. Interview by Eli Cohen, February 1996.

Lanik, Gail, GE Capital. Interview by Noel Tichy and Eli Cohen, April 1996.

Lawrence, James, PepsiCo. Interview by Noel Tichy and Eli Cohen, March 1996.

LeMoyne, Rear Admiral Irve, late Deputy Commander in Chief United States Special Operations Command. Interview by Noel Tichy and Eli Cohen, January 1996.

Lucas, Wes, AlliedSignal. Interview by Eli Cohen and Charles Burck, February 1996.

McDonough, William, GE Appliances. Interview by Eli Cohen, June 1996.

Mitchell, Norm, former president of the Electrial Workers Union, Louisville, Kentucky. Interview by Eli Cohen, June 1996.

Moyer, Staff Sergeant Christopher, 1st Battalion 75th Ranger Regiment United States Army. Interview by Eli Cohen, February 1997.

Myers, Phil, ServiceMaster Inc. Interview by Noel Tichy and Eli Cohen, June 1996.

Nawratil, Franz, Hewlett-Packard. Interview by Noel Tichy and Eli Cohen, June 1996.

Nguy, Lieutenant, 1st Battalion 75th Ranger Regiment United States Army. Interview by Eli Cohen, February 1997.

Norriss, Paul, AlliedSignal. Interview by Charles Burck and Eli Cohen, February 1996.

Notebaert, Richard, Ameritech. Interview by Noel Tichy and Eli Cohen, March 1996.

Oliver, George, GE Appliances. Interview by Noel Tichy and Eli Cohen, May 1996.

Oxley, Brian, ServiceMaster Inc. Interview by Eli Cohen, January 1996.

Parks, Captain James, United States Special Operations Command. Interview by Noel Tichy and Eli Cohen, April 1996.

Payton, Randy, GE Appliances. Interview by Eli Cohen, June1996.

Petrovich, Mary, AlliedSignal. Interview by Charles Burck and Eli Cohen, February 1996.

Pfeiffer, Eckhard, Compaq Computer. Interview by Noel Tichy and Eli Cohen, March 1996.

Platt, Lewis, Hewlett-Packard. Interview by Noel Tichy, June 1996.

Pollard, C. William, ServiceMaster Inc. Interview by Noel Tichy and Eli Cohen, January 1996.

Porter, Ben, AlliedSignal. Interview by Eli Cohen, February 1996.

Poses, Fred, AlliedSignal. Interview by Charles Burck and Eli Cohen, February 1996.

Powell, Marian, GE Capital Rail Co. Interview by Eli Cohen, March 1996.

———. Interview by Noel Tichy and Eli Cohen, April 1996.

Quincannon, Captain Joseph, United States Special Operations Command. Interview by Noel Tichy and Eli Cohen, April 1996.

Rankin, Captain, 1st Battalion 75th Ranger Regiment United States Army. Interview by Eli Cohen, February 1997.

Richmond, Chris, GE Capital. Two interviews by Eli Cohen, April 1996.

Robolledo, Rogelio, PepsiCo. Interview by Noel Tichy and Eli Cohen, March 1996.

Runtagh, Helene, GE Information Systems. Interview by Eli Cohen and Lynda St. Clair, February 1996.

Ryan, Colonel Mike, United States Special Operations Command. Two interviews by Eli Cohen, April 1996.

Schmid, Staff Sergeant Leland, 1st Battalion 75th Ranger Regiment United States Army. Interview by Eli Cohen, February 1997.

Schroder, Sergeant Brian, 1st Battalion 75th Ranger Regiment United States Army. Interview by Eli Cohen, February 1997.

Sinclair, Christopher, PepsiCo. Interview by Noel Tichy and Eli Cohen, March 1996.

Smith, Rear Admiral Raymond C., Deputy Commander in Chief United States Special Operations Command. Interview by Eli Cohen, March 1996.

Smith, Charles, GE Appliances. Interview by Eli Cohen, June 1996.

Stankovich, Colonel Robert, United States Special Operations Command. Interview by Noel Tichy and Eli Cohen, April 1996.

Stearns, Robert, Compaq Computer. Interview by Noel Tichy and Eli Cohen, March 1996.

Stimac, Gary, Compaq Computer. Interview by Noel Tichy and Eli Cohen, March 1996.

Stonesifer, Richard, former Chief Executive Officer, GE Appliances. Interview by Noel Tichy and Eli Cohen, May 1996.

Suarez, Lucho, PepsiCo. Interview by Noel Tichy and Eli Cohen, March 1996.

Summe, Gregory, AlliedSignal. Interview by Charles Burck and Eli Cohen, February 1996.

Thompson, Peter, PepsiCo. Interview by Noel Tichy and Eli Cohen, March 1996.

Tiller, Tom, GE Appliances. Interview with Noel Tichy and Eli Cohen, May 1996.

Toole, Larry, GE Capital. Two interviews by Eli Cohen, April 1996.

Trotman, Alex, Ford. Interview by Noel Tichy and Eli Cohen, August 1995.

Vangal, Ramesh, PepsiCo. Interview by Noel Tichy and Eli Cohen, March 1996.

Walker, Robert, Hewlett-Packard. Interview by Noel Tichy and Eli Cohen, March 1996.

Wallace, Cara, Ameritech. Interview by Eli Cohen, February 1996.

Welch, John, General Electric. Interview by Noel Tichy and Ram Charan, March 1996.

Wendt, Gary, GE Capital. Interview by Noel Tichy and Eli Cohen, March 1996.

——. Interview by Noel Tichy, Ram Charan, and Charles Burck, June 1996.

Wickman, Doug, GE Appliances. Interview by Eli Cohen, June 1996.

Woodbury,David, EDS. Interview by Eli Cohen, January 1996.

Worthington, Rear Admiral George, Naval Special Warfare Command (Retired). Interview by Eli Cohen, January 1997.

Wrightington, Rich, GE Appliances. Interview by Eli Cohen, June 1996.

Wrightman, GE Appliances. Interview by Eli Cohen, June 1996.

Field Studies/Benchmarking Visits

Benchmarking visit by Ford Motor Company to Focus: HOPE, April 1996.

Cohen, Eli. "Instilling Leadership in Modern Warriors." Trip aboard the USS *Carl Vinson,* United States Navy, Pacific Ocean, March 1996.

——. "Leadership in Special Operations Forces." Trip to 1st Battalion, 75th Ranger Regiment, United States Army, Fort Benning, Georgia, February, 1997.

——. Quick Market Intelligence (QMI) benchmarking trip to GE Appliances, Louisville, Kentucky, June 1996.

Tichy, Noel, and Eli Cohen. Benchmarking visit by Royal Dutch/Shell to GE Power Systems, Schenectady, New York, November, 1995.

Articles

Aley, James, and Lenore Schiff. "The Theory That Made Microsoft." *FORTUNE,* 29 April 1996.

Alsop, Stewart. "Apple's Next Move Misses the Mark." *FORTUNE,* 3 February 1997.

Amano, Takuma. "The Internet Economy." *Wall Street Journal,* 17 October 1996.

Arnst, Catherine, and Stephanie Anderson. "Compaq: The Making of a Comeback." *Business Week,* 2 November 1992.

Arnst, Catherine, and Peter Coy. "AT&T: Will the Bad News Ever End?" *Business Week,* 7 October 1996.

Auerbach, Jon G. "Computer Firms Likely to Post Mixed Earnings." *Wall Street Journal,* 14 January 1997.

Bank, David. "HP to Unveil Pacts with Microsoft, Oracle, Netscape." *Wall Street Journal,* 3 December 1996.

Banks, Howard. "Stomach Share." *Forbes,* 18 November 1996.

Barrett, Amy, Peter Elstrom, and Catherine Arnst. "Vaulting the Walls with Wireless." *Business Week,* 20 January 1997.

Bennis, Warren. "Learning to Lead." *Executive Excellence,* 1 January 1996.

Berner, Robert. "Retired General Speeds Deliveries, Cuts Costs, Helps Sears Rebound." *Wall Street Journal,* 16 July 1996.

Blumenstein, Rebecca, and Gabriella Stern. "GM Decides to Reposition . . ." *New York Times,* 30 August 1996.

Bongiorno, Lori. "The Pepsi Regeneration." *Business Week*, 11 March 1996.

Boudreaux, Donald J. "Microsoft Is a Competitor, Not a 'Predator.'" *Wall Street Journal,* 7 October 1996.

Bradsher, Keith. "What's New at G.M.? Cars, for a Change." *New York Times*, 8 September 1996.

Britt, Russ. "Are SGI's Woes Fleeting or Result of Bad Strategy?" *Investor's Business Daily,* 2 October 1996.

——. "Can a Newly Pared Apple Still Produce Hit Products?" *Investor's Business Daily,* 26 March 1997.

Brown, Eryn, and Janice Maloney. "Married . . . with Internet?" *FORTUNE,* 30 September 1996.

Brown, Tom. "In-House Training Is Nothing to Sniff At." *Wall Street Journal*, 15 April 1996.

Burke, Jonathan. "Northwest Passage." *The Red Herring*, 1 August 1996.

Burrows, Peter. "The Soul of a New Machine: Too Little, Too Late." *Business Week*, 13 January 1997.

Button, Kate. "King of Compaq." *Computer Weekly*, 30 September 1993.

Cauley, Leslie. "Ameritech's Net Climbs 38% as Profit Before One-Time Items Increases 10%." *Wall Street Journal,* 14 January 1997.

——. "IBM Plans to Oust John Akers as Chief/Tradition Proves to Be His Undoing." *USA Today,* 27 January 1993.

Clark, Don. "Microsoft Creates New Executive Group, Realigns Duties of Two Star Managers." *Wall Street Journal,* 4 December 1996.

CNN *Moneyline.* 28 October 1993.

Collins, James C., and Porras, Jerry I. "Building a Visionary Company." *Waters Information Service,* 1 January 1995.

Cortese, Amy, and Sager, Ira. "Lou Gerstner Unveils His Battle Plan." *BusinessWeek,* 4 April 1994.

Courter, Sheila A. "Big Companies Keep on Firing People but Hire Almost as Many, Study Finds." *Wall Street Journal*, 21 October 1996.

Damore, Kelly. "HP Vows to Become One of Top 3 PC Vendors by 1997 Through Aggressive Strategies." *Computer Reseller News,* 26 June 1995.

Darlin, Damon. "Intel's Palace." *Forbes,* 9 September 1996.

Dobrzynski, Judith. "Rethinking IBM." *BusinessWeek,* 4 October 1993.

Dougherty, Sheila. "Who's News—James Lawrence." *Wall Street Journal,* 20 September 1996.

Dugan, I. Jeanne. "The Best Performers." *Business Week,* 24 March 1997.

Eastwood, Alison. "HP's CEO Faces Up to Support Issues." *Computing Canada,* 1 September 1995.

Economist. "Boom and Gloom in Germany." 5 April 1997.

Economist. "A Busted Flush." 25 January 1997.

Economist. "Crossed Lines." 29 March 1997.

Economist. "Microsoft v. Netscape 'Freer Than Free.'" 17 August 1996.

Economist. "Mr. Creativity." 17 August 1996.

Economist. "Science and Technology—Rambo Rambus." 8 February 1997.

Economist. "The Texas Computer Massacre." 2 July 1994.

Economist. "Toyota on the March." 22 March 1997.

Economist. "Weighing the Case for the Network Computer." 18 January 1997.

Einstein, David. "Anonymous, Inc. No Personalities, No Pizzazz. Great Products. No Problem." *Marketing Computers,* 1 April 1995.

——. "Apple Stopped Shipment of Faulty Laptops." *San Francisco Chronicle,* 15 September 1995.

Elstrom, Peter. "Telecom's Pit Bull." *Business Week,* 1 July 1996.

Federal News Service. 2 March 1994.

Fialka, John J. "An Admiral Turns Big Guns on Waste at Norfolk, VA., Base." *Wall Street Journal,* 19 August 1996.

Financial Times. "Suddenly, Growth Is All the Rage." 24 August 1996.

Fisher, Anne B., and Erin Davies. "Market Value Added—Creating Stockholder Wealth." *FORTUNE,* 11 December 1995.

Forbes. "The Forbes 500." 21 April 1997.

FORTUNE. "The Chainsaw Legacy." 25 November 1996.

FORTUNE. "The FORTUNE 500." 29 April 1996.

Franco, Alberto. "De Rigueur, or Rigor Mortis?" *Latin Finance,* no. 81.

Frank, Robert. "Cola-War Casualty 'How Pepsi's Charge into Brazil Fell Short of Its Ambitious Goals.'" *Wall Street Journal,* 30 August 1996.

——. "PepsiCo's Critics Worry the Glass Is Still Half Empty." *Wall Street Journal,* 30 September 1996.

——. "PepsiCo Taps Outsider to Set Strategic Course." *Wall Street Journal,* 19 September 1996.

Frons, Marc, and Scott Scredon. "Coke's Man on the Spot." *Business Week,* 29 July 1985.

Gabrial, Trip. "Personal Trainers to Buff the Boss's People Skills." *New York Times,* 28 April 1996.

Garber, Joseph R. "The Year's Best Multimedia." *Forbes,* 1 July 1996.

Gillooly, Brian. "Compaq: Staying #1 in PC's." *Electronic Business Buyer,* 1 September 1994.

——. "Eckhard Pfeiffer." *Computer Reseller News,* 1994.

——. "HP's New Course." *Information Week,* 20 March 1995.

Goizueta, Roberto C., CEO, The Coca-Cola Company, "Remarks to the American Bankers Association." *The American Banker,* 5 November 1986.

Goldberg, Aaron. "Never Mind Gates, It's Platt Who's Gonna Lay You Flat." *PCWeek,* 5 June 1995.

Gomes, Lee. "Delays in Programming Force Apple to Offer Copland Piecemeal on Internet." *Wall Street Journal,* 8 August 1996.

——. "Herein Lies the Worm." *Wall Street Journal,* 18 October 1996.

——. "HP to Unveil Workstations Using a 'Wintel' System." *Wall Street Journal,* 26 August 1996.

Gove, Alex. "Going Hollywood." *The Red Herring,* 1 June 1996.

——. "Keeping Up with the Jones's" *The Red Herring,* 1 September 1996.

——. "www.bathwater.com" *The Red Herring,* 1 June 1996.

Grady, Barbara. "Kodak Replaces CEO Over Turnaround Efforts." *Reuters Business Report,* 6 August 1993.

Grove, Andrew S. "How (and Why) to Run a Meeting." *FORTUNE,* 11 July 1983.

——. "Is the Internet Overhyped?" *Forbes,* 23 September 1996.

Gunther, Mark, and Henry Goldblatt. "How GE Made NBC No. 1." *FORTUNE,* 3 February 1997.

Henderson, Tom. "Engineering Change." *Corporate Detroit Magazine,* July 1995.

——. "Tech Trek." *Corporate Detroit Magazine,* July 1995.

Hill, G. Christian. "Telecommunications—It's War." *Wall Street Journal,* 16 September 1996.

Horne, Alistair. "The Fateful Decisions of a Rookie President (About Truman's War)." *Wall Street Journal,* 9 August 1996.

Huey, John. "The World's Best Brand." *Time,* 31 May 1993.

Hutheesing, Nikhil. "David Amelio versus Goliath Gates." *Forbes,* 16 December 1996.

——. "Try It, You'll Like It." *Forbes,* 1 July 1996.

Intel News Release. 16 January 1996.

Intel News Release. 15 April 1996.

Intel News Release. 14 January 1997.

Investor's Business Daily. "Internet Stocks Suffering a Terminal Illness?" 25 April 1997.

Investor's Business Daily. "The Real Thing: Coke's Unbeatable Record." 19 May 1995.

Jenkins, Holman W., Jr. "The Rise of Public Pension Funds." *Wall Street Journal,* 6 April 1996.

Judge, Paul C. "Why the Fastest Chip Didn't Win." *Business Week,* 28 April 1997.

Kahn, Sharon. "Should GE Be Busted Up? Taking a Look at the Breakup Value of the World's Most Valuable Company." *Global Finance,* 1 May 1996.

Keen, Lieutenant Colonel P. K., and Captain James Larsen. "Ranger Company Night Live-Fire Raid." *Infantry,* September/October 1996.

Keller, John J. "The 'New' AT&T Faces Daunting Challenges." *Wall Street Journal,* 1 September 1996.

Kelley, Chris. "Detroit Program Tackles Inner-City Renewal from Within." *Dallas Morning News,* 5 December 1995.

Kirkpatrick, David. "IBM Is Back with New PCs and a New Attitude." *FORTUNE,* 11 November 1996.

——. "Intel's Amazing Profit Machine." *FORTUNE,* 17 February 1997.

——. "The PC Boom Isn't Over (Despite What You May Have Read)." *FORTUNE,* 29 April 1996.

——. "The Revolution at Compaq Computer." *FORTUNE,* 14 December 1992.

Kirkpatrick, David, and Joyce E. Davis. "Why Compaq Is Mad at Intel." *FORTUNE,* 31 October 1994.

Kitfield, James. "New World Warriors." *Government Executive,* November 1995.

Kosella, Rita. "Solving the DEC Puzzle." *Forbes,* 5 May 1997.

Levy, Steven. "The Microsoft Century." *Newsweek,* 2 December 1996.

Lieber, Ronald. "Who Are the Real Wealth Creators?" *FORTUNE,* 9 December 1996.

Locke, Thomas. "U S WEST Retreating from Plan." *Denver Business Journal,* 9 December 1994.

Loomis, Carol J. "Dinosaurs?" *FORTUNE,* 22 February 1993.

——. "King John Wears an Uneasy Crown." *FORTUNE,* 11 January 1993.

Loomis, Carol J., and Suzanne Barlyn. "AT&T Has No Clothes." *FORTUNE,* 5 February 1996.

Losee, Stephanie. "How Compaq Keeps the Magic Going." *FORTUNE,* 21 February 1994.

Lowenstein, Roger. "His Life in Turnaround." *Wall Street Journal,* 7 October 1996.

Lublin, Joann, and Oscar Suris. "'Chainsaw Al' Now Aspires to Be 'Al the Builder.'" *Wall Street Journal,* 9 April 1997.

Maira, Arun N., and Robert M. Curtice. "From Process Management to Complexity Management." *Arthur D. Little,* 19 December 1995.

Manager Magazin [German]. "General Jack." 1 August 1996.

Maney, Kevin. "Rocky Times at U S WEST/Phone Company Blazes Trail, Hits Potholes." *USA Today,* 27 October 1995.

McClenahen, John S. "52 Fiefdoms No More." *Industry Week,* 20 January 1997.

McDermontt, Daren. "Singapore Swing: Krugman Was Right Stung by a Professor, the Island Starts an Efficiency Drive." *Wall Street Journal,* 23 October 1996.

McWilliams, Gary. "Can DEC Beat the Big Blue Blues?" *Business Week,* 13 August 1990.

——. "Compaq: There's No End to Its Drive." *Business Week,* 17 February 1997.

——. "Crunch Time at DEC." *Business Week,* 4 May 1992.

Meyer, Michael. "Rethinking High Tech." *Newsweek*, 28 April 1997.

Morris, Betsy. "The Wealth Builders." *FORTUNE,* 11 December 1995.

Morrison, David J. "Retail's Shrinking Middle." *Wall Street Journal,* 21 October 1996.

Moukheiber, Zina. "Windows NT—NEVER!" *Forbes*, 23 September 1996.

Mulligan, Mike. "Two Sides to Bulls' 'Triangle.'" *Chicago Sun-Times*, 17 December 1992.

Naj, Amal Kumar. "Hennessy Is Retiring at Allied-Signal Inc., Sooner Than Expected." *Wall Street Journal,* 27 June 1991.

Nee, Eric. "Eckhard Pfeiffer: An Interview." *Upside*, 1 January 1995.

New York Times. "Life on the Bottom Rung: Top Executives Remember." 8 September 1996.

Nikkei Business. "Creating High Quality Services from a Manufacturer's Perspective, Regardless of Financial Service Categories." 8 July 1996.

Nocera, Joseph. "Confessions of a Corporate Killer." *FORTUNE,* 30 September 1996.

Norman, James. "Slow Payoff." *Forbes,* 27 February 1995.

Oliver, Suzanne. "The Battle of the Credit Cards." *Forbes,* 1 July 1996.

Ortega, Bob. "Life Without Sam." *Wall Street Journal,* 4 January 1995.

Palmer, Jay. "Still Shining." *Barron's,* 11 December 1995.

Pennar, Karen. "How Many Smarts Do You Have?" *Business Week,* 16 September 1996.

Pepper, Jon. "Ex-GM Chief Lloyd Reuss Now Devotes His Time to Shaping Lives Instead of Steel." *The Detroit News,* 24 December 1995.

Perkins, Anthony B. "William the Conqueror." *The Red Herring*, 1 August 1996.

Peters, Tom. "Brave Leadership." *Executive Excellence*, 1 January 1996.

Petzinger, Thomas, Jr. "Does Al Dunlap Mean Business, or Is He Just Plain Mean?" *Wall Street Journal,* 30 August 1996.

Pittsburgh Post-Gazette. "Up with Upsizing." 10 March 1996.

Pontin, Jason, and Christopher J. Alden. "The IntelNet." *The Red Herring,* 1 August 1996.

Port, Otis, et al. "The Silicon Age? It's Just Dawning." *Business Week*, 9 December 1996.

Ramstad, Evan. "Ambitious Compaq Invades the Market for Workstations." *Wall Street Journal,* 29 October 1996.

——. "Compaq Profit Jumps 43% as Sales Strengthen, Component Costs Decrease." *Wall Street Journal,* 17 October 1996.

Rebello, Kathy. "Bill's Quiet Shopping Spree." *Business Week,* 13 January 1997.

——. "Inside Microsoft." *Business Week,* 15 July 1996.

The Red Herring. "Active X vs. Java (Letter to Bill Gates) (Internet Dilemma)." 1 August 1996.

Ricks, Thomas E. "Defense Secretary Hints He May Resign." *Wall Street Journal,* 14 October 1996.

Rigdon, Joan E. "HP Goes for Blood Against IBM." *Wall Street Journal,* 23 September 1994.

Rigdon, Joan Indiana. "Netscape Forms Firm for Net Software for Appliances, Hoping to Set Standard." *Wall Street Journal,* 26 August 1996.

Rose, Robert. "Kentucky Plant Workers Are Cranking Out Good Ideas." *Wall Street Journal,* 13 August 1996.

Rosenberg, Robert. "One by One, Corporate Giants Fall." *Boston Globe,* 27 Janaury 1993.

Ross, Philip E. "Moore's Second Law." *Forbes,* 25 March 1996.

Sandberg, Jared. "Microsoft Plans to Spend Big on the Internet." *Wall Street Journal,* 15 November 1996.

Schlender, Brent. "Paradise Lost." *FORTUNE,* 19 February 1996.

Schendler, Brent, and Sheree R. Curry. "Software Is Everywhere." *FORTUNE,* 10 June 1996.

Schmitt, Julie. "World's Leading Chipmaker Sculpting New PC Universe." *USA Today,* 18 November 1996.

Schoenberg, Eric J. "Cyberdeals: Internet M&A." *The Red Herring,* 1 June 1996.

Sellers, Patricia. "How Coke Is Kicking Pepsi's Can." *FORTUNE,* October 28, 1996.

——. "Why Pepsi Needs to Become More Like Coke." *FORTUNE,* 3 March 1997.

ServiceMaster press release. "ServiceMaster Achieves 26th Consecutive Year of Growth in Revenues and Profits." 23 January 1997.

Shales, Amity. "A National Case of the Jitters." *Wall Street Journal,* 4 June 1996.

Sherman, Stratford, and Ani Hadjian. "How Tomorrow's Leaders Are Learning Their Stuff." *FORTUNE,* 27 November 1995.

Shirouzu, Norihiko. "For Coca-Cola in Japan, Things Go Better with Milk." *Wall Street Journal,* 20 January 1997.

Sprout, Allison L., and Sheree R. Curry. "Waiting to Download." *FORTUNE,* 5 August 1996.

Stewart, Bill. "Blazers Regroup After Injuries." United Press International, 3 May 1990.

Takahashi, Dean. "Intel, Compaq, and Others Join Forces . . ." *Wall Street Journal,* 28 March 1997.

——. "Intel Shifts Its Focus to Long-Term, Original Research." *Wall Street Journal,* 26 August 1996.

Taylor, Alex, III. "Why DETROIT Can't Make Money on Cars." *FORTUNE,* 9 September 1996.

Tichy, Noel M. "Bob Knowling's Change Manual." *Fast Company*, April/May 1997.

Tichy, Noel M., and Ram Charan. "How Creativity Can Take Wing at Edge of Chaos." *Wall Street Journal,* 19 October 1996.

Tichy, Noel, and Christopher DeRose. "Roger Enrico's Master Class." *FORTUNE,* 27 November 1995.

Tichy, Noel M., and Stratford Sherman. "A Master Class in Radical Change." *FORTUNE,* 13 December 1993.

USA Today. "Chainsaw's Self-Portrait." 30 August 1996.

Wall Street Journal. "Centennial Journal: Chicago's Poisoned Tylenol Scare, 1982." 29 October 1989.

Wall Street Journal. "Technology—The Corporate Connection." Section R, 18 January 1996.

Wall Street Journal. "World Business—Empire Building." Section R, 26 September 1996.

Wal-Mart press release. "Wal-Mart Announces Expansion Plans." 10 October 1995.

Wal-Mart press release. "Wal-Mart Reports Record Sales and Income for the Third Quarter." 14 November 1995.

Welles, Edward O. "Why Every Company Needs a Story." *Inc.,* 1 May 1996.

White, Joseph B. "'The Witch Doctors' Those Gurus in the Boardroom." *Wall Street Journal,* 1 November 1996.

Young, Jeffrey. "The George S. Patton of Software." *Forbes,* 27 January 1997.

Ziegler, Bart, and Don Clark. "Microsoft Gives Technology Away to Beat Rival." *Wall Street Journal,* 2 October 1996.

Books and Academic Journal Articles

Bennis, Warren. "Learning to Lead." *Executive Excellence* (January 1996).

Bowen, H. Kent, et al. "Make Projects the School for Leaders." *Harvard Business Review* (1 October 1994).

Bowlby, John. *Loss.* Vol 3 of *Attachment and Loss.* New York: Basic Books, 1980.

Brandenburger, Adam M. "Inside Intel." *Harvard Business Review* (November/ December 1996).

Bridges, William. *Jobshift.* Reading, Mass.: Addison-Wesley, 1994.

Burns, James MacGregor. *Leadership.* New York: Harper & Row, Torchbooks, 1978.

Carroll, Paul. *Big Blues.* New York: Random House, 1993.

Cohen, Eli D., Lynda St. Clair, and Noel M. Tichy. "Leadership Development as a Strategic Initiative." *Handbook for Business Strategy 1996.* New York: Faulkner & Gray, 1997.

Cohen, Eli, and Noel M. Tichy. "How Leaders Develop Leaders." *Training and Development* (1 March 1997).

Collins, James C., and Jerry I. Porras. *Built to Last.* New York: Harper-Collins, 1995.

——. "Organizational Vision and Visionary Organizations." *California Management Review* (fall 1991).

Conger, Jay A. "Leaders: Born or Bred?" in *Frontiers of Leadership: An Essential Reader.* Edited by M. Syrett and C. Hogg. Oxford: Blackwell Publishers, 1992.

Drucker, Peter. *Managing in a Time of Great Change.* New York: Dutton, Truman Talley Books, 1995.

Eden, D. "Leadership and Expectations: Pygmalion Effects and Other Self-Fulfilling Prophecies in Organizations." *Leadership Quarterly* (winter 1992): 271–305.

——. "Self-Fulfilling Prophecy as a Management Tool: Harnessing Pygmalion." *Academy of Management Review* (January 1984): 64–73.

Enrico, Roger, and Jesse Kornbluth. *The Other Guy Blinked: How Pepsi Won the Cola Wars.* New York: Bantam Books, 1996.

Ettore, Barbara. "GE Brings a New Washer to Life." *AMA Management Review* (September 1995).

Gardner, Howard. *Leading Minds: An Anatomy of Leadership.* New York: Basic Books, 1996.

Gardner, John William. *On Leadership.* New York: Free Press, 1990.

Gertz, Dwight L., and Joao P. A. Baptista. *Grow to Be Great.* New York: The Free Press, 1995.

Grove, Andrew S. *High Output Management.* New York: Random House, 1983.

——. *One-on-One with Andy Grove: How to Manage Your Boss, Yourself, and Your Coworkers.* New York: G. P. Putnam's Sons, 1987.

——. *Only the Paranoid Survive: How to Exploit the Crisis Points That Challenge Every Company and Career.* New York: Doubleday, Currency, 1996.

Hambrick, Donald C. "The Top Management Team: Key to Strategic Success." *California Management Review* (fall 1987).

Hartley, Robert F. *Management Mistakes and Successes.* New York: Wiley, 1991.

Hornstein, Harvey. *Managerial Courage: Revitalizing Your Company Without Sacrificing Your Job.* New York: Wiley, 1986.

Jackson, Phil. *Sacred Hoops.* New York: Hyperion, 1995.

Jasinowski, Jerry, and Robert Hamrin. *Making It in America.* New York: Simon & Schuster, 1995.

Katz, Donald. *Just Do It.* New York: Random House, 1994.

Katzenbach, Jon R., and Douglas K. Smith. "The Discipline of Teams." *Harvard Business Review* (March/April 1993).

Keen, Sam. *Fire in the Belly.* New York: Bantam Books, 1991.

——. *Hymns to an Unknown God.* New York: Bantam Books, 1994.

Kim, W. Chan, and Renee A. Mauborgne. "Parables of Leadership." *Harvard Business Review* (July/August 1992).

Kübler-Ross, Elisabeth. *On Death and Dying.* New York: Macmillan Publishing Company, 1969.

Latham, G. P., and G. A. Yukl. "A Review of Research on the Application of Goal Setting in Organizations." *Academy of Management Journal* (December 1975): 824–845.

Locke, E. A., and G. P. Latham. *A Theory of Goal Setting and Task Performance.* Englewood Cliffs, N.J.: Prentice Hall, 1990.

Mills, Daniel Quinn. *Broken Promises.* Boston: Harvard Business School Press, 1996.

Moody's Handbook of Common Stocks. New York: Moody's Investor Services, 1989.

Nadler, David A., and Michael L. Tushman. "Beyond the Charismatic Leader: Leadership & Organizational Change." *California Management Review* (winter 1990).

O'Reilly, Charles. "Corporations, Culture, & Commitment: Motivation & Social Control in Organizations." *California Management Review* (summer 1989).

Oren, Harari. "Turn Your Organization into a Hotbed of Ideas." *AMA Management Review* (1 November 1995).

Peters, Tom. "Get Innovative or Get Dead." *California Management Review* (winter 1991).

Peters, Tom, and Robert Waterman. *In Search of Excellence.* New York: Harper & Row, 1982.

Pollard, C. William. *Soul of the Firm.* New York: HarperBusiness, 1996.

Quinn, Robert E. *Beyond Rational Management: Mastering the Paradoxes and Competing Demands of High Performance.* San Francisco: Jossey-Bass, 1988.

Quinn, Robert E., et al. *Becoming a Master Manager: A Competency Framework.* New York: Wiley, 1990.

Rhodes, Robert James. *Winston Churchill His Complete Speeches 1897–1963.* Vols. IV and VII. New York: Chelsea House, 1974.

Schein, Edgar H. *Organizational Culture and Leadership.* San Francisco: Jossey-Bass, 1992.

Sheehy, Gail. *New Passages: Mapping Your Life Across Time.* New York: Random House, 1995.

Spain, Patrick, and James Talbot. *Hoover's Handbook of American Companies 1996.* Austin, Tex.: The Reference Press, 1996.

Tichy, Noel M. "Simultaneous Transformation and CEO Succession." *Organizational Dynamics* (summer 1996).

Tichy, Noel M., and Ram Charan. "The CEO as Coach: An Interview with Allied-Signal's Lawrence A. Bossidy." *Harvard Business Review* (March/April 1995).

Tichy, Noel M., and Christopher DeRose. "The Pepsi Challenge." *Training & Development* (May 1996): 58.

Tichy, Noel M., and Mary Anne Devanna. *The Transformational Leader.* New York: Wiley, 1986.

Tichy, Noel M., and Stratford Sherman. *Control Your Destiny or Someone Else Will.* New York: Doubleday, Currency, 1993.

Wack, Pierre. "Scenarios: Shooting the Rapids." *Harvard Business Review* (November/December 1985).

——. "Scenarios: Uncharted Waters Ahead." *Harvard Business Review* (September/October 1985).

Womack, James. *The Machine That Changed the World.* New York: HarperPerennial, 1991.

Worthington, George R. "Whither Naval Special Warfare?" *Proceedings* (January 1996).

Harvard Business School Cases

"Coca-Cola Versus Pepsi-Cola (A)." 9-387-108. 1987.

"Coca-Cola Versus Pepsi-Cola (B)." 9-387-109. 1987.

"Coca-Cola Versus Pepsi-Cola (C)." 9-387-110. 1987.

"Compaq Computer Corporation." 9-491-011. 1990 (revised 1991).

"Continuous Casting Investments at USX Corporation." 9-697-020. 1996.

"General Electric: Reg Jones and Jack Welch." N9-391-144. 1991.

"General Electric: Jack Welch's Second Wave." N9-391-248. 1991.

"Hewlett-Packard: Challenging the Entrepreneurial Culture." 9-384-035. 1983.

"Hewlett-Packard: Corporate, Group, and Divisional Manufacturing (A)." 9-691-001. 1991.

"The Intel Pentium Chip Controversy (A)." 9-196-091. 1995 (revised 1996).

"The Intel Pentium Chip Controversy (B)." 9-196-092. 1995.

"Jack Welch: General Electric's Revolutionary." 9-394-065. 1993 (revised 1994).

"Jack Welch: General Elctric's Revolutionary Teaching Note." 5-395-232. 1995.

"The Job of the General Manager." 9-388-035. 1987.

"John Sculley at Apple Computer (A)." 9-486-001. 1985 (revised 1987).

"Johnson & Johhnson: The Tylenol Tragedy." 9-583-043. 1982 (revised 1992).

"Managing Change: Course Overview." N9-494-042. 1993.

"Microsoft, 1995." 9-795-147. 1995 (revised 1996).

"Microsoft, 1995 Teaching Note." 5-796-071. 1995.

"Nike (E)." 9-385-033. 1984 (revised 1995).

"Nike (E) Teaching Notes." 5-385-100. 1984 (revised 1985).

"Nike (E1)." 9-385-034. 1984.

"Nike (E2)." 9-385-035. 1984.

"Nike (E3)." 9-385-036. 1984.

"Nike Introduction Teaching Notes." 5-385-162. 1984.

"Nike—Series Overview." 9-385-024. 1984.

"Nike Summary Teaching Note." 5-385-163. 1984.

"Nike in Transition (A): The Ascendancy of Bob Woodell." 9-392-105. 1992 (revised 1993).

"Nike in Transition (B): Phil Knight Returns." 9-392-106. 1992 (revised 1994).

"Nike in Transition (C): A Second COO." 9-392-107. 1992 (revised 1994).

"Note on the U.S. Soft Drink Industry in 1986." 9-387-107. 1987

"Pepsi: The Indian Challenge." 9-793-060. 1993 (revised 1995).

"PepsiCo Bottling in Mexico." 9-293-137. 1993 (revised 1994).

"PepsiCo. International." 9-592-055. 1991.

"Pepsi-Cola (A)." 9-579-108. 1978 (revised 1986).

"Pepsi-Cola Fountain Beverage Division: Marketing Organization." 9-589-045. 1988.

"Pepsi-Cola Fountain Beverage Division: Tea Breeze." 9-589-060. 1988 (revised 1989).

"Pepsi-Cola United Kingdom (A)." 9-584-052. 1983 (revised 1985).

"Pepsi-Cola U.S. Beverages (A)." 9-390-034. 1989 (revised 1991).

"Pepsi-Cola U.S. Beverages (B)." 9-390-035. 1989 (revised 1991).

"PepsiCo and Madonna." 9-590-038. 1990.

"PepsiCo's Restaurants." 9-794-078. 1994 (revised 1995).

"PepsiCo: A View from the Corporate Office." 9-694-078. 1994.

"Pepsi's Regeneration, 1990–1993." 9-395-048. 1994 (revised 1996).

"Phil Knight Manging NIKE's Transformation." 9-394-012. 1993 (revised 1994).

"Restructuring European Petrochemicals: Royal Dutch/Shell Group." 9-385-206. 1984 (revised 1985).

"The ServiceMaster Company." 9-693-042. 1992 (revised 1993).

"ServiceMaster Industries Inc." 9-388-064. 1987 (revised 1988).

"Strategic Countermoves: Coca-Cola vs. Pepsi." 9-795-133. 1995.

"3M: Profile of an Innovating Company." 9-395-016. 1995.

"USX Corporation." 9-296-050. 1996.

Stanford Business School Cases

"Apple Computer (A)." BP-229(A). 1983.

"Apple Computer (B)." BP-229(B). 1983.

"Apple Computer: The First Ten Years." BP-245. 1985.

"Apple Computer—Strategic Investment Group." SM-21. 1995.

"Southwest Airlines (A)." HR-1A. 1994.

Company Profiles/Analyst Reports

"Analyst Report: Compaq Computer Corporation." Prudential Securities. November 2, 1995.

"Analyst Report: Compaq Computer Corporation." Salomon Brothers. December 5, 1995.

"Analsyt Report: Compaq Computer Corporation." PNC Institutional Investment Service. November 8, 1995.

"Analyst Report: Compaq Computer Corporation." Natwest Securities Corporation. September 29, 1995.

"Analyst Report: Compaq Computer Corporation." Lehman Brothers. September 22, 1995.

"Analyst Report: Compaq Computer Corporation." Merrill Lynch Capital Markets. September 21, 1995.

"Analyst Report: Compaq Computer Corporation." Pershing Division, Donaldson Lufkin & Jenrette. September 1, 1995.

"Analyst Report: Compaq Computer Corporation." Salomon Brothers. December 5, 1995.

"Analyst Report: Compaq Computer Corporation." PNC Institutional Investment Service. November 8, 1995.

"Analyst Report Summary: GE Appliances." C.S. First Boston. January 22, 1996.

"Analyst Report: GE Capital Services." Salomon Brothers. January 23, 1996.

"Analyst Report: GE Power Systems." Salomon Brothers. January 23, 1996.

"Analyst Report: Hewlett-Packard." Dean Witter Reynolds. November 29, 1995.

"Analyst Report: Hewlett-Packard." Merrill Lynch Capital Markets. November 30, 1995.

"Analyst Report: ServiceMaster." Goldman Sachs. March 6, 1995.

"Analyst Report: ServiceMaster." Merrill Lynch. October 31, 1995.

"Analyst Report: ServiceMaster." Brean Murray, Foster Securities Inc. April 26, 1996.

"Analyst Report: ServiceMaster." Standard & Poor's. November 5, 1995.

"Analyst Report: Wal-Mart." Natwest Securities Corporation. September 20, 1995.

"Analyst Report: Wal-Mart." William Blair & Company. September 8, 1995.

"Analyst Report: Wal-Mart." Sanford C. Bernstein & Co. August 31, 1995.

"Analyst Report: Wal-Mart." Interstate/Johnson Lane. August 28, 1995.

"Analyst Report: Wal-Mart." A. G. Edwards & Sons. August 25, 1995.

"Analyst Report: Wal-Mart." C.S. First Boston. August 21, 1995.

"Company Profile: General Electric Company." *FORTUNE Business Reports.* February 1995.

"Company Profile: Microsoft Corporation." *FORTUNE Business Reports.* February 1995.

"Company Profile: The News Corporation Limited." *FORTUNE Business Reports.* February 1995.

"Company Profile: Royal Dutch Petroleum Company." *FORTUNE Business Reports.* February 1995.

Speeches/Presentations

Bossidy, Lawrence A., AlliedSignal. "America's Economic Survival: What We Need to Do Now." Remarks to the Commonwealth Club of California, San Francisco, California, June 21, 1995.

——. "America's Corporations Are Back in the Lead. Can They Stay Ahead?" Remarks to the Economic Club of Detroit, February 14, 1994.

——. "Critical People Issues for Tomorrow's Successful Companies." Remarks to the Human Resource Planning Society, Orlando, Florida, April 10, 1995.

——. "Restructuring Action Plan." Security Analysts Presentation, AlliedSignal, October 9, 1991.

——. "Mastering Change." Remarks to the McDonnell Douglas Masters Program, Long Beach, California, July 1, 1993.

——. "NAFTA: Right for America." United States House of Representatives Sub-committee on Trade Committee of Ways and Means, September 15, 1993.

——. Keynote address to the Colgate University Fund, Campaign Kickoff Dinner, Hamilton, New York, September 17, 1994.

——. Speech to the Florida A&M University School of Business and Industry, October 18, 1994.

——. "Survival Tactics for the CEO." Remarks to the Boston College CEO Club, November 1, 1994.

——. Remarks at Senior Management Meeting, November 19, 1991.

——. Remarks at Senior Management Meeting, November 12, 1992.

——. Remarks at Senior Management Meeting, November 17, 1993.

——. Remarks at Senior Management Meeting September 19, 1994.

——. Remarks at Senior Management Meeting, May 1994.

——. Remarks at Senior Management Meeting, November 1994.

——. Remarks at Senior Management Meeting, May 1995.

——. Remarks at Senior Management Meeting, November 1995.

Boykin, Colonel William G. "The Origins of the United States Special Operations Command."

Calloway, Wayne. Suggested remarks, Experiencing PepsiCo., June 22, 1995.

Cantu, Carlos. Speech on values and profits, Orlando, Florida, December 2, 1995.

Cunningham, Father William, co-founder Focus: HOPE. Acceptance speech at the University of Michigan Business Leadership Awards, 1995.

——. Speech to executives for Ford Leadership Program, April 22, 1996.

Dammerman, Dennis D. "A Decade of Opportunity." Speech to the National Association of Black Accountants, St. Louis, Missouri, June 28, 1991.

——. Speech at the Delaware Valley FMP/ISMP graduation, July 13, 1988.

Downing, General Wayne. "Duty and the Warrior." Lecture to United States Military Academy, 1992.

——. "Leadership." Presentation to the United States Military Academy, January 5, 1995.

——. "Warrior . . . Or Milicrat?" Presentation notes, November 6, 1985.

Enrico, Roger. Remarks at Senior Management Meeting, Lake George, New York, July 9, 1994.

Knowling, Robert, U S WEST. Speech to the Michigan Business School, August 1996.

Notebaert, Richard C., Ameritech. "The New Rules of Telecommunications." Speech to Young Executives Club, Chicago, Illinois, May 24, 1994.

——. "Lessons in Leadership." Speech to the Young Executives Club, Chicago, Illinois, March 24, 1994.

——. "Leadership." Slides presented to the Executive Forum, 1996.

Oliver, George, GE Appliances. "Successful Leaders."

Pepper, John, Procter & Gamble. Speech to the Michigan Business School, July 1996.

Pfieffer, Eckhard, Compaq Computer. "The PC-Centered Digital Revolution Now Touches Every Age Group and Every Room of Your Home." Speech at the Winter Consumer Electronics Show, Las Vegas, Nevada, January 5, 1996.

——. "Compaq: The Computer Company for the Enterprise and the Home." Speech to the Innovate Forum 95, October 17, 1995.

——. "Escaping the Commodity Trap." Speech to Agenda 96: The Executive Conference, October 12, 1995.

——. "How Compaq Is Reshaping Itself Continuously." Speech to the Korean Management Association, September 12, 1995.

——. "Leadership at Compaq." Speech at the GE Corporate Executive Council Meeting, March 21, 1995.

——. "The PC: A Universal Tool for Home and Business." Speech at the PC Expo, New York, New York, June 20, 1995.

Pollard, C. William, ServiceMaster Inc. Speech to the Michigan Business School, August 1996.

Stearns, Robert, Compaq Computer. "Speech on Innovation of Companies."

———. "Innovation." Presentation notes.

Stimac, Gary, Compaq Computer. Innovate 95 Keynote speech, October 1995.

Stonesifer, Richard, GE Appliances. "Core Values of GE Appliances."

———. Speech to the Michigan Business School, October 1995.

Welch, John F., Jr., General Electric. Remarks at Operating Managers Conference, Boca Raton, Florida, January 1991.

———. Remarks at Operating Managers Conference, Boca Raton, Florida, January 1994.

———. Remarks at Operating Managers Conference, Boca Raton, Florida, January 1997.

Wendt, Gary. "Growth: How to Get It!" GE Capital presentation.

Worthington, George R. "Leadership: A Brief List of Traits." January 30, 1996.

Internal Information/Documents

AlliedSignal Aerospace. *Horizons,* vol. VIII, no. 5, July 1995.

———. *Horizons,* vol. VIII, no. 6, August/September 1995.

———. *Horizons,* vol. VIII, no. 7, October 1995.

———. *Horizons*, vol. VIII, no. 8, November/December 1995.

———. *Horizons,* vol. IX, no. 1, January/February 1996.

———. *Horizons Special,* March 1996.

———. *Horizons: Update*, February 1996.

AlliedSignal. *Up Words Clearinghouse,* Janaury/February 1996.

AlliedSignal Aerospace. "1995 Goals and Flight Path." 1995.

"AlliedSignal Linkage Kit." May 1995.

"AlliedSignal's Transformational Story." Handbook accompanying the *Mastering Revolutionary Change* video series.

AlliedSignal. "Committed to Customer Service and Manufacturing Excellence." Promotional material.

AlliedSignal. "Cultural Evolution at Allied Signal." Internal presentation.

AlliedSignal. "Key Elements in the Total Quality Plan." Internal presentation.

AlliedSignal. "Total Quality at AlliedSignal." Internal presentation.

AlliedSignal Aerospace. "TQS/IPDS: Working Together Better and Faster Than Ever Before."

AlliedSignal. "Vision, Commitment, Values."

AlliedSignal. "World Class Leadership Development." Internal presentation.

AlliedSignal. "Worldwide Employee Survey Results." June 1993.

AlliedSignal. Annual Meeting/First Quarter Report, 1995.

AlliedSignal. Second Quarter Report, 1995.

AlliedSignal. Third Quarter Report, 1995.

Biography, Mary Petrovich, AlliedSignal.

Bossidy, Lawrence A. "CEO Commentary." AlliedSignal, February 22, 1994.

——. "CEO Commentary." AlliedSignal, March 17, 1994.

——. "CEO Commentary." AlliedSignal, April 19, 1994.

——. "CEO Commentary." AlliedSignal, May 24, 1994.

——. "CEO Commentary." AlliedSignal, July 12, 1994.

——. "CEO Commentary." AlliedSignal, September 7, 1994.

——. "CEO Commentary." AlliedSignal, October 13, 1994.

——. "CEO Commentary." AlliedSignal, March 1, 1995.

——. "CEO Commentary." AlliedSignal, April 3, 1995.

——. "CEO Commentary." AlliedSignal, May 1995.

——. "CEO Commentary." AlliedSignal, June 1995.

——. "CEO Commentary." AlliedSignal, July 1995.

——. "CEO Commentary." AlliedSignal, August 1995.

——. "CEO Commentary." AlliedSignal, September 1995.

——. "CEO Commentary." AlliedSignal, October 1995.

——. "CEO Commentary." AlliedSignal, November 1995.

——. "CEO Commentary." AlliedSignal, December 1995.

——. "CEO Commentary." AlliedSignal, January 1996.

Clawson, C. J. "1996 Goals." AlliedSignal Automotive Memorandum, January 15, 1996.

Ameritech. "Team Ameritech: Values for Winning."

Ameritech. "1996 Cultural Environment—Leadership Model." 1996.

The Coca-Cola Company. "Our Mission and Our Commitment." February 1994.

The Coca-Cola Company. "1995 Mid-Year Report." July 1995.

Compaq Computer Corporation. Robert W. Stearns biography.

Compaq Computer Corporation. Ross A. Cooley biography.

Compaq Computer Corporation. Gary Stimac biography.

Compaq Computer Corporation. Hans W. Gutsch biography.

Compaq 1995–1996 Environmental Report.

Focus: HOPE Program Information on Fast Track and Machinist Training Institute, 1996.

"GE Appliances Fact Sheet." February 27, 1996.

"GE Historical Timeline."

"GE Organizational Charts."

"GE Products and Services." January 1995.

Welch, John F. "Handwritten Exhibit." General Electric.

Hewlett-Packard. Lewis E. Platt biography.

Hewlett-Packard. Richard C. Watts biography.

Hewlett-Packard. Robert P. Wayman biography.

Hewlett-Packard. Franz X. Nawratil biography.

Hewlett-Packard. Debra L. Dunn biography.

Hewlett-Packard. Richard E. Belluzo biography.

Hewlett-Packard. Byron J. Anderson biography.

Hewlett-Packard. Edward W. Barnholt biography.

Hewlett-Packard. George B. Cobbe biography.

Hewlett-Packard. Manuel F. Diaz biography.

Hewlett-Packard. Ann M. Livermore biography.

Hewlett-Packard. Pete Peterson biography.

Hewlett-Packard. Alex Sozonoff biography.

"IntelVIEW." Intel publication, fall 1995.

Johnson & Johnson. Credo, 1996.

Johnson & Johnson. Credo, 1989.

Johnson & Johnson. Credo, 1979.

Johnson & Johnson. Credo, 1948.

Burke, James E., CEO, Johnson & Johnson. "Challenge." A letter issued to Johnson & Johnson employees during meetings from December 8–10, 1975.

Enrico, Roger. "Executive Leadership: Building the Business." PepsiCo presentation, 1995.

Royal Dutch/Shell. "Shell Business Framework." Internal document.

USCINCSOC Quality Award application, 1997.

United States Navy. Rear Admiral Raymond C. Smith biography.

United States Special Operations Command. General Wayne A. Downing biography.

United States Special Operations Command. Rear Admiral Irve C. LeMoyne biography.

Downing, General Wayne. "Reinventing License."

Kearney, Lieutenant Colonel Francis H., III. "The Impact of Leaders on Organizational Culture: A 75th Ranger Regiment Case Study." United States Army War College Strategy Research Project, 1996.

"A Briefing to General Shelton on Total Quality Leadership." January 10, 1996.

United States Special Operations Command. "Goals."

United States Special Operations Command. "Special Operations Forces Truths."

United States Special Operations Command. "Values, Vision, and Mission."

1997 USSOCOM Military Equal Opportunity Climate Survey.

United States Special Operations Command Logo.

United States Special Operations Command (USSOCOM) Fiscal Year 1996 Briefing presented to Noel Tichy and Eli Cohen, January 1996.

U S WEST. "Shareowner Investment Plan." October 10, 1995.

U S WEST. "U S WEST Media Group 1995 Financials."

U S WEST. "U S WEST Communications Group 1995 Financials."

Wal-Mart. "Wal-Mart: Making a Difference in Hometowns and America."

Wal-Mart. "Wal-Mart: The Story of Wal-Mart."

Wal-Mart. "Wal-Mart: The Retail Divisions."

Annual Reports/SEC Filings/Compact Disclosures

AlliedSignal 1992 Annual Report.

AlliedSignal 1993 Annual Report.

AlliedSignal 1994 Annual Report.

AlliedSignal 1995 Annual Report.

AlliedSignal 1996 Annual Report.

AlliedSignal 1992 Form 10-K.

America Online 1995 Annual Report.

Ameritech 1993 Annual Report.

Ameritech 1994 Annual Report.

Ameritech 1995 Annual Report.

Avenue International Company Profile—Financial Statement Analysis.

Citicorp 1993 Annual Report.

The Coca-Cola Company 1982 Annual Report.

The Coca-Cola Company 1983 Annual Report.

The Coca-Cola Company 1984 Annual Report.

The Coca-Cola Company 1985 Annual Report.

The Coca-Cola Company 1986 Annual Report.

The Coca-Cola Company 1987 Annual Report.

The Coca-Cola Company 1989 Annual Report.

The Coca-Cola Company 1991 Annual Report.

The Coca-Cola Company 1992 Annual Report.

The Coca-Cola Company 1993 Annual Report.

The Coca-Cola Company 1994 Annual Report.

The Coca-Cola Company 1995 Annual Report.

The Coca-Cola Company 10-K report 1995.

The Coca-Cola Company 10-Q report, March 31, 1996.

The Coca-Cola Company Compact Disclosure.

Compaq 1993 Annual Report.

Compaq 1994 Annual Report.

Compaq 1995 Annual Report.

Compaq 10-K report 1996.

Compaq Compact Disclosure.
General Electric 1987 Annual Report.
General Electric 1988 Annual Report.
General Electric 1989 Annual Report.
General Electric 1990 Annual Report.
General Electric 1991 Annual Report.
General Electric 1992 Annual Report.
General Electric 1993 Annual Report.
General Electric 1994 Annual Report.
General Electric 1995 Annual Report.
General Electric 1996 Annual Report.
Hewlett-Packard 1994 Annual Report.
Hewlett-Packard 1995 Annual Report.
Intel 1993 Annual Report.
Intel 1994 Annual Report.
Intel 1995 Annual Report.
Intel 10-K report 1995.
Intel 10-Q report, April 1, 1995.
Intel 10-Q report, September 30, 1995.
Intel 10-Q report, March 30, 1996.
PepsiCo, Inc. 1992 Annual Report.
PepsiCo, Inc. 1993 Annual Report.
PepsiCo, Inc. 1994 Annual Report.
PepsiCo, Inc. 1995 Annual Report.
ServiceMaster 1994 Annual Report.
ServiceMaster 1995 Annual Report.
Starbucks Compact Disclosure.
U S WEST 1993 Annual Report.
U S WEST 1994 Annual Report.
U S WEST 1995 Annual Report.
U S WEST 10-K report, 1995.
U S WEST 10-Q report, March 31, 1996.
Wal-Mart 1995 Annual Report.
Wal-Mart 10-Q report, July 31, 1995.
Wal-Mart 10-K report, 1995.
Wal-Mart Compact Disclosure.

Web Sites

Financial Highlights. Coca-Cola Annual Report [Online]. Available:
http://www.cocacola.com/co/financial96.html [1997, May 20].

George Catlett Marshall. *United States Information Agency/The Marshall Plan* [Online]. Available:
http://www.usia.gov/topical/pol/marshall/mp-bio.htm [1997, May 20].

Sam Keen. *Putnam-Berkley* [Online]. Available:
http://www.putnam.com/authors/sam_keen/author.html [1997, June 8].

John F. Welch. *GE History* [Online]. Available:
http://www.ge.com/ibhisjfw.htm [1997, May 20].

120 Years of Innovation. *GE History* [Online]. Available:
http://www.ge.com/ibhis0.htm [1997, May 20].

Electronic Databases

Bloomberg Financial Markets

Center for Research in Securities Market Index Database

Schoch, Claude. Compact Disclosure database. Version 4.5F, October 1995, Digital Library Systems Inc.

Compustat

Videos

Aguilar, Francis J. "James Burke, Johnson & Johnson. Philosophy and Culture (Abridged). A Question and Answer Session with Advanced Management Program Participants." Harvard Business School video, 1984.

AlliedSignal. "Total Quality Today." Company video.

Ameritech. "Special Report—Breakthrough Leadership." Company video, January 1993.

Ameritech. "Announcement Employee Telecast." Company video, February 1996.

Ameritech News Broadcast, February 1996.

Bossidy, Lawrence, AlliedSignal. *FORTUNE* 500 Forum Interview, November 1996.

Bossidy, Lawrence, AlliedSignal. Report to Employees, October 1992.

Bossidy, Lawrence, AlliedSignal. TQM Introduction. Company video.

CBS This Morning documentary on the Navy SEALs, April 29–May 3, 1996.

Compaq. "4th Quarter Company Meeting." Company video, November 1995.

Focus: HOPE. "1995 Overview." Company video, June 1995.

Focus: HOPE. "Center for Advanced Technologies." Company video, June 1995.

Focus: HOPE, Commodity Supplemental Forum. "The Challenge Continues." Company video, June 1995.

Focus: HOPE. "Guaranteeing America's Future." Company video, June 1995.

Frontline. "The Gulf War." PBS documentary, June 1995.

GE Appliances. "Save the Park." Company video.

GE Capital. "GE Capital Teleconference." Company video, January 1996.

GE Corporate. "Welch, John—Stern: Meet the CEO's." Teaching materials.

GE/Pepsi/USSOCOM. "Afternoon Discussion." Workshop presentation, April 1996.

GE/Pepsi/USSOCOM. "Closing Comments by Participants." Workshop presentation, April 1996.

MacNeil-Lehrer News Hour 1992 segment on Focus: HOPE.

Tichy, Noel, and Stratford Sherman. *Mastering Revolutionary Change* a *Fortune* video series. Video House Publishing, 1994.

United States Special Operations Command. "Downing, General Wayne—Briefing, Saudi Bombing." News broadcast, September 1996.

United States Special Operations Command. "USSOCOM—'A Global Commitment' & Humanitarian Video."

"Profits & Promise—Reworking One American Dream." Round table discussion.

Index

▲ HarperBusiness ESSENTIALS

Business Classics for the Inquisitive Executive

THE INNOVATOR'S DILEMMA
Clayton M. Christensen
A *NEW YORK TIMES*, *WALL STREET JOURNAL*, AND *BUSINESSWEEK* BESTSELLER
ISBN 0-06-052199-6 (paperback)

"The book to read among mainstream managers trying to dope out an Internet strategy."
                                                                        —New York Times

THE INTELLIGENT INVESTOR: *Revised Edition*
Benjamin Graham
ISBN 0-06-055566-1 (paperback)

First published in 1949, this is the definitive book on investing due to Graham's timeless philosophy of "value investing." *Now with new commentary by Jason Zweig.*

THE WISDOM OF TEAMS: *Creating the High-Performance Organization*
Jon R. Katzenbach & Douglas K. Smith
ISBN 0-06-052200-3 (paperback) • ISBN 1-55994-967-8 (audio)

"A thoughtful and well-written book filled with fascinating examples. . . .
You'll be hard-pressed to find a better guide." —John Byrne, *BusinessWeek*

INDECENT EXPOSURE: *A True Story of Hollywood and Wall Street*
David McClintick
With a Foreword by James B. Stewart and a new Afterword by the author
A NATIONAL BOOK AWARD FINALIST AND NATIONAL BESTSELLER
ISBN 0-06-050815-9 (paperback)

"Fascinating. . . . One of the best-reported and best-written business adventures
ever published." *—BusinessWeek*

BUILT TO LAST: *Successful Habits of Visionary Companies*
James C. Collins & Jerry I. Porras
ISBN 0-06-051640-2 (paperback) • ISBN 0-694-51479-9 (audio)

"One of the most eye-opening business studies since *In Search of Excellence*."
                                                                        —Kevin Maney, *USA Today*

THE EFFECTIVE EXECUTIVE
Peter F. Drucker
ISBN 0-06-051607-0 (paperback)

"An imaginative book. . . . A survival manual on how to escape organization traps."
                                                                        —Wall Street Journal

☰ HarperBusiness E S S E N T I A L S

Business Classics for the Inquisitive Executive

CROSSING THE CHASM
Marketing and Selling High-Tech Products to Mainstream Customers
Geoffrey A. Moore
ISBN 0-06-051712-3 (paperback) • PerfectBound e-book

"A must-read for marketing executives, CEOs, and especially venture capitalists."
—Jeff Miller, President, Documentum

THE LEADERSHIP ENGINE
How Winning Companies Build Leaders at Every Level
Noel M. Tichy with Eli Cohen
A *WALL STREET JOURNAL* BESTSELLER
ISBN 0-88730-931-3 (paperback) • ISBN 0-694-51881-6 (audio) • PerfectBound e-book

Practical advice from the acclaimed authority on organizational transformation.

REENGINEERING THE CORPORATION
A Manifesto for Business Revolution
Michael Hammer and James Champy
ISBN 0-06-055953-5 (paperback) • PerfectBound e-book

"May well be the best-written, most well-reasoned business book for the managerial
masses since *In Search of Excellence*." —*BusinessWeek*

LEADERS: *Strategies for Taking Charge*
Warren G. Bennis & Burt Nanus
ISBN 0-06-055954-3 (paperback)

"An insightful book that should be read by every manager aspiring to be a true leader. . . .
One of the most important books of its type in a long time." —*Chicago Tribune*

BARBARIANS AT THE GATE: *The Fall of RJR Nabisco*
Bryan Burrough and John Helyar
ISBN 0-06-053635-7 (paperback)

"The fascinating inside story of the largest corporate takeover in American history. . . .
It reads like a novel." —*Today Show*

**Don't miss the next book by your favorite author.
Sign up for AuthorTracker by visiting *www.AuthorTracker.com*.**

Available wherever books are sold, or call 1-800-331-3761 to order.